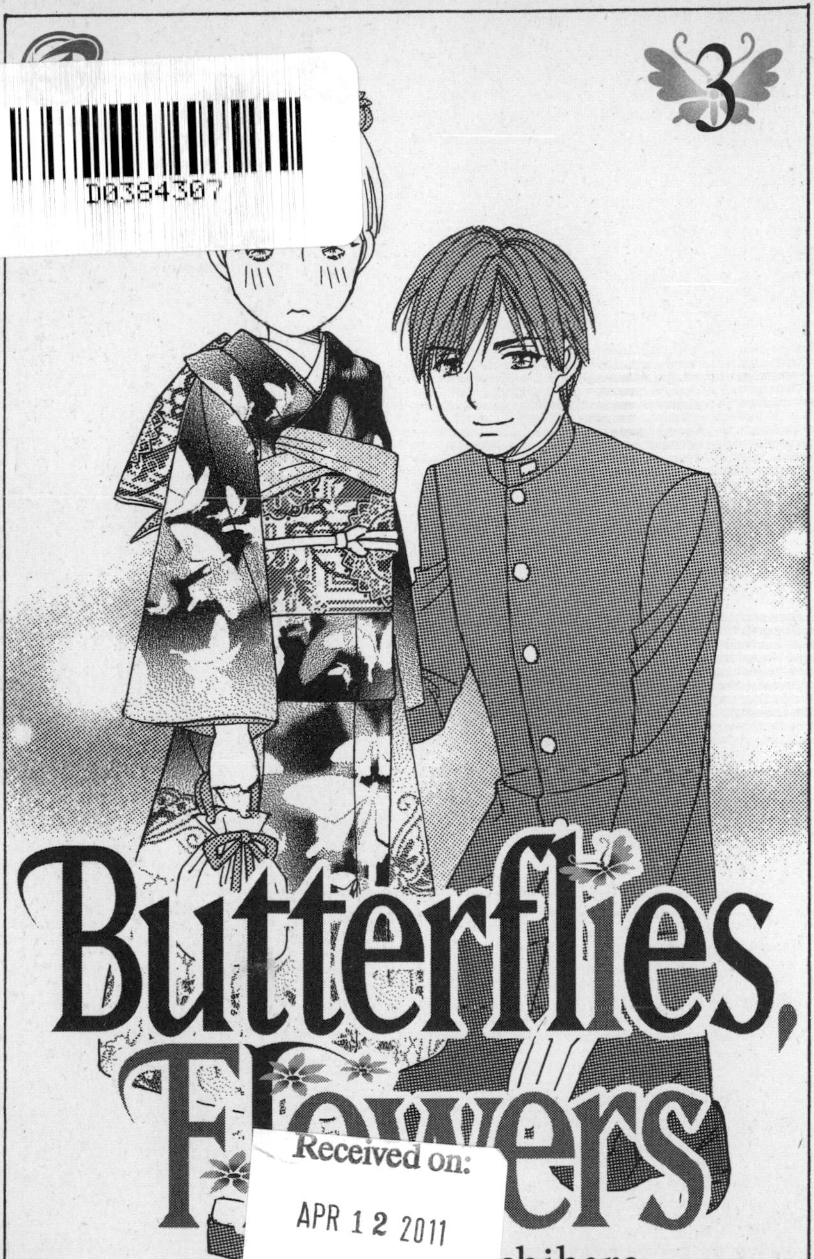

3

Butterflies, Flowers

Sto shihara

chi-Go-San. With Cha-chan.

Butterflies, Flowers 3

Characters

◆Choko Kuze
She's an office worker from an upper-class family who used to be rich. Domoto usually gets the better of her, but at times, she brings out her "aristocratic girl's resolve."

Story Thus Far

◆Choko's family used to be extremely rich until 13 years ago when they went bankrupt. Now they're just a working-class family running a soba shop.

◆Choko starts working in the Administration Department of a real estate company. But being unskilled, Choko finds herself being pushed around by the senior staff and the mean Director Domoto...

◆Domoto's father used to be a servant who worked for the Kuze family. The director is actually "Cha-chan," the boy who looked after Choko when she was small!

◆Masayuki Domoto

The Director whom Choko loves. He's the son of a former servant to the Kuze family. He is a rather high-handed supervisor, but he supports Choko in her private life. Her childhood nickname for him is "Cha-chan."

◆Genzaburo Suou

He's a veteran office worker in the Administration Department and a good friend of Domoto. He's a guy, but he usually cross-dresses.

◆Domoto tells Choko that he will protect her with his life. Choko finds out what it's like to be in love. But Domoto continues to treat her as if she were a child...

◆Choko tries to get Domoto to accept her as an adult. Makie, the niece of the president and CEO, goes after Domoto, but this only brings Choko and Domoto closer together. The two start dating.

◆Although Choko and Domoto have started dating, the couple is unable to consummate their relationship...

Butterflies, Flowers

Contents

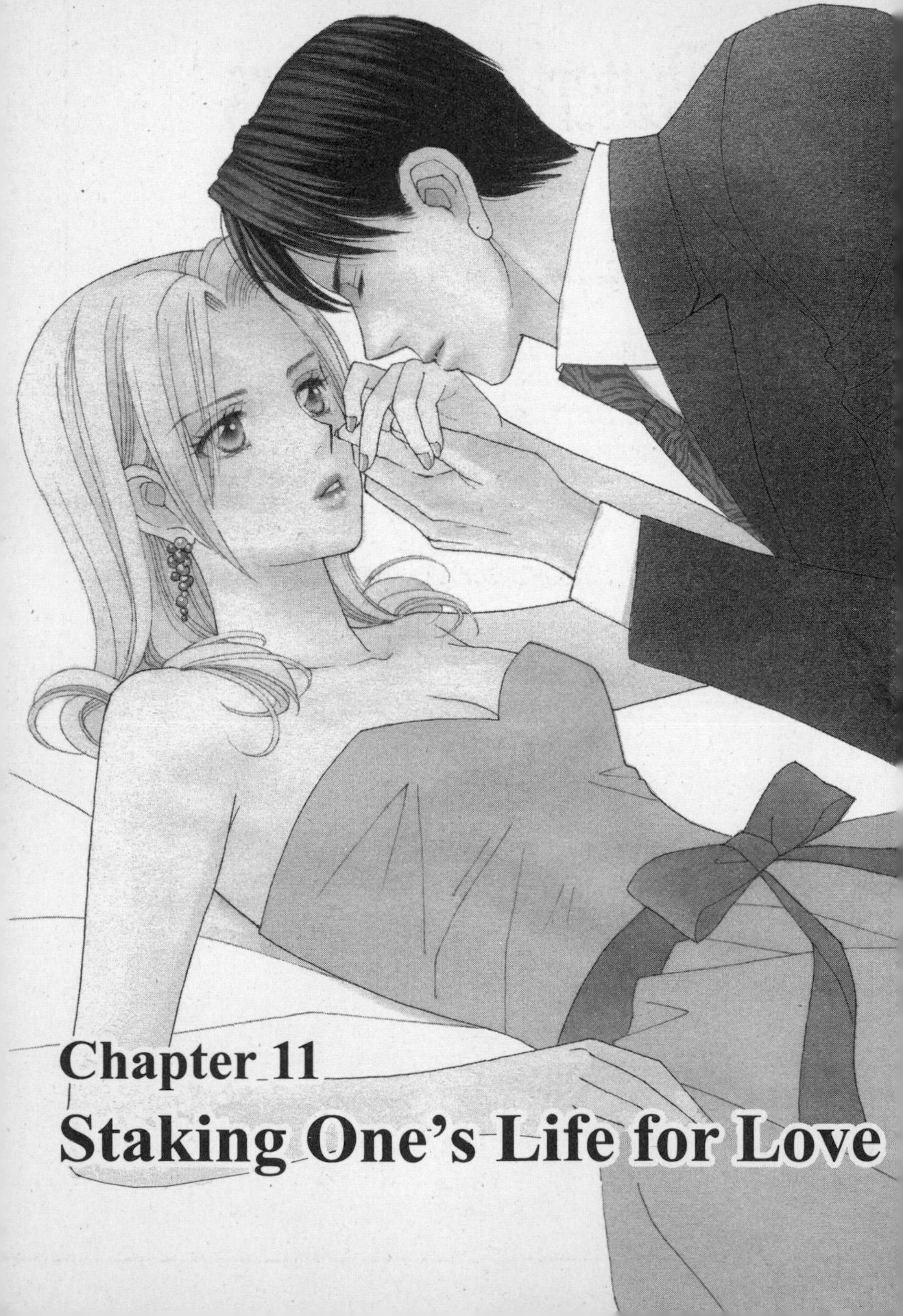

Chapter 11
Staking One's Life for Love

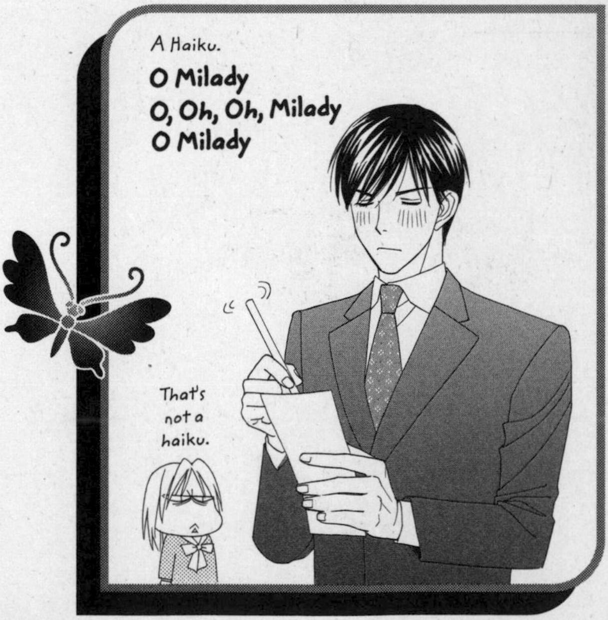
A Haiku.
O Milady
O, Oh, Oh, Milady
O Milady
That's not a haiku.

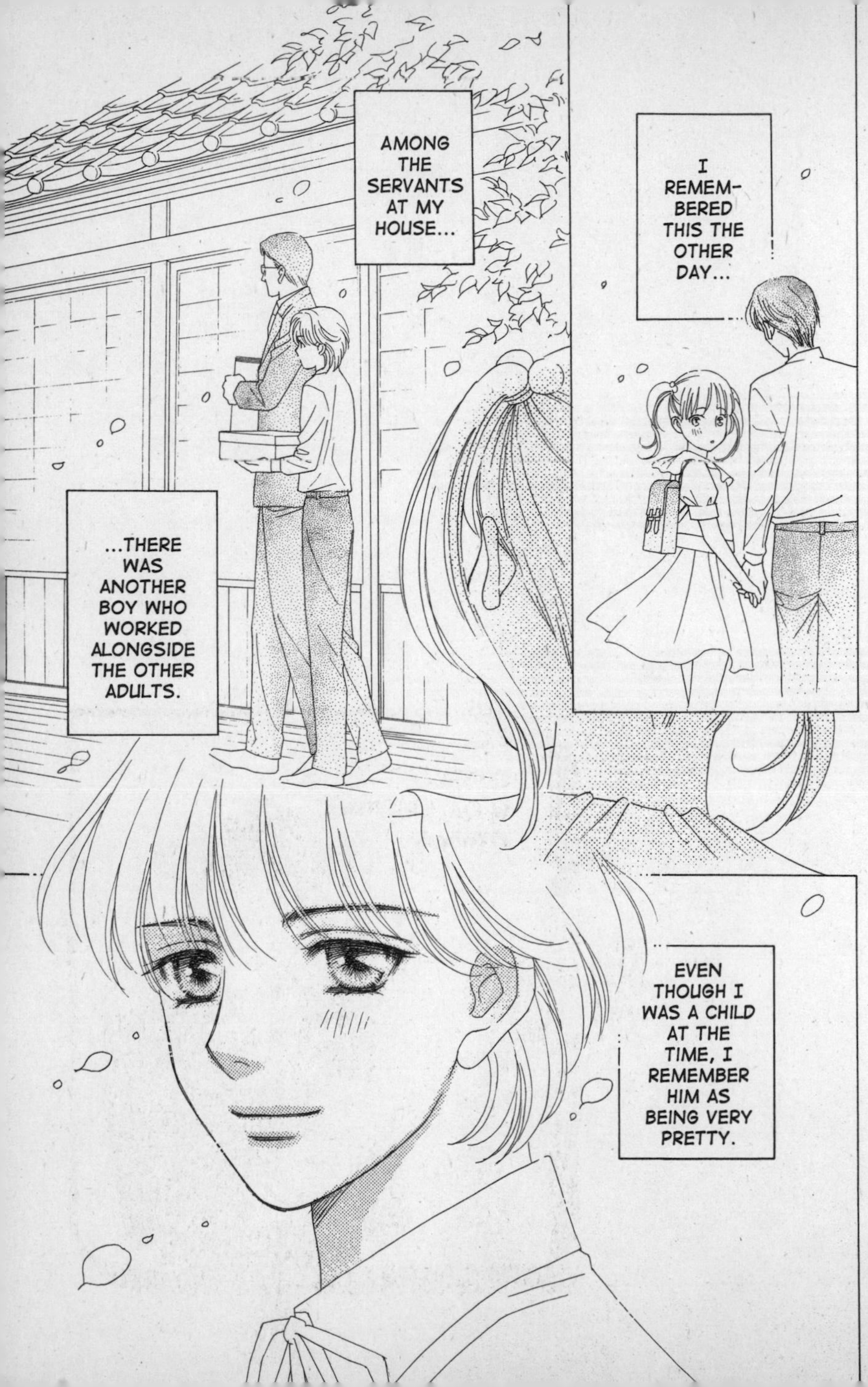
I REMEMBERED THIS THE OTHER DAY...
AMONG THE SERVANTS AT MY HOUSE...
...THERE WAS ANOTHER BOY WHO WORKED ALONGSIDE THE OTHER ADULTS.
...EVEN THOUGH I WAS A CHILD AT THE TIME, I REMEMBER HIM AS BEING VERY PRETTY.

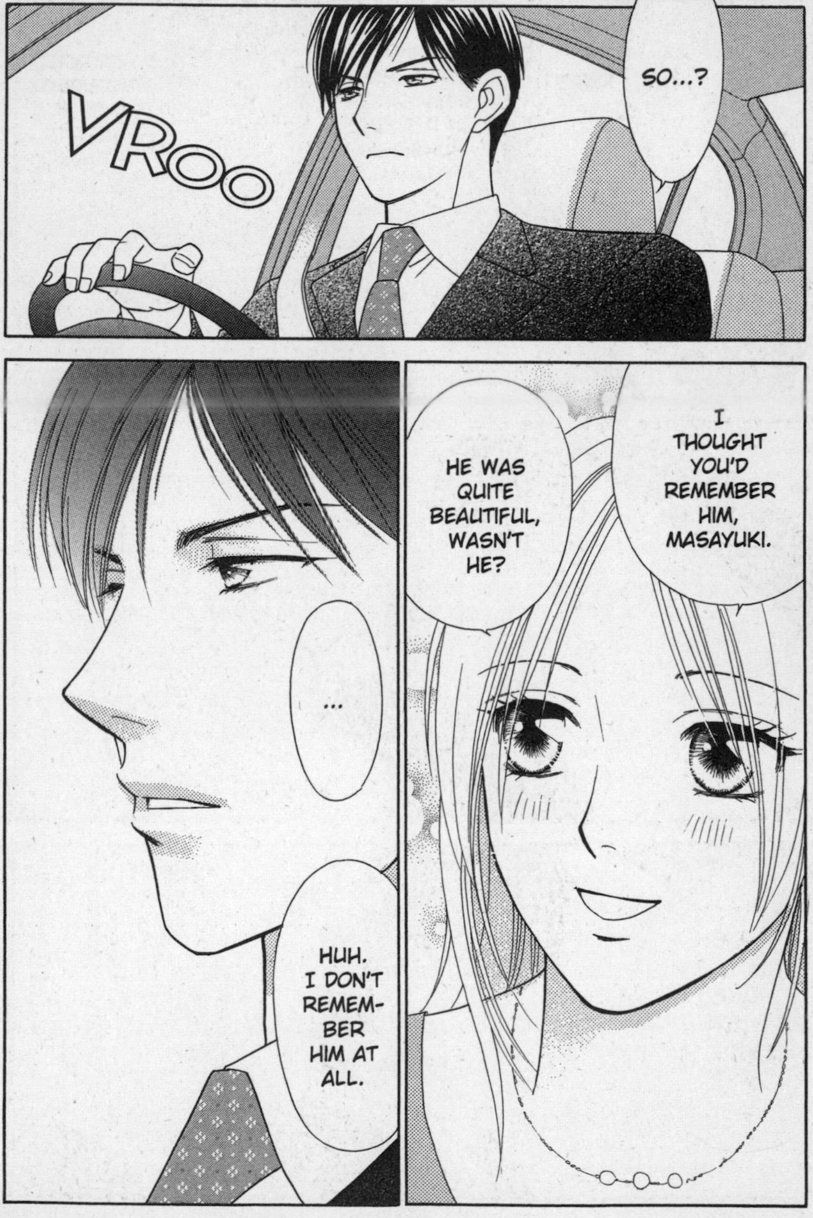
SO...?
VROOO
I THOUGHT YOU'D REMEMBER HIM, MASAYUKI.
HE WAS QUITE BEAUTIFUL, WASN'T HE?
...
HUH. I DON'T REMEMBER HIM AT ALL.

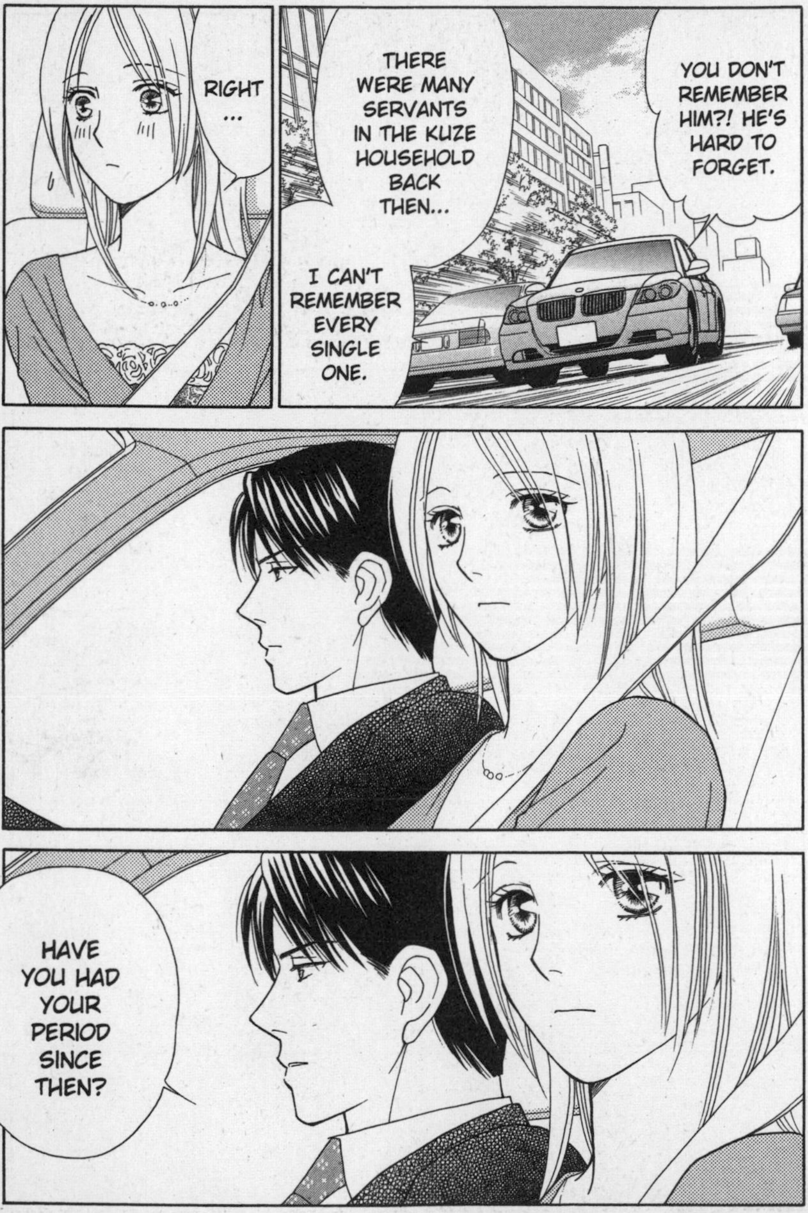
YOU DON'T REMEMBER HIM?! HE'S HARD TO FORGET.
THERE WERE MANY SERVANTS IN THE KUZE HOUSEHOLD BACK THEN...
I CAN'T REMEMBER EVERY SINGLE ONE.
RIGHT ...
HAVE YOU HAD YOUR PERIOD SINCE THEN?

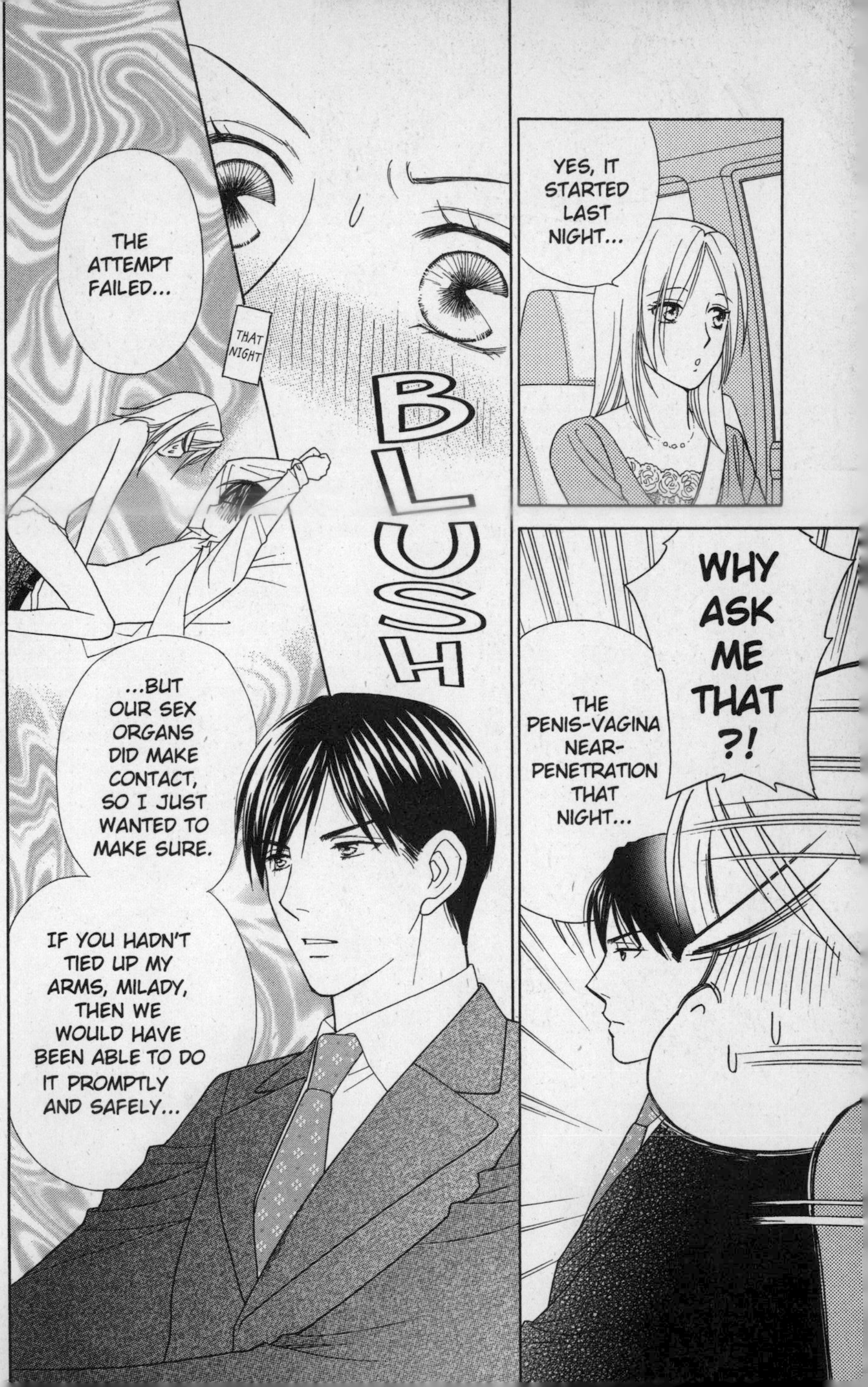
YES, IT STARTED LAST NIGHT...
WHY ASK ME THAT?!
THE PENIS-VAGINA NEAR-PENETRATION THAT NIGHT...
THE ATTEMPT FAILED...
THAT NIGHT
BLUSH
...BUT OUR SEX ORGANS DID MAKE CONTACT, SO I JUST WANTED TO MAKE SURE.
IF YOU HADN'T TIED UP MY ARMS, MILADY, THEN WE WOULD HAVE BEEN ABLE TO DO IT PROMPTLY AND SAFELY...

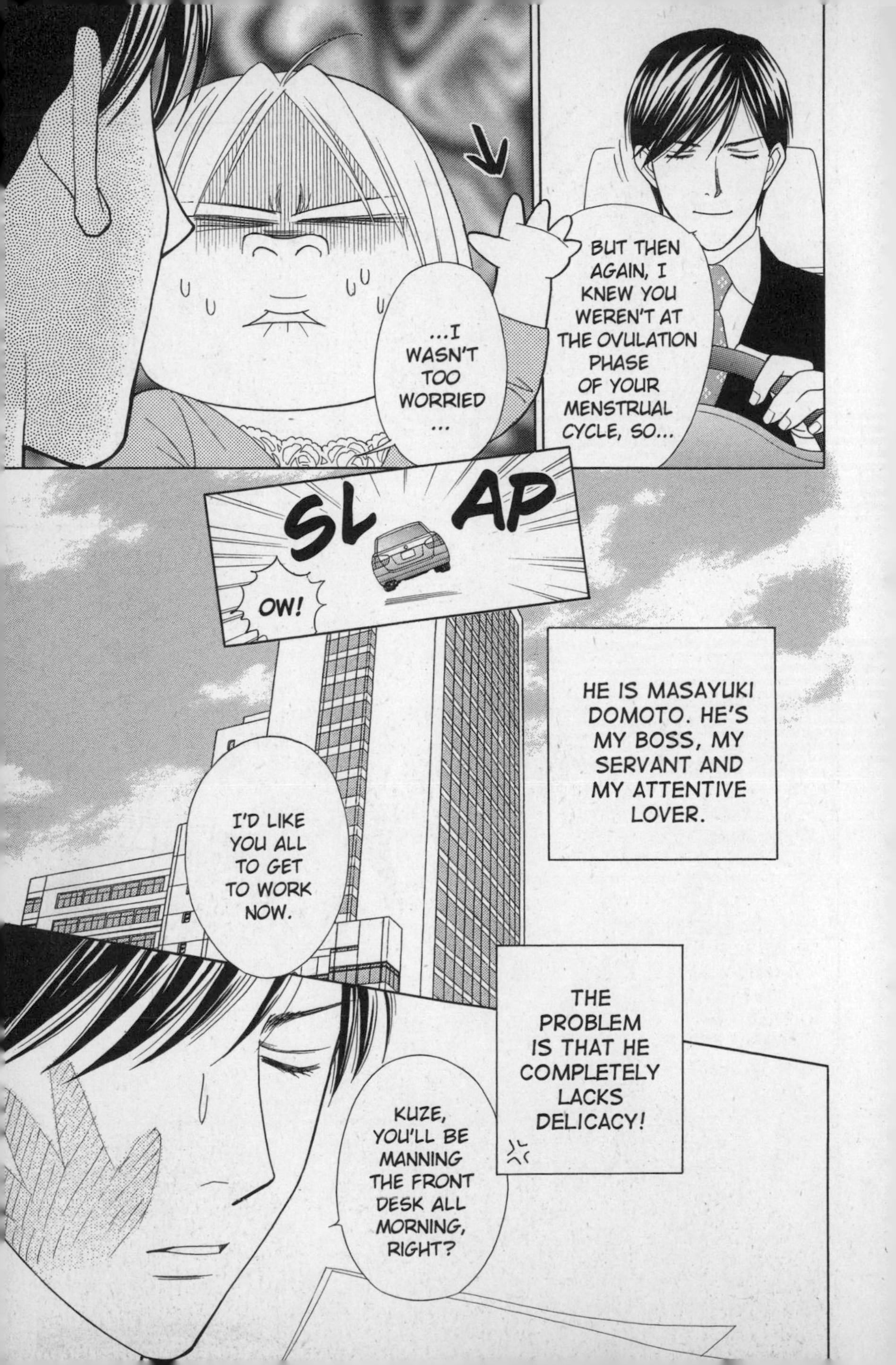
BUT THEN AGAIN, I KNEW YOU WEREN'T AT THE OVULATION PHASE OF YOUR MENSTRUAL CYCLE, SO...
...I WASN'T TOO WORRIED ...
SLAP
OW!
HE IS MASAYUKI DOMOTO. HE'S MY BOSS, MY SERVANT AND MY ATTENTIVE LOVER.
I'D LIKE YOU ALL TO GET TO WORK NOW.
THE PROBLEM IS THAT HE COMPLETELY LACKS DELICACY!
KUZE, YOU'LL BE MANNING THE FRONT DESK ALL MORNING, RIGHT?

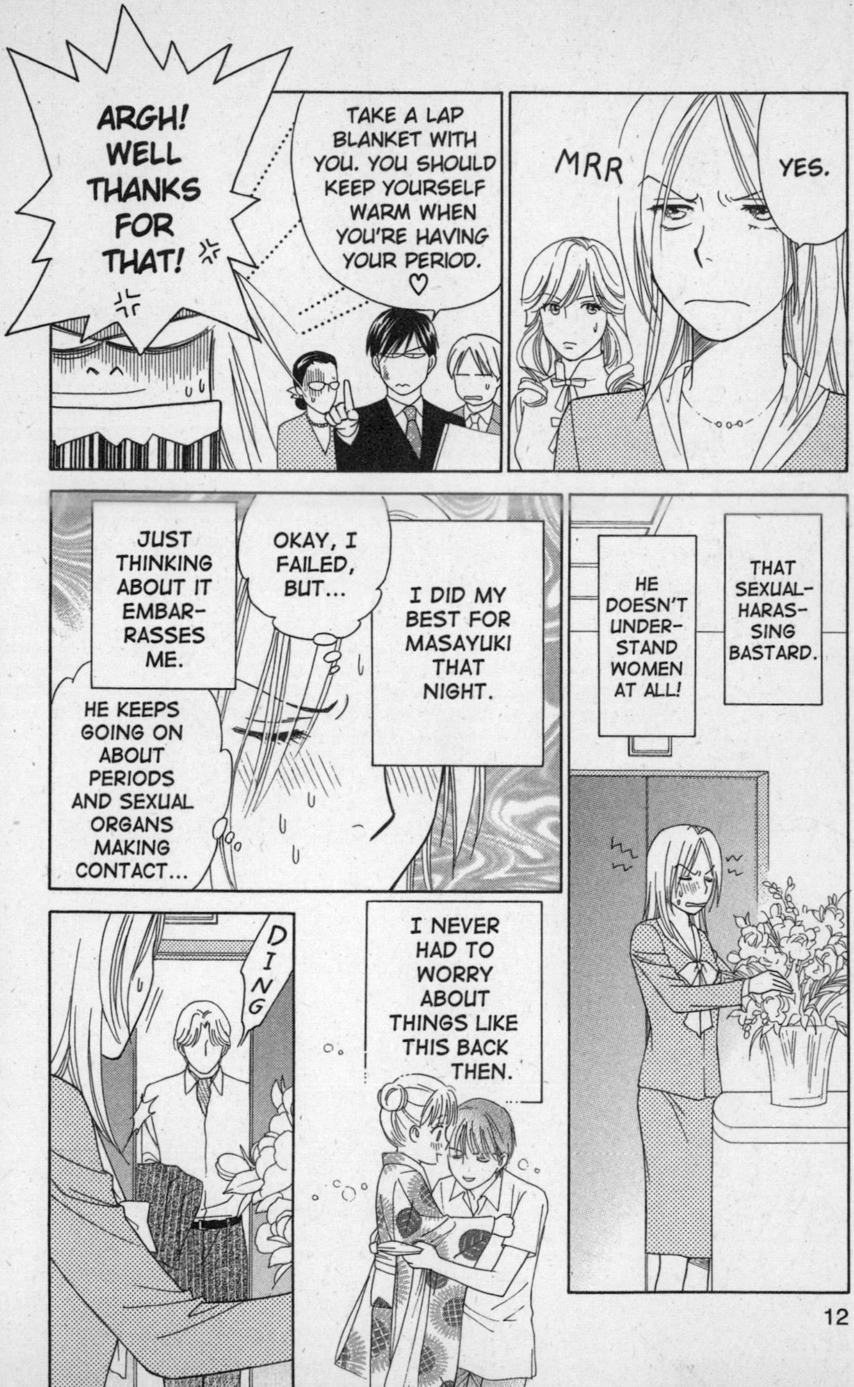
YES.
MRR
TAKE A LAP BLANKET WITH YOU. YOU SHOULD KEEP YOURSELF WARM WHEN YOU'RE HAVING YOUR PERIOD. ♡
ARGH! WELL THANKS FOR THAT!
THAT SEXUAL-HARASSING BASTARD.
HE DOESN'T UNDERSTAND WOMEN AT ALL!
I DID MY BEST FOR MASAYUKI THAT NIGHT.
OKAY, I FAILED, BUT...
JUST THINKING ABOUT IT EMBARRASSES ME.
HE KEEPS GOING ON ABOUT PERIODS AND SEXUAL ORGANS MAKING CONTACT...
I NEVER HAD TO WORRY ABOUT THINGS LIKE THIS BACK THEN.
DING

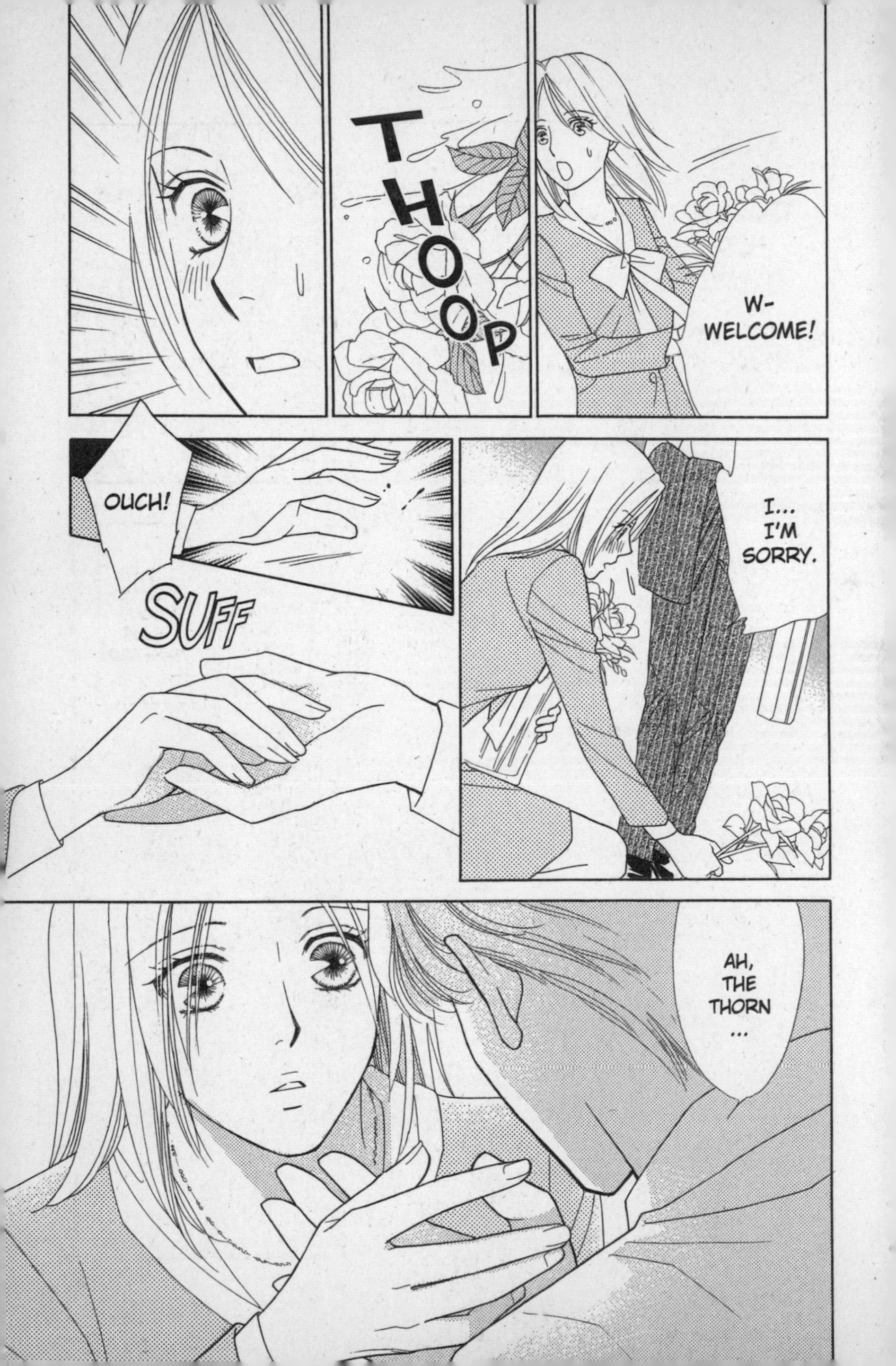
W- WELCOME!
THOOP
I... I'M SORRY.
OUCH!
SUFF
AH, THE THORN ...

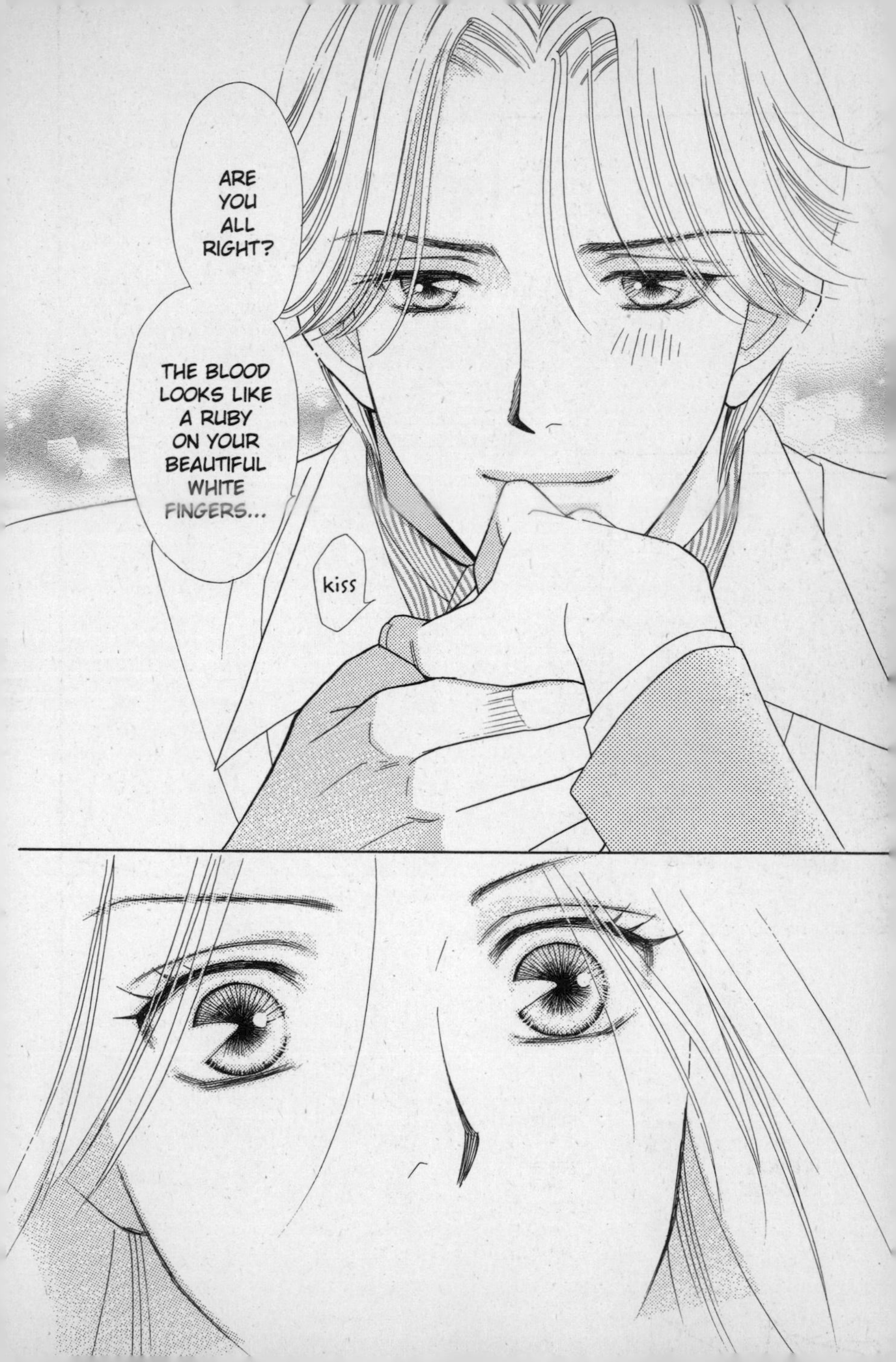
ARE YOU ALL RIGHT?
THE BLOOD LOOKS LIKE A RUBY ON YOUR BEAUTIFUL WHITE FINGERS...
kiss

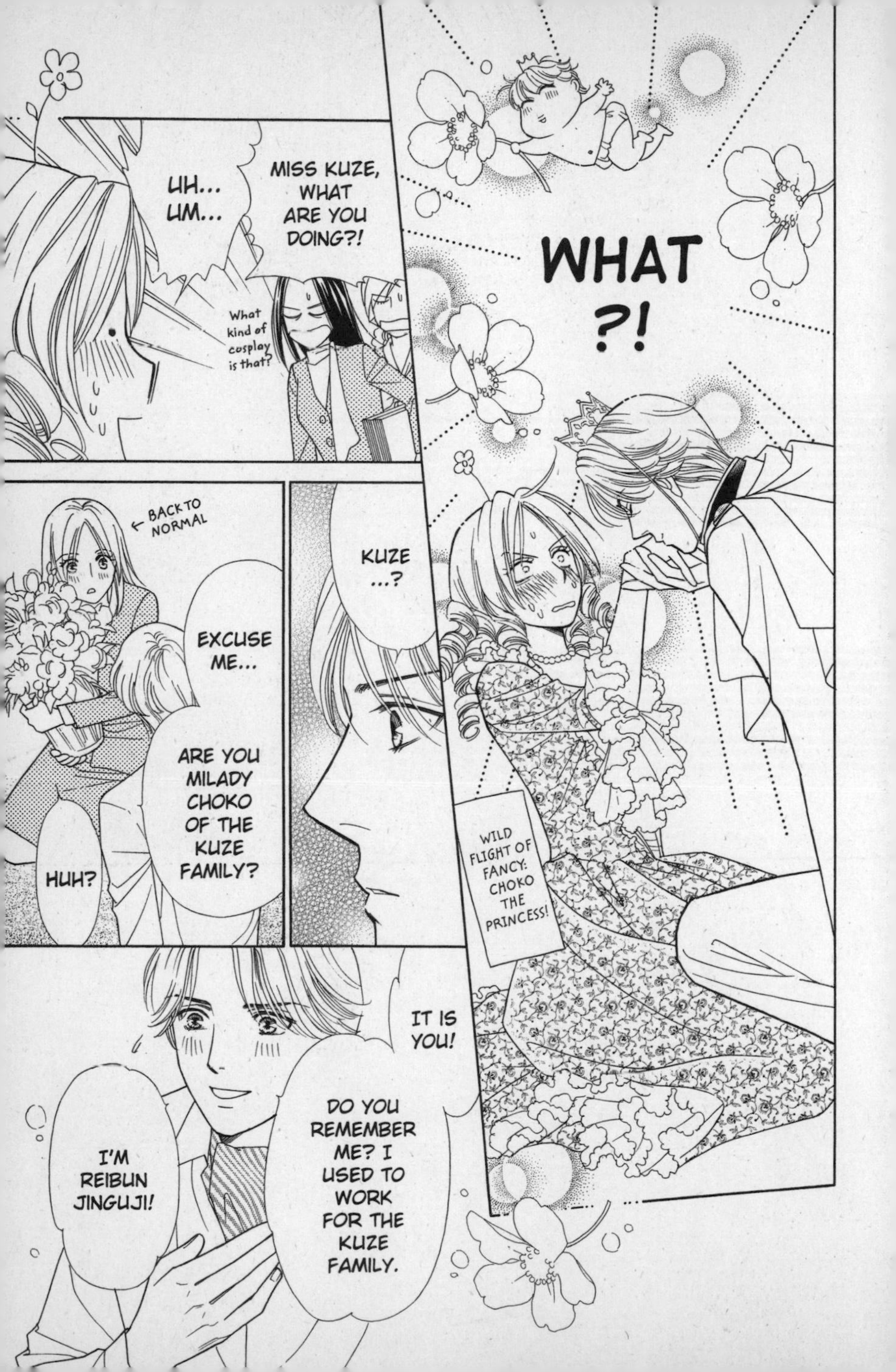
WHAT ?!
WILD FLIGHT OF FANCY: CHOKO THE PRINCESS!
MISS KUZE, WHAT ARE YOU DOING?!
UH... UM...
What kind of cosplay is that?
KUZE ...?
EXCUSE ME...
ARE YOU MILADY CHOKO OF THE KUZE FAMILY?
← BACK TO NORMAL
HUH?
IT IS YOU!
DO YOU REMEMBER ME? I USED TO WORK FOR THE KUZE FAMILY.
I'M REIBUN JINGUJI!

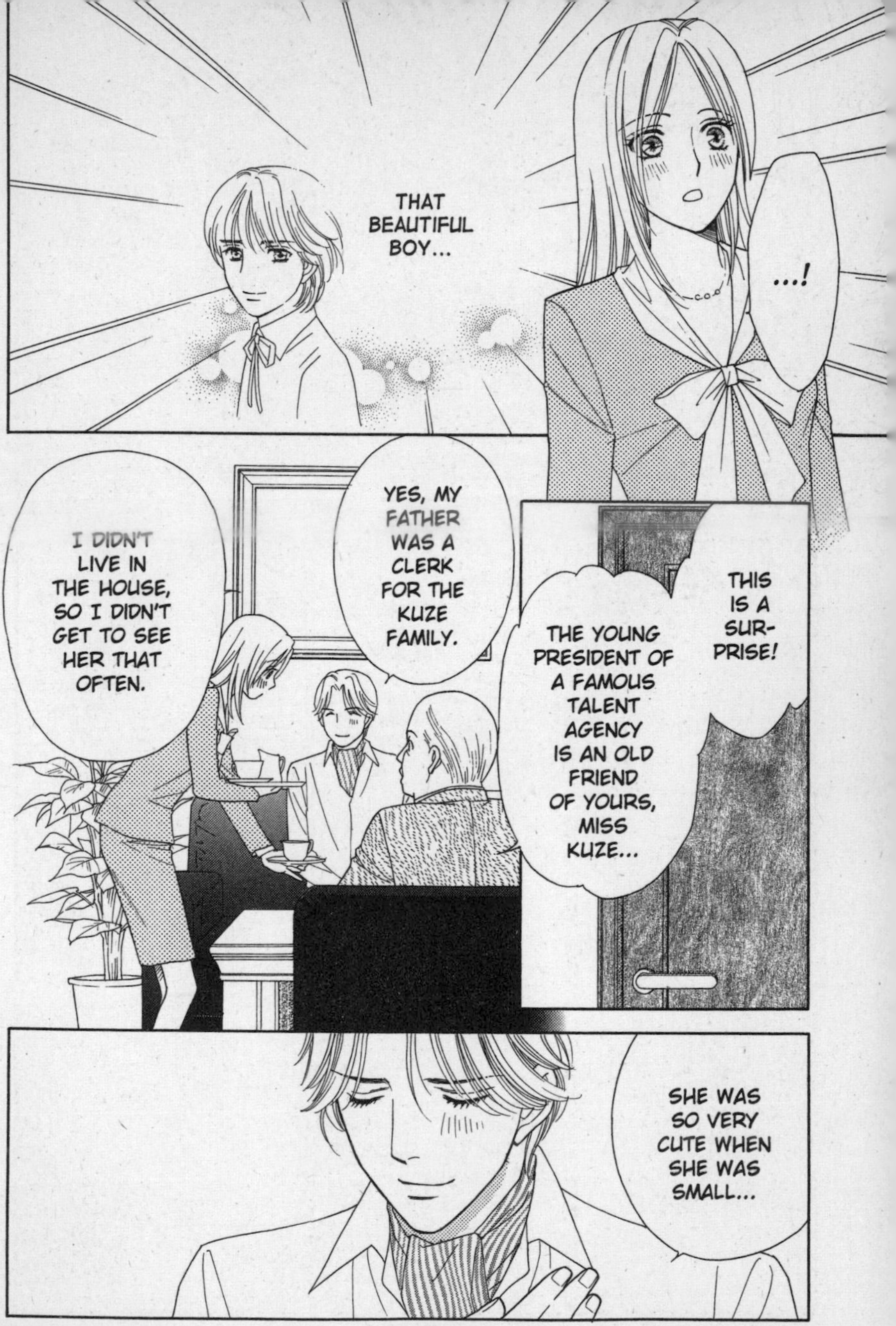
...!
THAT BEAUTIFUL BOY...
THIS IS A SURPRISE!
THE YOUNG PRESIDENT OF A FAMOUS TALENT AGENCY IS AN OLD FRIEND OF YOURS, MISS KUZE...
YES, MY FATHER WAS A CLERK FOR THE KUZE FAMILY.
I DIDN'T LIVE IN THE HOUSE, SO I DIDN'T GET TO SEE HER THAT OFTEN.
SHE WAS SO VERY CUTE WHEN SHE WAS SMALL...

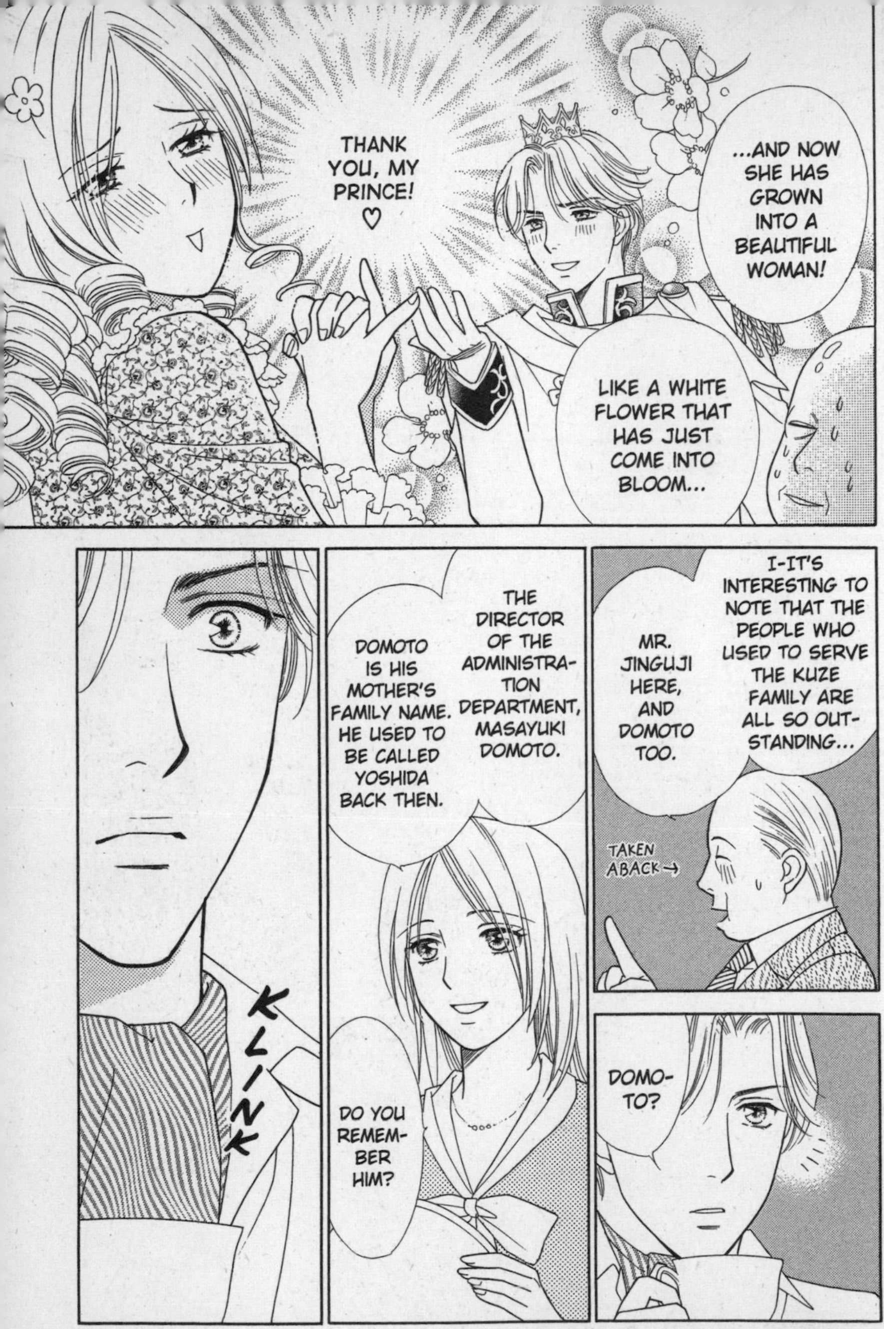
...AND NOW SHE HAS GROWN INTO A BEAUTIFUL WOMAN!
LIKE A WHITE FLOWER THAT HAS JUST COME INTO BLOOM...
THANK YOU, MY PRINCE! ♡
I-IT'S INTERESTING TO NOTE THAT THE PEOPLE WHO USED TO SERVE THE KUZE FAMILY ARE ALL SO OUT-STANDING...
MR. JINGUJI HERE, AND DOMOTO TOO.
TAKEN ABACK →
DOMO-TO?
THE DIRECTOR OF THE ADMINISTRA-TION DEPARTMENT, MASAYUKI DOMOTO.
DOMOTO IS HIS MOTHER'S FAMILY NAME. HE USED TO BE CALLED YOSHIDA BACK THEN.
DO YOU REMEM-BER HIM?
KLINK

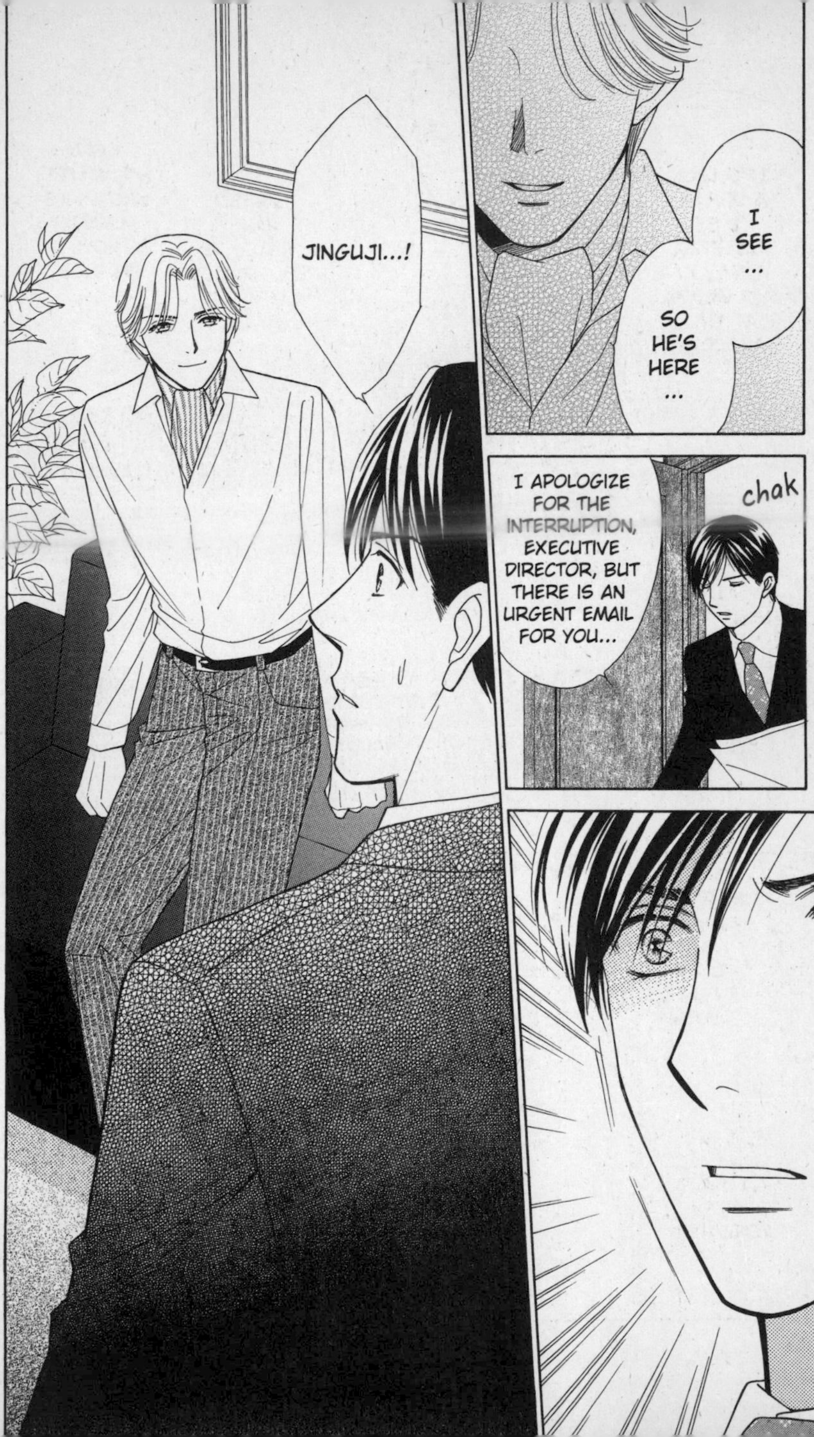
I SEE ...
SO HE'S HERE ...
I APOLOGIZE FOR THE INTERRUPTION, EXECUTIVE DIRECTOR, BUT THERE IS AN URGENT EMAIL FOR YOU...
chak
JINGUJI...!

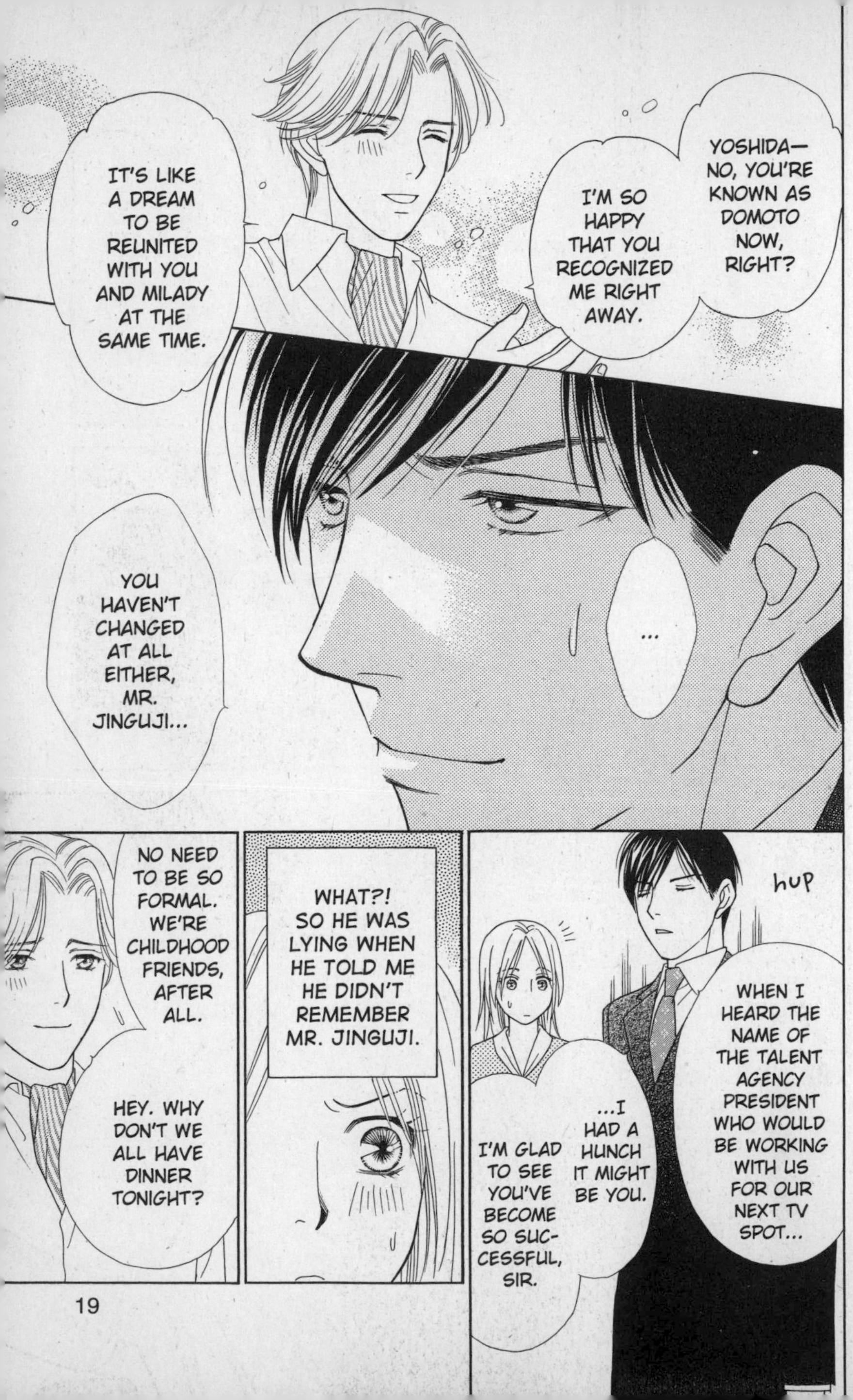
YOSHIDA—NO, YOU'RE KNOWN AS DOMOTO NOW, RIGHT?
I'M SO HAPPY THAT YOU RECOGNIZED ME RIGHT AWAY.
IT'S LIKE A DREAM TO BE REUNITED WITH YOU AND MILADY AT THE SAME TIME.
...
YOU HAVEN'T CHANGED AT ALL EITHER, MR. JINGUJI...
hup
WHEN I HEARD THE NAME OF THE TALENT AGENCY PRESIDENT WHO WOULD BE WORKING WITH US FOR OUR NEXT TV SPOT...
...I HAD A HUNCH IT MIGHT BE YOU.
I'M GLAD TO SEE YOU'VE BECOME SO SUC-CESSFUL, SIR.
WHAT?! SO HE WAS LYING WHEN HE TOLD ME HE DIDN'T REMEMBER MR. JINGUJI.
NO NEED TO BE SO FORMAL. WE'RE CHILDHOOD FRIENDS, AFTER ALL.
HEY. WHY DON'T WE ALL HAVE DINNER TONIGHT?

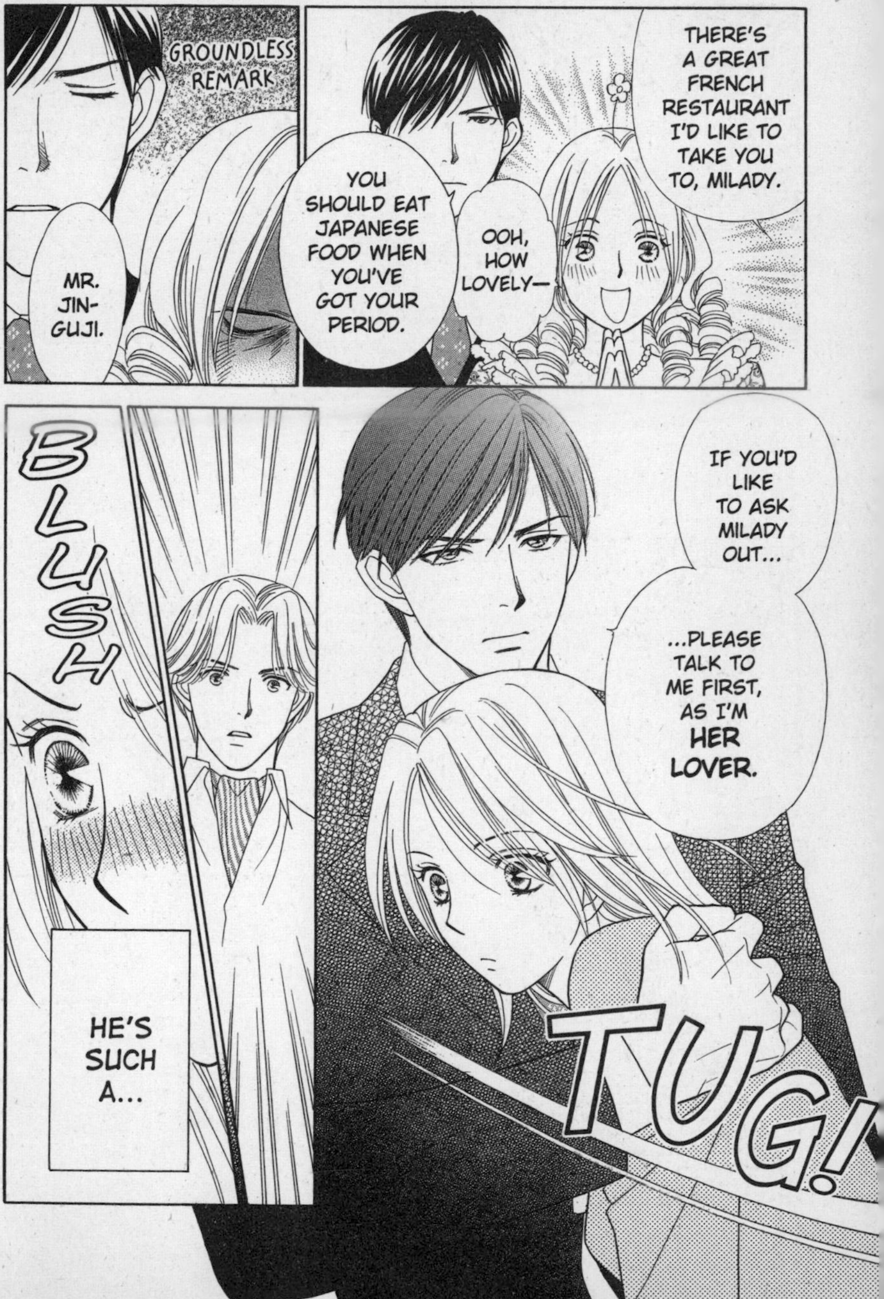
THERE'S A GREAT FRENCH RESTAURANT I'D LIKE TO TAKE YOU TO, MILADY.
OOH, HOW LOVELY—
YOU SHOULD EAT JAPANESE FOOD WHEN YOU'VE GOT YOUR PERIOD.
GROUNDLESS REMARK
MR. JIN-GUJI.
IF YOU'D LIKE TO ASK MILADY OUT...
...PLEASE TALK TO ME FIRST, AS I'M **HER LOVER.**
TUG!
BLUSH
HE'S SUCH A...

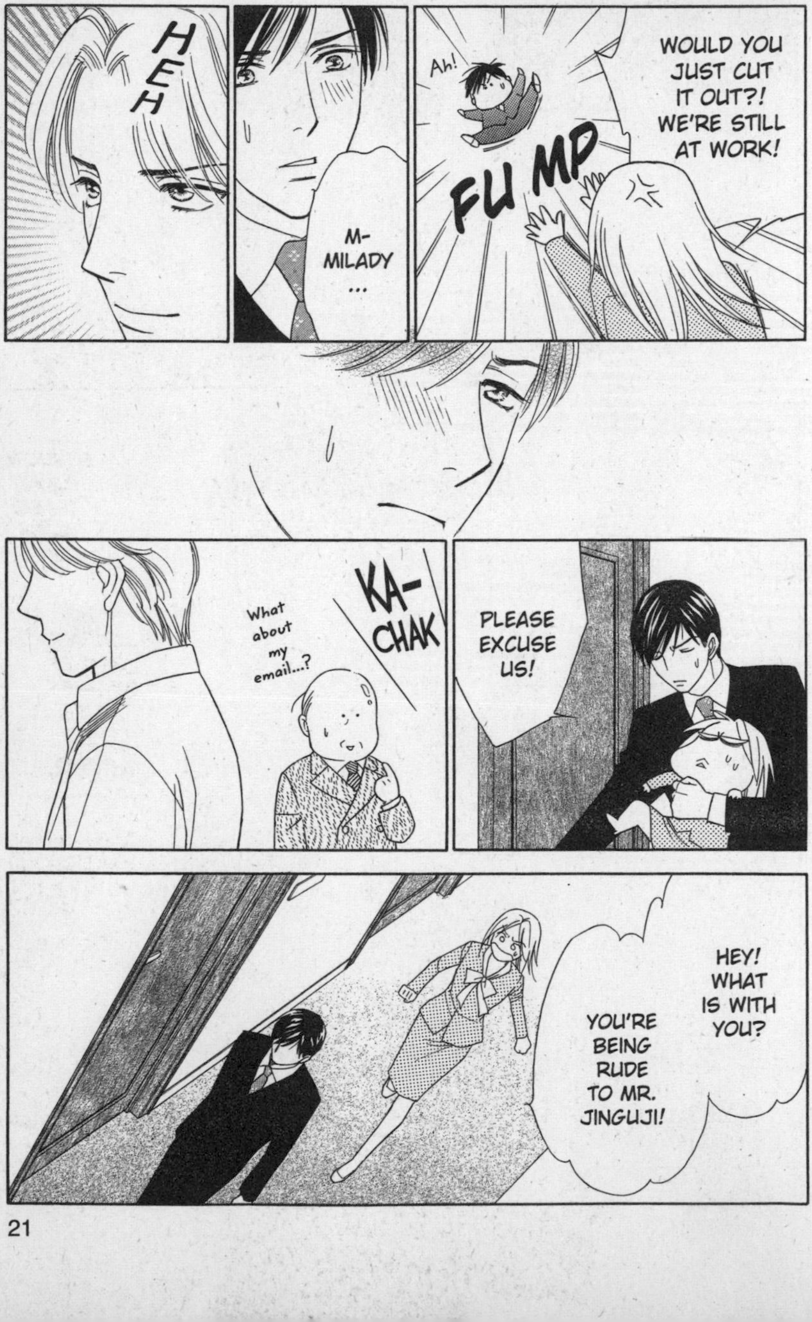
WOULD YOU JUST CUT IT OUT?! WE'RE STILL AT WORK!
Ah!
FUMP
M-MILADY ...
HEH
PLEASE EXCUSE US!
KA-CHAK
What about my email...?
HEY! WHAT IS WITH YOU?
YOU'RE BEING RUDE TO MR. JINGUJI!

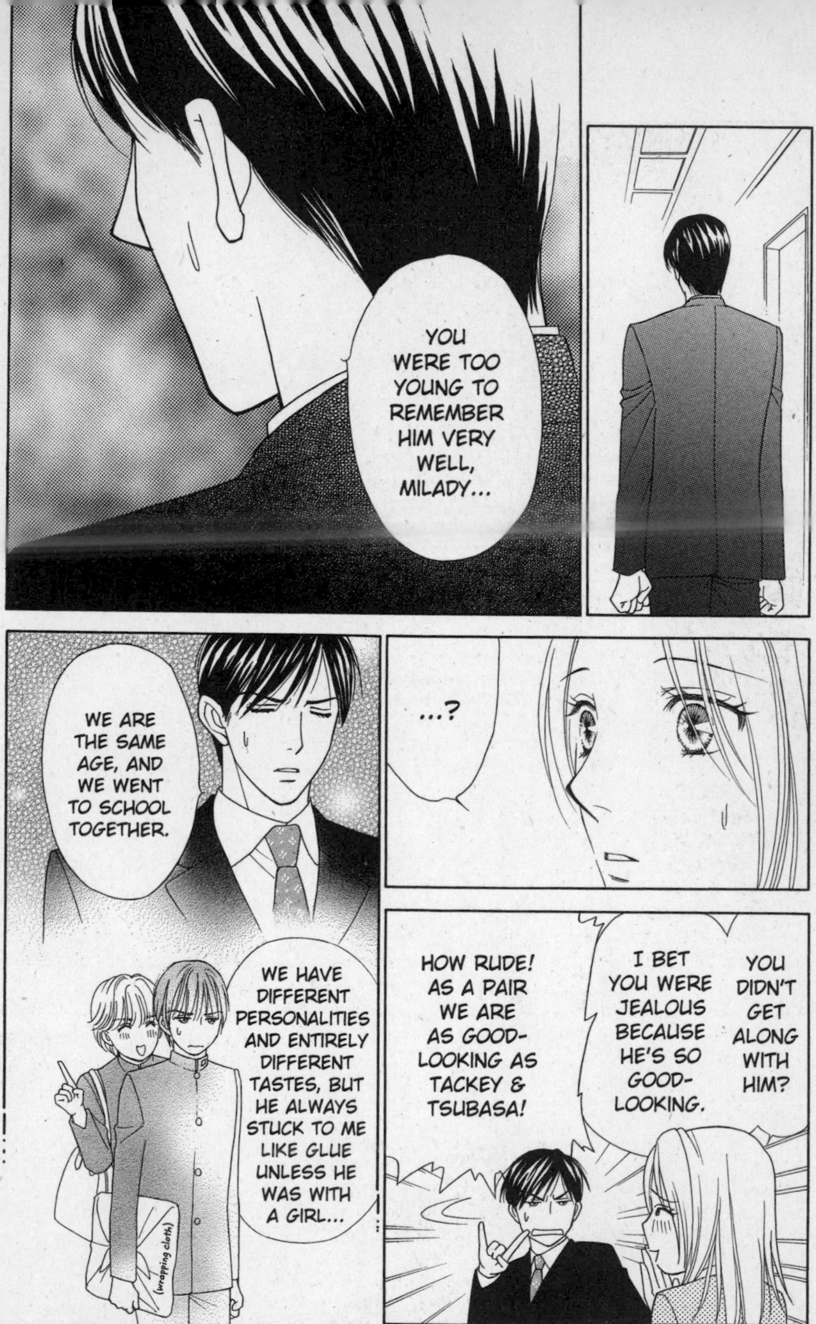
YOU WERE TOO YOUNG TO REMEMBER HIM VERY WELL, MILADY...
...?
YOU DIDN'T GET ALONG WITH HIM?
I BET YOU WERE JEALOUS BECAUSE HE'S SO GOOD-LOOKING.
HOW RUDE! AS A PAIR WE ARE AS GOOD-LOOKING AS TACKEY & TSUBASA!
WE ARE THE SAME AGE, AND WE WENT TO SCHOOL TOGETHER.
WE HAVE DIFFERENT PERSONALITIES AND ENTIRELY DIFFERENT TASTES, BUT HE ALWAYS STUCK TO ME LIKE GLUE UNLESS HE WAS WITH A GIRL...
(wrapping cloth)

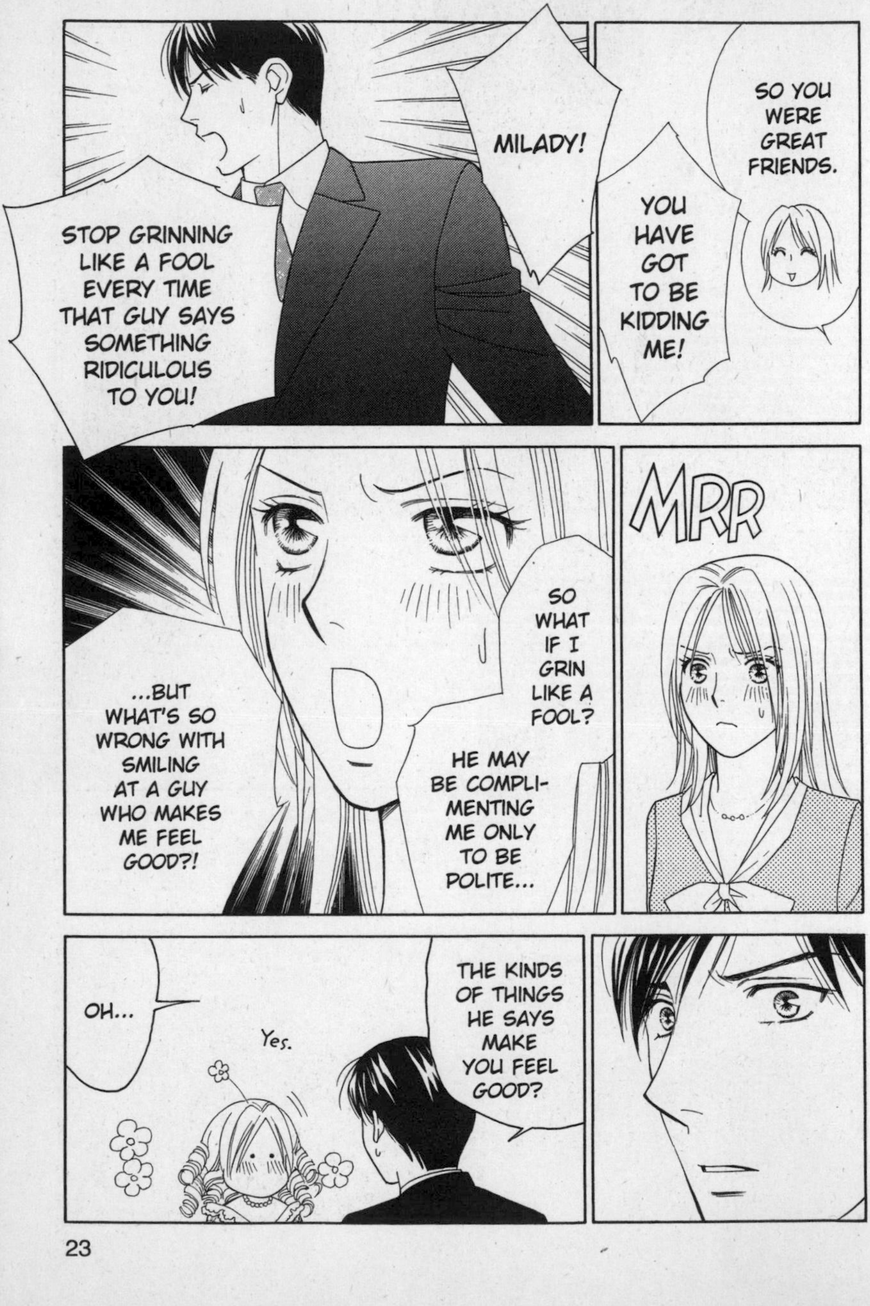
SO YOU WERE GREAT FRIENDS.
YOU HAVE GOT TO BE KIDDING ME!
MILADY!
STOP GRINNING LIKE A FOOL EVERY TIME THAT GUY SAYS SOMETHING RIDICULOUS TO YOU!
MRR
SO WHAT IF I GRIN LIKE A FOOL?
HE MAY BE COMPLI-MENTING ME ONLY TO BE POLITE...
...BUT WHAT'S SO WRONG WITH SMILING AT A GUY WHO MAKES ME FEEL GOOD?!
THE KINDS OF THINGS HE SAYS MAKE YOU FEEL GOOD?
Yes.
OH...

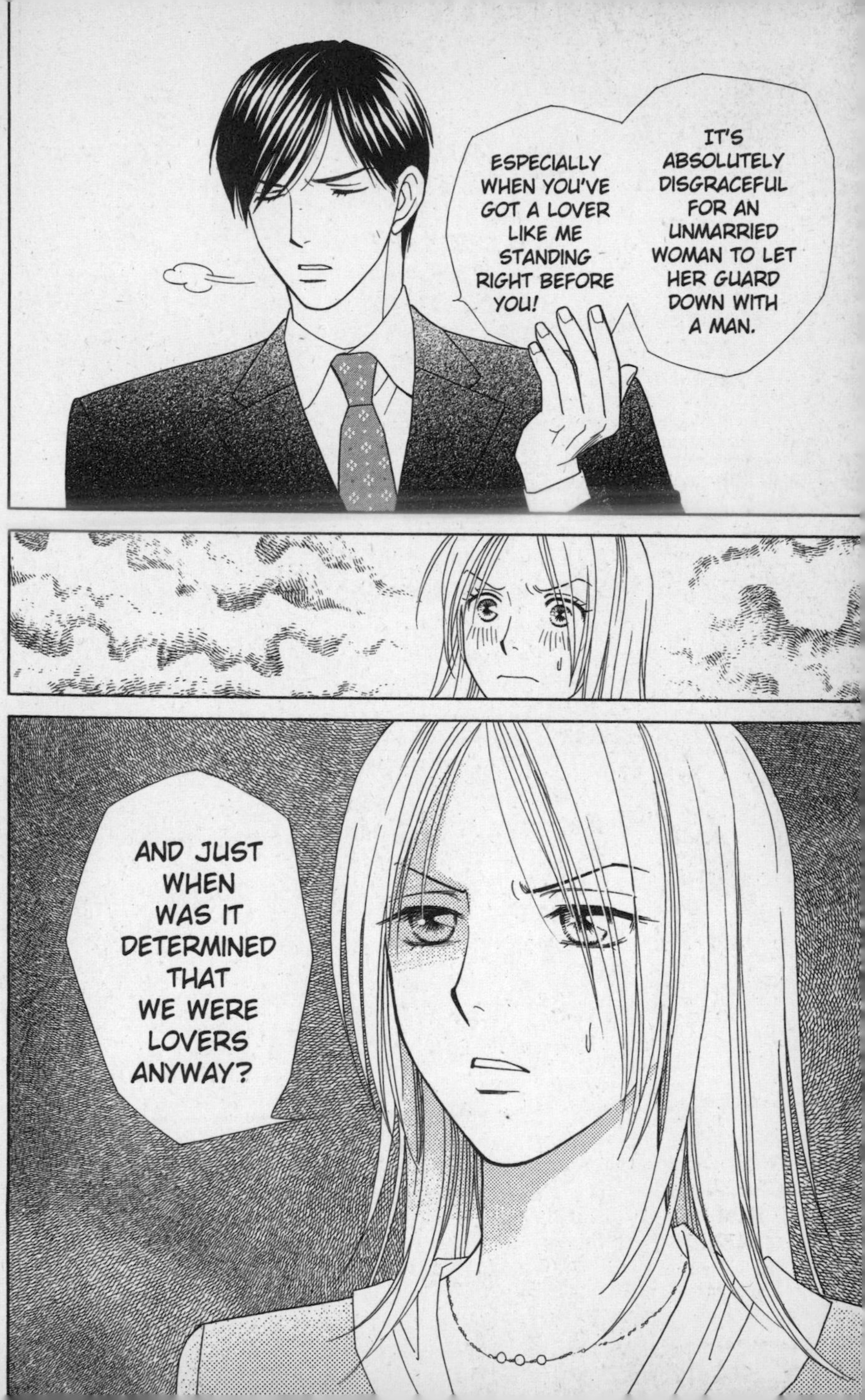
IT'S ABSOLUTELY DISGRACEFUL FOR AN UNMARRIED WOMAN TO LET HER GUARD DOWN WITH A MAN.
ESPECIALLY WHEN YOU'VE GOT A LOVER LIKE ME STANDING RIGHT BEFORE YOU!
AND JUST WHEN WAS IT DETERMINED THAT WE WERE LOVERS ANYWAY?

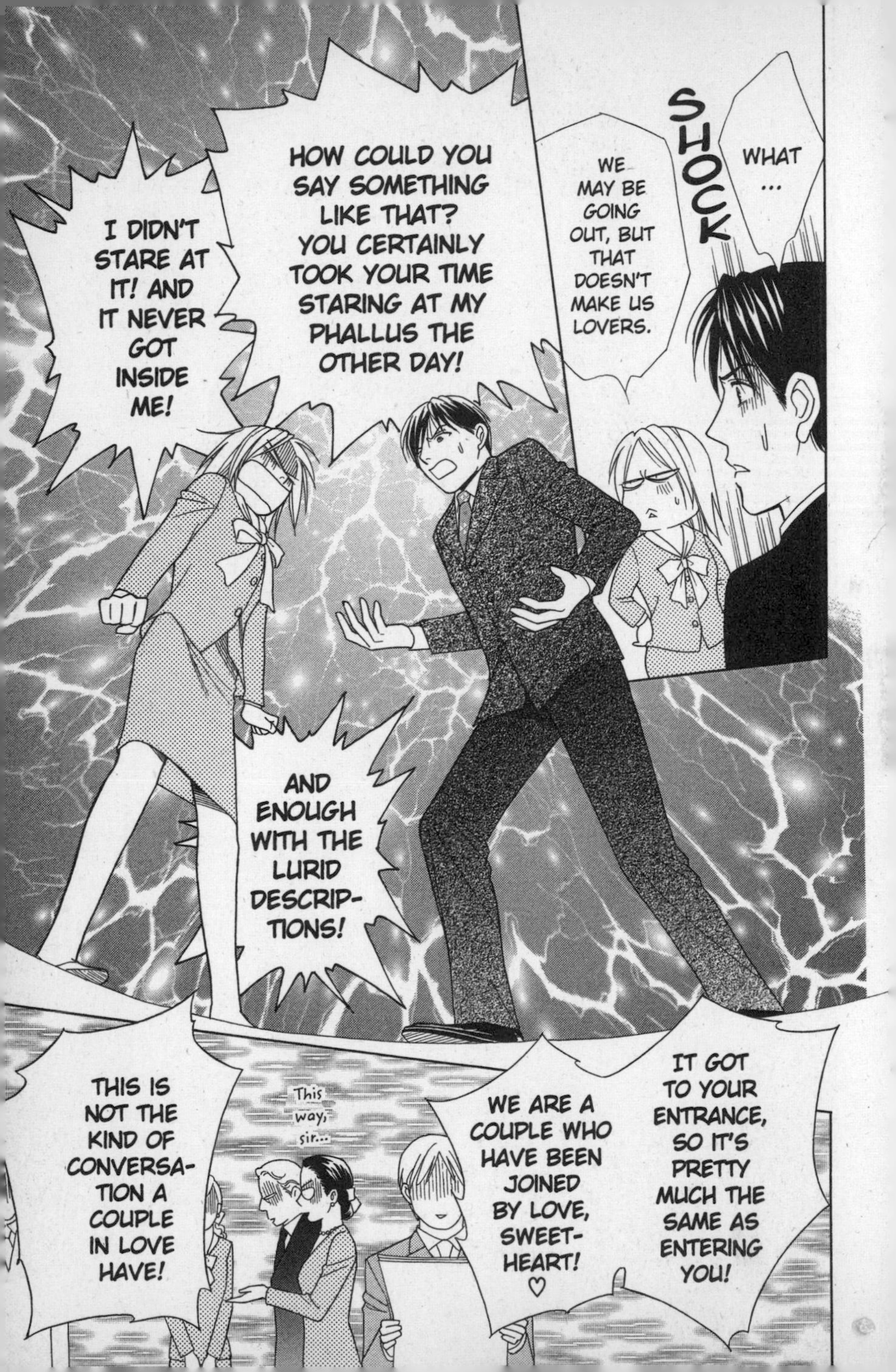
WHAT ...
SHOCK
WE MAY BE GOING OUT, BUT THAT DOESN'T MAKE US LOVERS.
HOW COULD YOU SAY SOMETHING LIKE THAT? YOU CERTAINLY TOOK YOUR TIME STARING AT MY PHALLUS THE OTHER DAY!
I DIDN'T STARE AT IT! AND IT NEVER GOT INSIDE ME!
AND ENOUGH WITH THE LURID DESCRIPTIONS!
IT GOT TO YOUR ENTRANCE, SO IT'S PRETTY MUCH THE SAME AS ENTERING YOU!
WE ARE A COUPLE WHO HAVE BEEN JOINED BY LOVE, SWEETHEART! ♡
This way, sir...
THIS IS NOT THE KIND OF CONVERSATION A COUPLE IN LOVE HAVE!

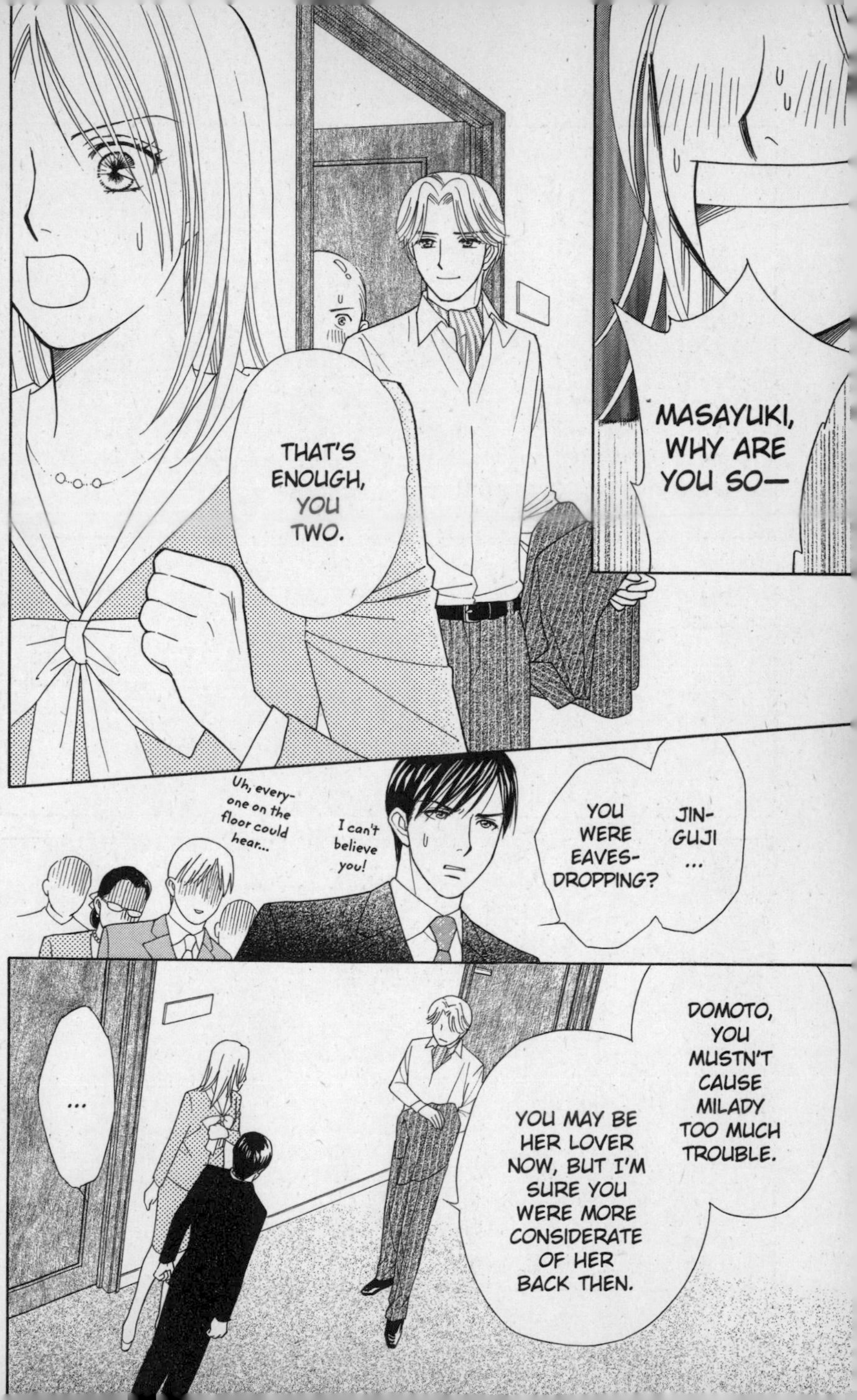
MASAYUKI, WHY ARE YOU SO—
THAT'S ENOUGH, YOU TWO.
JIN-GUJI ...
YOU WERE EAVES-DROPPING?
I can't believe you!
Uh, every-one on the floor could hear...
DOMOTO, YOU MUSTN'T CAUSE MILADY TOO MUCH TROUBLE.
YOU MAY BE HER LOVER NOW, BUT I'M SURE YOU WERE MORE CONSIDERATE OF HER BACK THEN.
...

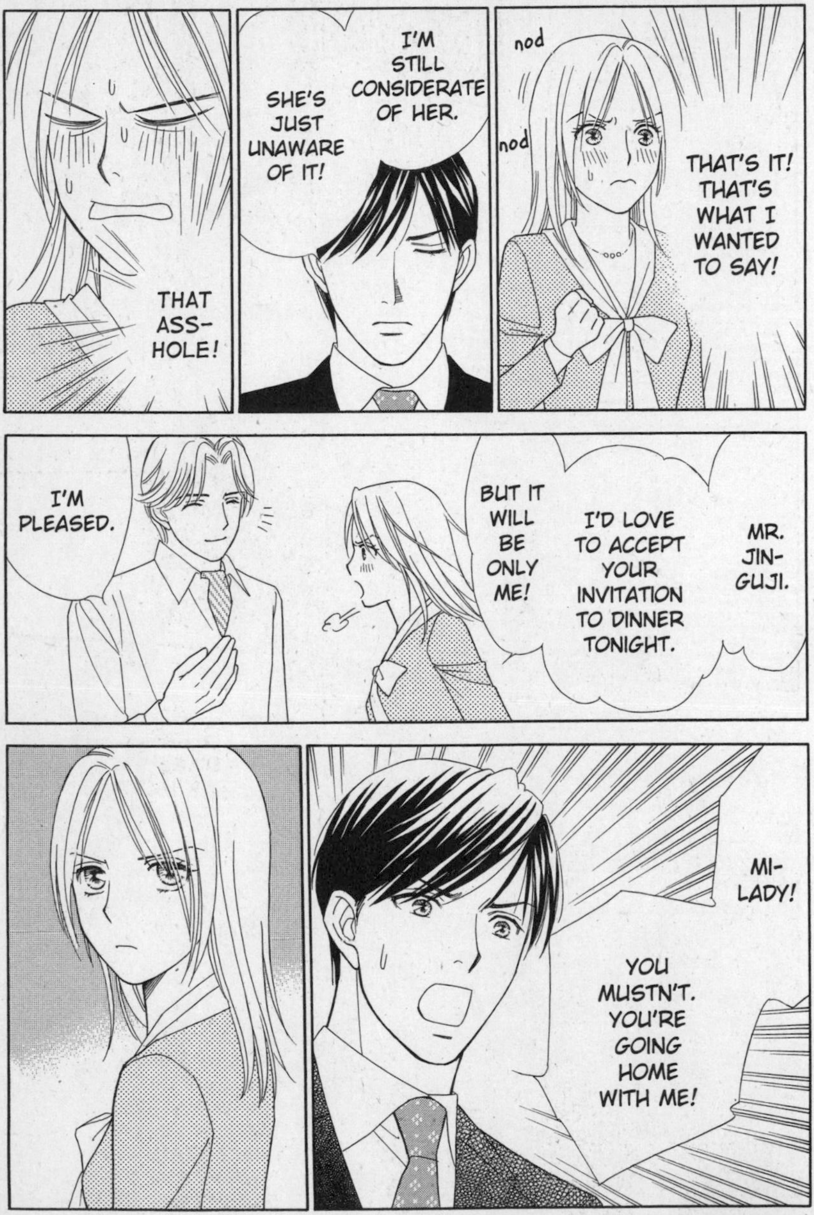
nod
nod
THAT'S IT! THAT'S WHAT I WANTED TO SAY!
I'M STILL CONSIDERATE OF HER.
SHE'S JUST UNAWARE OF IT!
THAT ASS-HOLE!
MR. JIN-GUJI.
I'D LOVE TO ACCEPT YOUR INVITATION TO DINNER TONIGHT.
BUT IT WILL BE ONLY ME!
I'M PLEASED.
MI-LADY!
YOU MUSTN'T. YOU'RE GOING HOME WITH ME!

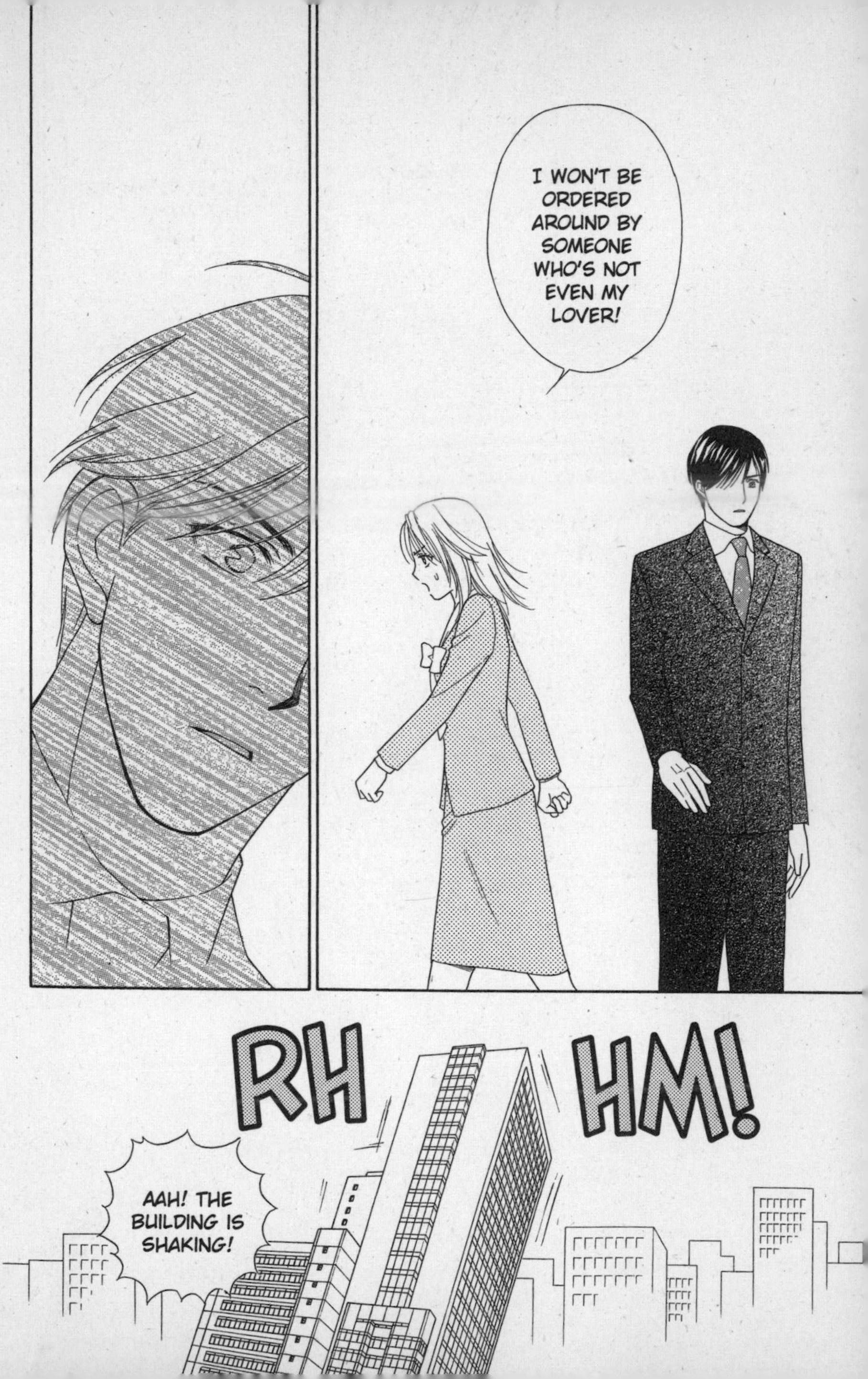
I WON'T BE ORDERED AROUND BY SOMEONE WHO'S NOT EVEN MY LOVER!
RH HM!
AAH! THE BUILDING IS SHAKING!

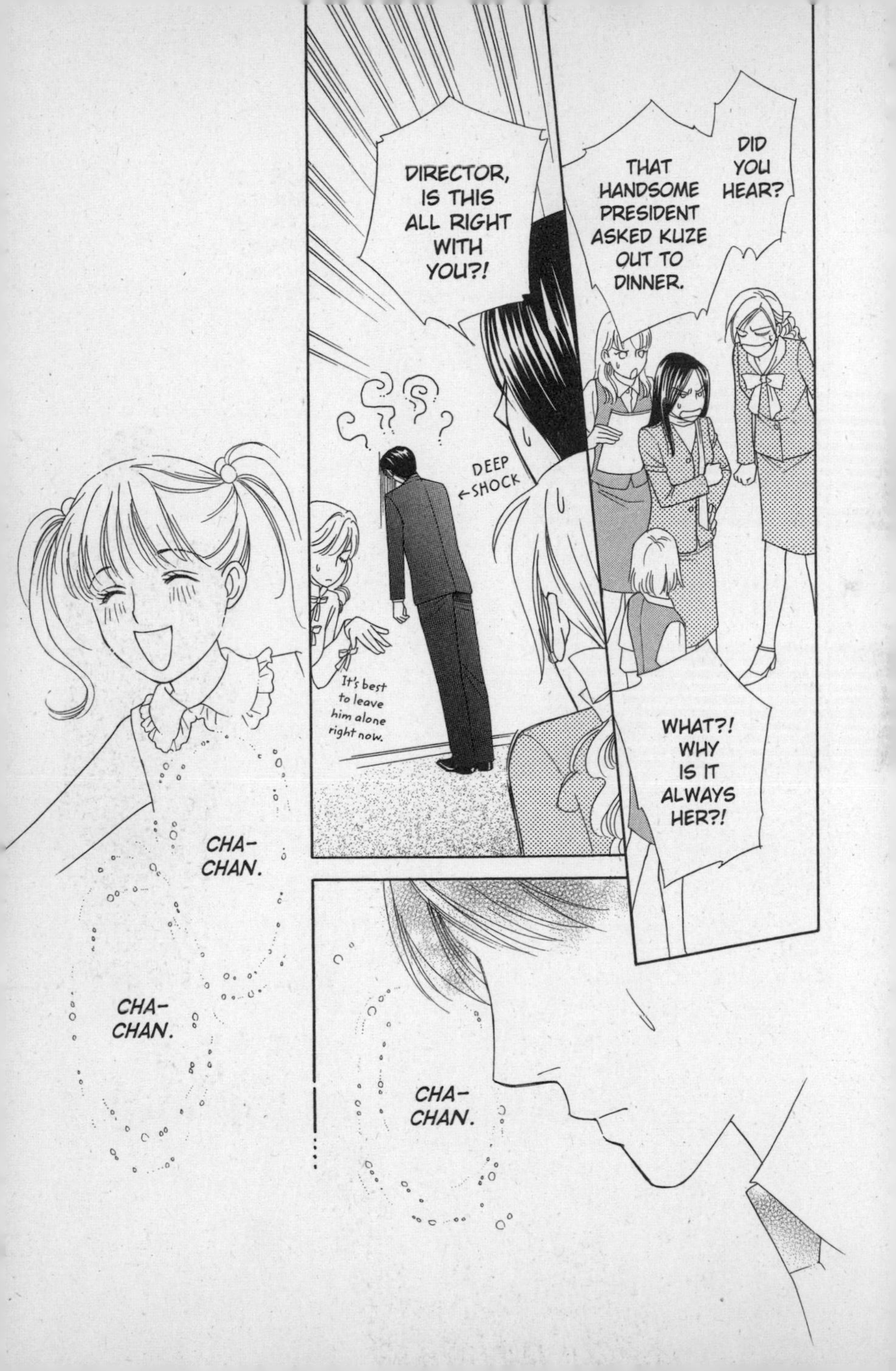
DID YOU HEAR?
THAT HANDSOME PRESIDENT ASKED KUZE OUT TO DINNER.
WHAT?! WHY IS IT ALWAYS HER?!
DIRECTOR, IS THIS ALL RIGHT WITH YOU?!
DEEP ←SHOCK
It's best to leave him alone right now.
CHA-CHAN.
CHA-CHAN.
CHA-CHAN.

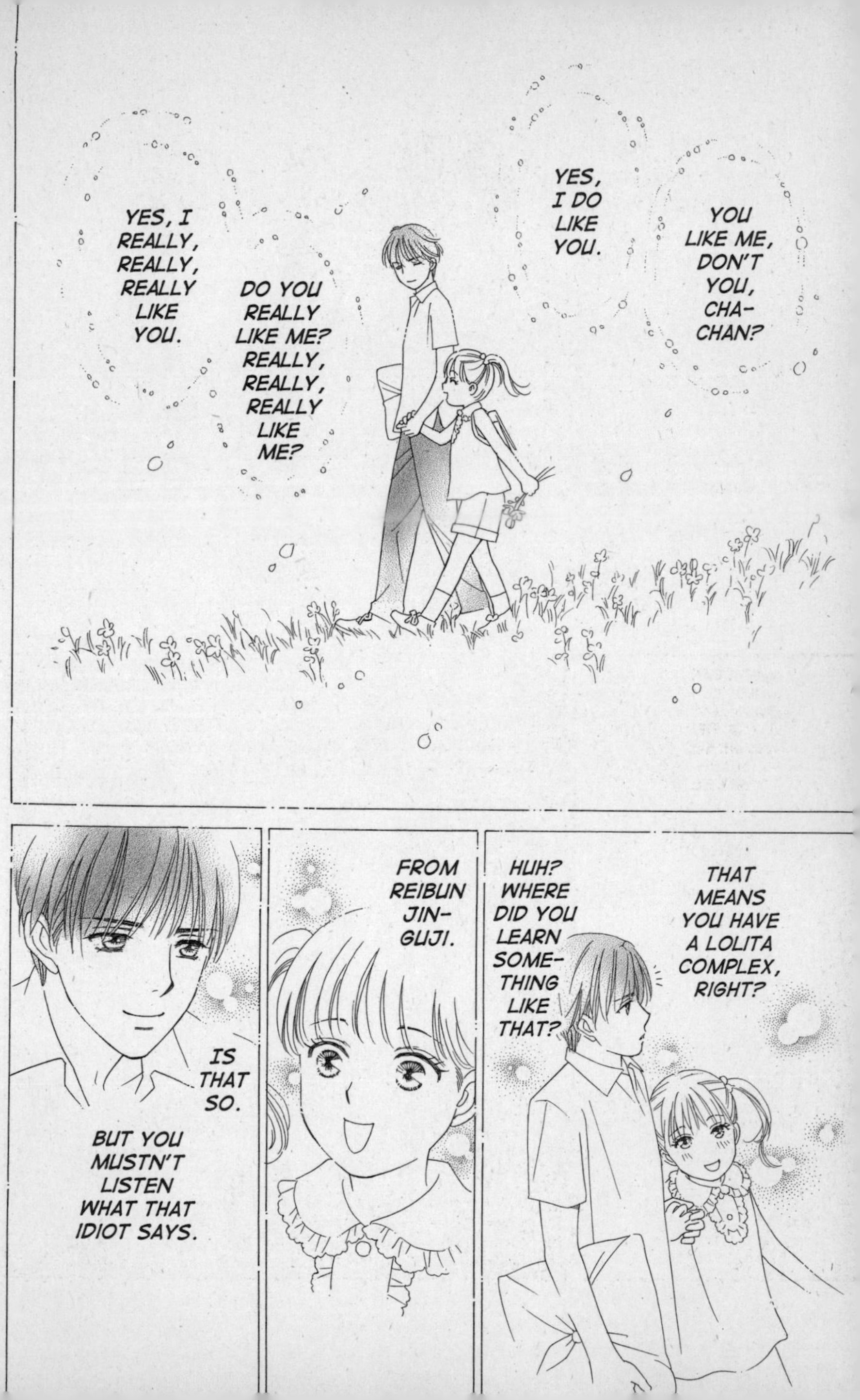
YOU LIKE ME, DON'T YOU, CHA-CHAN?
YES, I DO LIKE YOU.
DO YOU REALLY LIKE ME? REALLY, REALLY, REALLY LIKE ME?
YES, I REALLY, REALLY, REALLY LIKE YOU.
THAT MEANS YOU HAVE A LOLITA COMPLEX, RIGHT?
HUH? WHERE DID YOU LEARN SOME-THING LIKE THAT?
FROM REIBUN JIN-GUJI.
IS THAT SO.
BUT YOU MUSTN'T LISTEN WHAT THAT IDIOT SAYS.

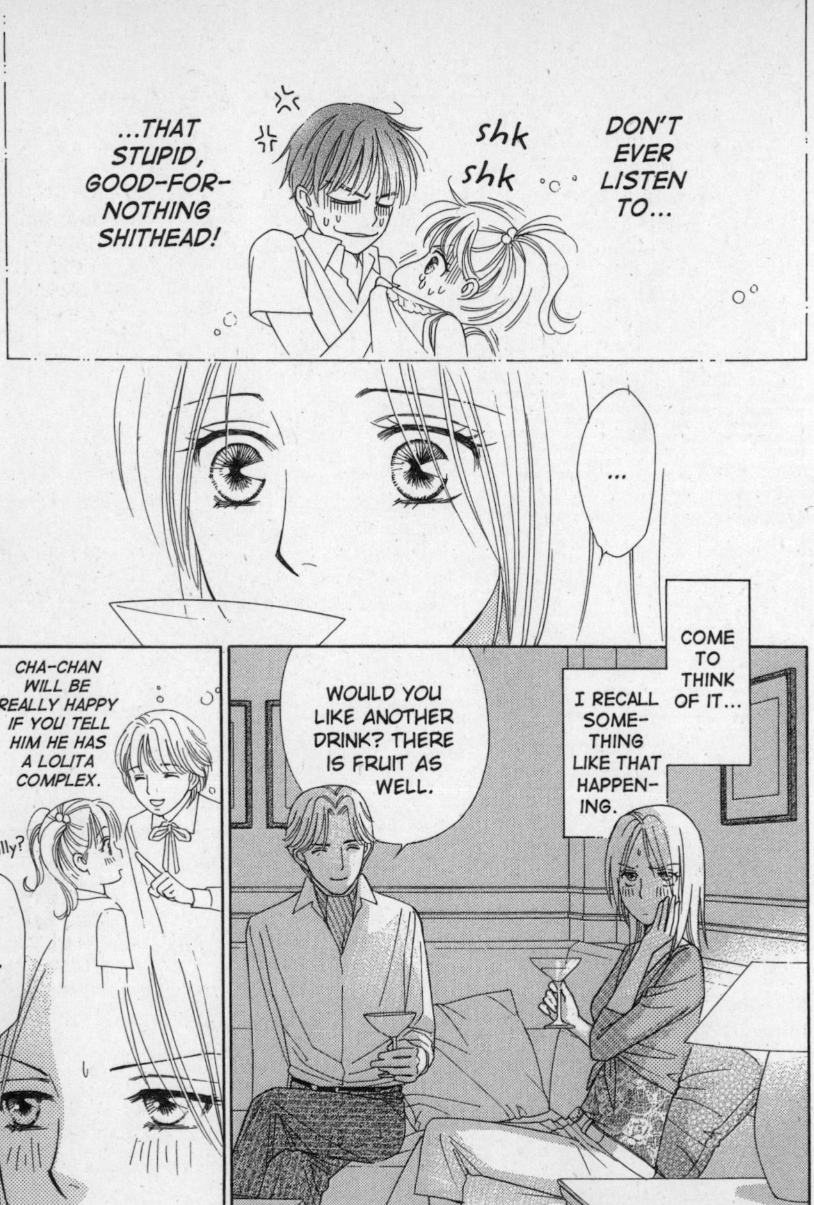
DON'T EVER LISTEN TO...
shk shk
...THAT STUPID, GOOD-FOR-NOTHING SHITHEAD!
...
COME TO THINK OF IT...
I RECALL SOMETHING LIKE THAT HAPPENING.
WOULD YOU LIKE ANOTHER DRINK? THERE IS FRUIT AS WELL.
CHA-CHAN WILL BE REALLY HAPPY IF YOU TELL HIM HE HAS A LOLITA COMPLEX.
Really?
...

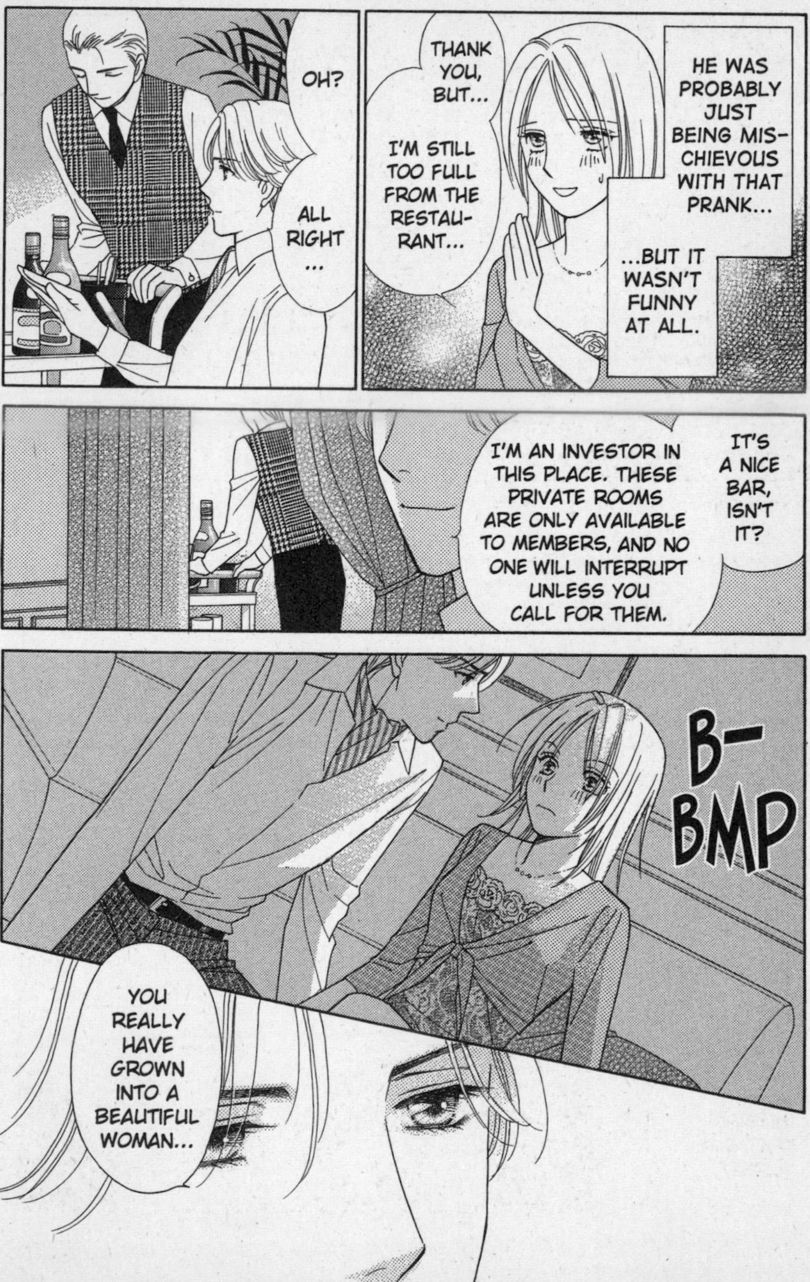
HE WAS PROBABLY JUST BEING MIS-CHIEVOUS WITH THAT PRANK...
...BUT IT WASN'T FUNNY AT ALL.
THANK YOU, BUT...
I'M STILL TOO FULL FROM THE RESTAU-RANT...
OH?
ALL RIGHT...
IT'S A NICE BAR, ISN'T IT?
I'M AN INVESTOR IN THIS PLACE. THESE PRIVATE ROOMS ARE ONLY AVAILABLE TO MEMBERS, AND NO ONE WILL INTERRUPT UNLESS YOU CALL FOR THEM.
B-BMP
YOU REALLY HAVE GROWN INTO A BEAUTIFUL WOMAN...

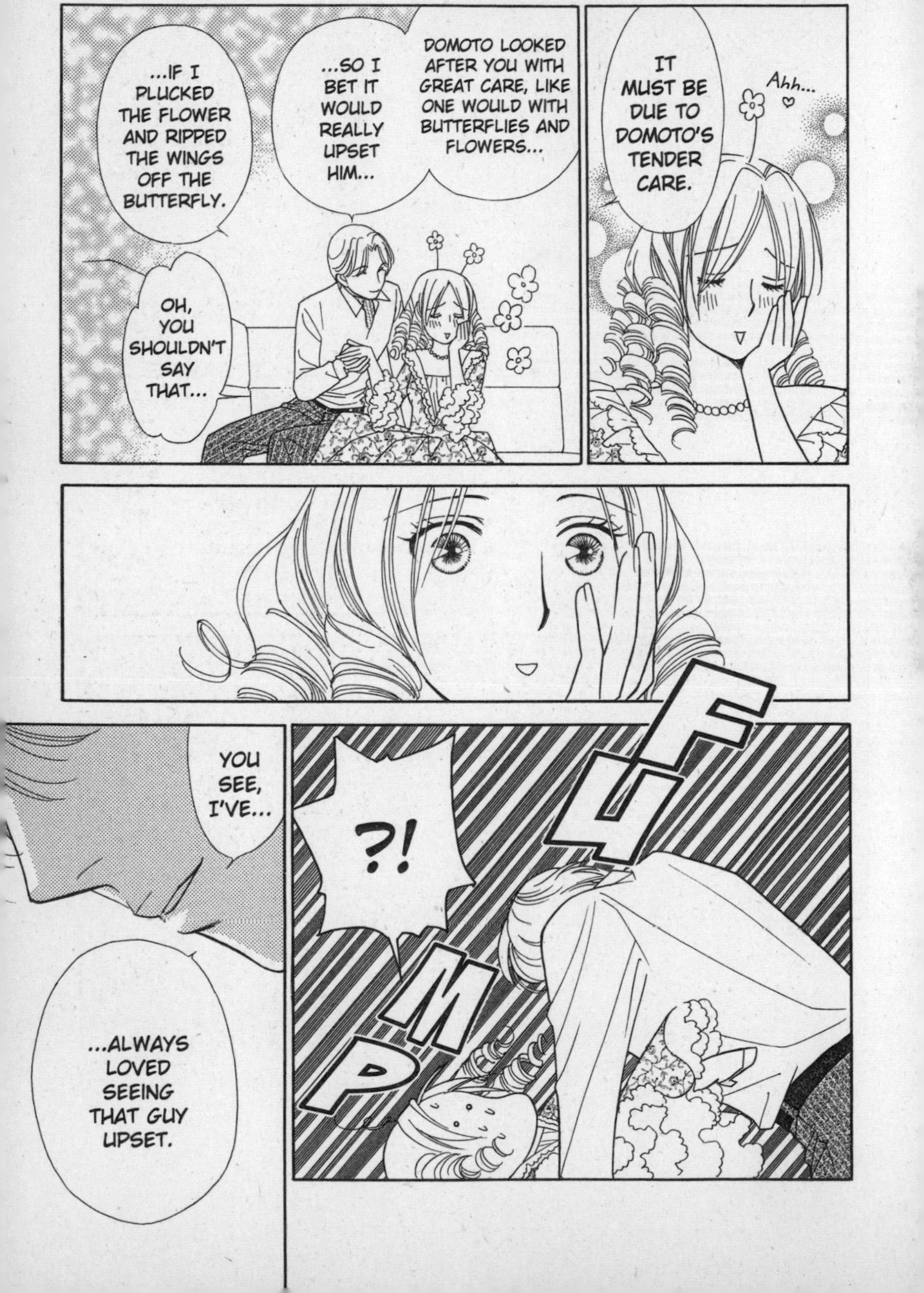
IT MUST BE DUE TO DOMOTO'S TENDER CARE.
Ahh...
DOMOTO LOOKED AFTER YOU WITH GREAT CARE, LIKE ONE WOULD WITH BUTTERFLIES AND FLOWERS...
...SO I BET IT WOULD REALLY UPSET HIM...
...IF I PLUCKED THE FLOWER AND RIPPED THE WINGS OFF THE BUTTERFLY.
OH, YOU SHOULDN'T SAY THAT...
FUMP
?!
YOU SEE, I'VE...
...ALWAYS LOVED SEEING THAT GUY UPSET.

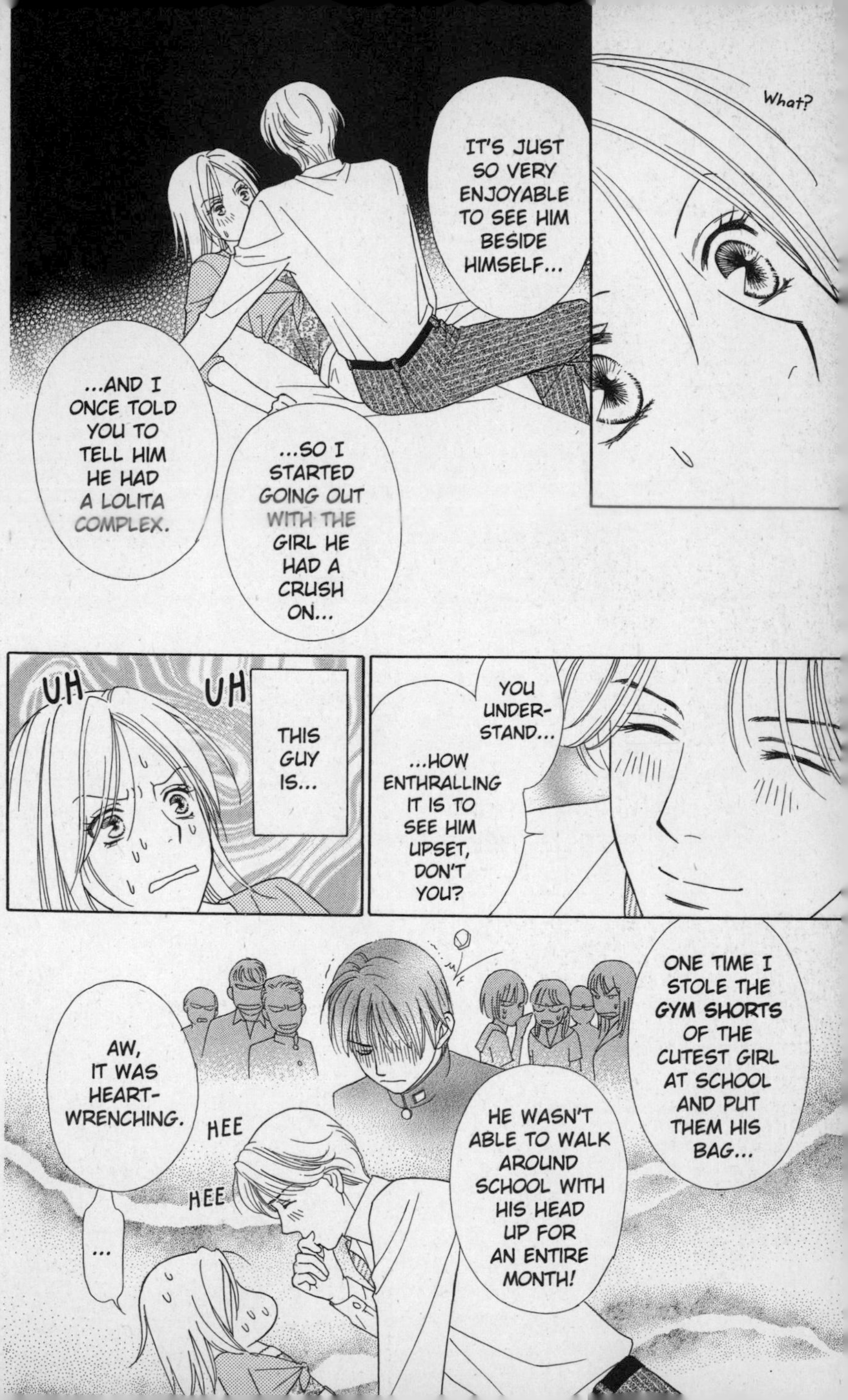

What?
IT'S JUST SO VERY ENJOYABLE TO SEE HIM BESIDE HIMSELF...
...SO I STARTED GOING OUT WITH THE GIRL HE HAD A CRUSH ON...
...AND I ONCE TOLD YOU TO TELL HIM HE HAD A LOLITA COMPLEX.
YOU UNDER-STAND...
...HOW ENTHRALLING IT IS TO SEE HIM UPSET, DON'T YOU?
UH
UH
THIS GUY IS...
ONE TIME I STOLE THE GYM SHORTS OF THE CUTEST GIRL AT SCHOOL AND PUT THEM HIS BAG...
HE WASN'T ABLE TO WALK AROUND SCHOOL WITH HIS HEAD UP FOR AN ENTIRE MONTH!
HEE
HEE
AW, IT WAS HEART-WRENCHING.
...

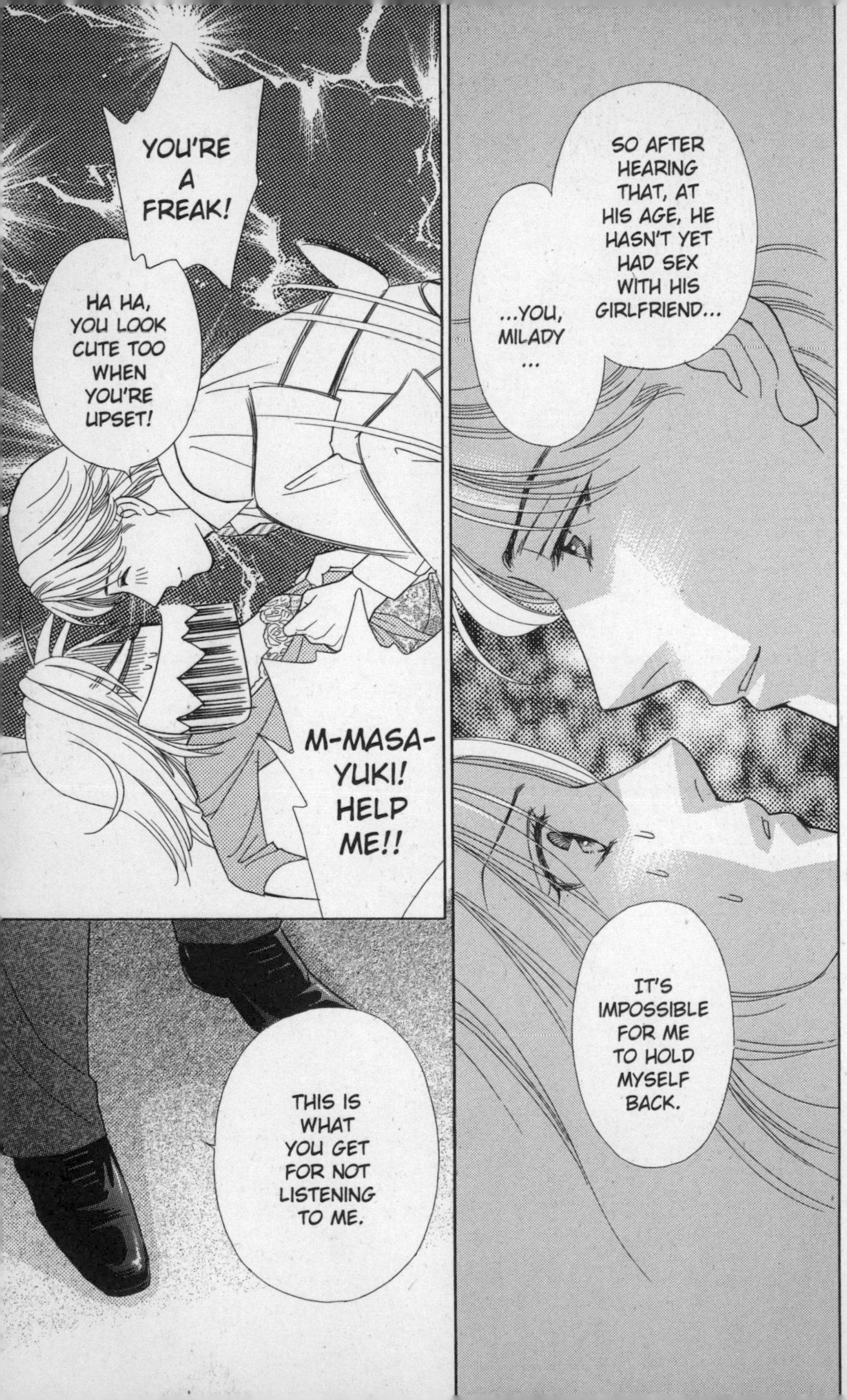
SO AFTER HEARING THAT, AT HIS AGE, HE HASN'T YET HAD SEX WITH HIS GIRLFRIEND...
...YOU, MILADY ...
IT'S IMPOSSIBLE FOR ME TO HOLD MYSELF BACK.
YOU'RE A FREAK!
HA HA, YOU LOOK CUTE TOO WHEN YOU'RE UPSET!
M-MASA-YUKI! HELP ME!!
THIS IS WHAT YOU GET FOR NOT LISTENING TO ME.

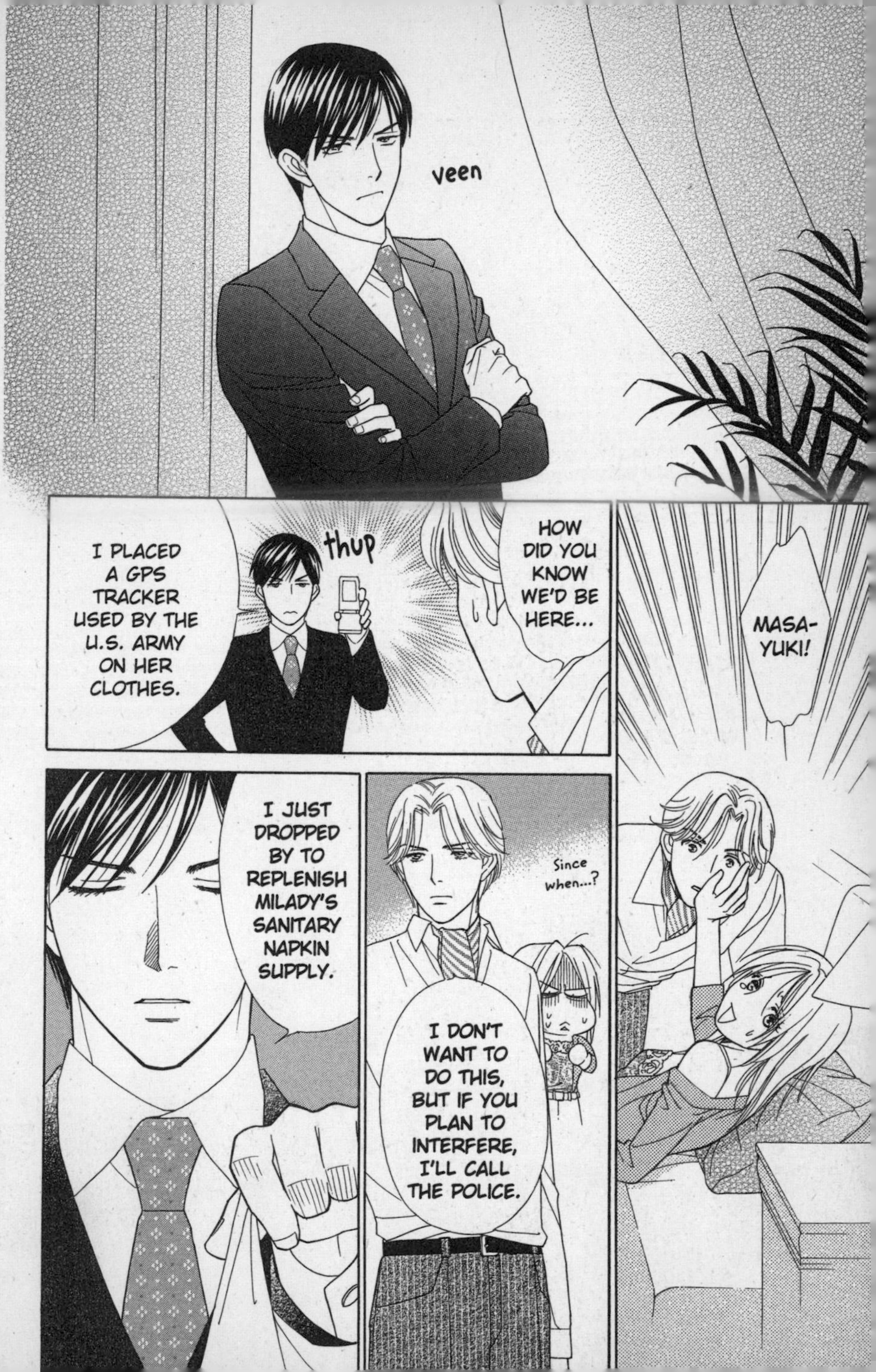
veen
MASA-YUKI!
HOW DID YOU KNOW WE'D BE HERE...
thup
I PLACED A GPS TRACKER USED BY THE U.S. ARMY ON HER CLOTHES.
Since when...?
I DON'T WANT TO DO THIS, BUT IF YOU PLAN TO INTERFERE, I'LL CALL THE POLICE.
I JUST DROPPED BY TO REPLENISH MILADY'S SANITARY NAPKIN SUPPLY.

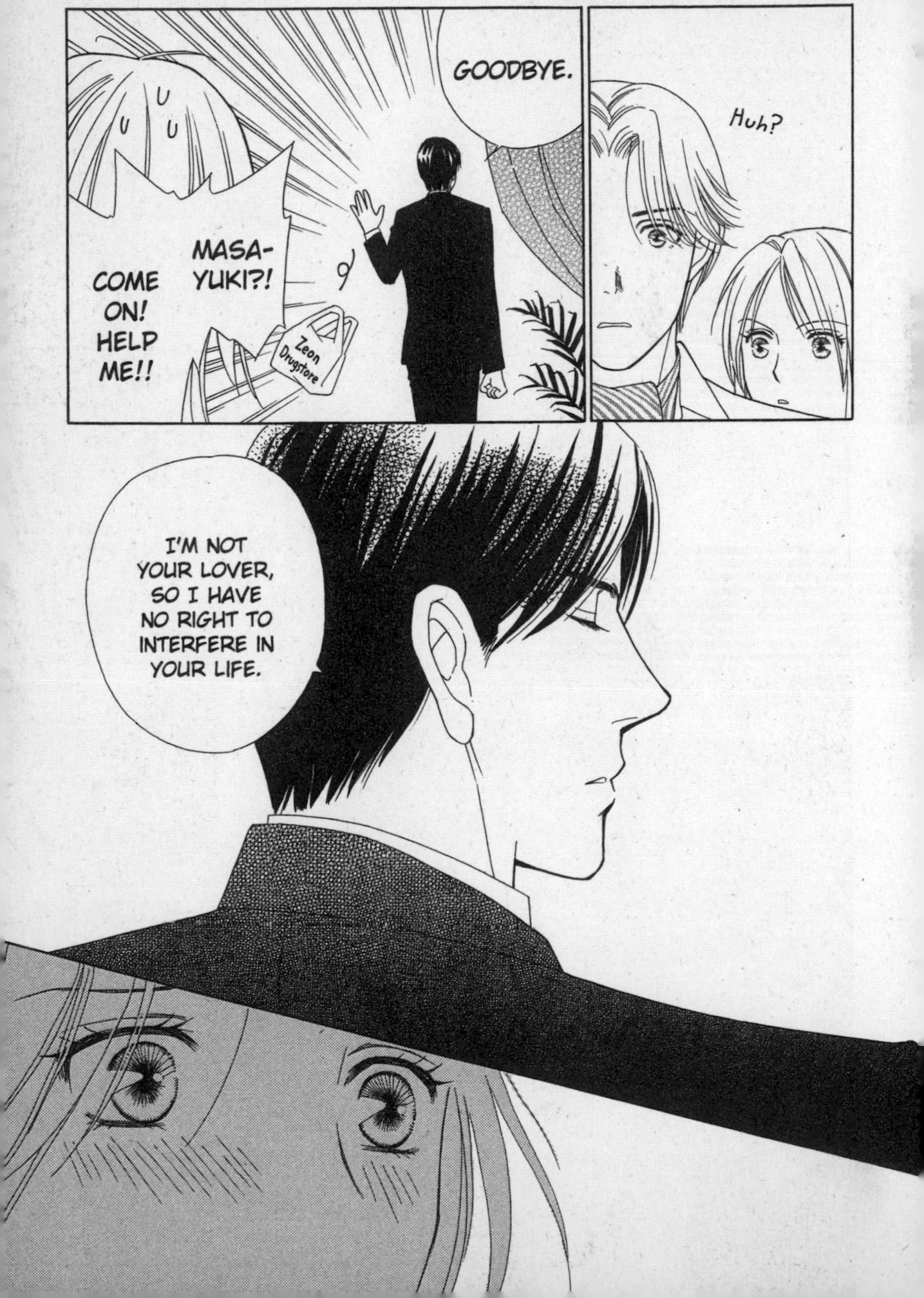
Huh?
GOODBYE.
MASA-YUKI?!
COME ON! HELP ME!!
Zeon Drugstore
I'M NOT YOUR LOVER, SO I HAVE NO RIGHT TO INTERFERE IN YOUR LIFE.

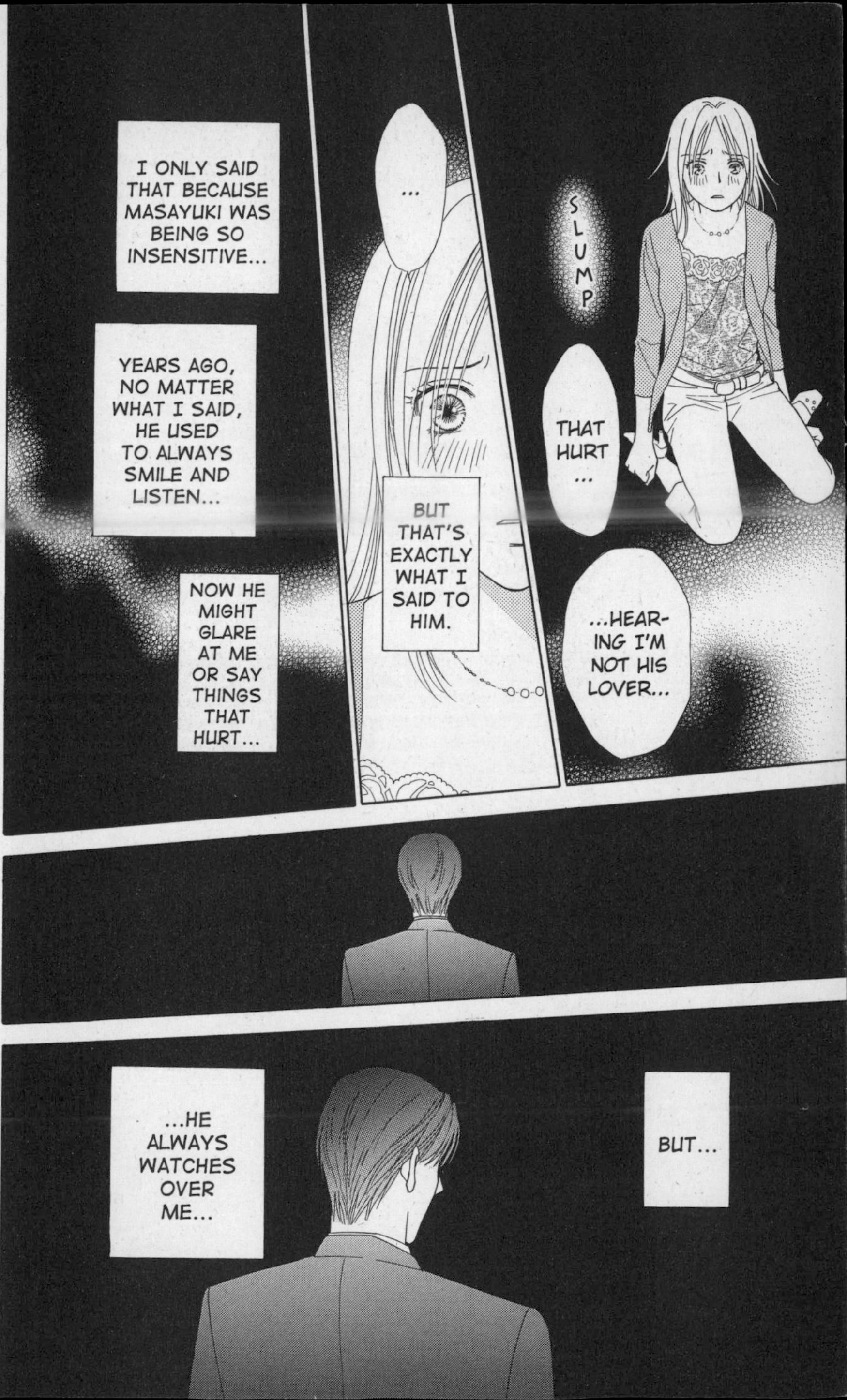
SLUMP
THAT HURT...
...HEARING I'M NOT HIS LOVER...
...
BUT THAT'S EXACTLY WHAT I SAID TO HIM.
I ONLY SAID THAT BECAUSE MASAYUKI WAS BEING SO INSENSITIVE...
YEARS AGO, NO MATTER WHAT I SAID, HE USED TO ALWAYS SMILE AND LISTEN...
NOW HE MIGHT GLARE AT ME OR SAY THINGS THAT HURT...
BUT...
...HE ALWAYS WATCHES OVER ME...

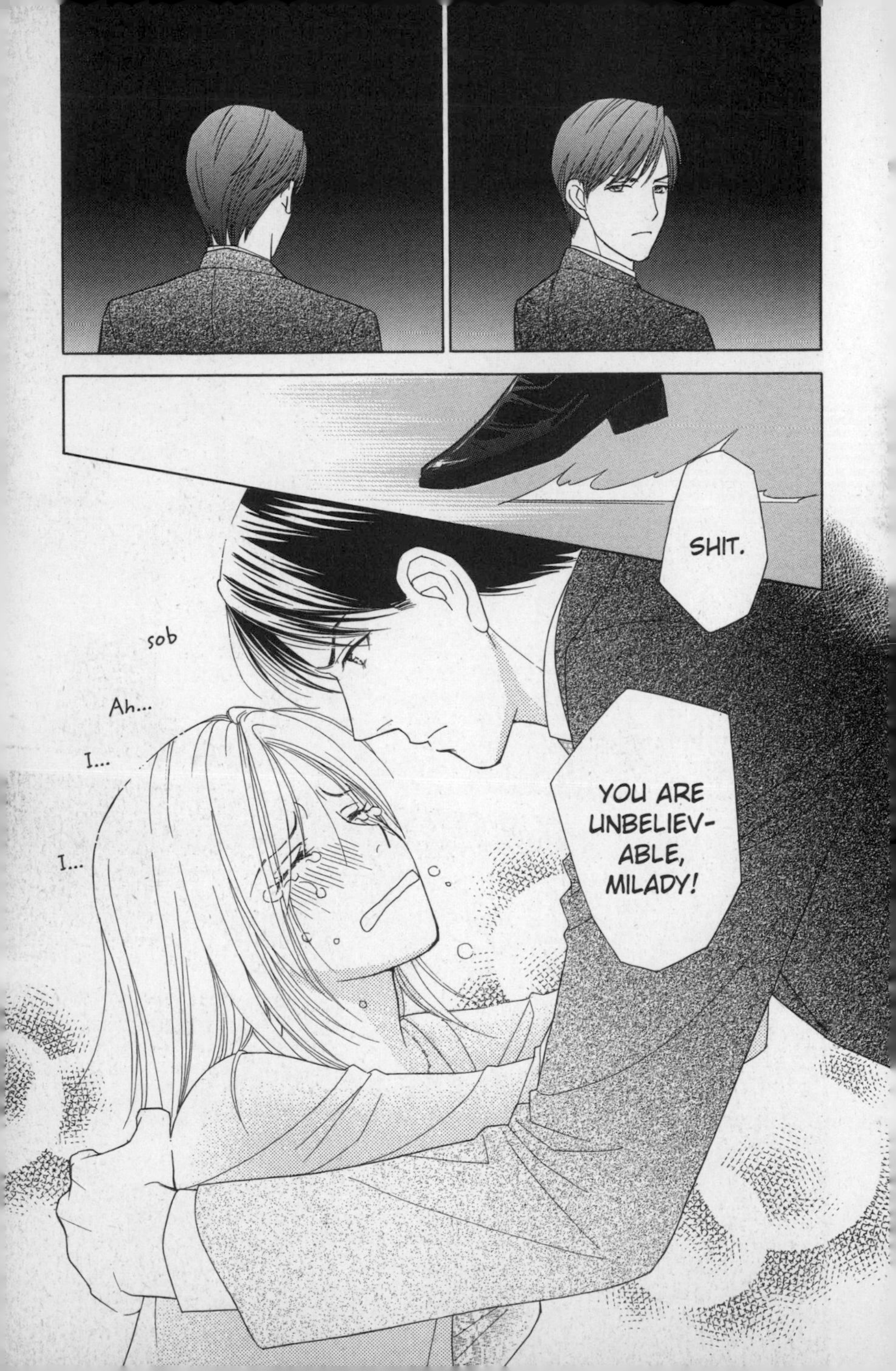
SHIT.
YOU ARE UNBELIEV-ABLE, MILADY!
sob
Ah...
I...
I...

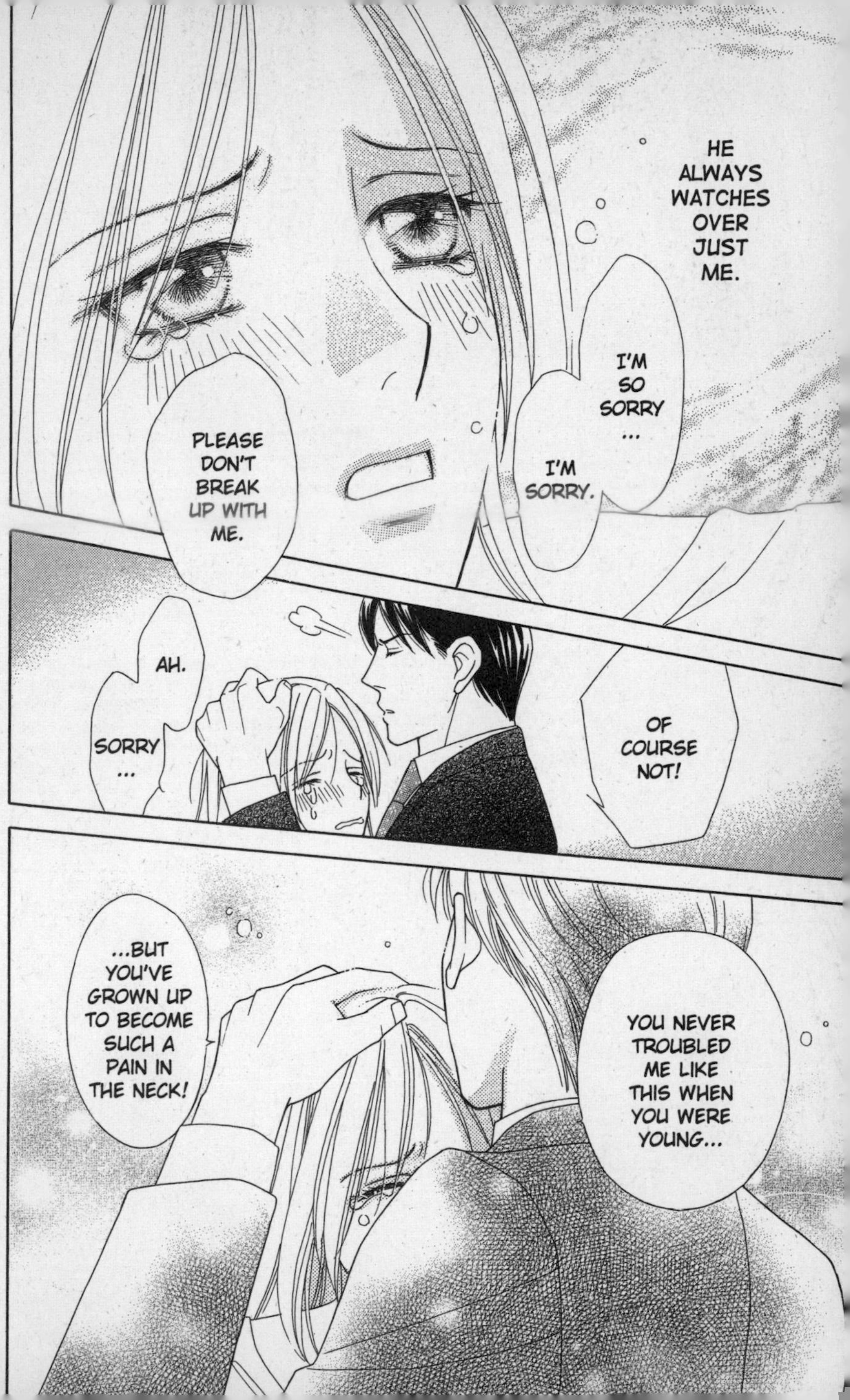
HE ALWAYS WATCHES OVER JUST ME.
I'M SO SORRY...
I'M SORRY.
PLEASE DON'T BREAK UP WITH ME.
OF COURSE NOT!
AH.
SORRY...
YOU NEVER TROUBLED ME LIKE THIS WHEN YOU WERE YOUNG...
...BUT YOU'VE GROWN UP TO BECOME SUCH A PAIN IN THE NECK!

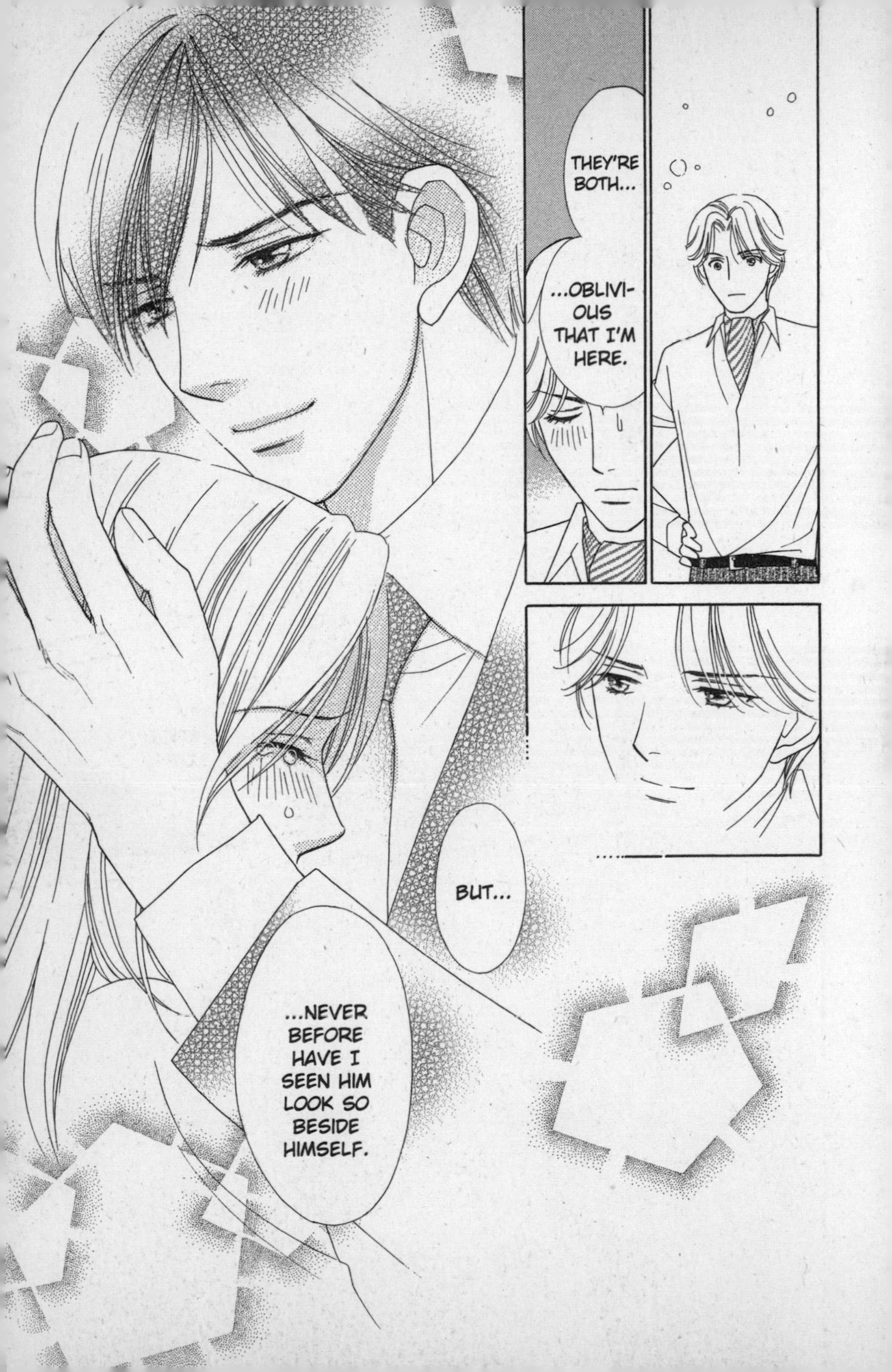

THEY'RE BOTH...
...OBLIVI-OUS THAT I'M HERE.
......
BUT...
...NEVER BEFORE HAVE I SEEN HIM LOOK SO BESIDE HIMSELF.

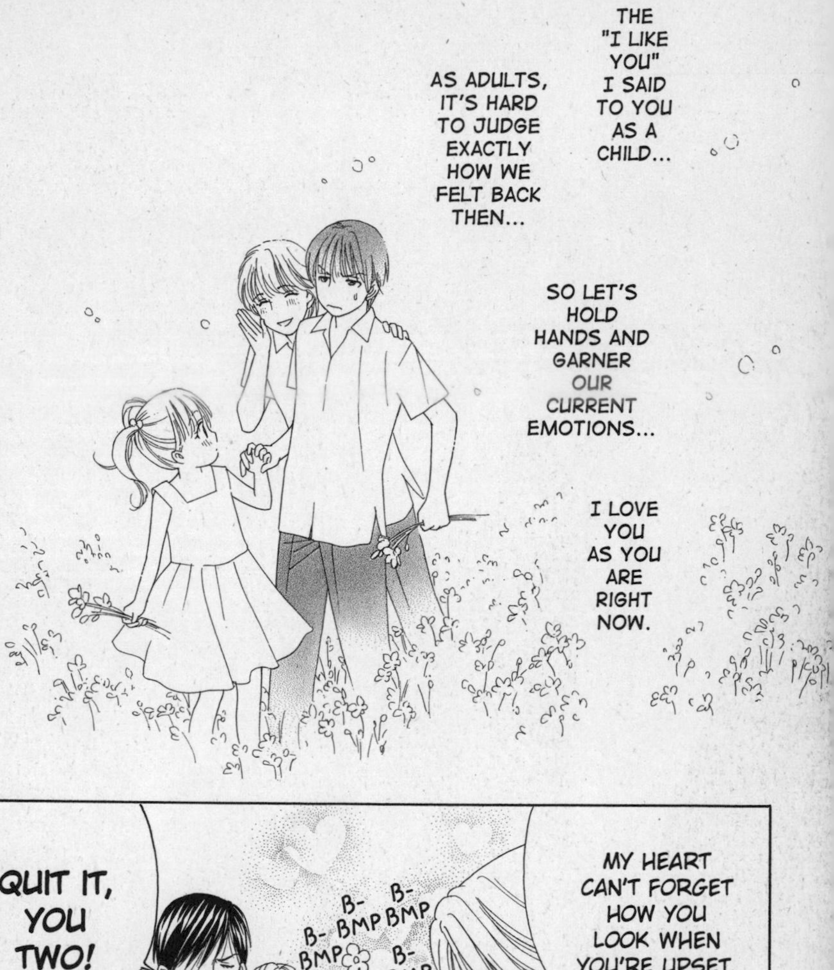
THE "I LIKE YOU" I SAID TO YOU AS A CHILD...
AS ADULTS, IT'S HARD TO JUDGE EXACTLY HOW WE FELT BACK THEN...
SO LET'S HOLD HANDS AND GARNER OUR CURRENT EMOTIONS...
I LOVE YOU AS YOU ARE RIGHT NOW.

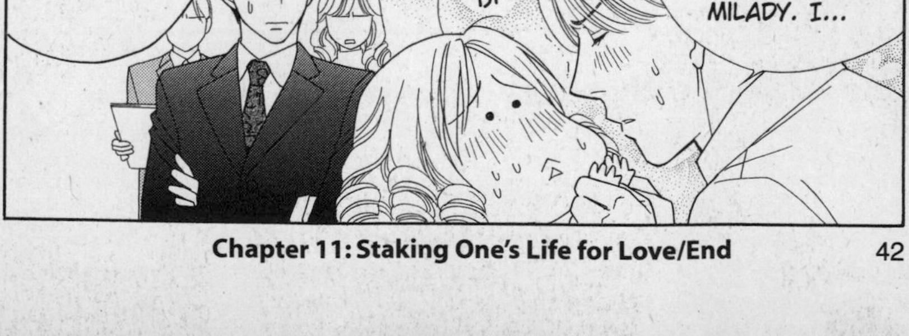
MY HEART CAN'T FORGET HOW YOU LOOK WHEN YOU'RE UPSET, MILADY. I...
B-BMP
B-BMP
B-BMP
B-BMP
QUIT IT, YOU TWO!

Chapter 11: Staking One's Life for Love/End

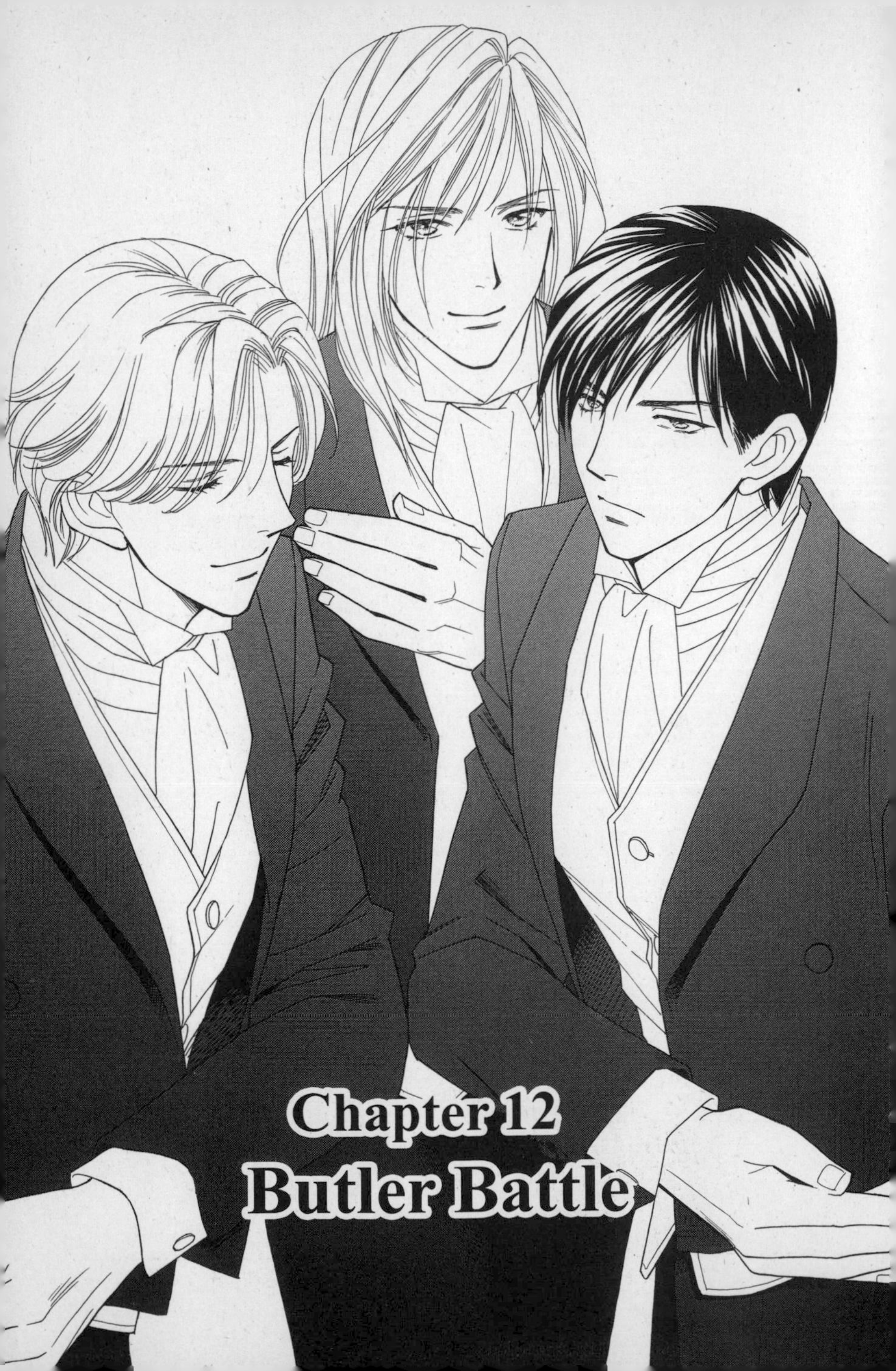
Chapter 12
Butler Battle

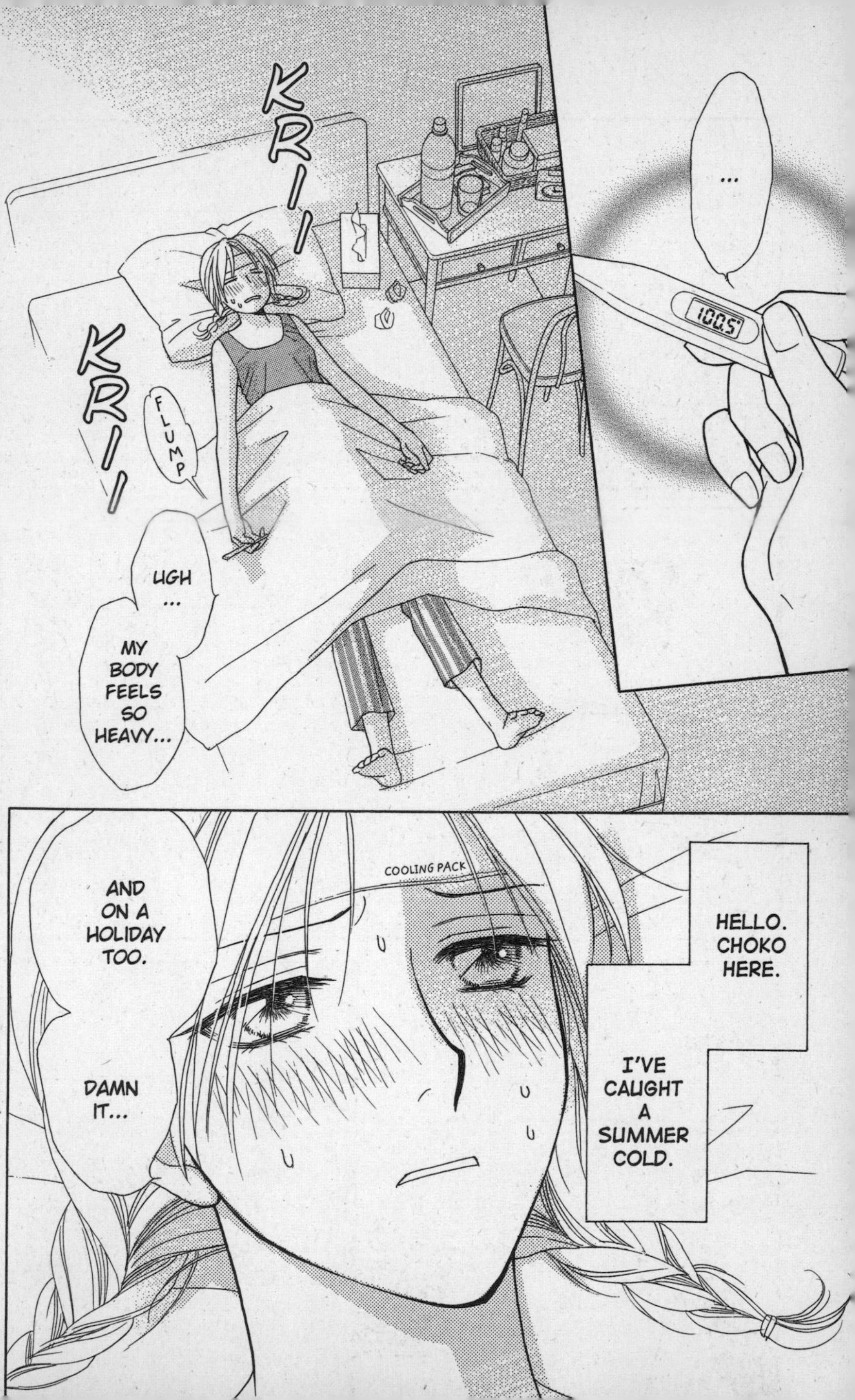
...
100.5°
KRI-I
KRI-I
FLUMP
UGH ...
MY BODY FEELS SO HEAVY...
HELLO. CHOKO HERE.
I'VE CAUGHT A SUMMER COLD.
COOLING PACK
AND ON A HOLIDAY TOO.
DAMN IT...

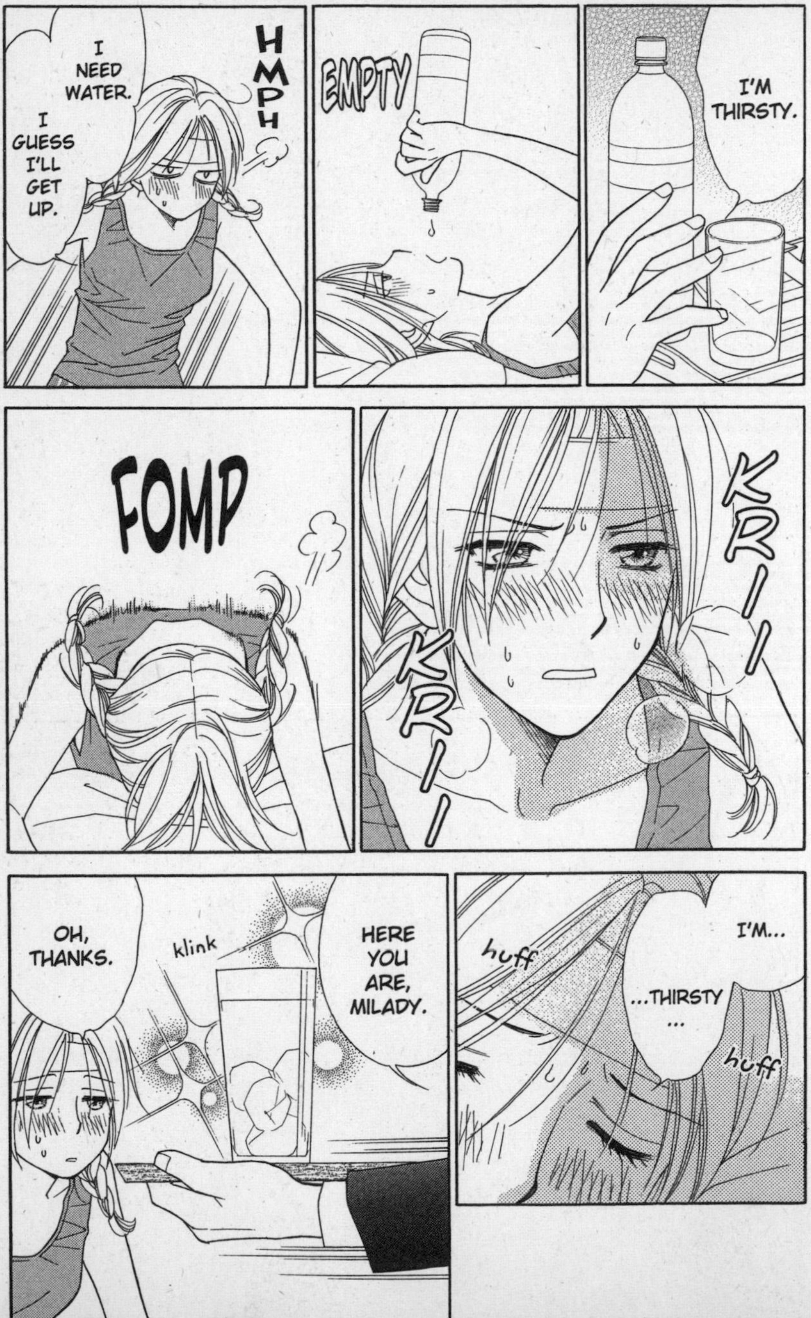
I'M THIRSTY.
EMPTY
HMPH
I NEED WATER.
I GUESS I'LL GET UP.
KRI-I
KRI-I
FOMP
I'M...
...THIRSTY ...
huff
huff
HERE YOU ARE, MILADY.
klink
OH, THANKS.

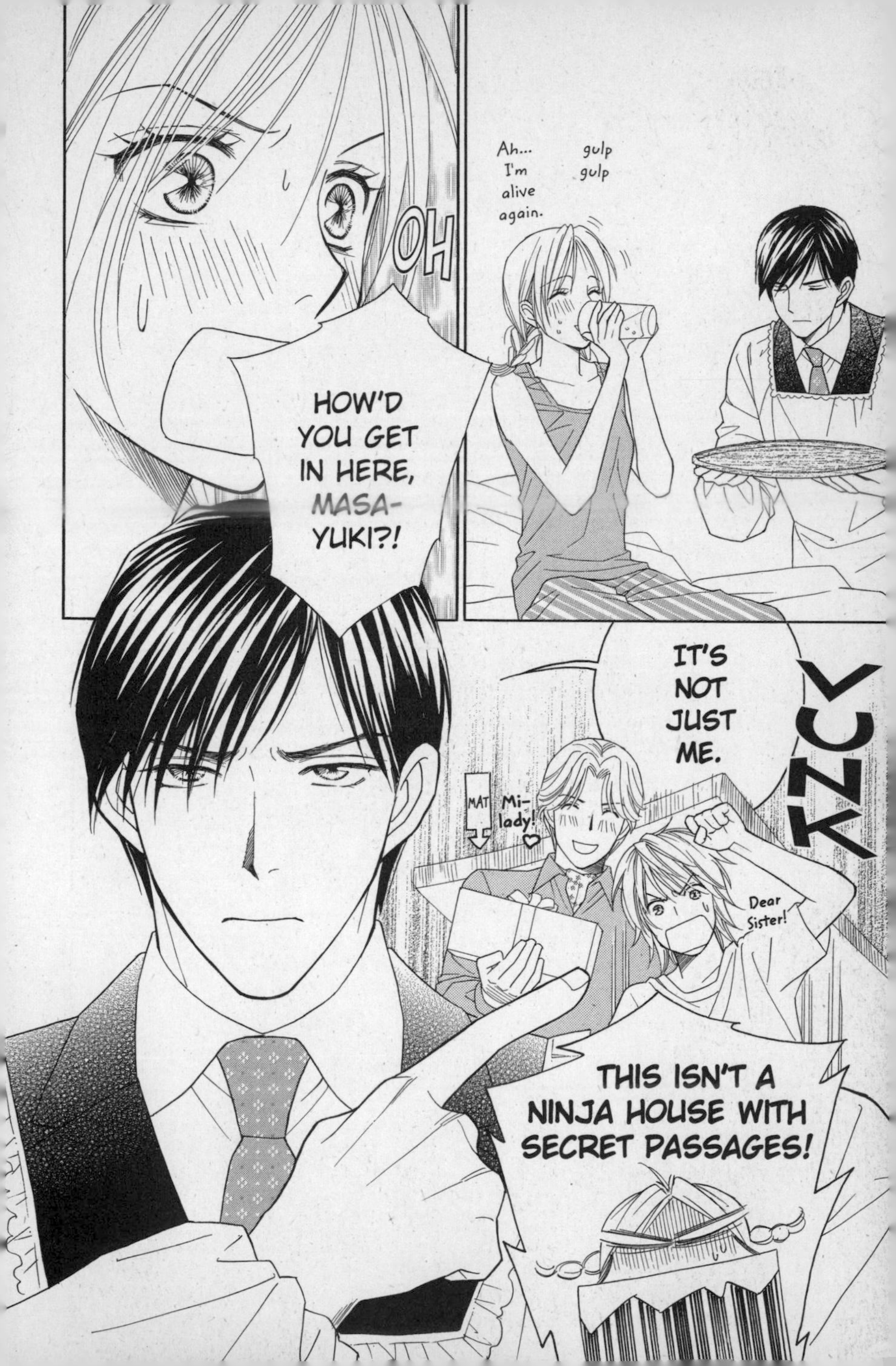
Ah... I'm alive again.
gulp gulp
OH
HOW'D YOU GET IN HERE, MASA-YUKI?!
IT'S NOT JUST ME.
MAT
Mi-lady!
Dear Sister!
THIS ISN'T A NINJA HOUSE WITH SECRET PASSAGES!

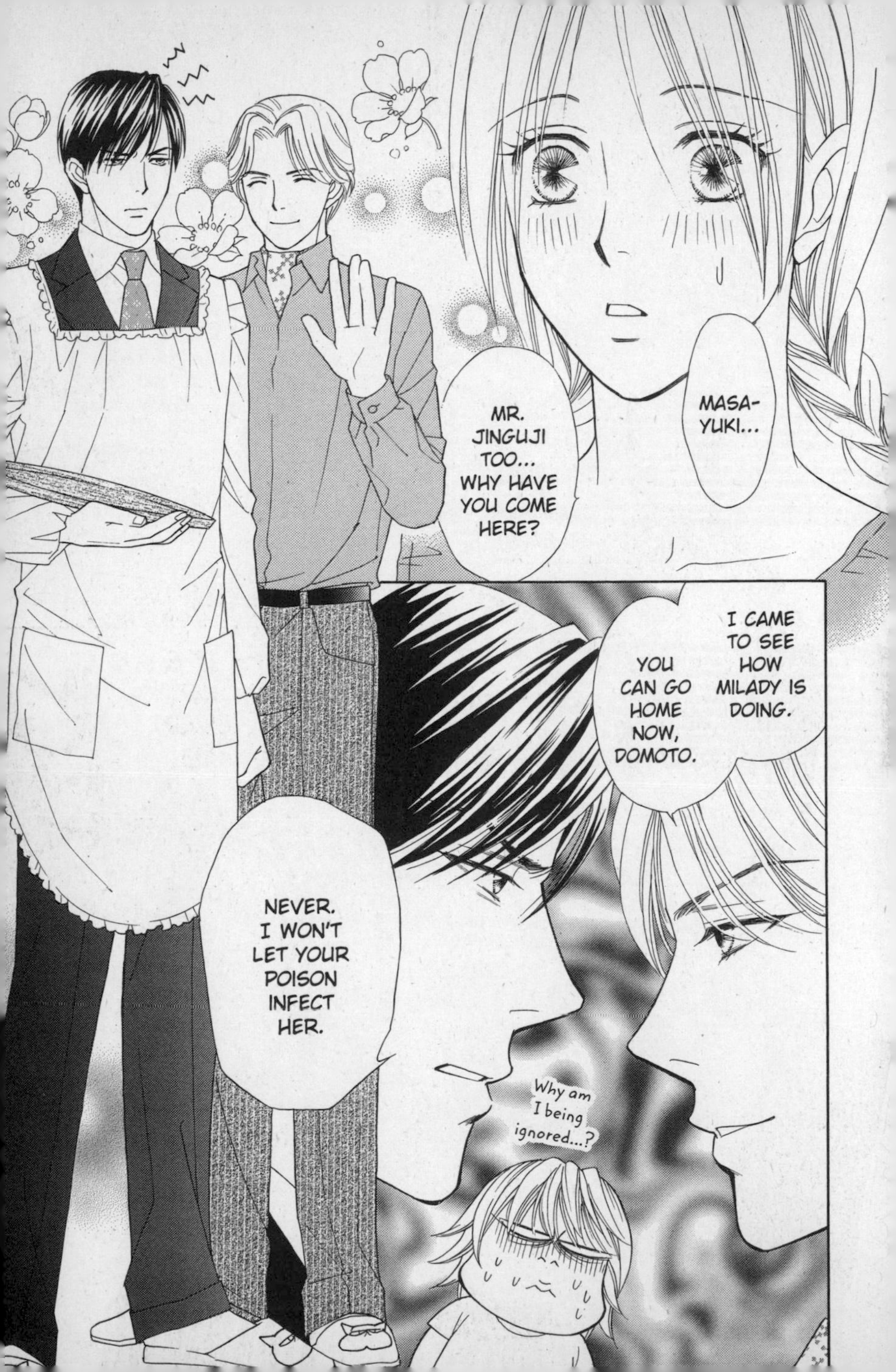
MASA-YUKI...
MR. JINGUJI TOO... WHY HAVE YOU COME HERE?
I CAME TO SEE HOW MILADY IS DOING.
YOU CAN GO HOME NOW, DOMOTO.
NEVER. I WON'T LET YOUR POISON INFECT HER.
Why am I being ignored...?

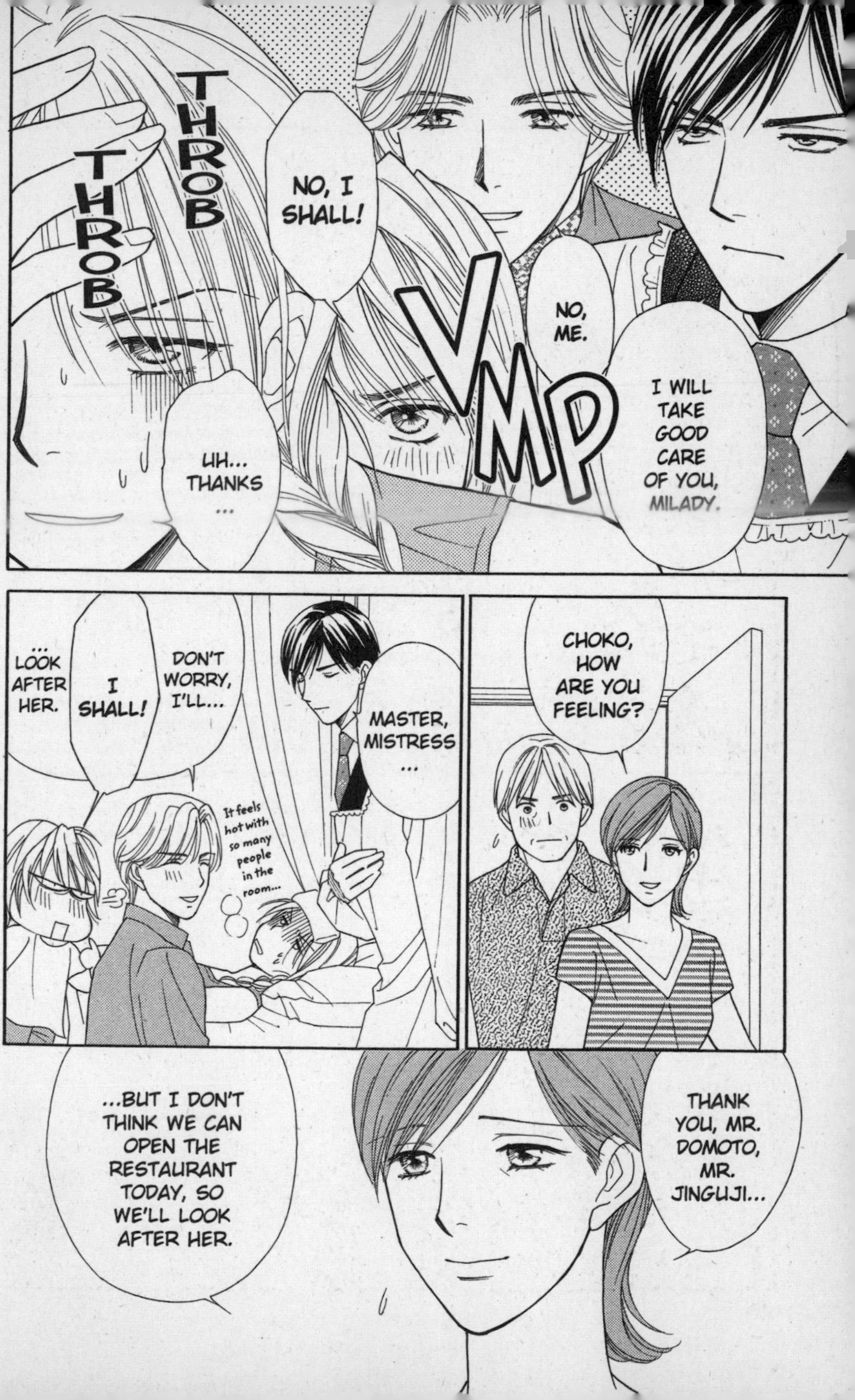
I WILL TAKE GOOD CARE OF YOU, MILADY.
NO, ME.
VMP
NO, I SHALL!
THROB THROB
UH... THANKS ...
CHOKO, HOW ARE YOU FEELING?
MASTER, MISTRESS ...
DON'T WORRY, I'LL...
I SHALL!
... LOOK AFTER HER.
It feels hot with so many people in the room...
THANK YOU, MR. DOMOTO, MR. JINGUJI...
...BUT I DON'T THINK WE CAN OPEN THE RESTAURANT TODAY, SO WE'LL LOOK AFTER HER.

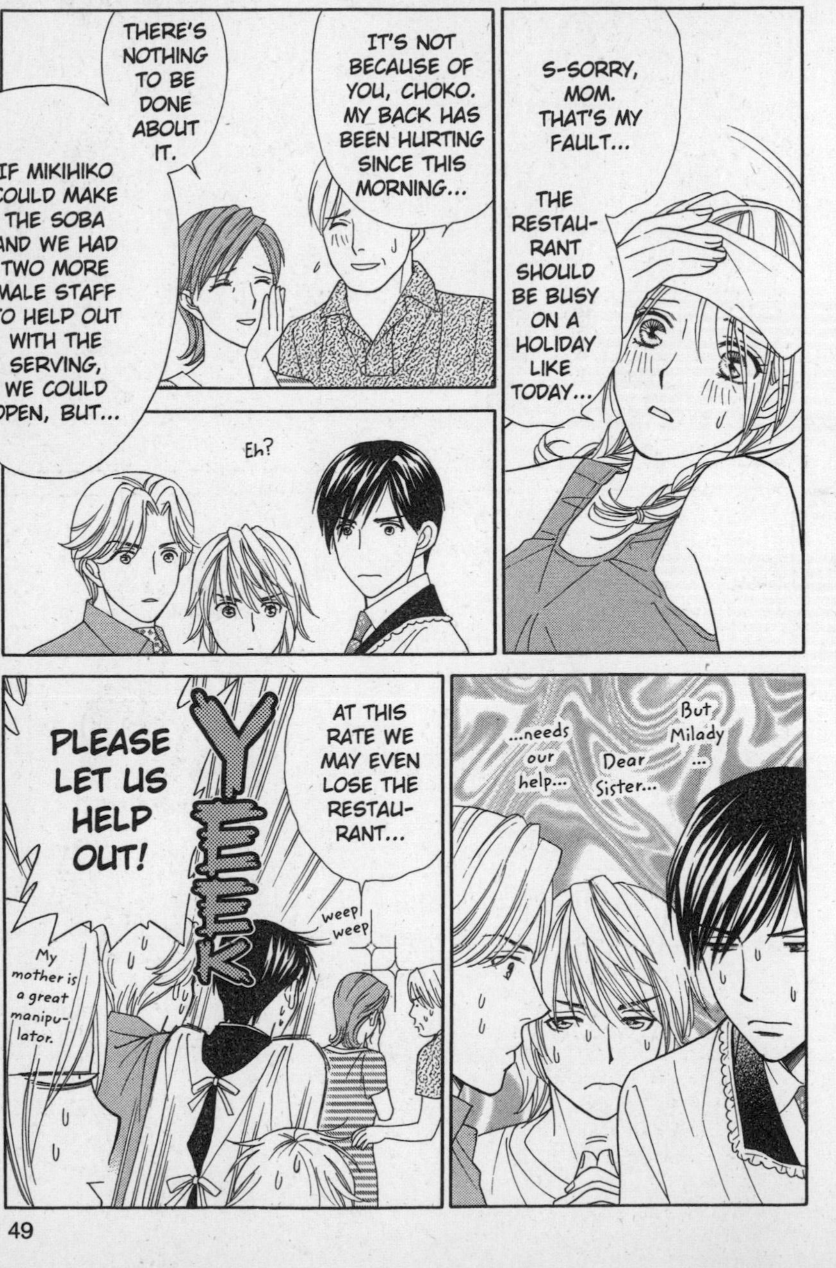
S-SORRY, MOM. THAT'S MY FAULT...
THE RESTAU-RANT SHOULD BE BUSY ON A HOLIDAY LIKE TODAY...
IT'S NOT BECAUSE OF YOU, CHOKO. MY BACK HAS BEEN HURTING SINCE THIS MORNING...
THERE'S NOTHING TO BE DONE ABOUT IT.
IF MIKIHIKO COULD MAKE THE SOBA AND WE HAD TWO MORE MALE STAFF TO HELP OUT WITH THE SERVING, WE COULD OPEN, BUT...
Eh?
But Milady...
Dear Sister...
...needs our help...
AT THIS RATE WE MAY EVEN LOSE THE RESTAU-RANT...
YEEK
PLEASE LET US HELP OUT!
weep weep
My mother is a great manipu-lator.

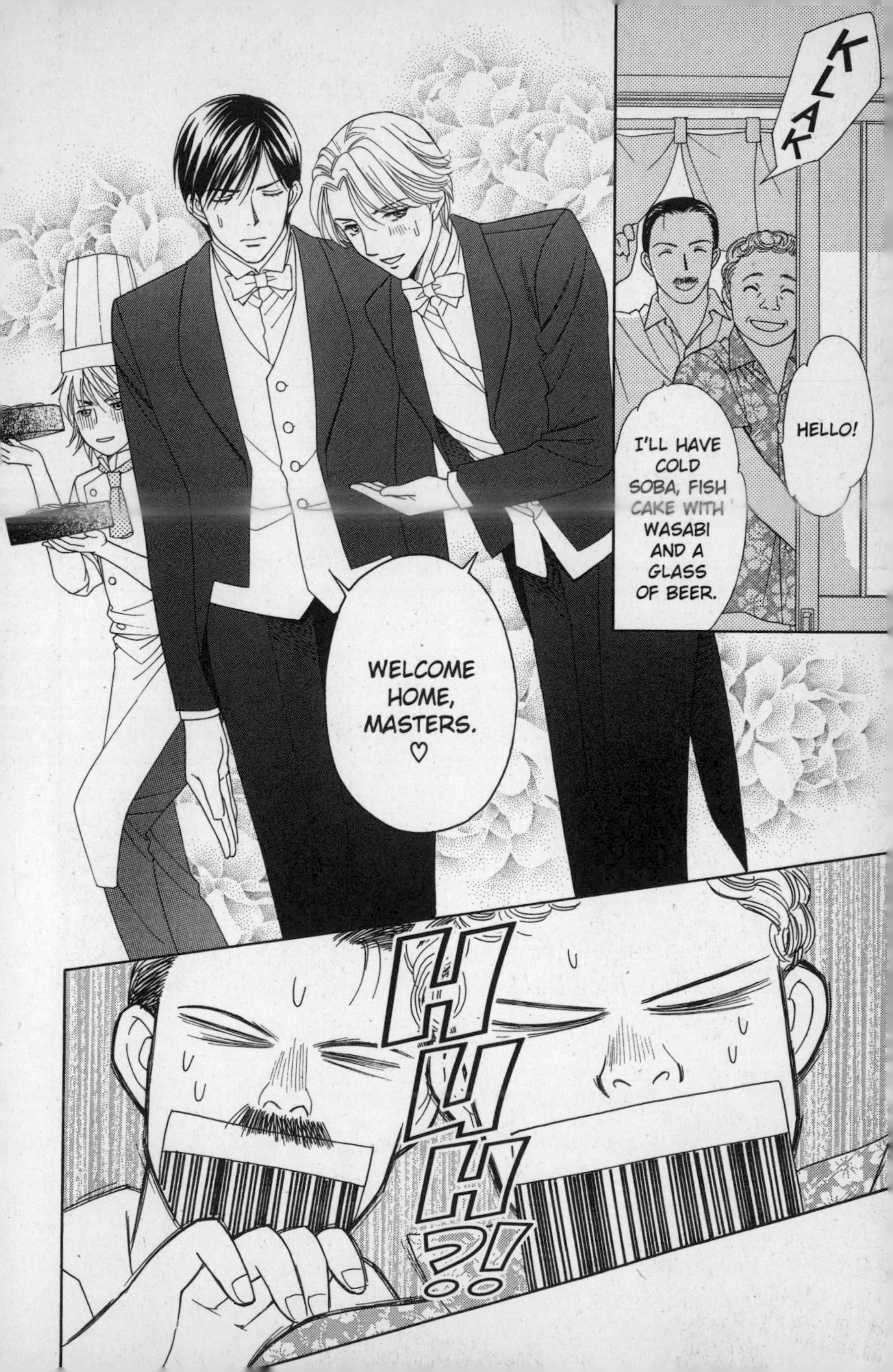
KLAK
HELLO!
I'LL HAVE COLD SOBA, FISH CAKE WITH WASABI AND A GLASS OF BEER.
WELCOME HOME, MASTERS. ♡
HUH?!

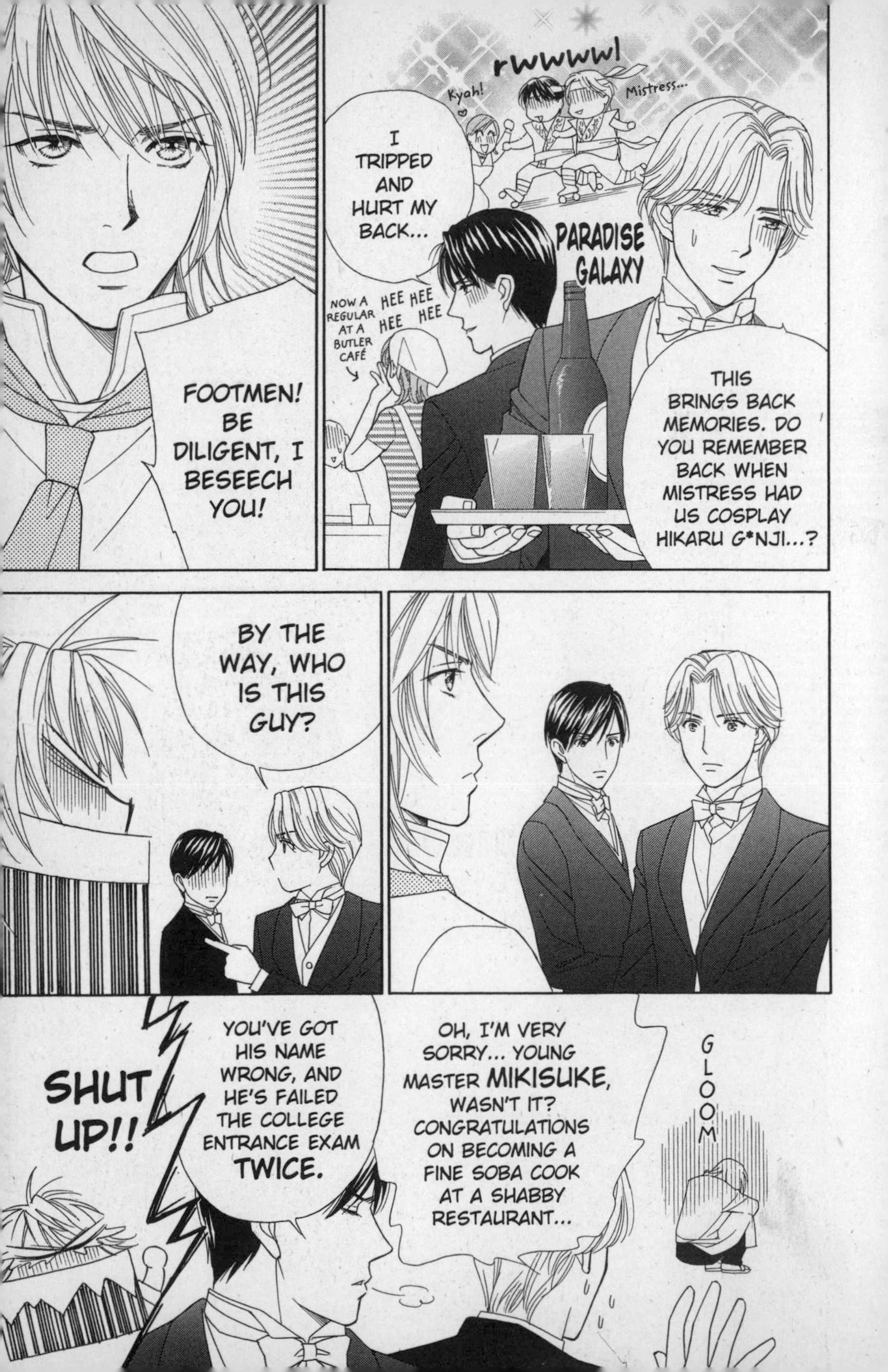
Mistress...
rwwwwl
Kyah!
THIS BRINGS BACK MEMORIES. DO YOU REMEMBER BACK WHEN MISTRESS HAD US COSPLAY HIKARU G*NJI...?
PARADISE GALAXY
I TRIPPED AND HURT MY BACK...
HEE HEE HEE HEE
NOW A REGULAR AT A BUTLER CAFÉ
FOOTMEN! BE DILIGENT, I BESEECH YOU!
BY THE WAY, WHO IS THIS GUY?
GLOOM
OH, I'M VERY SORRY... YOUNG MASTER MIKISUKE, WASN'T IT? CONGRATULATIONS ON BECOMING A FINE SOBA COOK AT A SHABBY RESTAURANT...
YOU'VE GOT HIS NAME WRONG, AND HE'S FAILED THE COLLEGE ENTRANCE EXAM TWICE.
SHUT UP!!

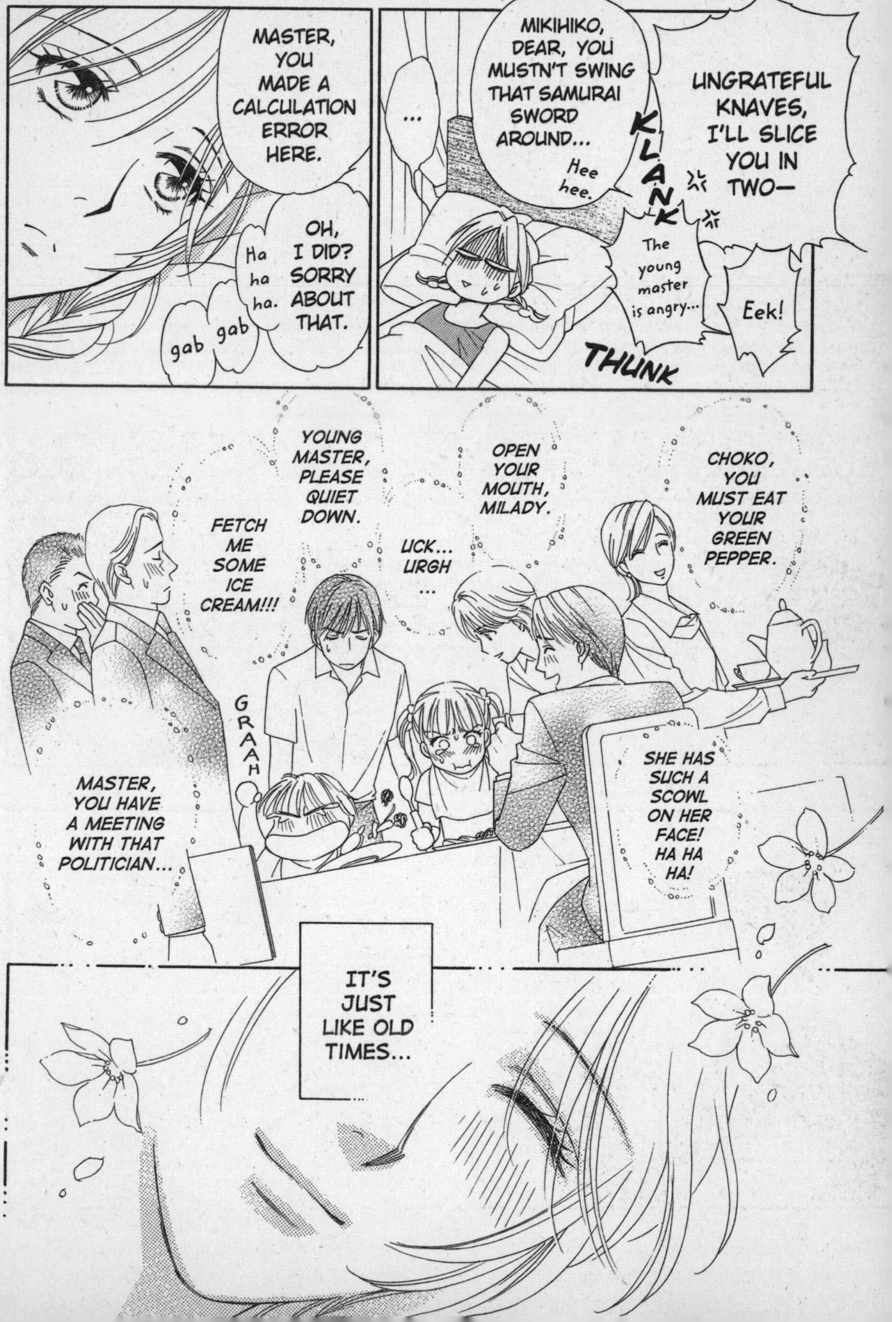
UNGRATEFUL KNAVES, I'LL SLICE YOU IN TWO—
MIKIHIKO, DEAR, YOU MUSTN'T SWING THAT SAMURAI SWORD AROUND...
KLANK
Hee hee.
The young master is angry...
Eek!
...
THUNK
MASTER, YOU MADE A CALCULATION ERROR HERE.
OH, I DID? SORRY ABOUT THAT.
Ha ha ha.
gab gab
CHOKO, YOU MUST EAT YOUR GREEN PEPPER.
OPEN YOUR MOUTH, MILADY.
UCK... URGH ...
YOUNG MASTER, PLEASE QUIET DOWN.
FETCH ME SOME ICE CREAM!!!
SHE HAS SUCH A SCOWL ON HER FACE! HA HA HA!
GRAAH
MASTER, YOU HAVE A MEETING WITH THAT POLITICIAN...
IT'S JUST LIKE OLD TIMES...

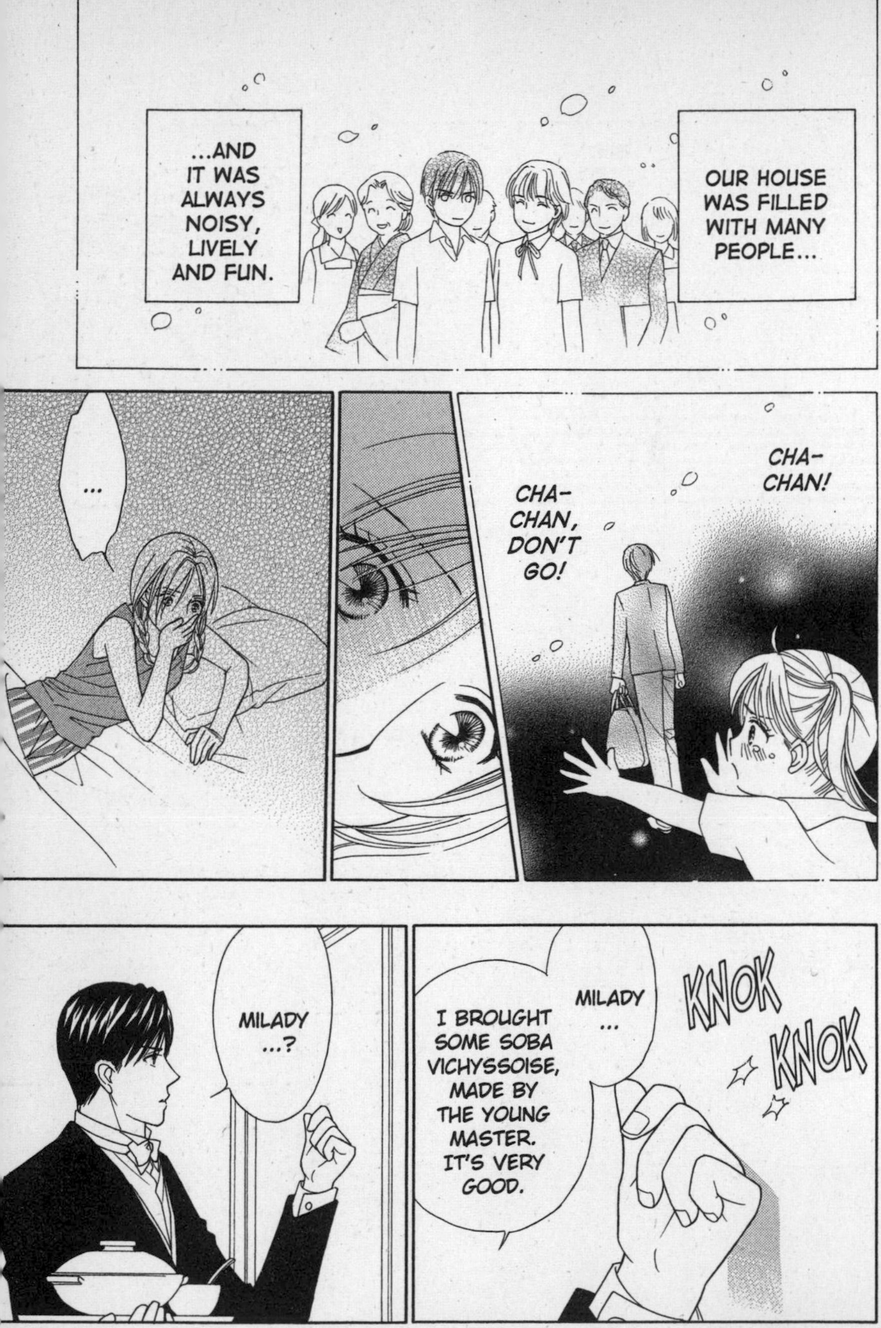

OUR HOUSE WAS FILLED WITH MANY PEOPLE...
...AND IT WAS ALWAYS NOISY, LIVELY AND FUN.
CHA-CHAN!
CHA-CHAN, DON'T GO!
...
KNOK KNOK
MILADY ...
I BROUGHT SOME SOBA VICHYSSOISE, MADE BY THE YOUNG MASTER. IT'S VERY GOOD.
MILADY ...?

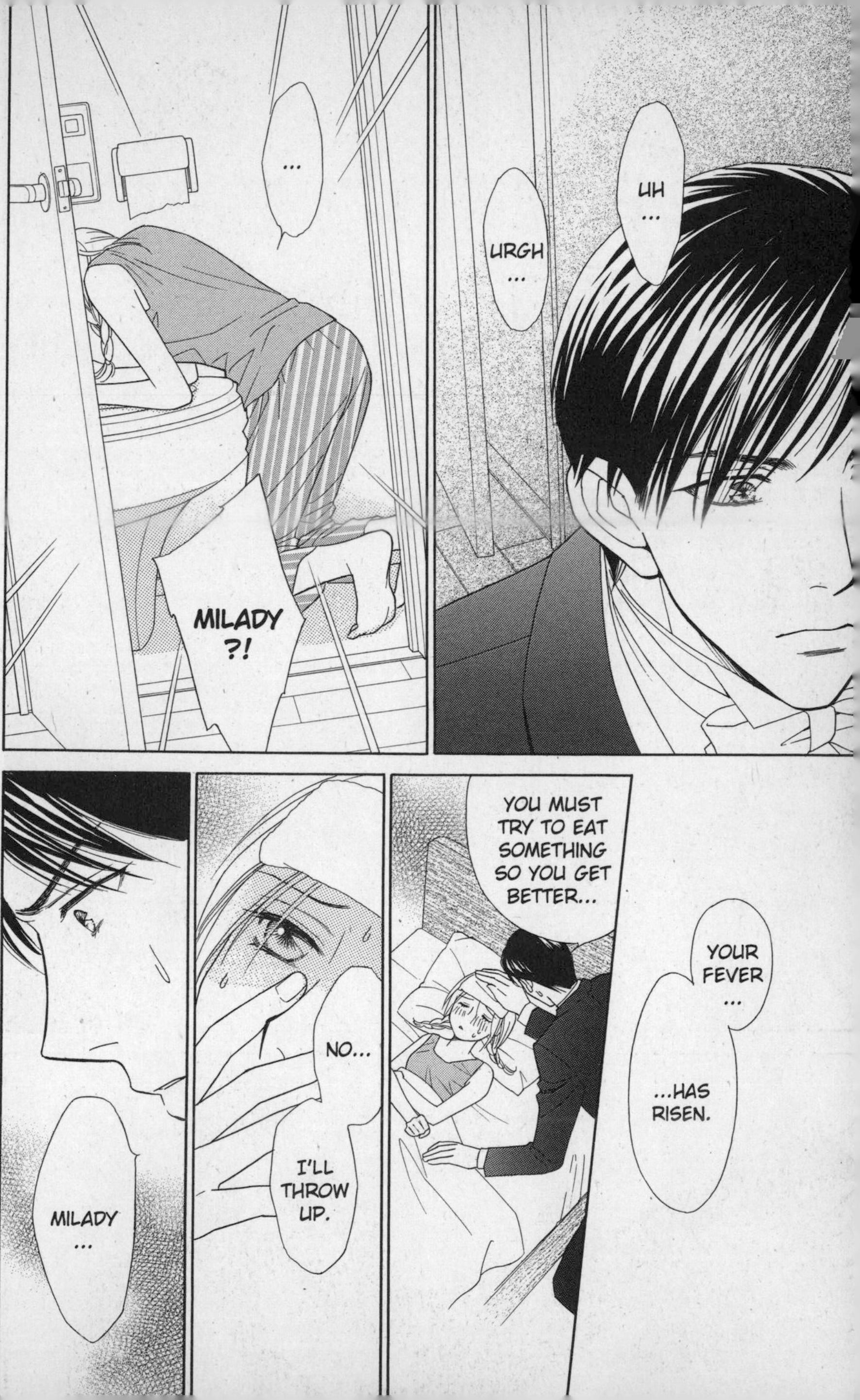
UH ...
URGH ...
...
MILADY ?!
YOUR FEVER ...
...HAS RISEN.
YOU MUST TRY TO EAT SOMETHING SO YOU GET BETTER...
NO...
I'LL THROW UP.
MILADY ...

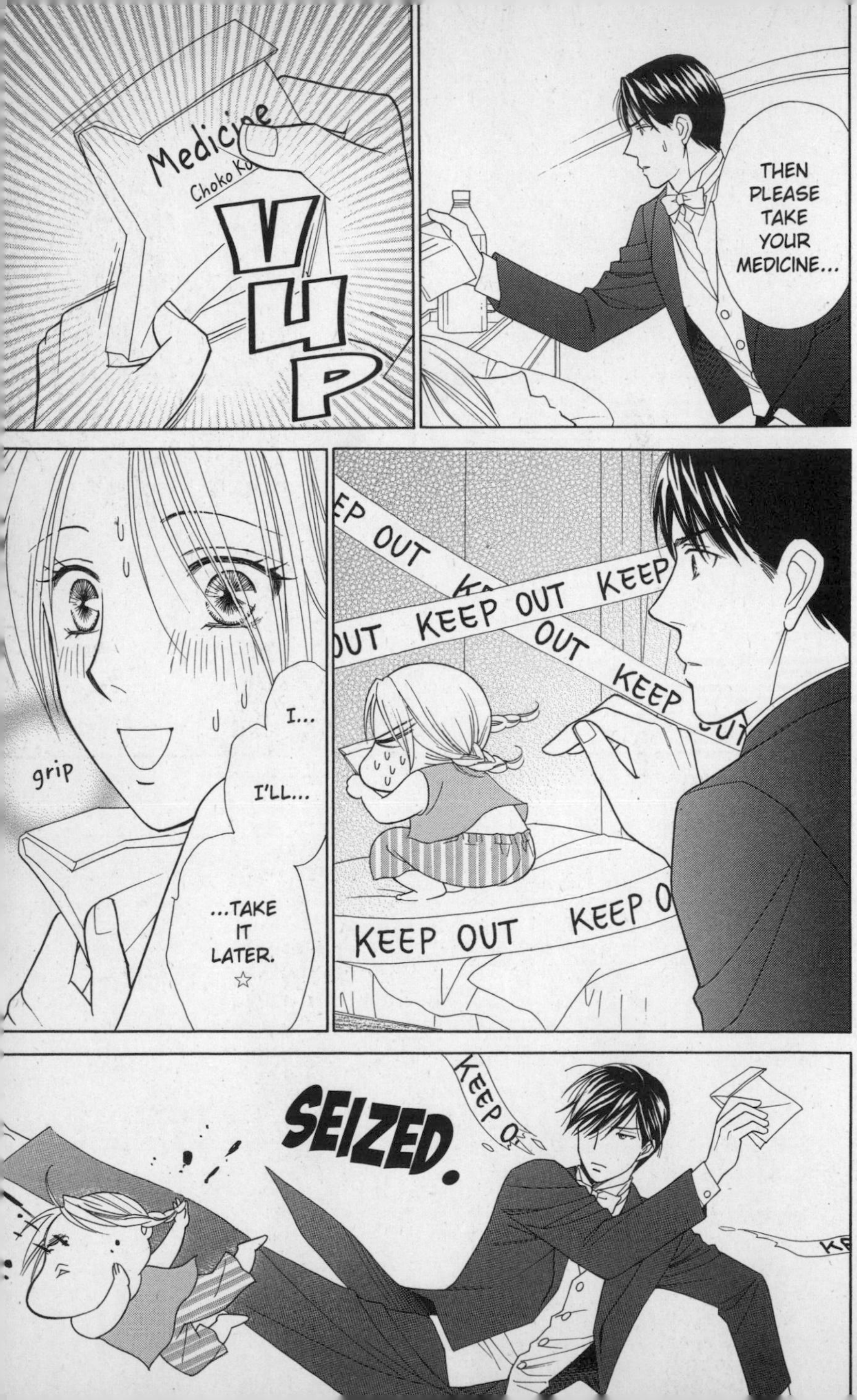
THEN PLEASE TAKE YOUR MEDICINE...
Medicine
Choko Ko
VUP
EP OUT
KEEP OUT KEEP
OUT
OUT
KEEP
KEEP OUT KEEP O
I...
I'LL...
...TAKE IT LATER. ☆
grip
SEIZED.
KEEP O

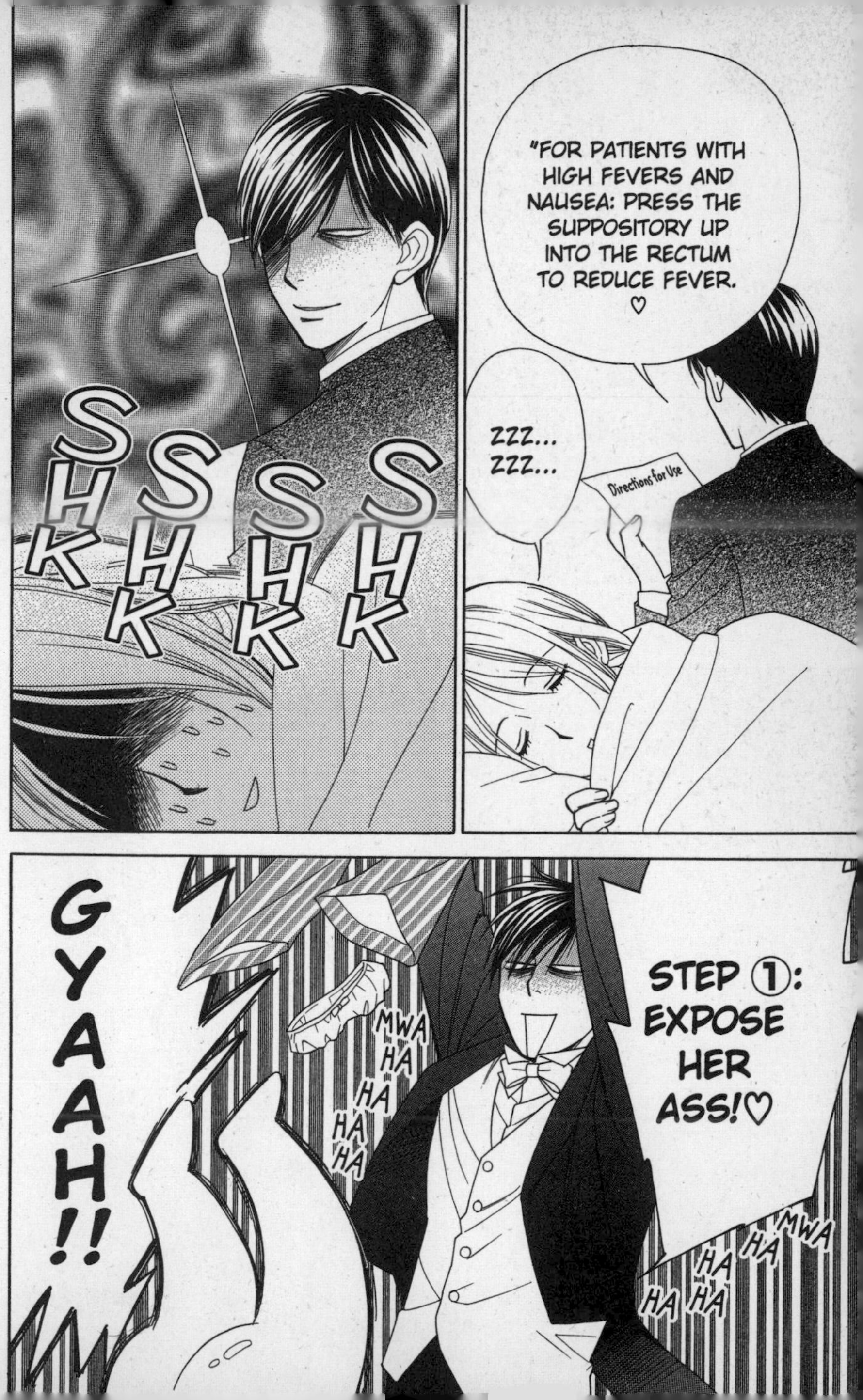
"FOR PATIENTS WITH HIGH FEVERS AND NAUSEA: PRESS THE SUPPOSITORY UP INTO THE RECTUM TO REDUCE FEVER. ♡
ZZZ... ZZZ...
Directions for Use
SHHK SHHK SHHK SHHK
STEP ①: EXPOSE HER ASS!♡
MWA HA HA HA HA
MWA HA HA HA HA
GYAAH!!

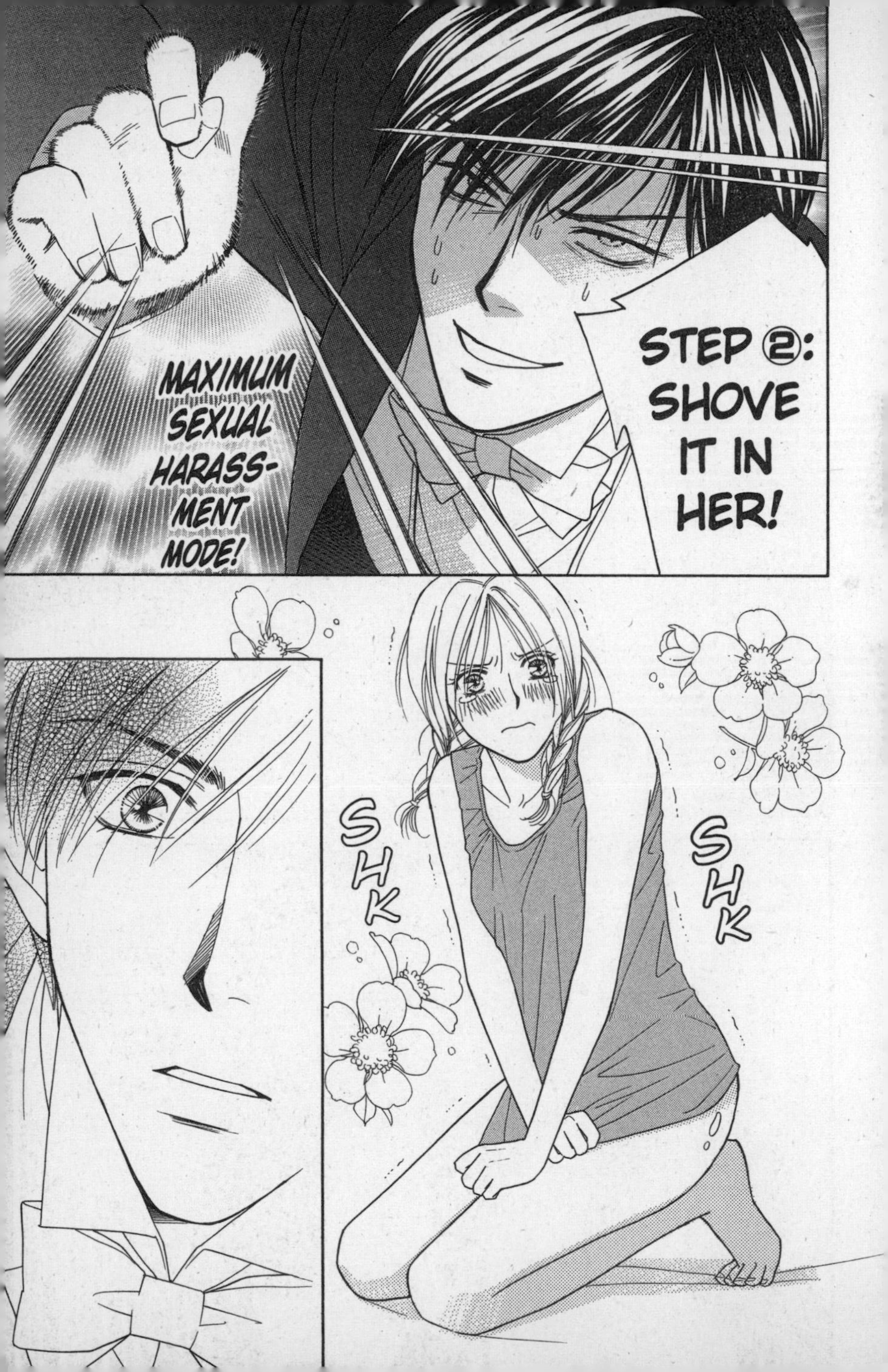
STEP ②: SHOVE IT IN HER!
MAXIMUM SEXUAL HARASS-MENT MODE!
SHK
SHK

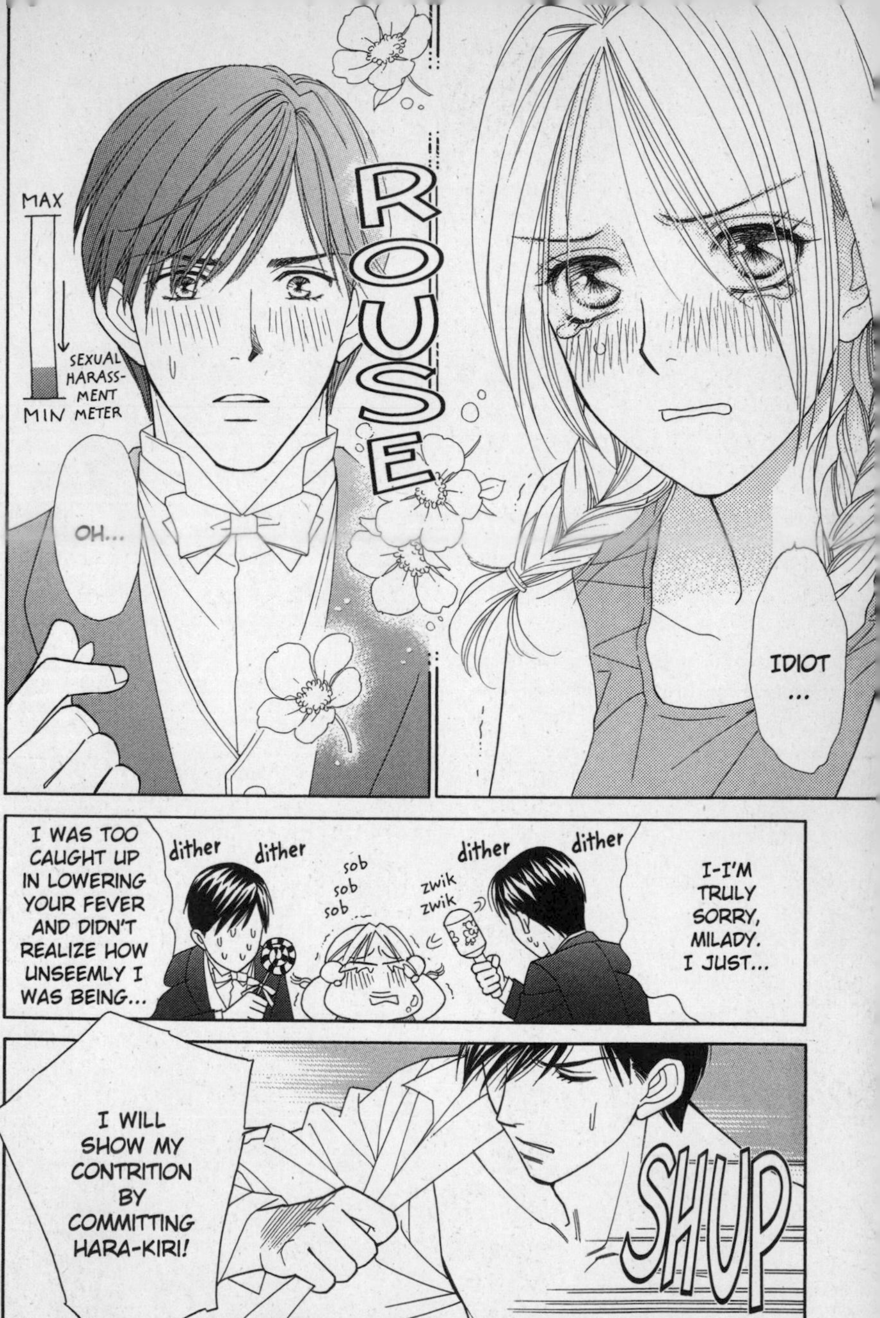
IDIOT ...
ROUSE
MAX
MIN
SEXUAL HARASSMENT METER
OH...
I-I'M TRULY SORRY, MILADY. I JUST...
dither dither
zwik zwik
sob sob sob
dither dither
I WAS TOO CAUGHT UP IN LOWERING YOUR FEVER AND DIDN'T REALIZE HOW UNSEEMLY I WAS BEING...
SHUP
I WILL SHOW MY CONTRITION BY COMMITTING HARA-KIRI!

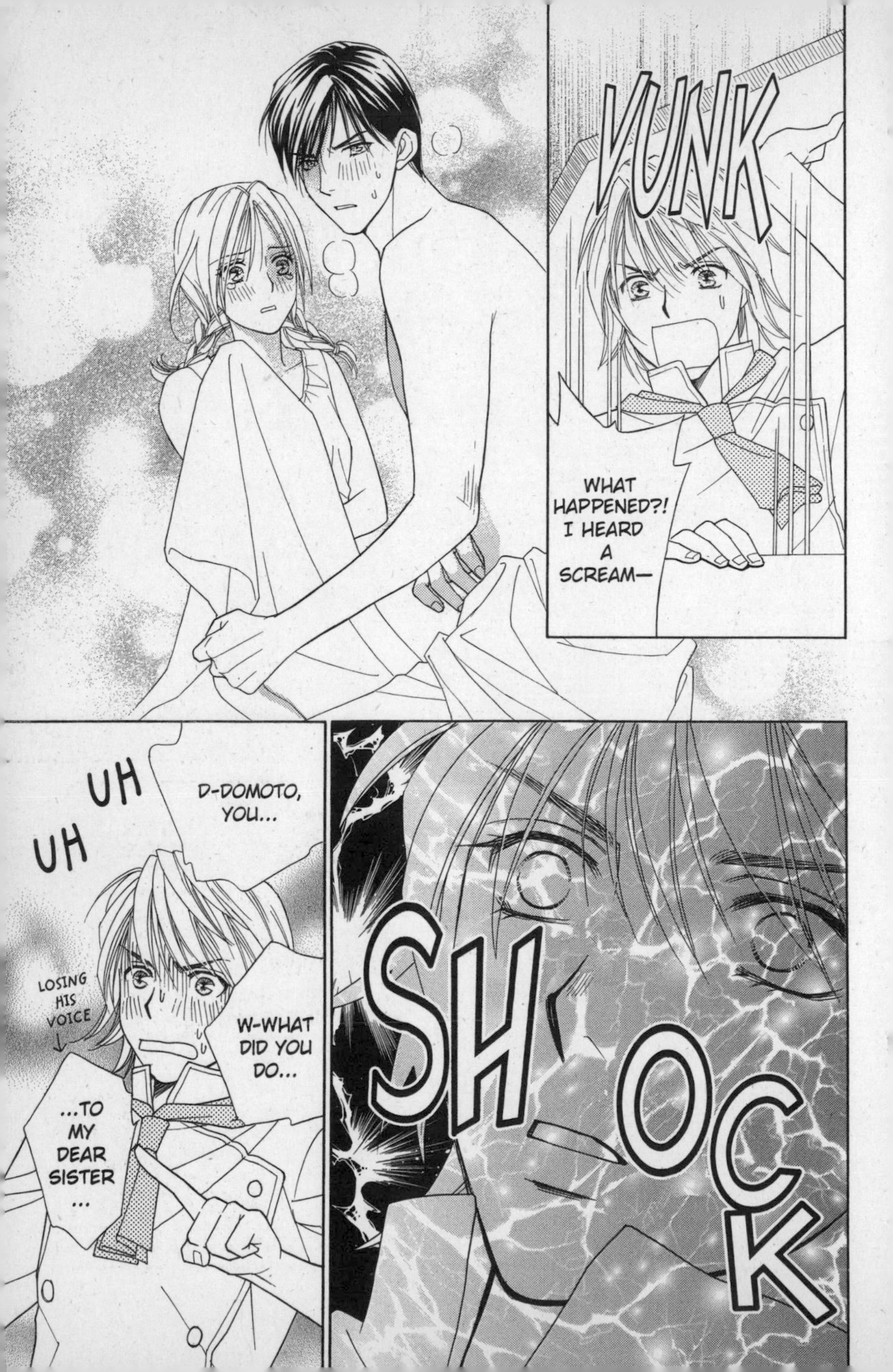
VUNK
WHAT HAPPENED?! I HEARD A SCREAM—
SHOCK
D-DOMOTO, YOU...
UH
UH
LOSING HIS VOICE
W-WHAT DID YOU DO...
...TO MY DEAR SISTER ...

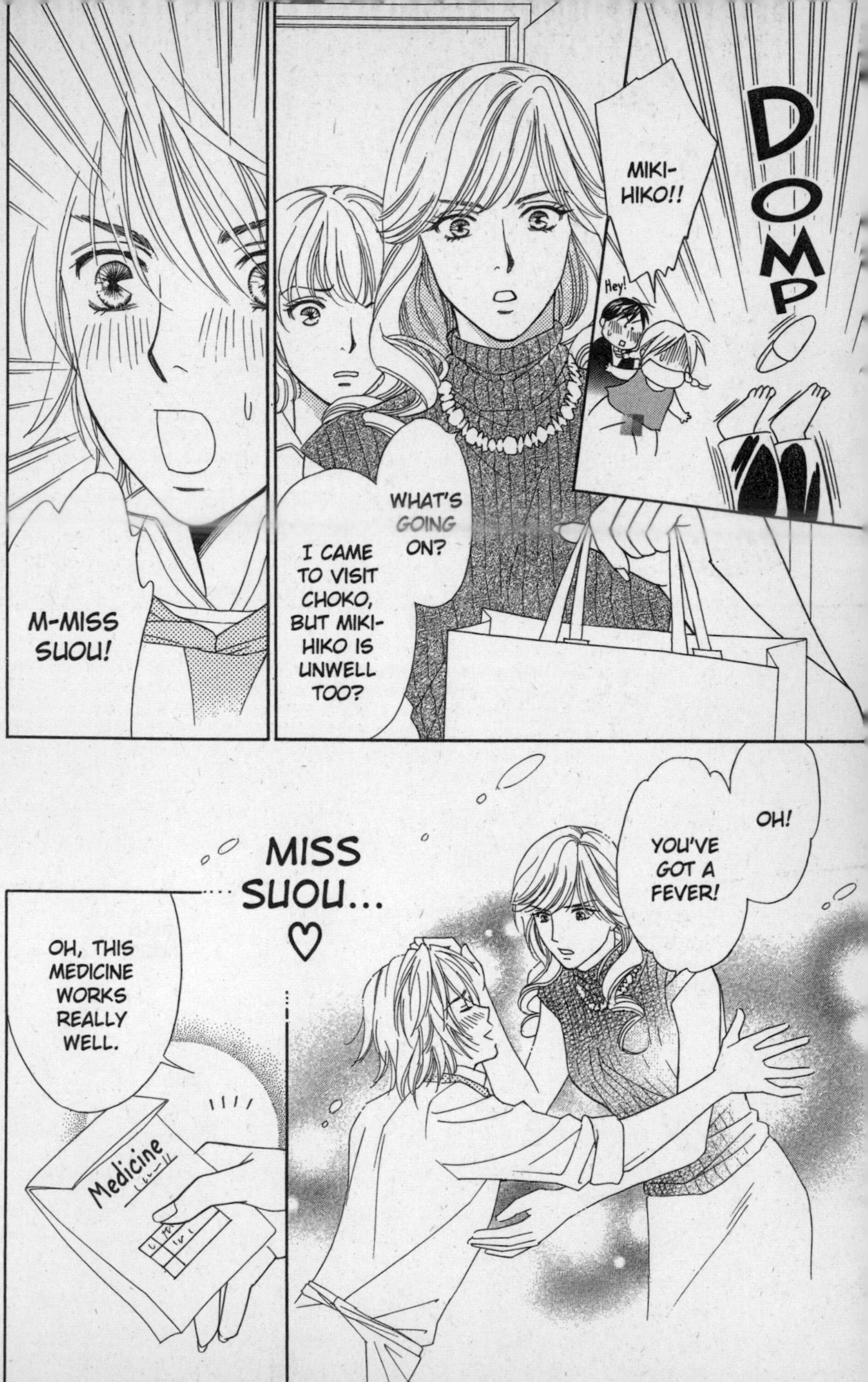
DOMP
MIKI-HIKO!!
Hey!
WHAT'S GOING ON?
I CAME TO VISIT CHOKO, BUT MIKI-HIKO IS UNWELL TOO?
M-MISS SUOU!
OH!
YOU'VE GOT A FEVER!
MISS SUOU... ♥
OH, THIS MEDICINE WORKS REALLY WELL.
Medicine

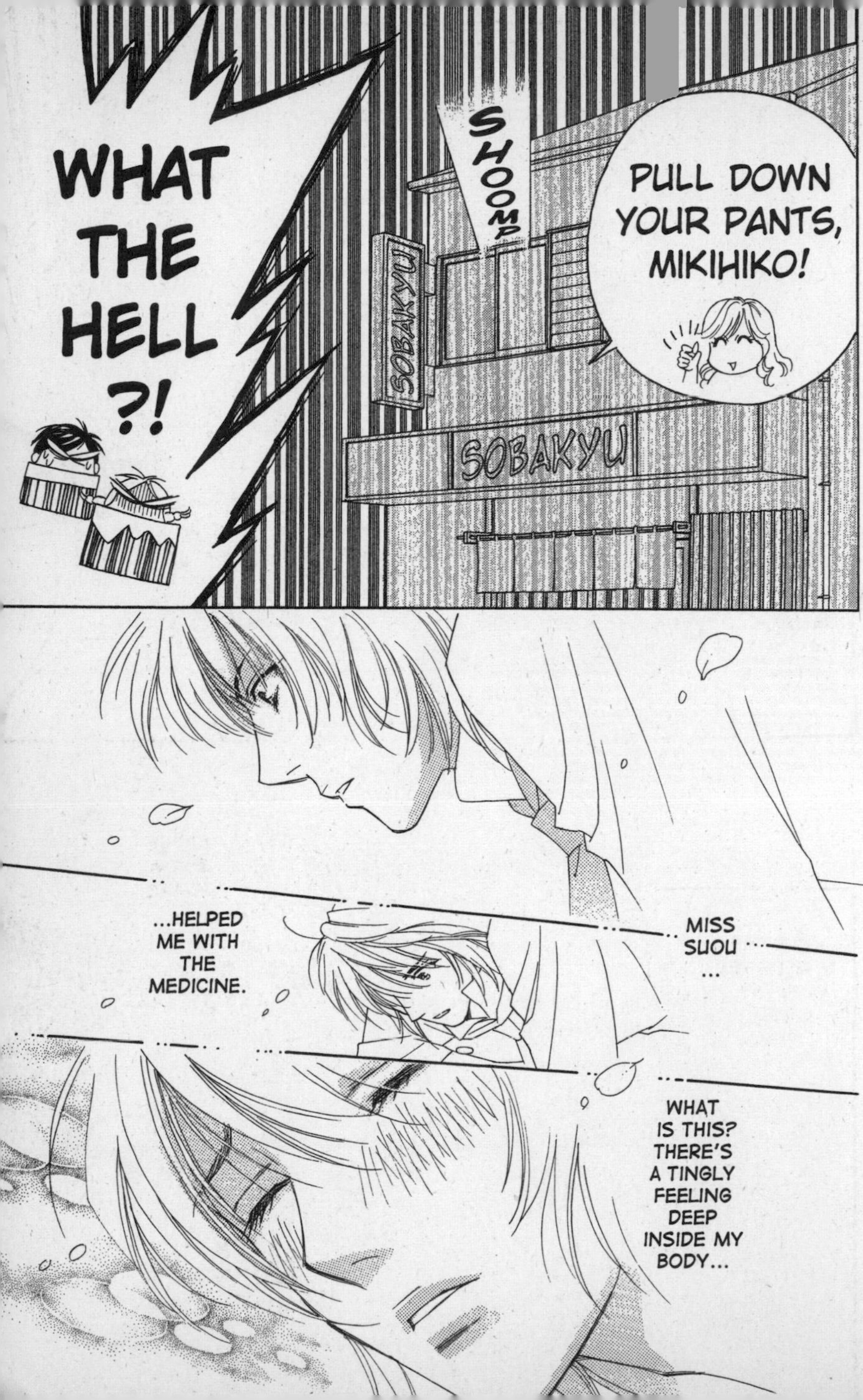

PULL DOWN YOUR PANTS, MIKIHIKO!
SHOOMP
SOBAKYU
SOBAKYU
WHAT THE HELL ?!
MISS SUOU ...
...HELPED ME WITH THE MEDICINE.
WHAT IS THIS? THERE'S A TINGLY FEELING DEEP INSIDE MY BODY...

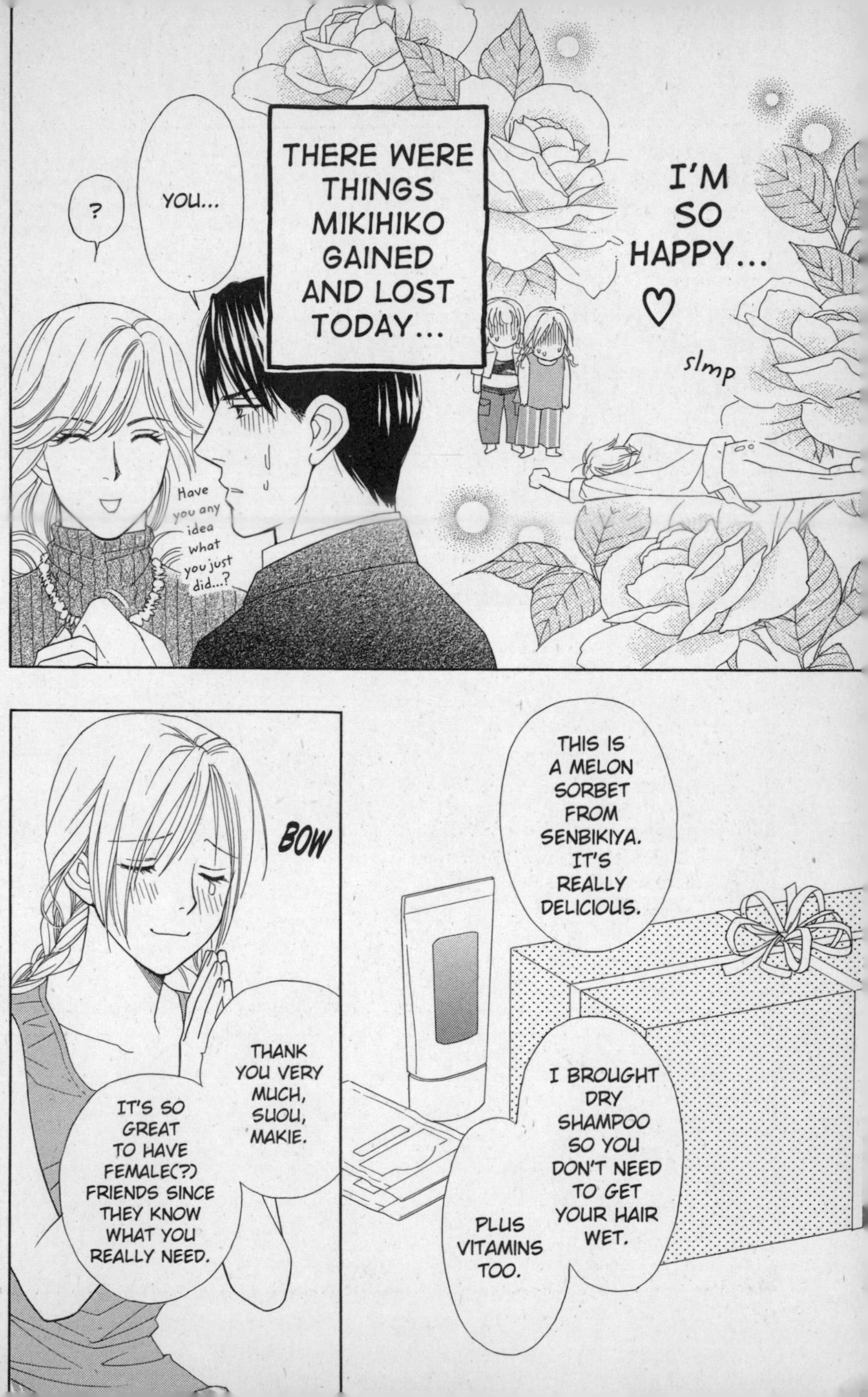
I'M SO HAPPY... ♡
slmp
THERE WERE THINGS MIKIHIKO GAINED AND LOST TODAY...
YOU...
?
Have you any idea what you just did...?
THIS IS A MELON SORBET FROM SENBIKIYA. IT'S REALLY DELICIOUS.
I BROUGHT DRY SHAMPOO SO YOU DON'T NEED TO GET YOUR HAIR WET.
PLUS VITAMINS TOO.
BOW
THANK YOU VERY MUCH, SUOU, MAKIE.
IT'S SO GREAT TO HAVE FEMALE(?) FRIENDS SINCE THEY KNOW WHAT YOU REALLY NEED.

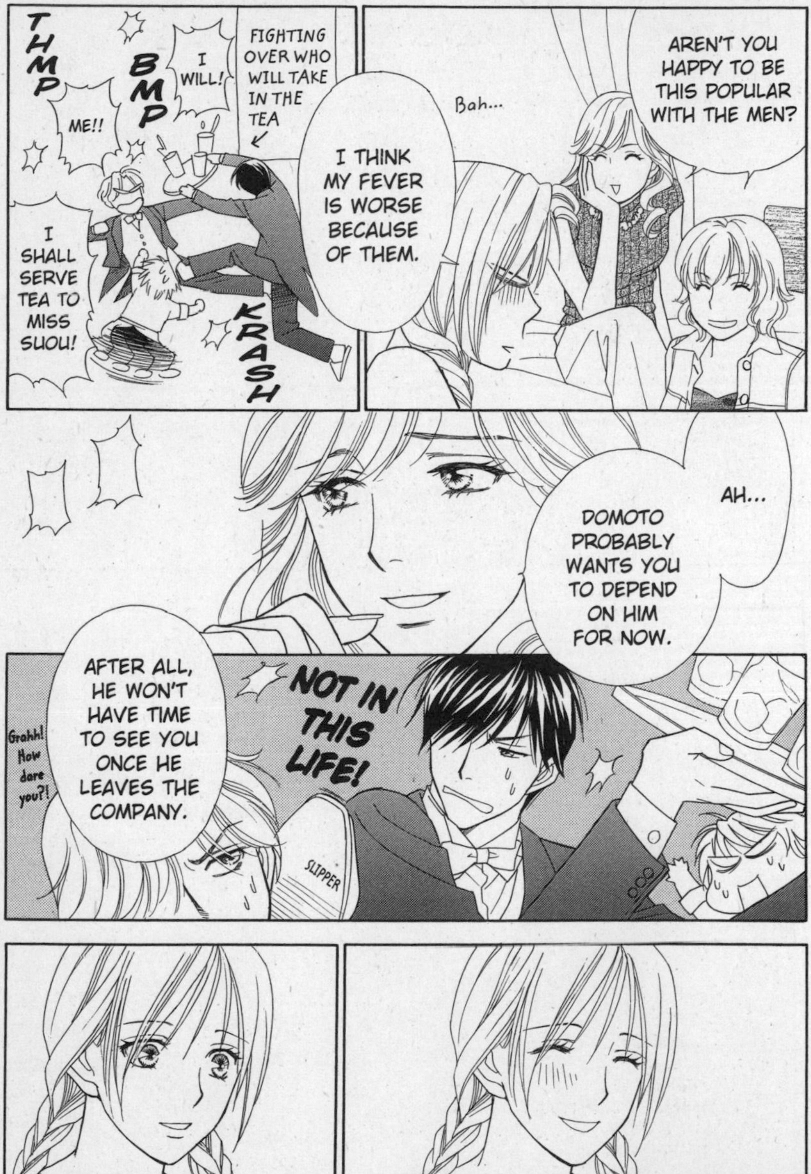
Bah...
AREN'T YOU HAPPY TO BE THIS POPULAR WITH THE MEN?
I THINK MY FEVER IS WORSE BECAUSE OF THEM.
FIGHTING OVER WHO WILL TAKE IN THE TEA
I WILL!
BMP
THMP
ME!!
I SHALL SERVE TEA TO MISS SUOU!
KRASH
AH...
DOMOTO PROBABLY WANTS YOU TO DEPEND ON HIM FOR NOW.
NOT IN THIS LIFE!
AFTER ALL, HE WON'T HAVE TIME TO SEE YOU ONCE HE LEAVES THE COMPANY.
Grahh! How dare you?!
SLIPPER

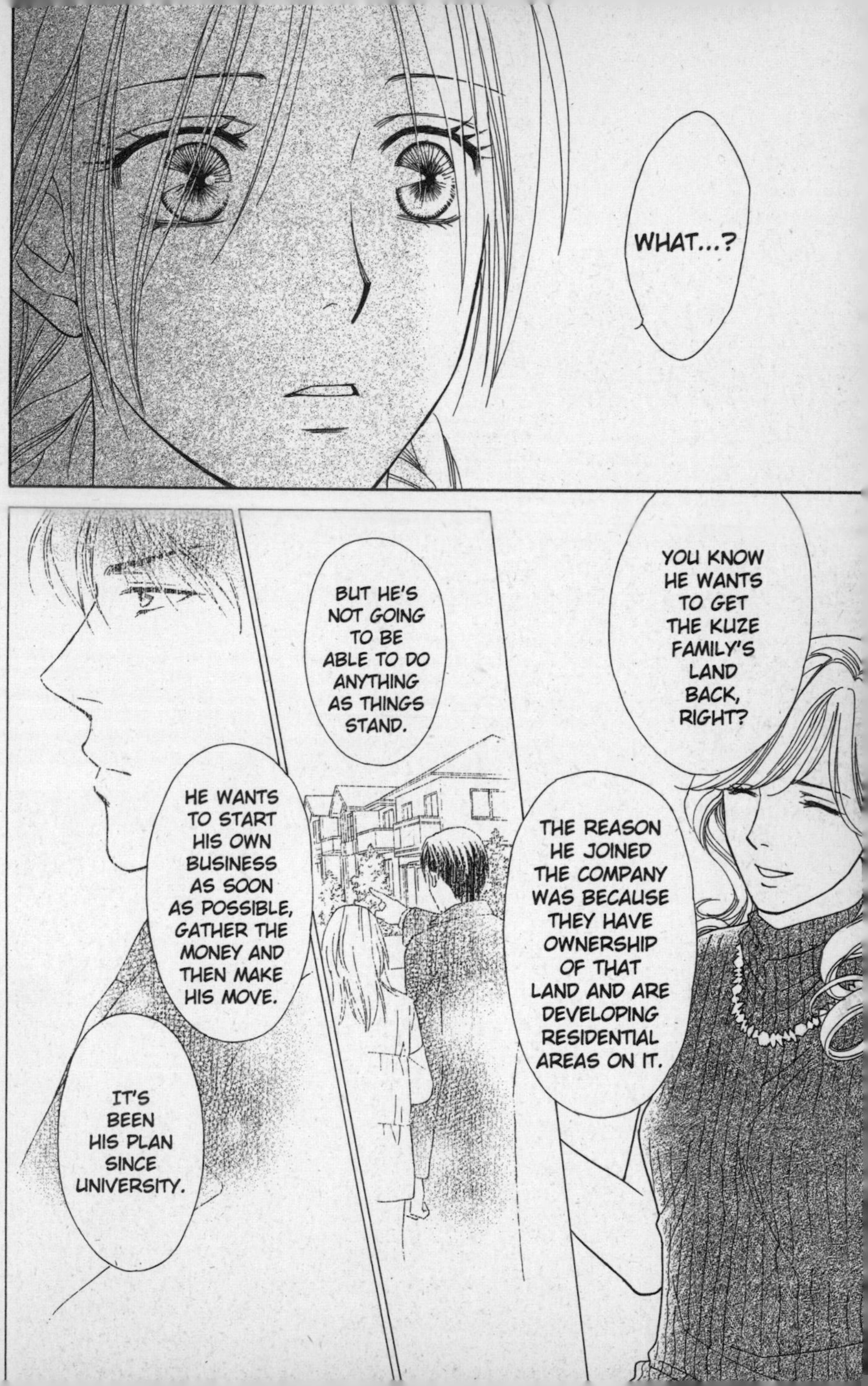
WHAT...?
YOU KNOW HE WANTS TO GET THE KUZE FAMILY'S LAND BACK, RIGHT?
THE REASON HE JOINED THE COMPANY WAS BECAUSE THEY HAVE OWNERSHIP OF THAT LAND AND ARE DEVELOPING RESIDENTIAL AREAS ON IT.
BUT HE'S NOT GOING TO BE ABLE TO DO ANYTHING AS THINGS STAND.
HE WANTS TO START HIS OWN BUSINESS AS SOON AS POSSIBLE, GATHER THE MONEY AND THEN MAKE HIS MOVE.
IT'S BEEN HIS PLAN SINCE UNIVERSITY.

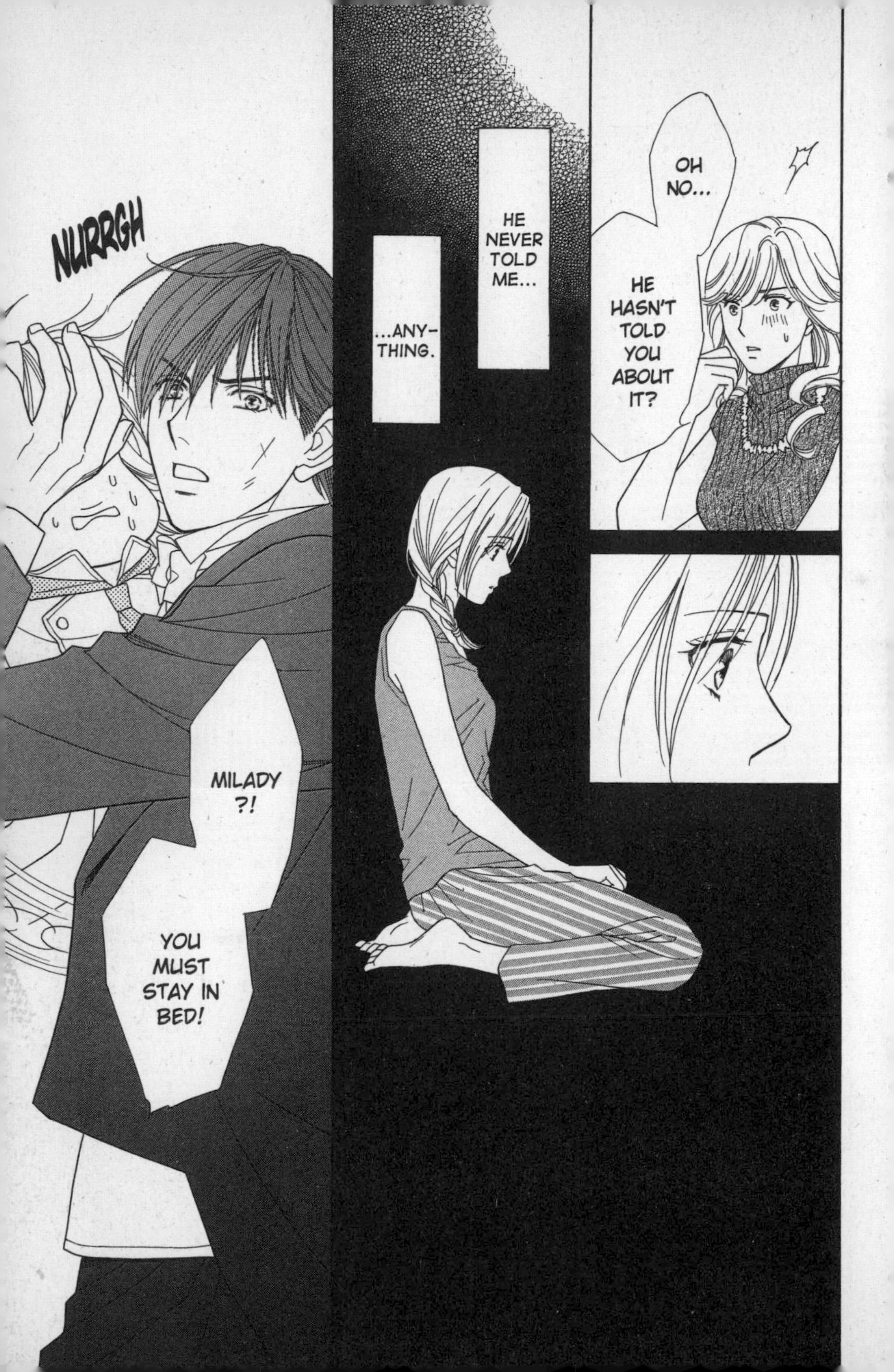
OH NO...
HE HASN'T TOLD YOU ABOUT IT?
HE NEVER TOLD ME...
...ANY-THING.
NURRGH
MILADY ?!
YOU MUST STAY IN BED!

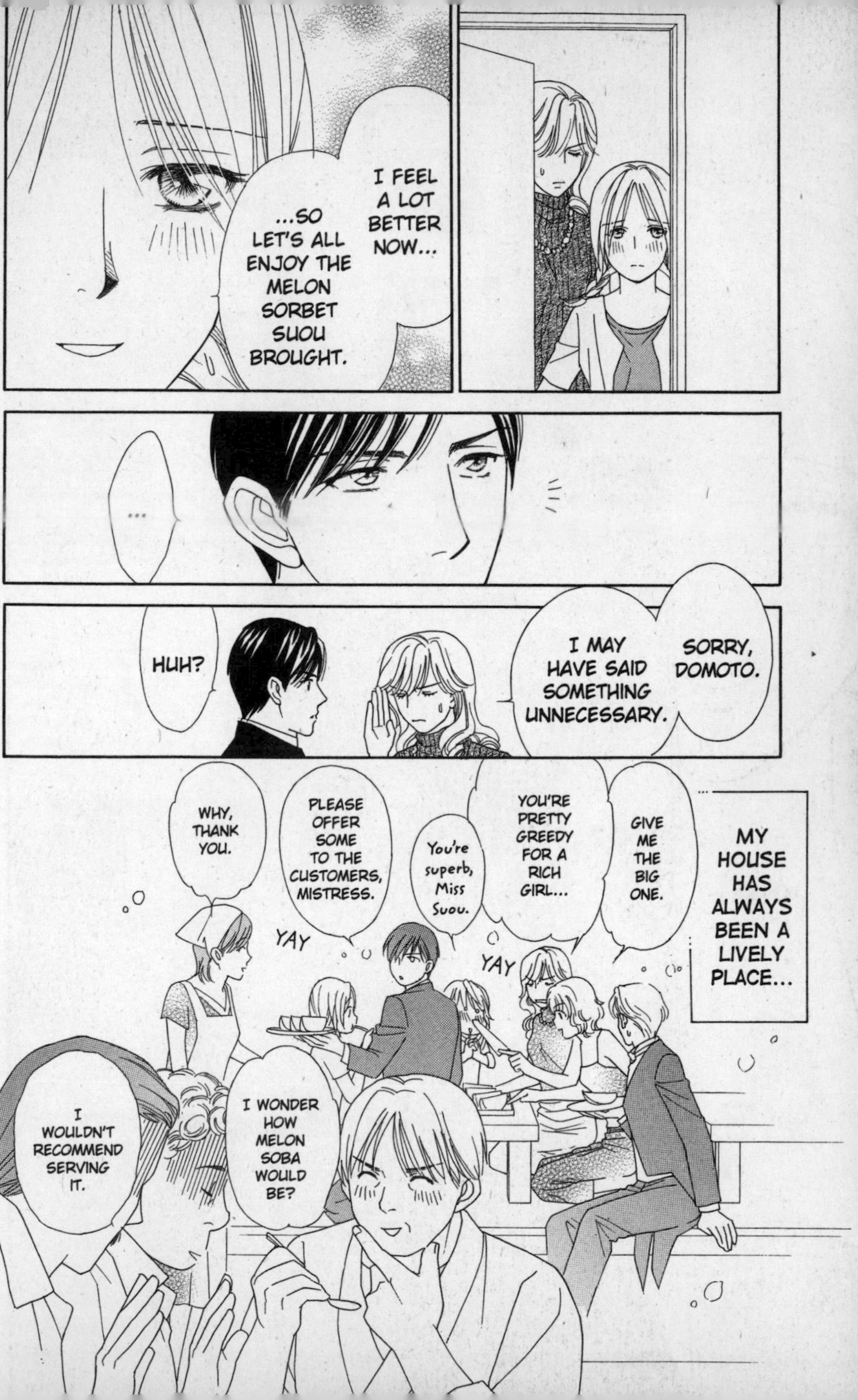
I FEEL A LOT BETTER NOW...
...SO LET'S ALL ENJOY THE MELON SORBET SUOU BROUGHT.
...
SORRY, DOMOTO.
I MAY HAVE SAID SOMETHING UNNECESSARY.
HUH?
...MY HOUSE HAS ALWAYS BEEN A LIVELY PLACE...
GIVE ME THE BIG ONE.
YOU'RE PRETTY GREEDY FOR A RICH GIRL...
YAY
You're superb, Miss Suou.
PLEASE OFFER SOME TO THE CUSTOMERS, MISTRESS.
YAY
WHY, THANK YOU.
I WONDER HOW MELON SOBA WOULD BE?
I WOULDN'T RECOMMEND SERVING IT.

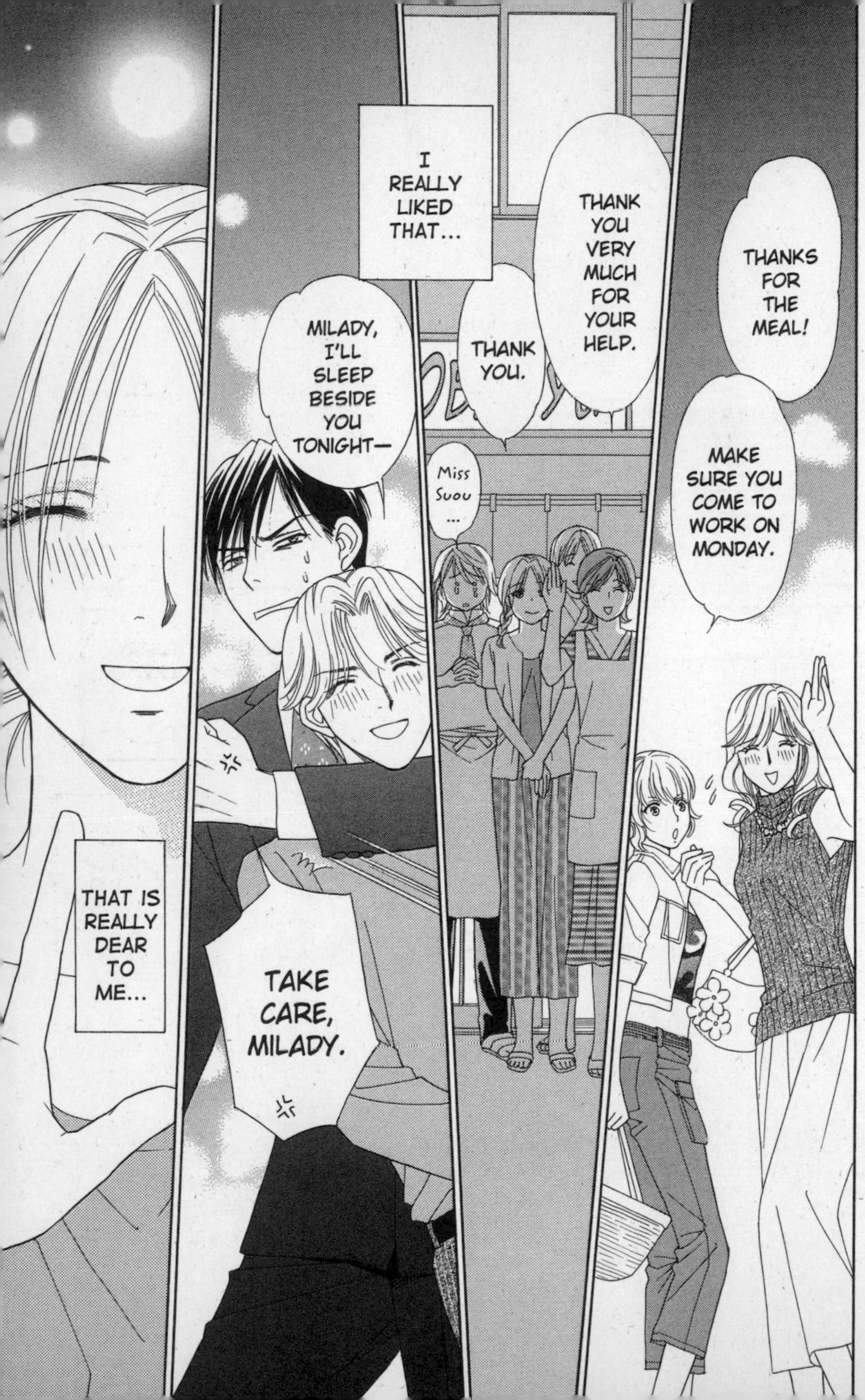
THANKS FOR THE MEAL!
MAKE SURE YOU COME TO WORK ON MONDAY.
THANK YOU VERY MUCH FOR YOUR HELP.
I REALLY LIKED THAT...
THANK YOU.
Miss Suou...
MILADY, I'LL SLEEP BESIDE YOU TONIGHT—
TAKE CARE, MILADY.
THAT IS REALLY DEAR TO ME...

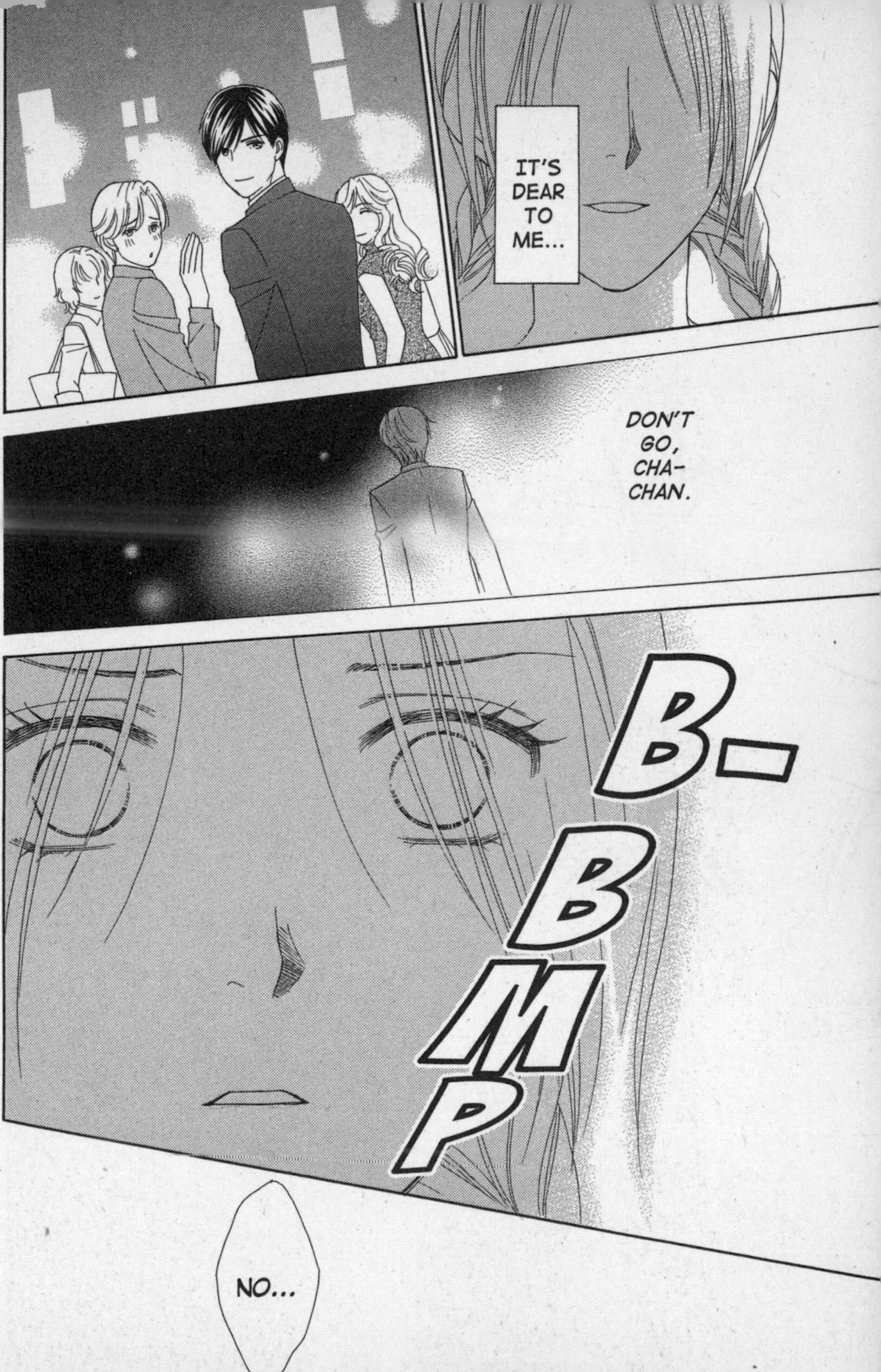
IT'S DEAR TO ME...
DON'T GO, CHA-CHAN.
B-BMP
NO...

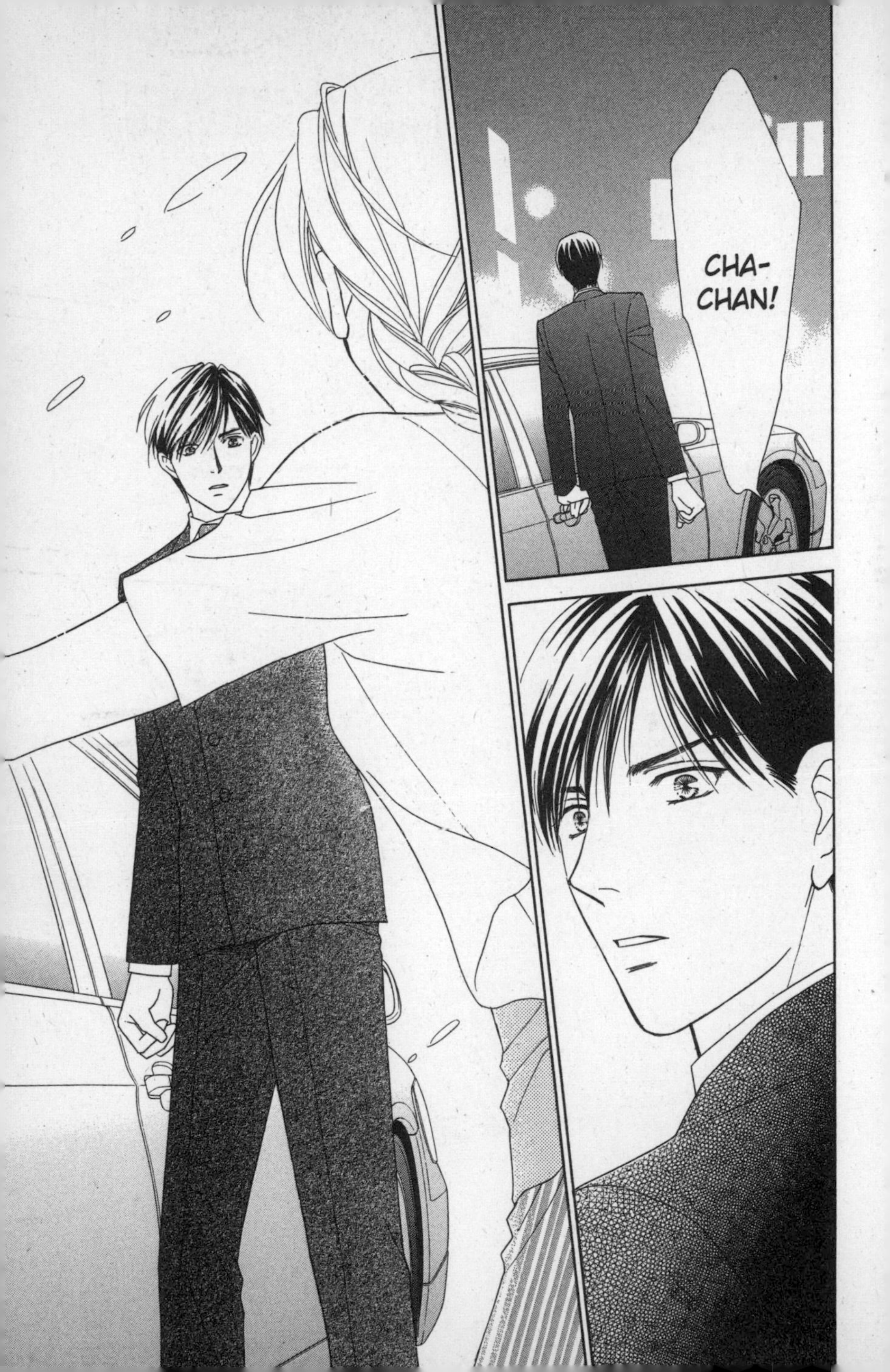
CHA-
CHAN!

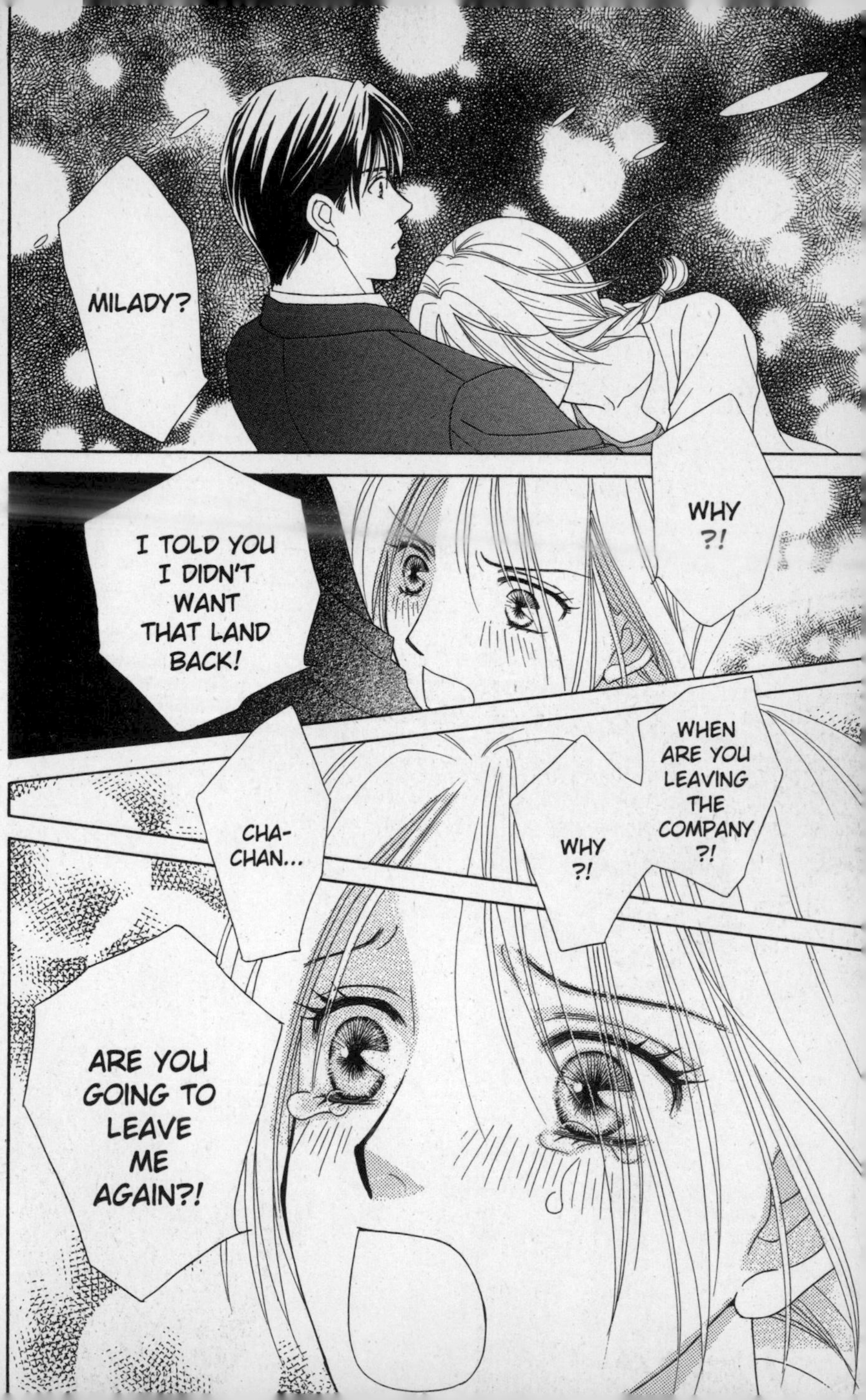
MILADY?
WHY ?!
I TOLD YOU I DIDN'T WANT THAT LAND BACK!
WHEN ARE YOU LEAVING THE COMPANY ?!
WHY ?!
CHA-CHAN...
ARE YOU GOING TO LEAVE ME AGAIN?!

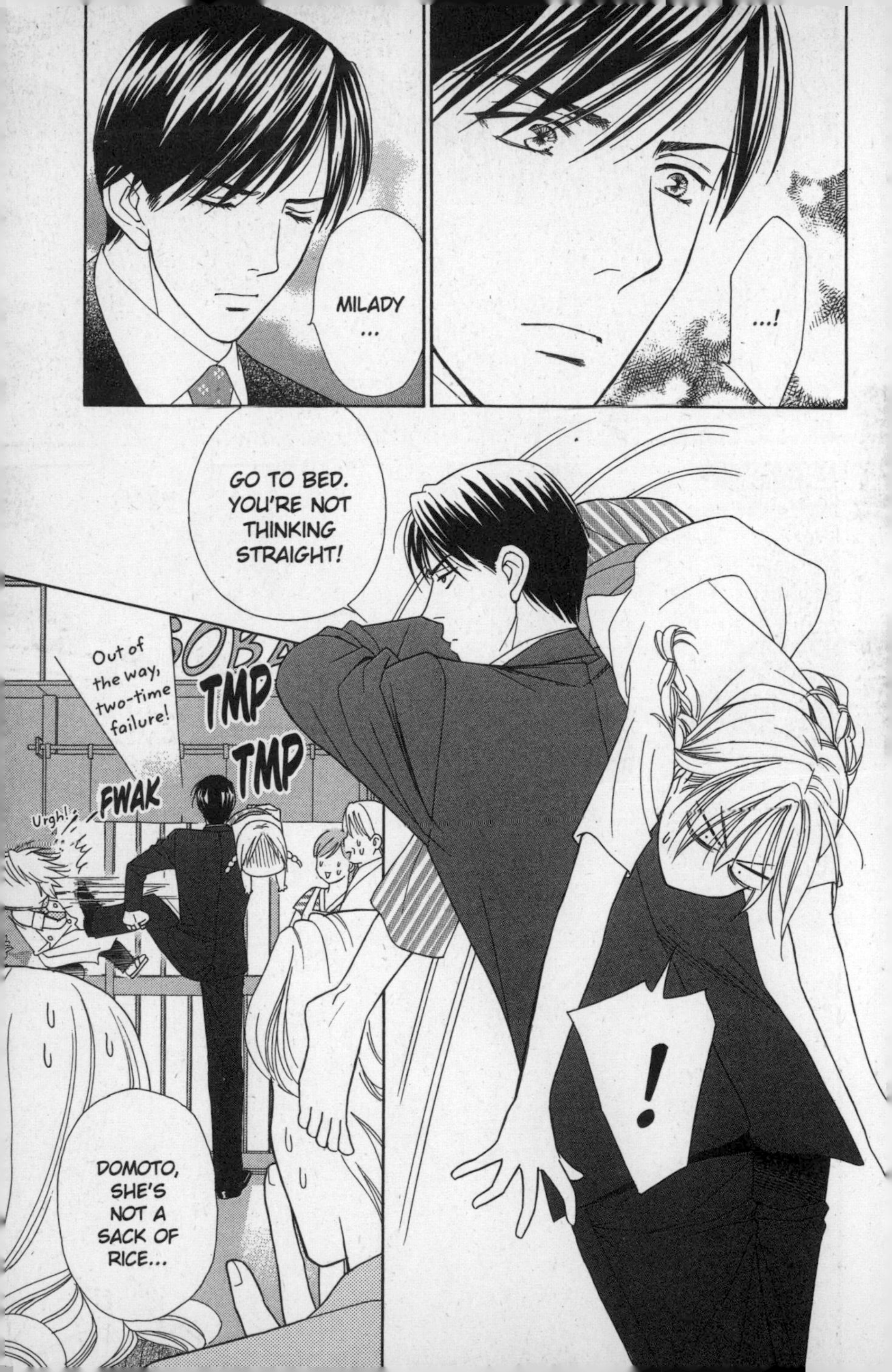
...!
MILADY ...
GO TO BED. YOU'RE NOT THINKING STRAIGHT!
!
TMP
TMP
Out of the way, two-time failure!
FWAK
Urgh!
DOMOTO, SHE'S NOT A SACK OF RICE...

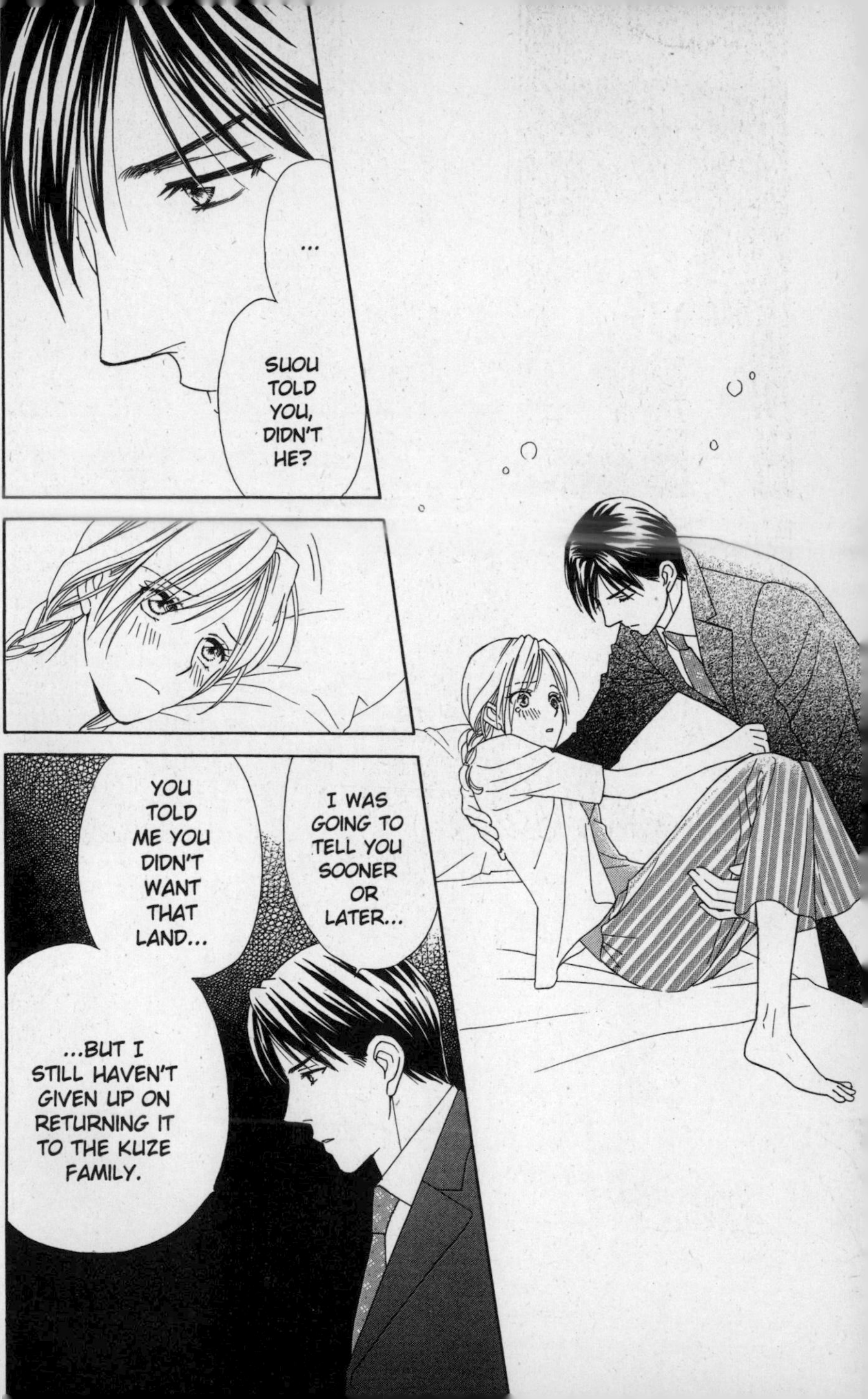
...
SUOU TOLD YOU, DIDN'T HE?
I WAS GOING TO TELL YOU SOONER OR LATER...
YOU TOLD ME YOU DIDN'T WANT THAT LAND...
...BUT I STILL HAVEN'T GIVEN UP ON RETURNING IT TO THE KUZE FAMILY.

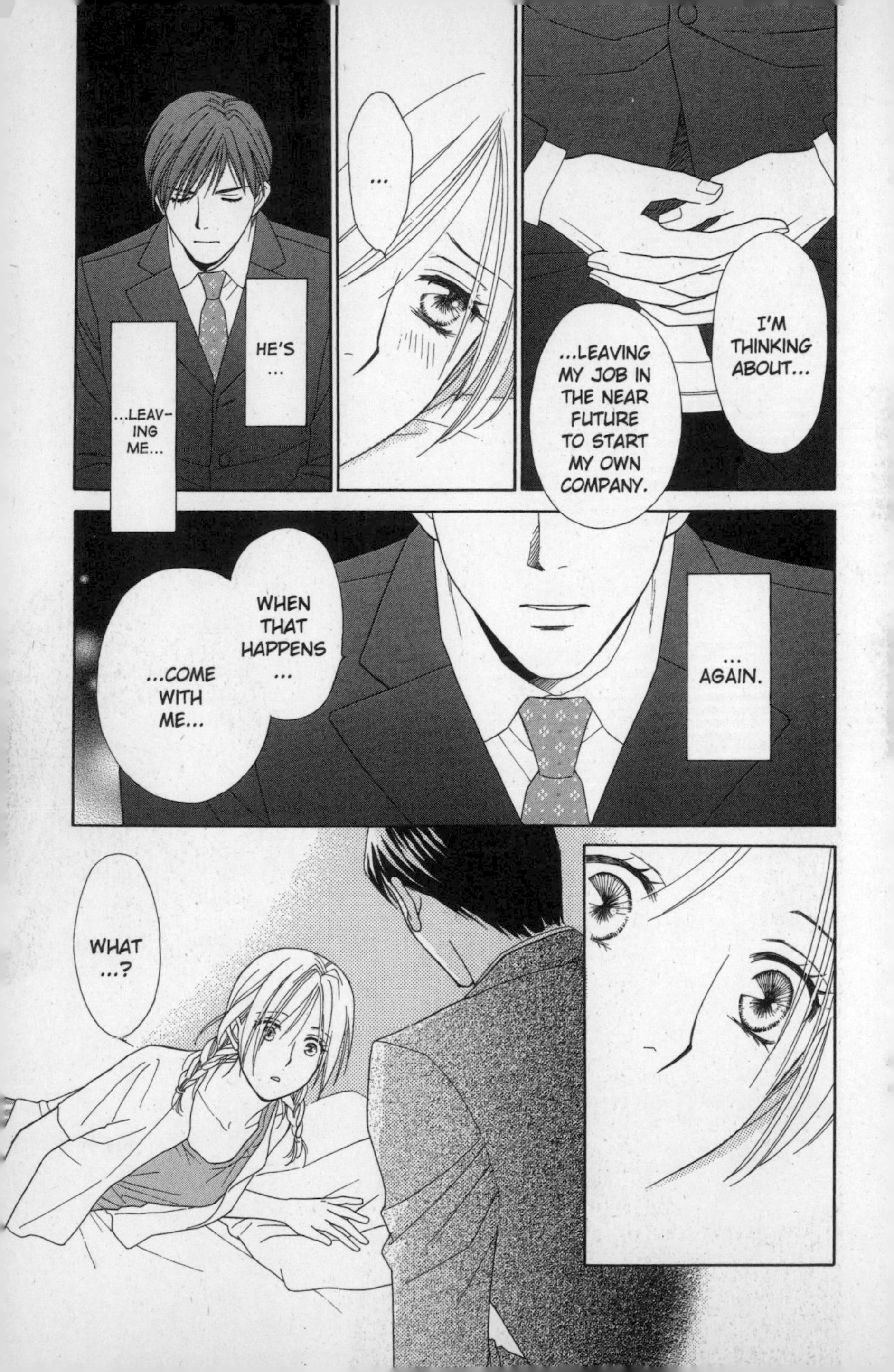
I'M THINKING ABOUT...
...LEAVING MY JOB IN THE NEAR FUTURE TO START MY OWN COMPANY.
...
HE'S ...
...LEAV- ING ME...
... AGAIN.
WHEN THAT HAPPENS ...
...COME WITH ME...
WHAT ...?

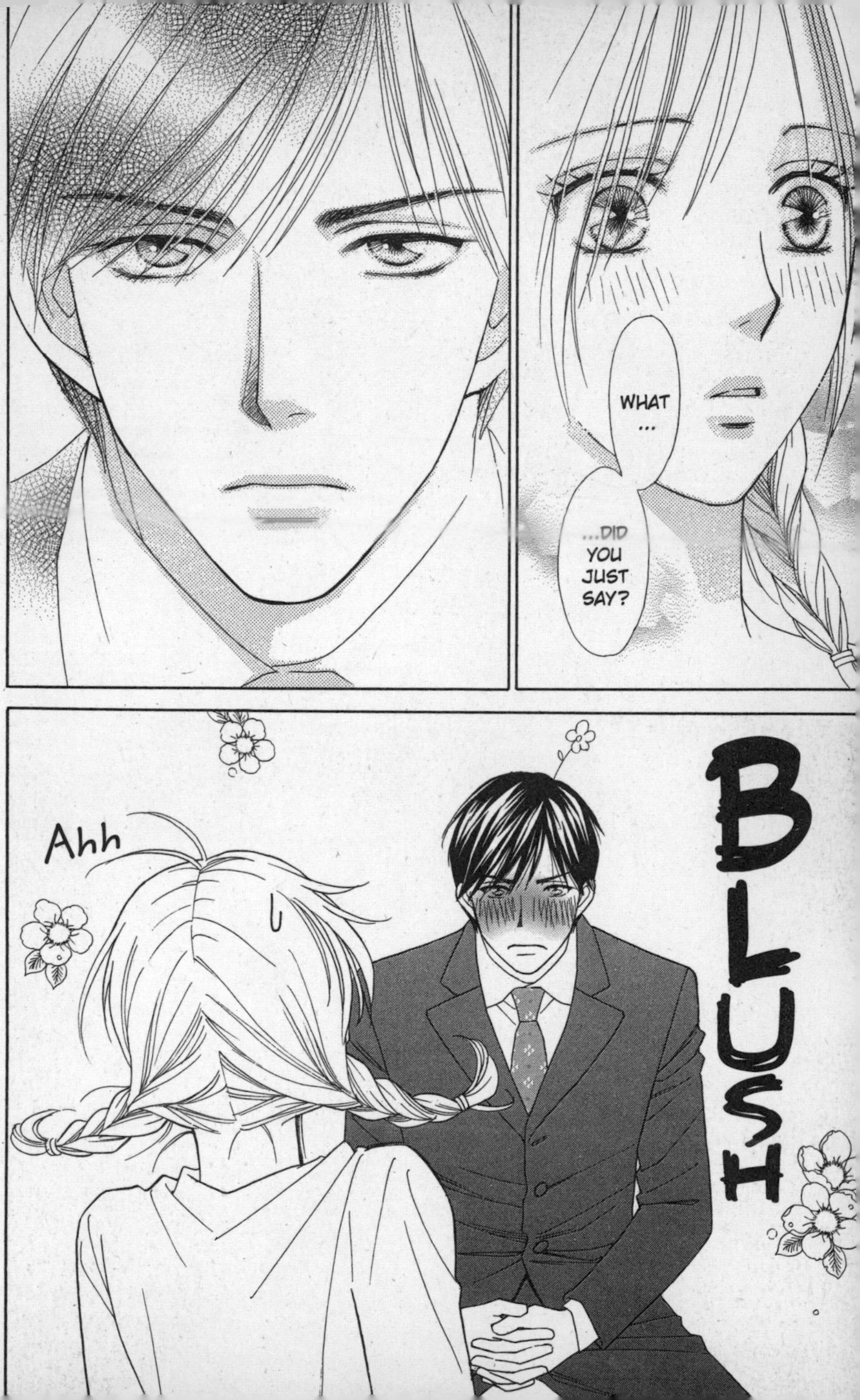
WHAT ...
...DID YOU JUST SAY?
BLUSH
Ahh

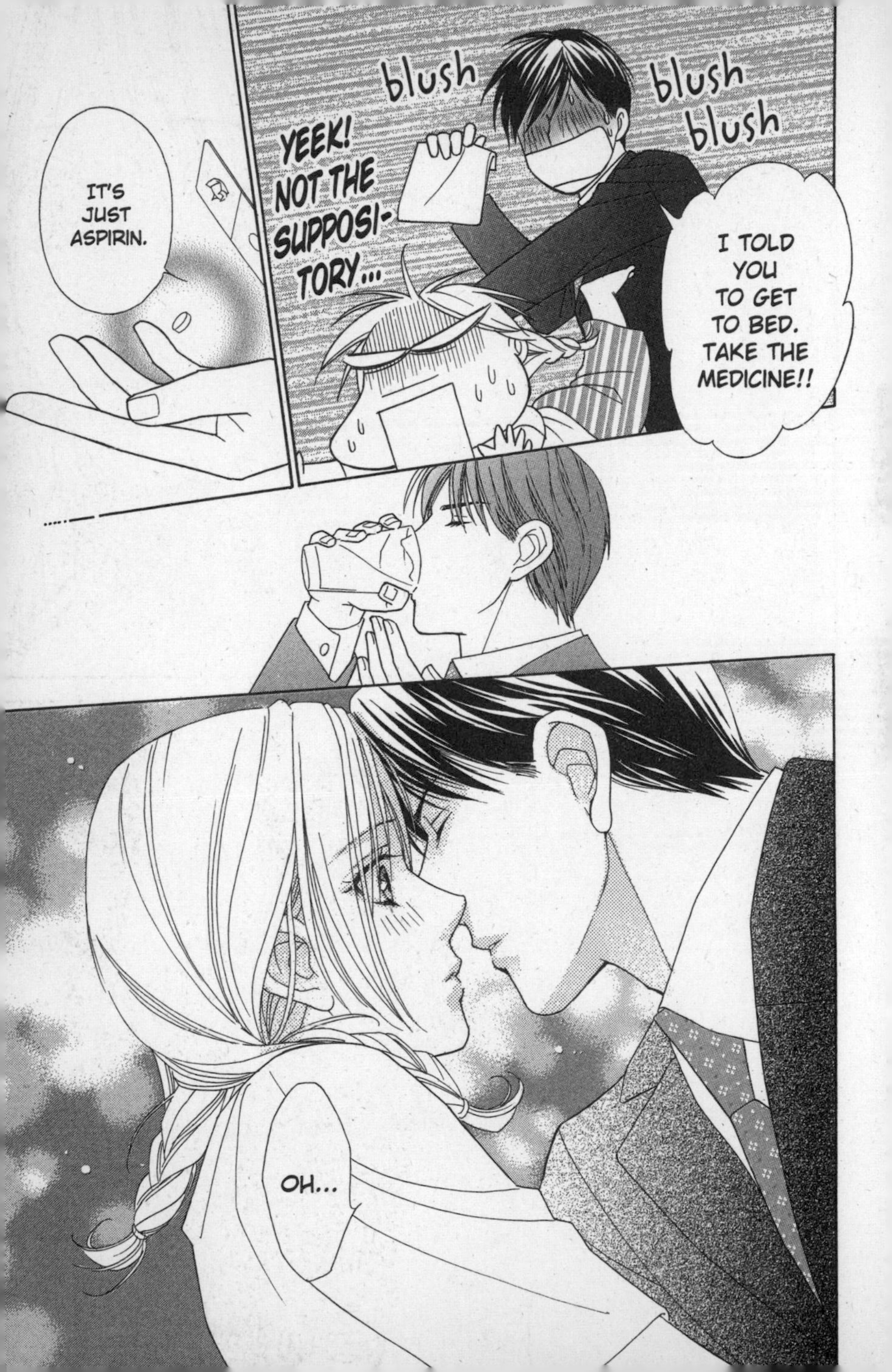
blush blush
blush
I TOLD YOU TO GET TO BED. TAKE THE MEDICINE!!
YEEK! NOT THE SUPPOSI-TORY...
IT'S JUST ASPIRIN.
.....—
OH...

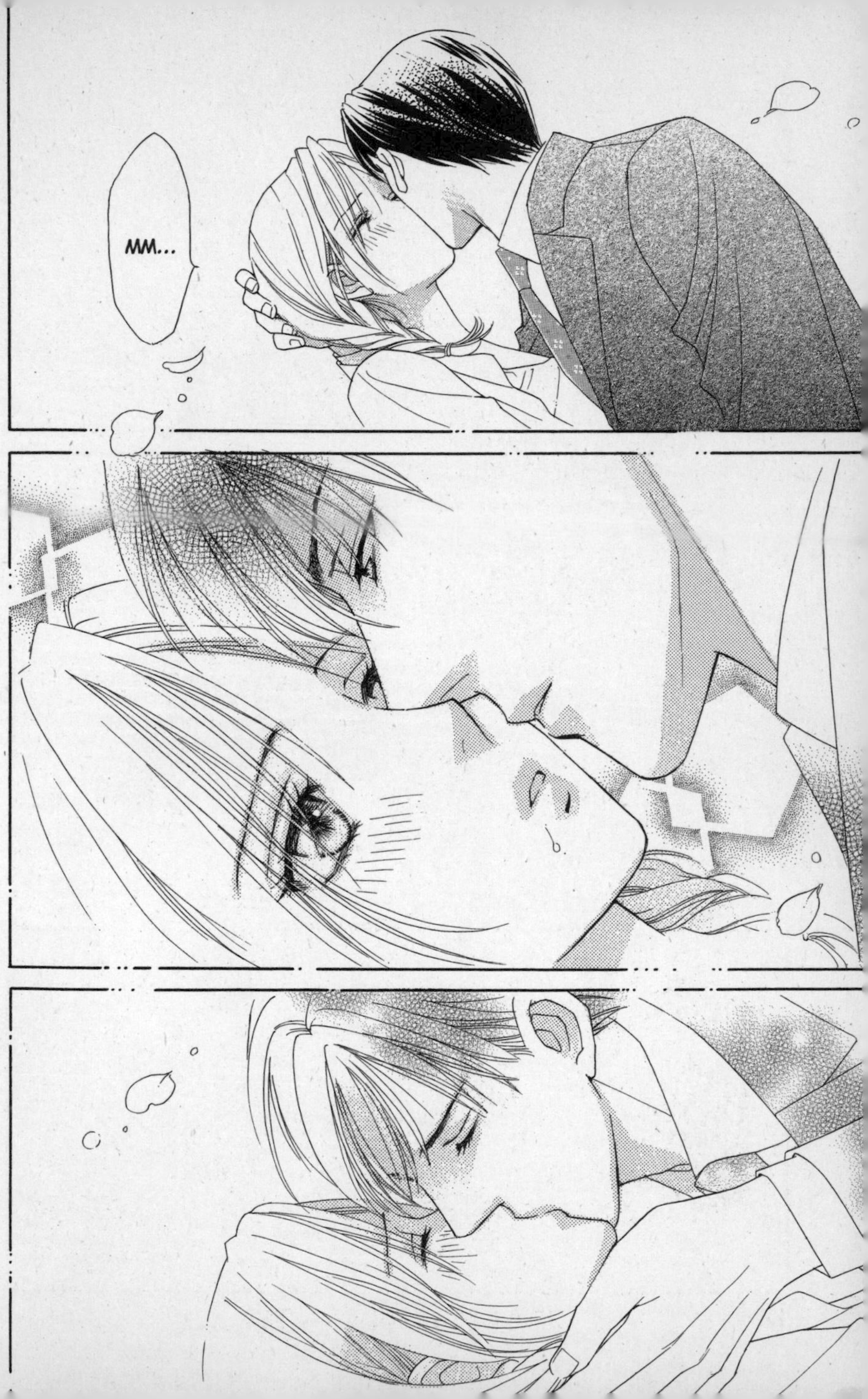
MM...

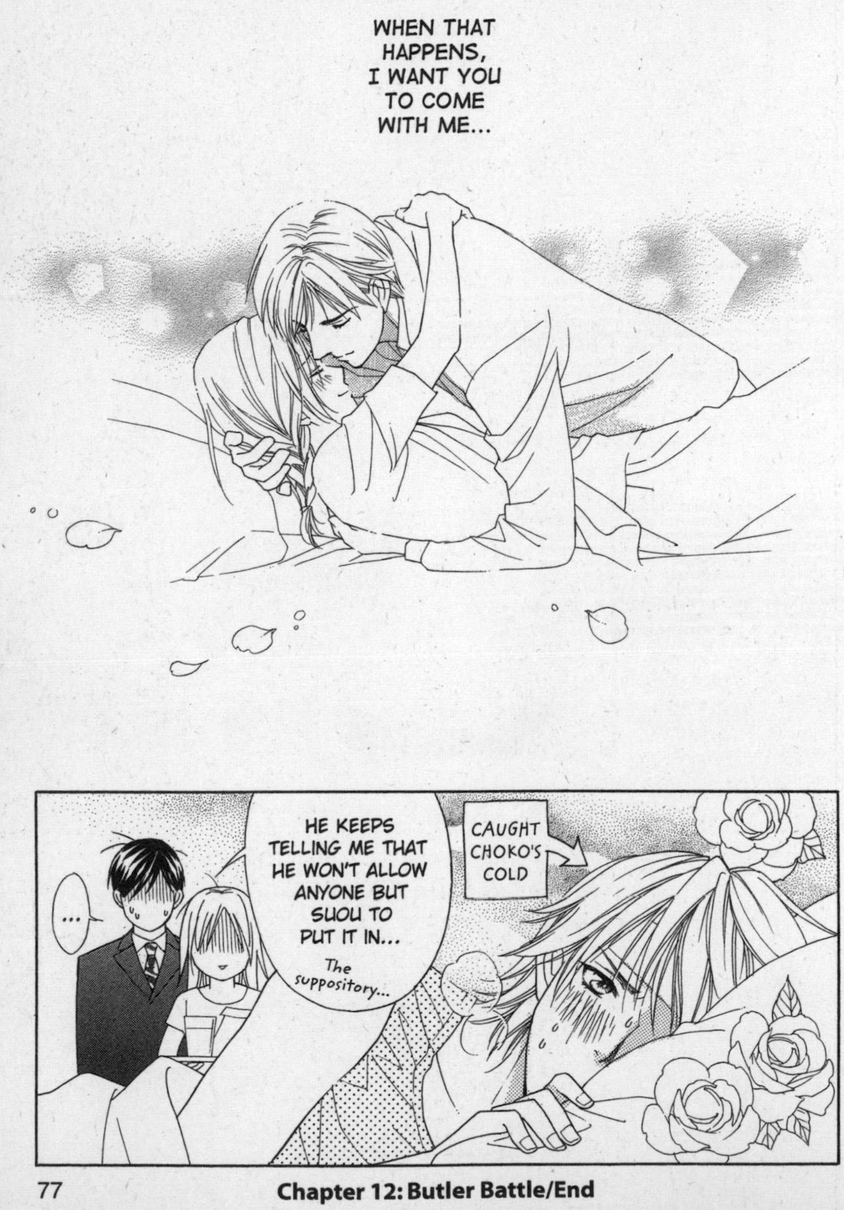
WHEN THAT HAPPENS, I WANT YOU TO COME WITH ME...
CAUGHT CHOKO'S COLD
HE KEEPS TELLING ME THAT HE WON'T ALLOW ANYONE BUT SUOU TO PUT IT IN...
The suppository...
...

MISCONSTRUED REMARK

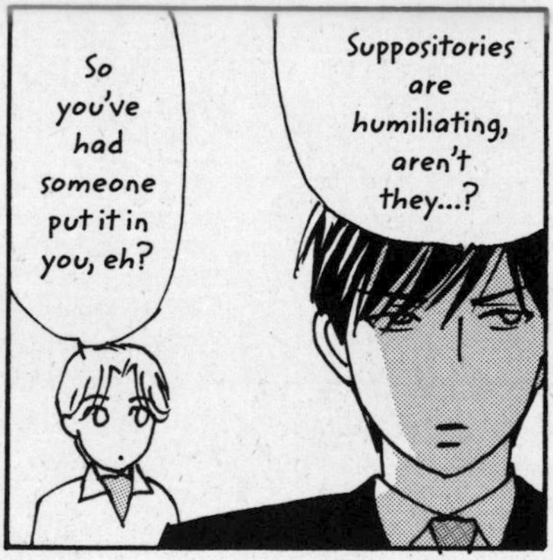

Suppositories are humiliating, aren't they...?
So you've had someone put it in you, eh?

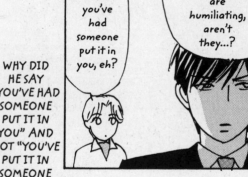

WHY DID HE SAY "YOU'VE HAD SOMEONE PUT IT IN YOU" AND NOT "YOU'VE PUT IT IN SOMEONE ELSE"?

Chapter 13

A Couple's Summer Story

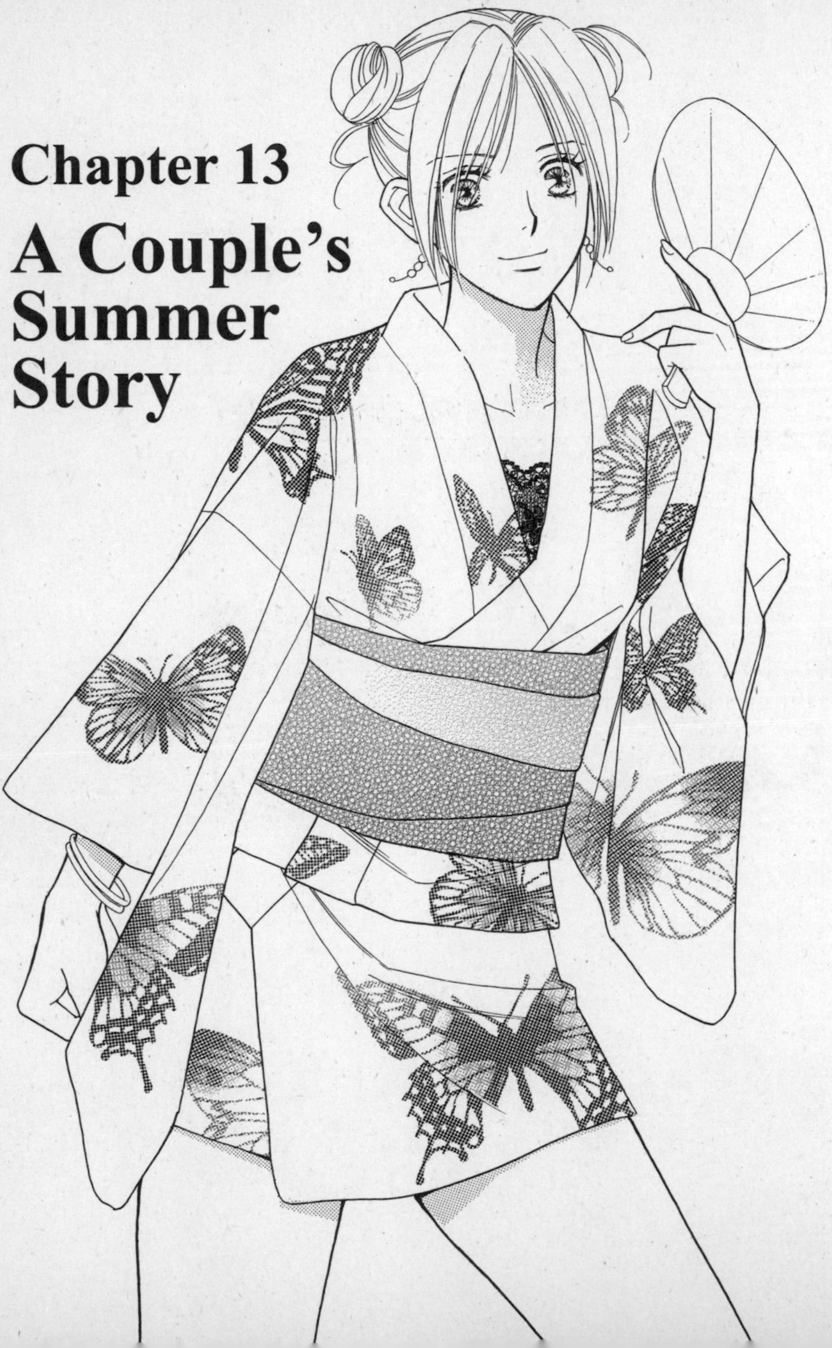

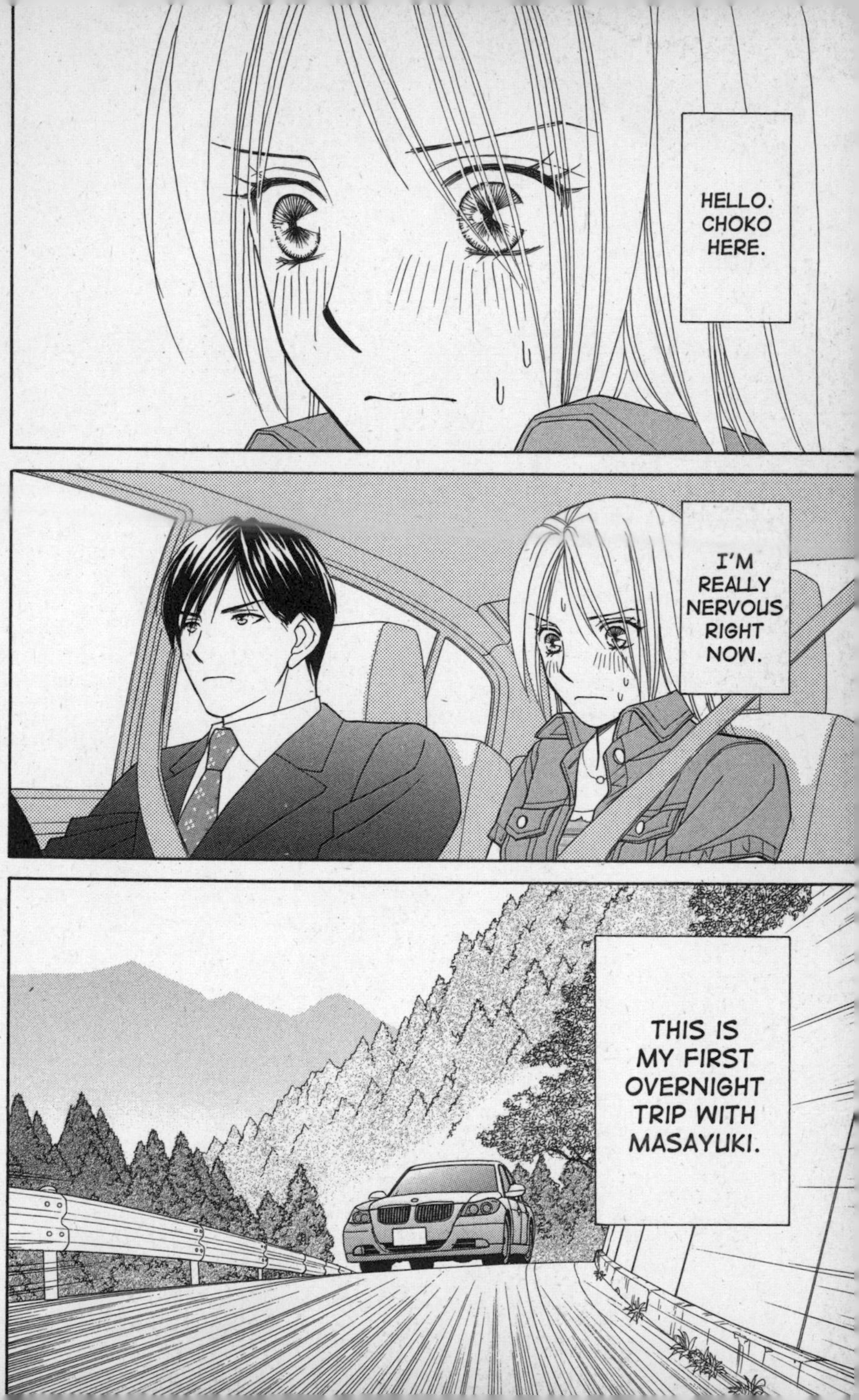
HELLO. CHOKO HERE.
I'M REALLY NERVOUS RIGHT NOW.
THIS IS MY FIRST OVERNIGHT TRIP WITH MASAYUKI.

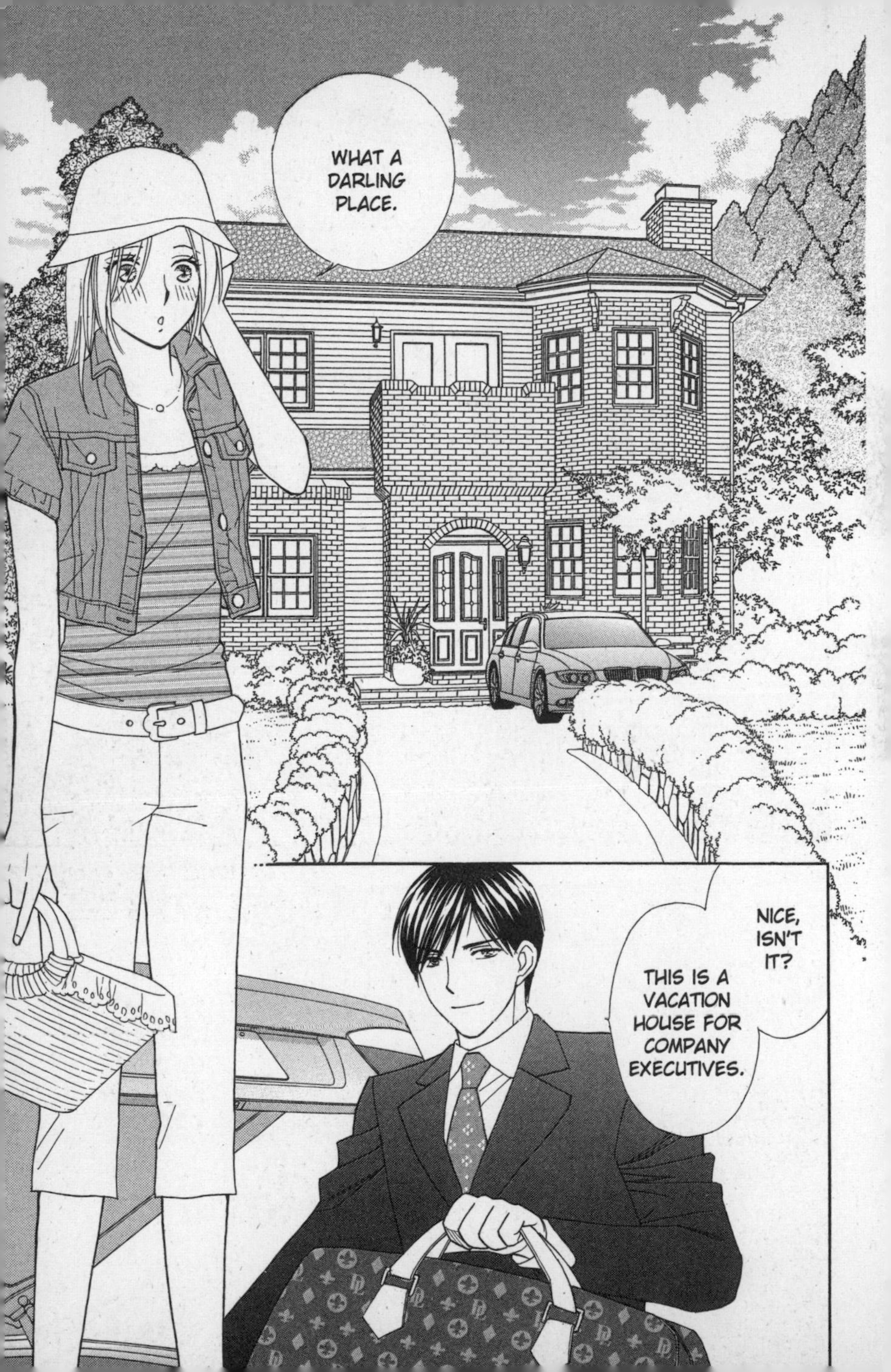
WHAT A DARLING PLACE.
NICE, ISN'T IT?
THIS IS A VACATION HOUSE FOR COMPANY EXECUTIVES.

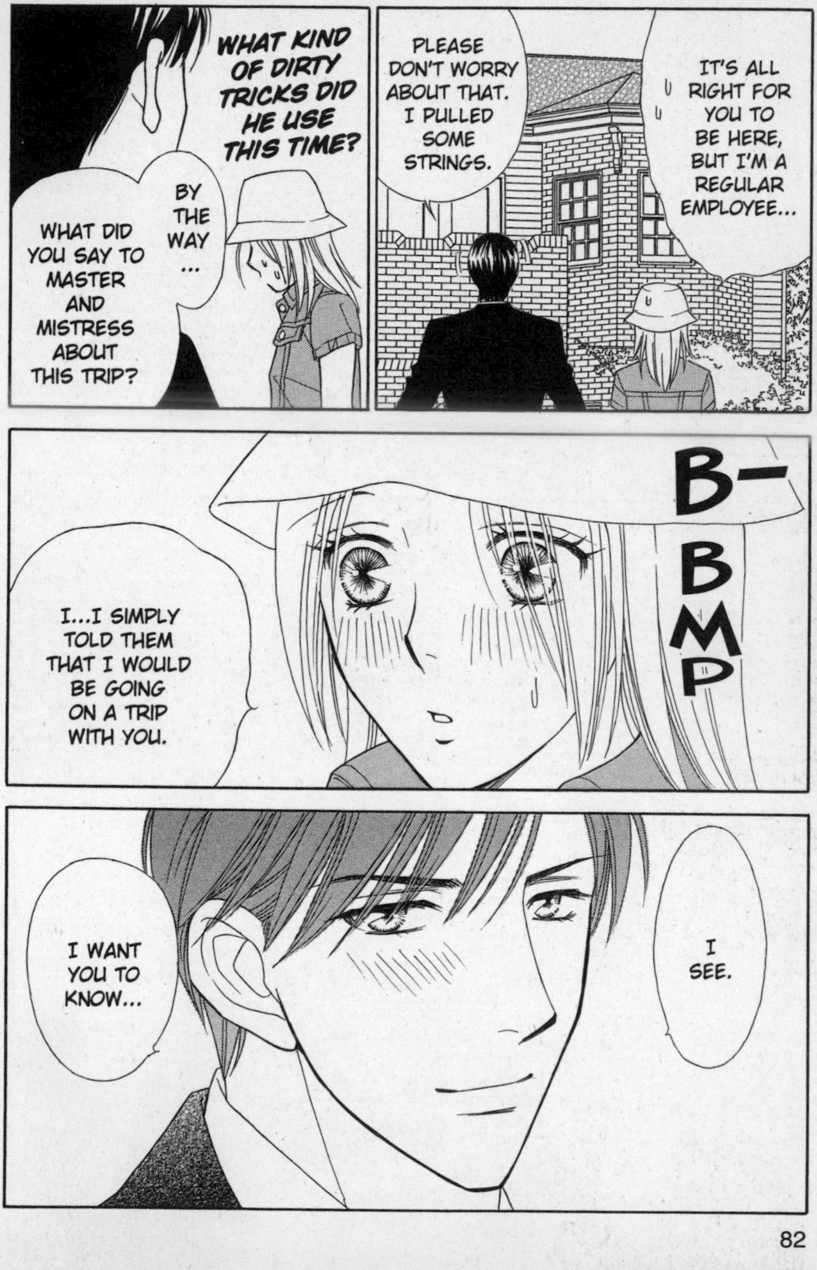
IT'S ALL RIGHT FOR YOU TO BE HERE, BUT I'M A REGULAR EMPLOYEE...
PLEASE DON'T WORRY ABOUT THAT. I PULLED SOME STRINGS.
WHAT KIND OF DIRTY TRICKS DID HE USE THIS TIME?
BY THE WAY ...
WHAT DID YOU SAY TO MASTER AND MISTRESS ABOUT THIS TRIP?
B-BMP
I...I SIMPLY TOLD THEM THAT I WOULD BE GOING ON A TRIP WITH YOU.
I SEE.
I WANT YOU TO KNOW...

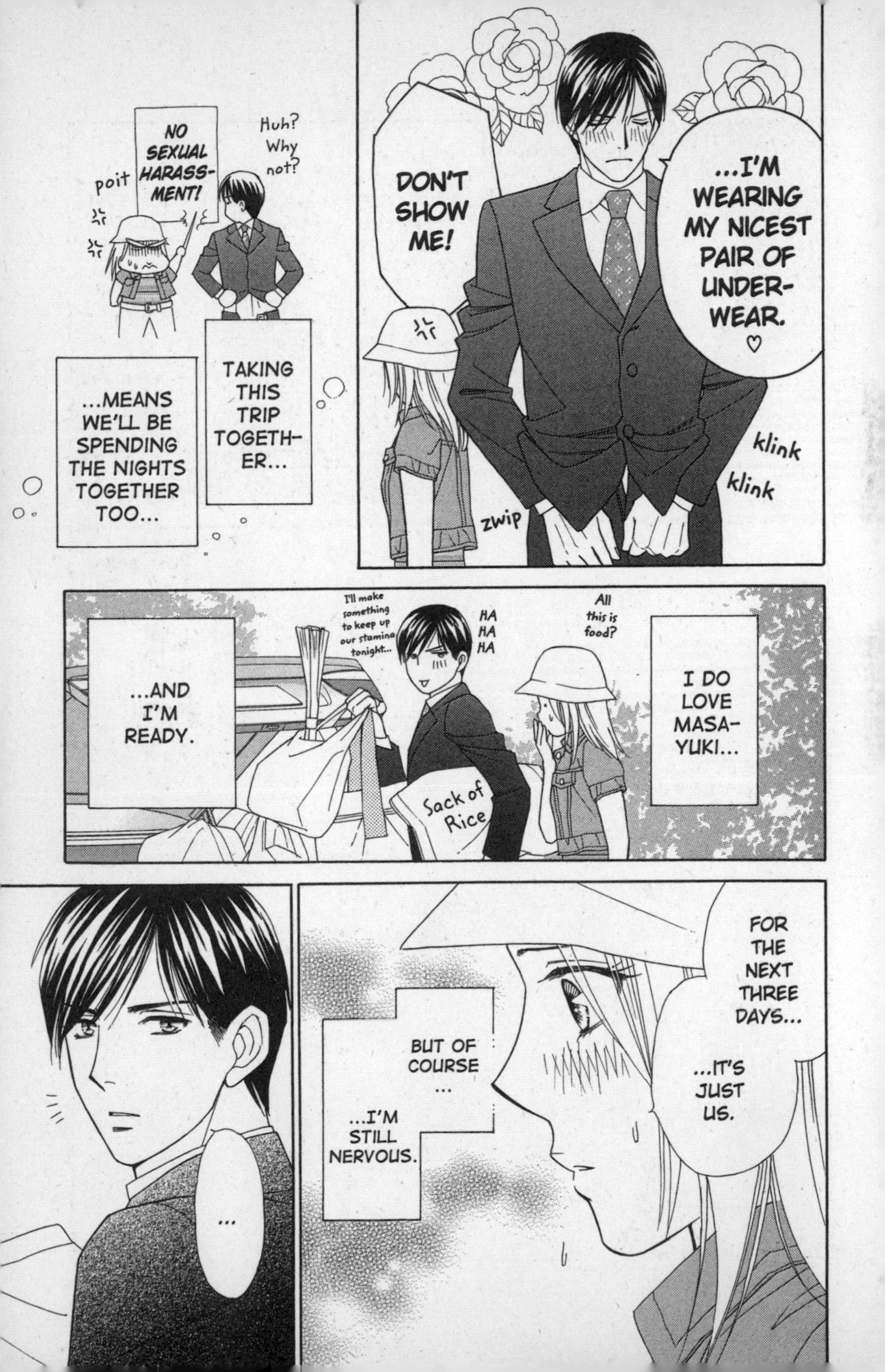
...I'M WEARING MY NICEST PAIR OF UNDER-WEAR. ♡
DON'T SHOW ME!
klink
klink
zwip
Huh? Why not?
NO SEXUAL HARASS-MENT!
poit
TAKING THIS TRIP TOGETH-ER...
...MEANS WE'LL BE SPENDING THE NIGHTS TOGETHER TOO...
I DO LOVE MASA-YUKI...
All this is food?
HA HA HA
I'll make something to keep up our stamina tonight...
Sack of Rice
...AND I'M READY.
FOR THE NEXT THREE DAYS...
...IT'S JUST US.
BUT OF COURSE...
...I'M STILL NERVOUS.
...

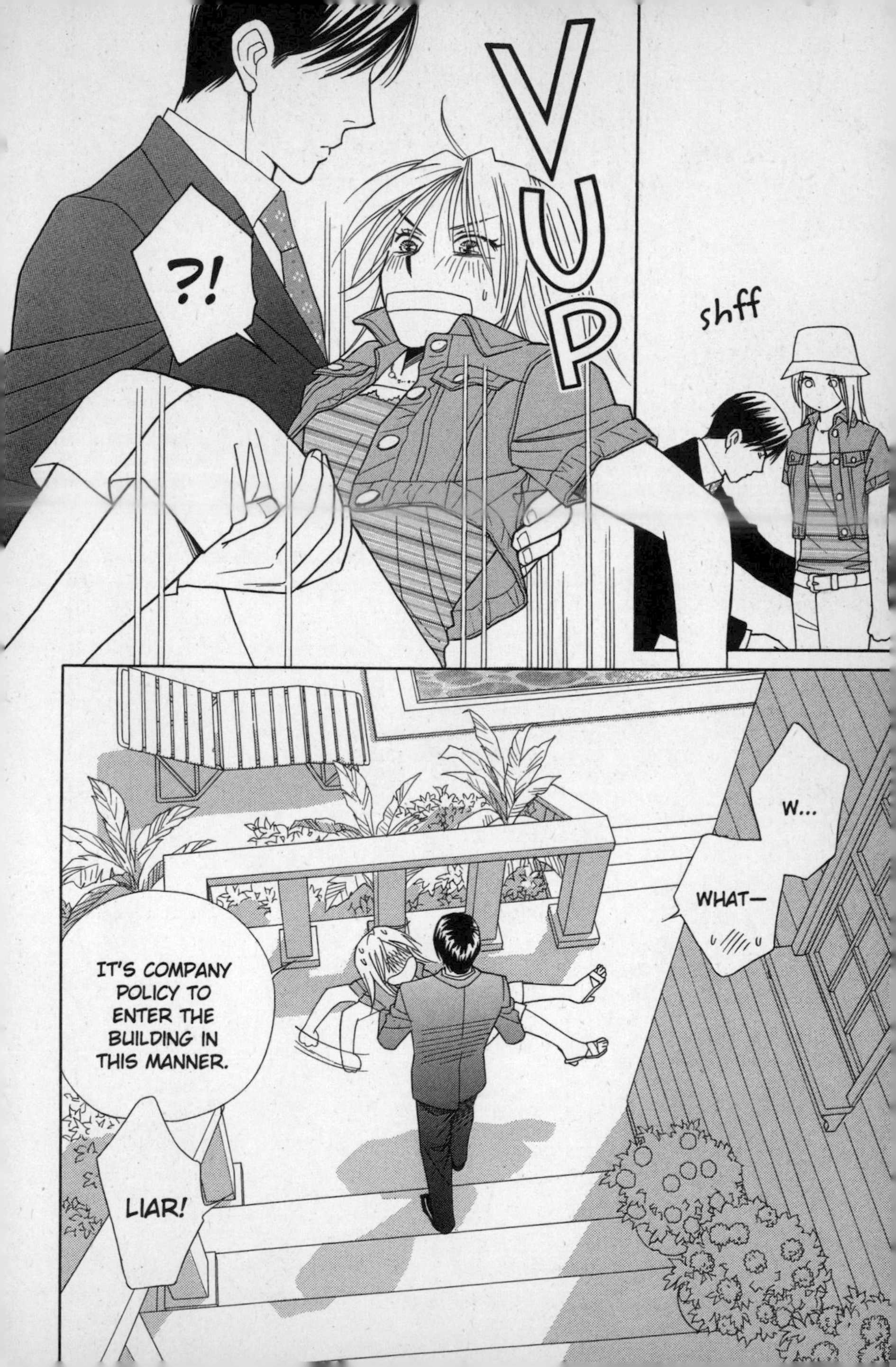
shff
VUP
?!
W...
WHAT—
IT'S COMPANY POLICY TO ENTER THE BUILDING IN THIS MANNER.
LIAR!

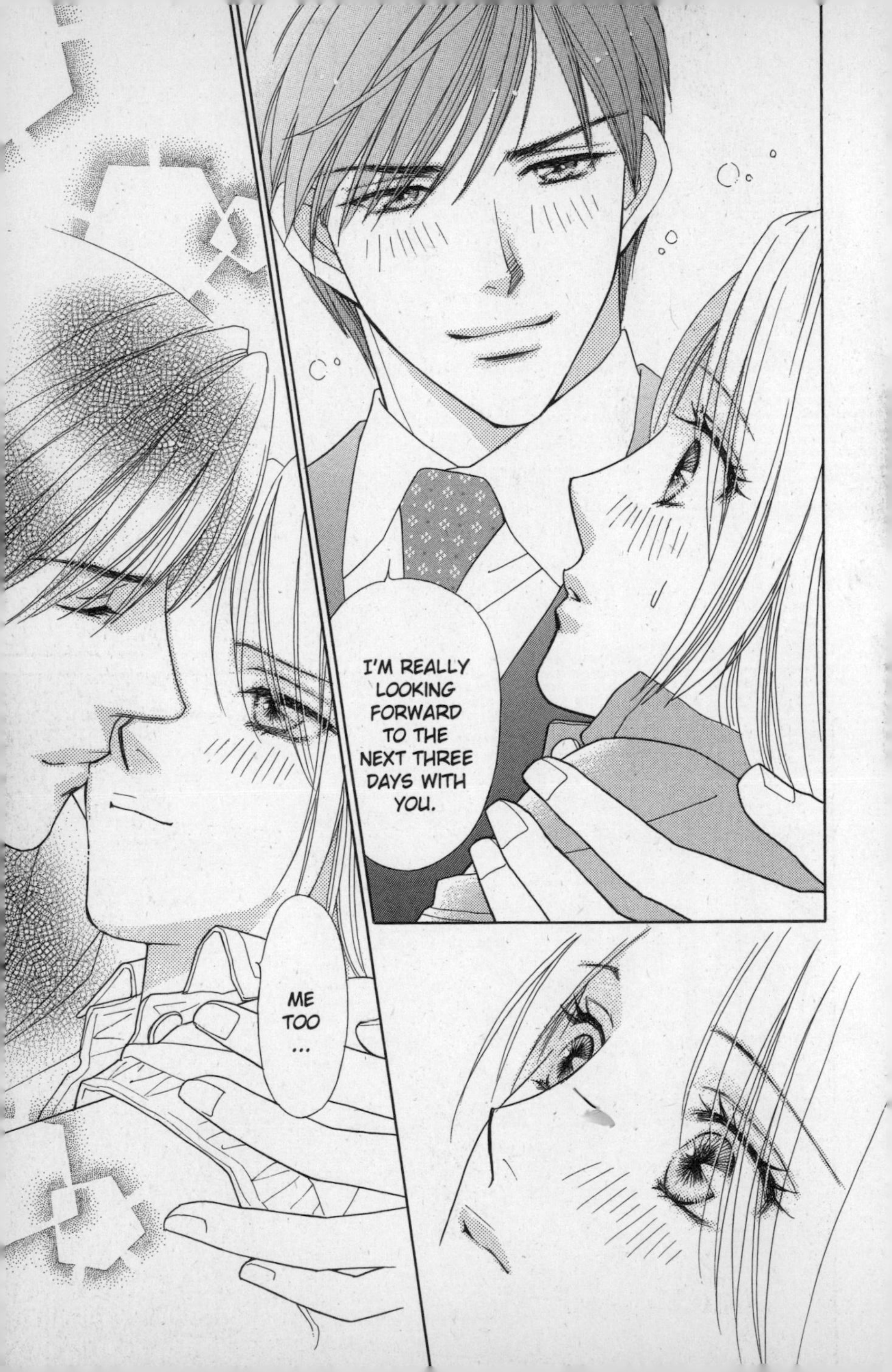
I'M REALLY LOOKING FORWARD TO THE NEXT THREE DAYS WITH YOU.
ME TOO ...

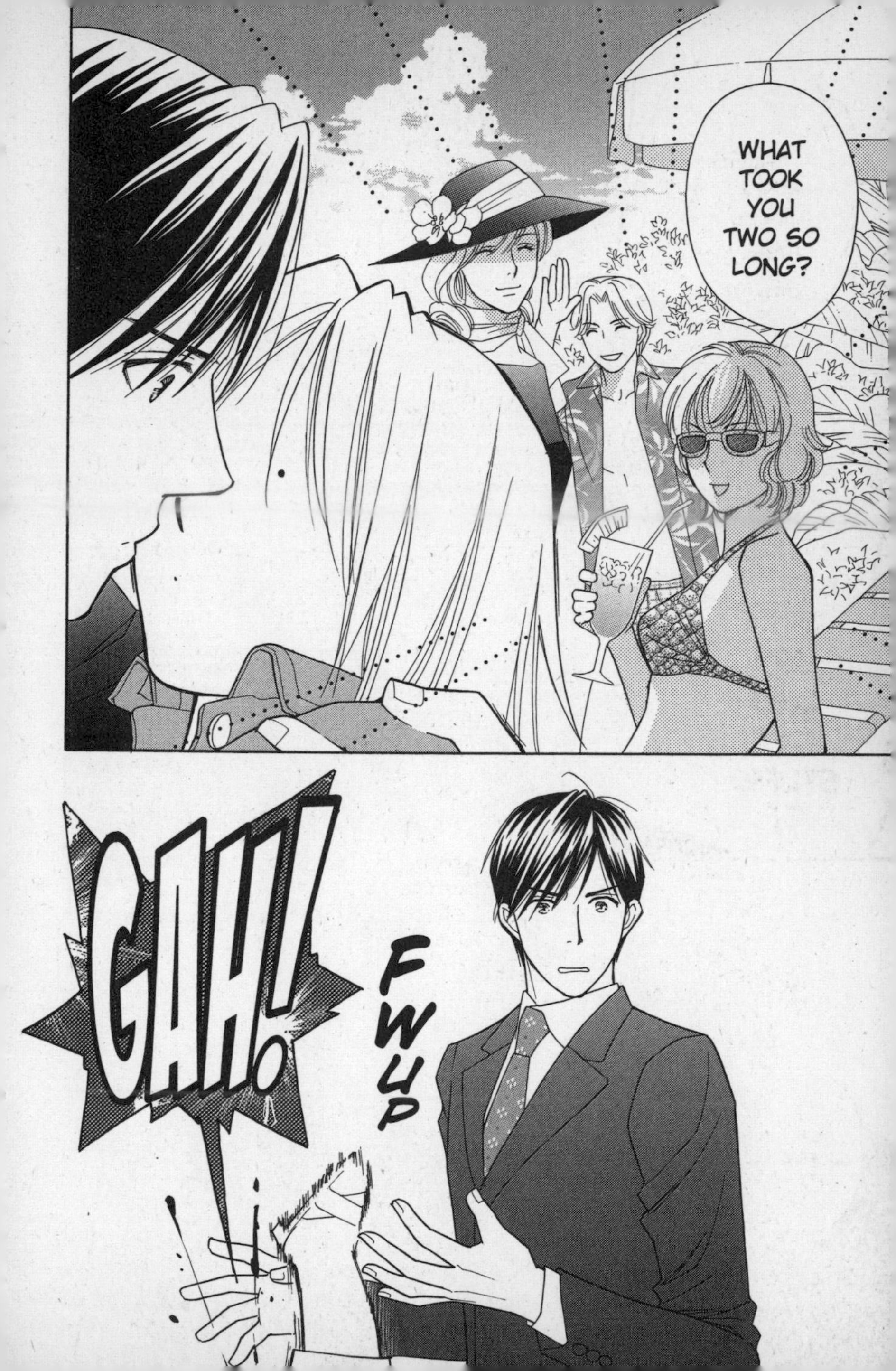
WHAT TOOK YOU TWO SO LONG?
GAH!
FWUP

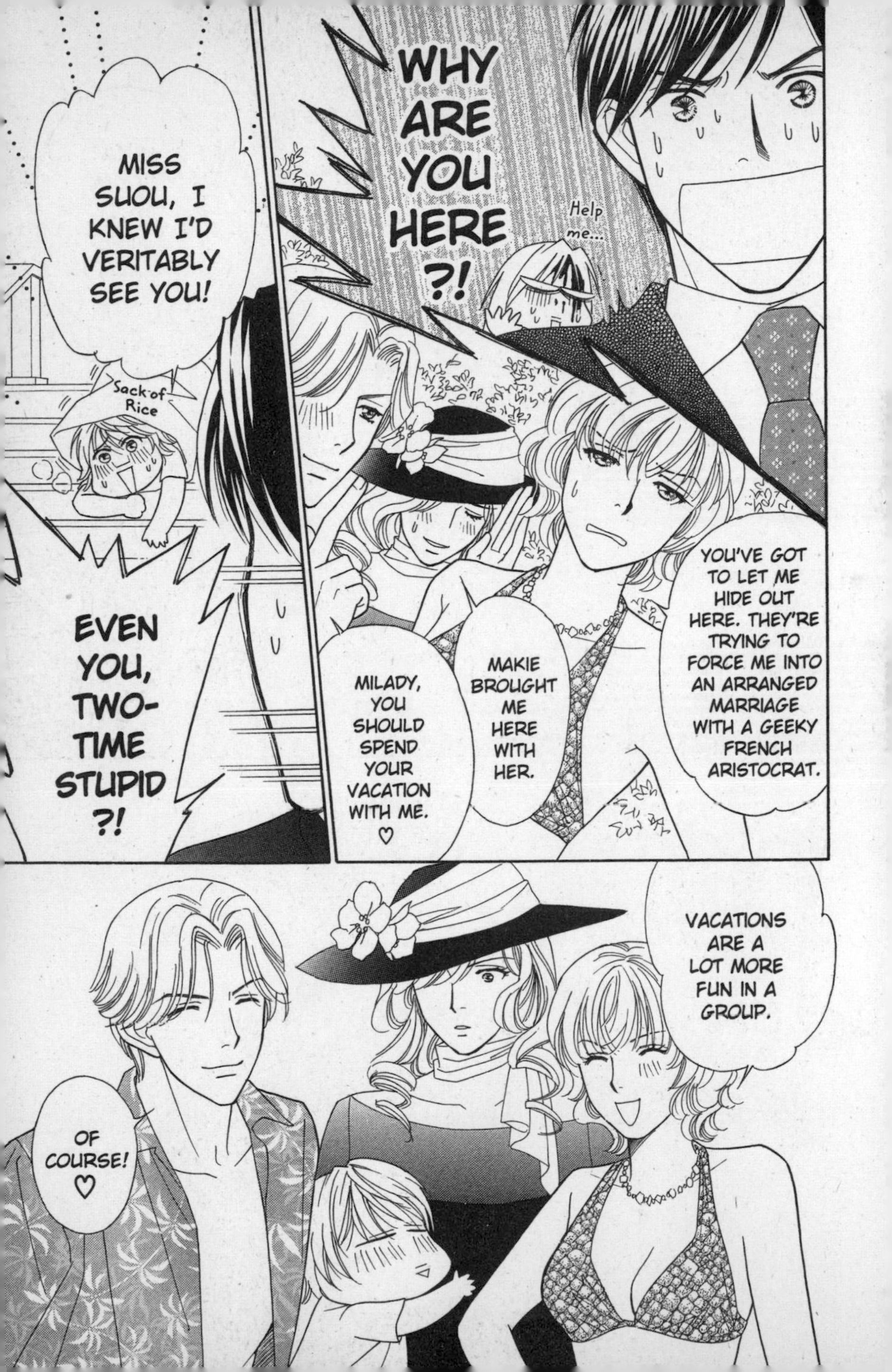
WHY ARE YOU HERE?!
Help me...
YOU'VE GOT TO LET ME HIDE OUT HERE. THEY'RE TRYING TO FORCE ME INTO AN ARRANGED MARRIAGE WITH A GEEKY FRENCH ARISTOCRAT.
MAKIE BROUGHT ME HERE WITH HER.
MILADY, YOU SHOULD SPEND YOUR VACATION WITH ME. ♡
MISS SUOU, I KNEW I'D VERITABLY SEE YOU!
Sack of Rice
EVEN YOU, TWO-TIME STUPID?!
VACATIONS ARE A LOT MORE FUN IN A GROUP.
OF COURSE! ♡

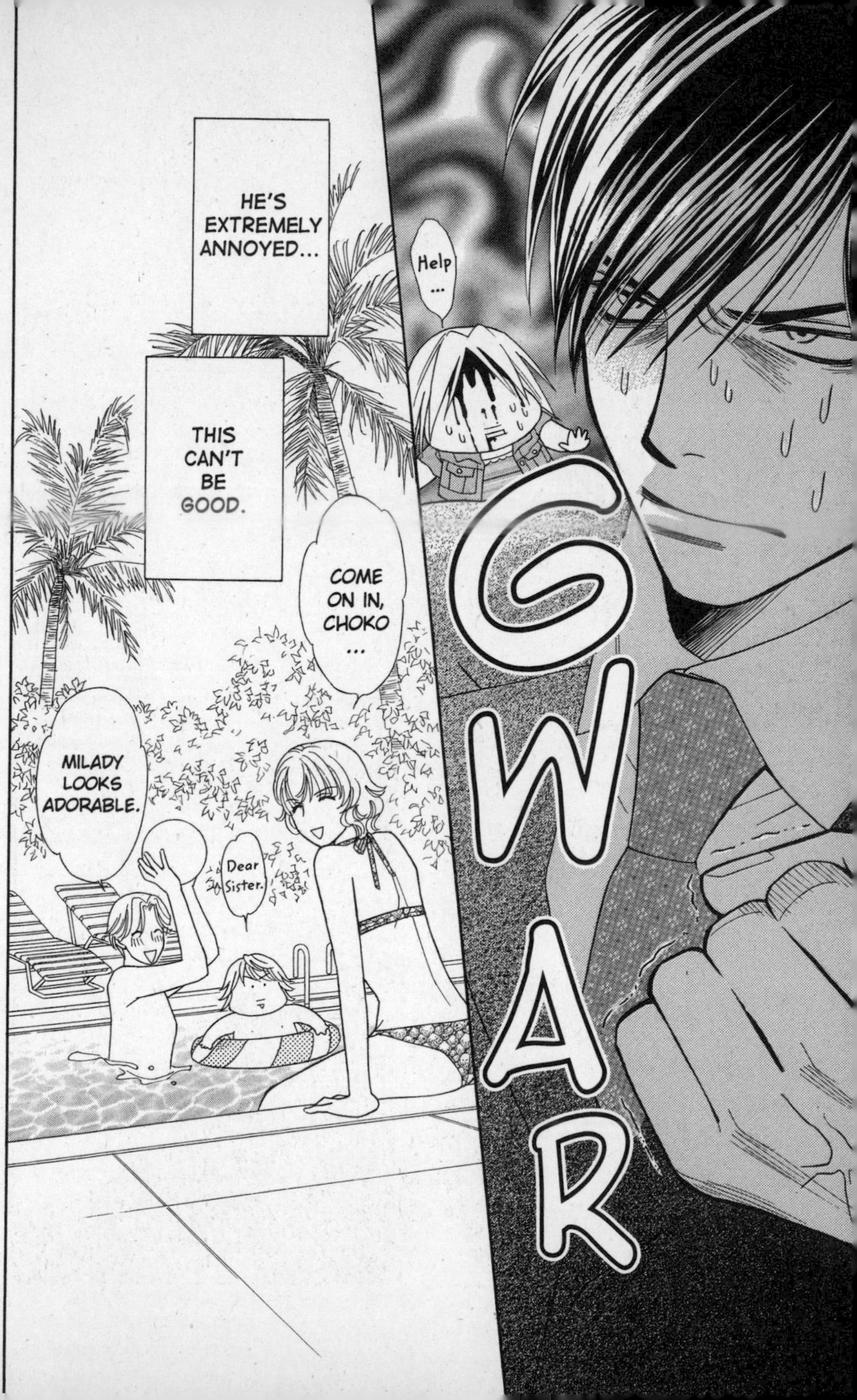
Help ...
GWAR
HE'S EXTREMELY ANNOYED...
THIS CAN'T BE GOOD.
COME ON IN, CHOKO ...
MILADY LOOKS ADORABLE.
Dear Sister.

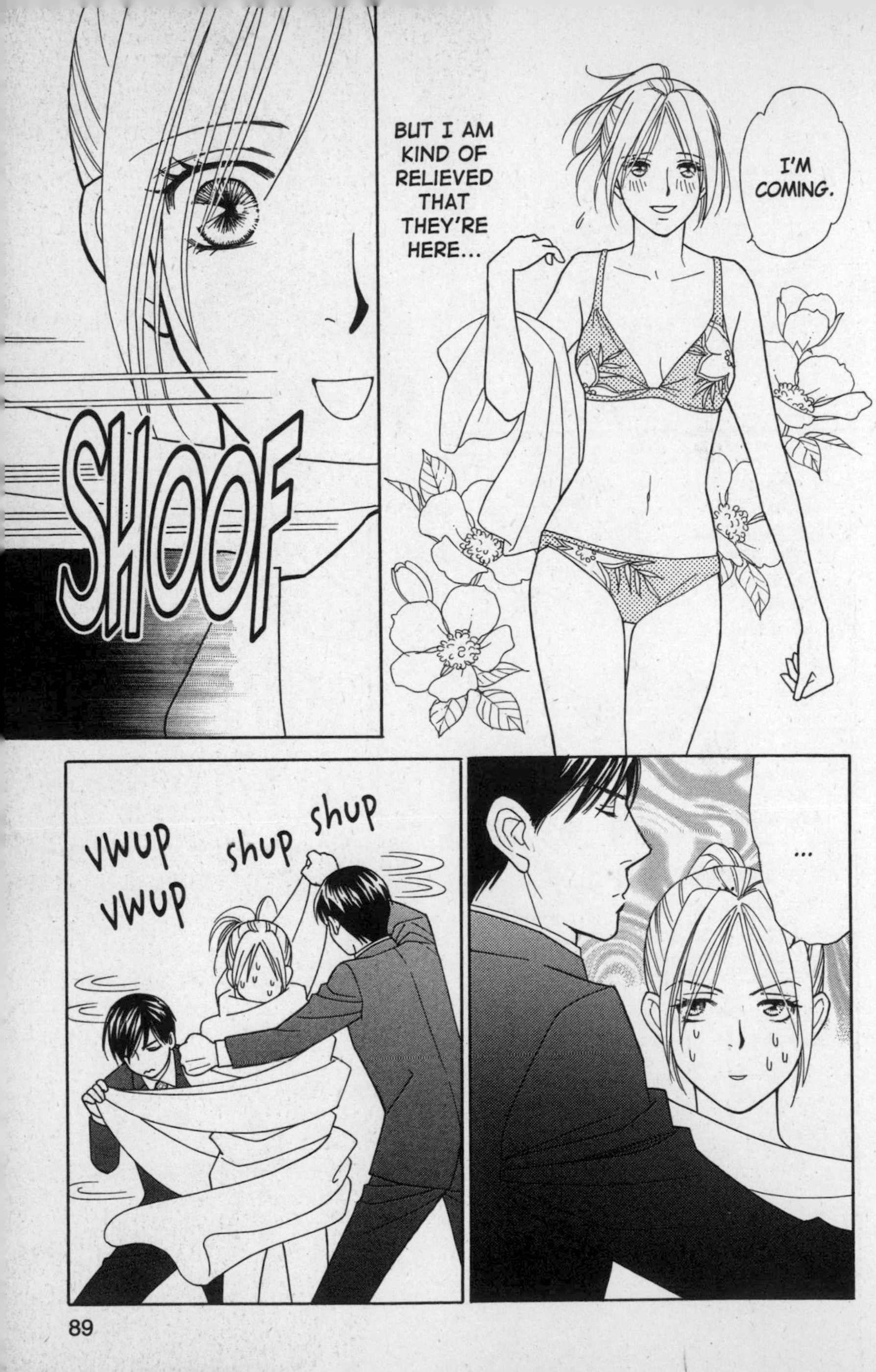
I'M COMING.
BUT I AM KIND OF RELIEVED THAT THEY'RE HERE...
SHOOF
...
shup
shup
vwup vwup

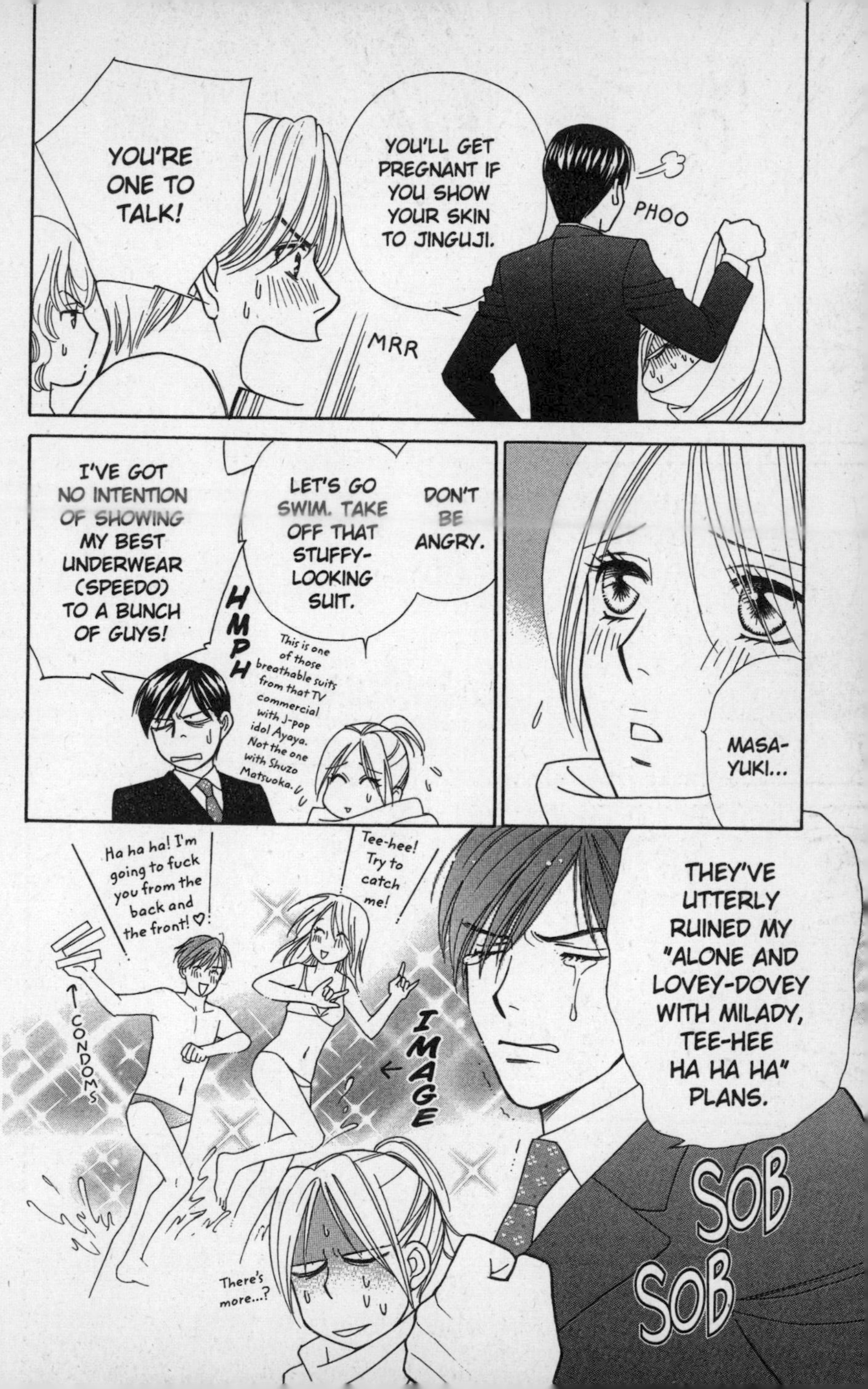

PHOO
YOU'LL GET PREGNANT IF YOU SHOW YOUR SKIN TO JINGUJI.
MRR
YOU'RE ONE TO TALK!
MASA-YUKI...
DON'T BE ANGRY.
LET'S GO SWIM. TAKE OFF THAT STUFFY-LOOKING SUIT.
HMPH
I'VE GOT NO INTENTION OF SHOWING MY BEST UNDERWEAR (SPEEDO) TO A BUNCH OF GUYS!
This is one of those breathable suits from that TV commercial with J-pop idol Ayaya. Not the one with Shuzo Matsuoka.
THEY'VE UTTERLY RUINED MY "ALONE AND LOVEY-DOVEY WITH MILADY, TEE-HEE HA HA HA" PLANS.
SOB SOB
IMAGE
Tee-hee! Try to catch me!
Ha ha ha! I'm going to fuck you from the back and the front! ♡
CONDOMS
There's more...?

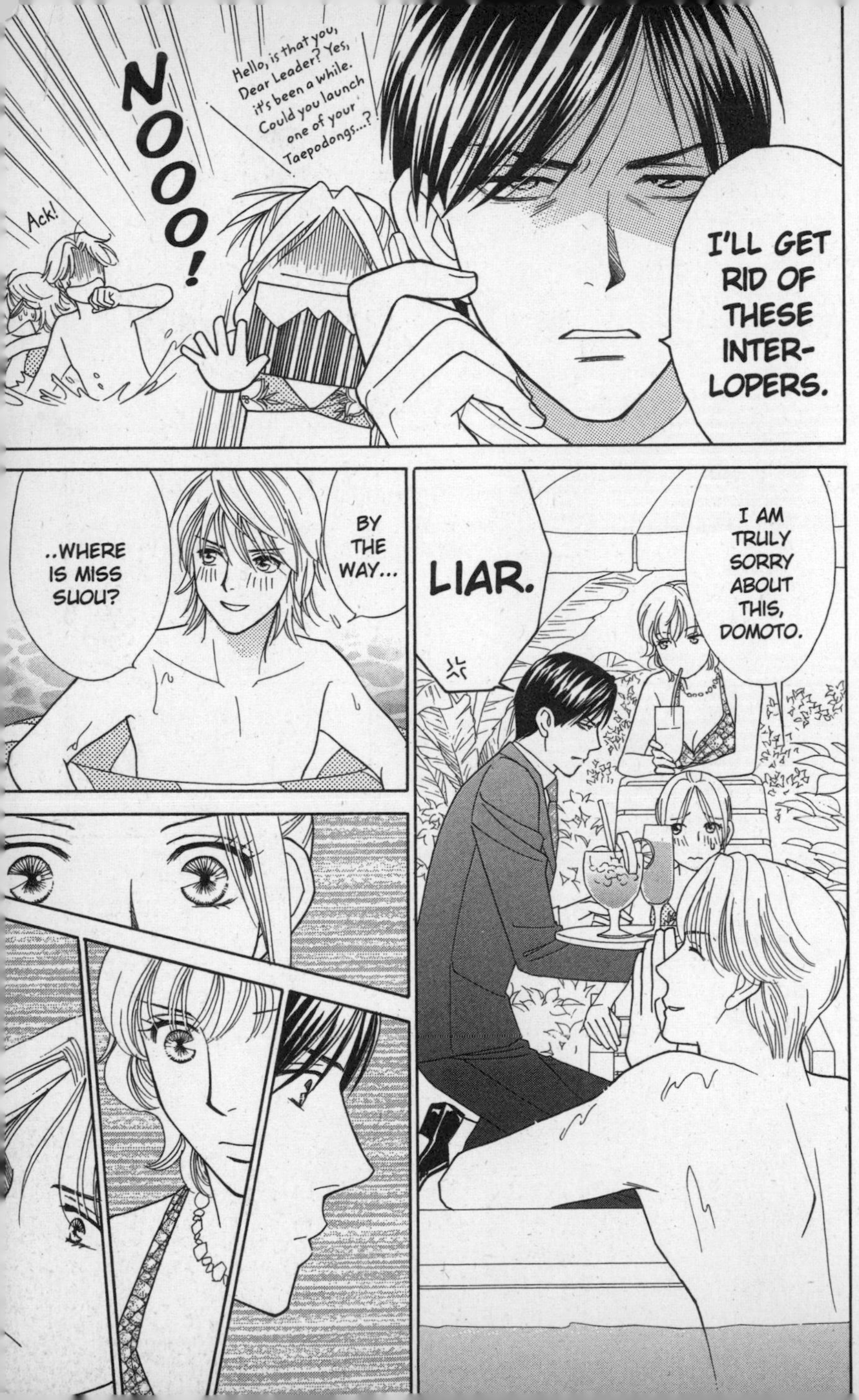
I'LL GET RID OF THESE INTER-LOPERS.
Hello, is that you, Dear Leader? Yes, it's been a while. Could you launch one of your Taepodongs...?
NOOOO!
Ack!
I AM TRULY SORRY ABOUT THIS, DOMOTO.
LIAR.
BY THE WAY...
..WHERE IS MISS SUOU?

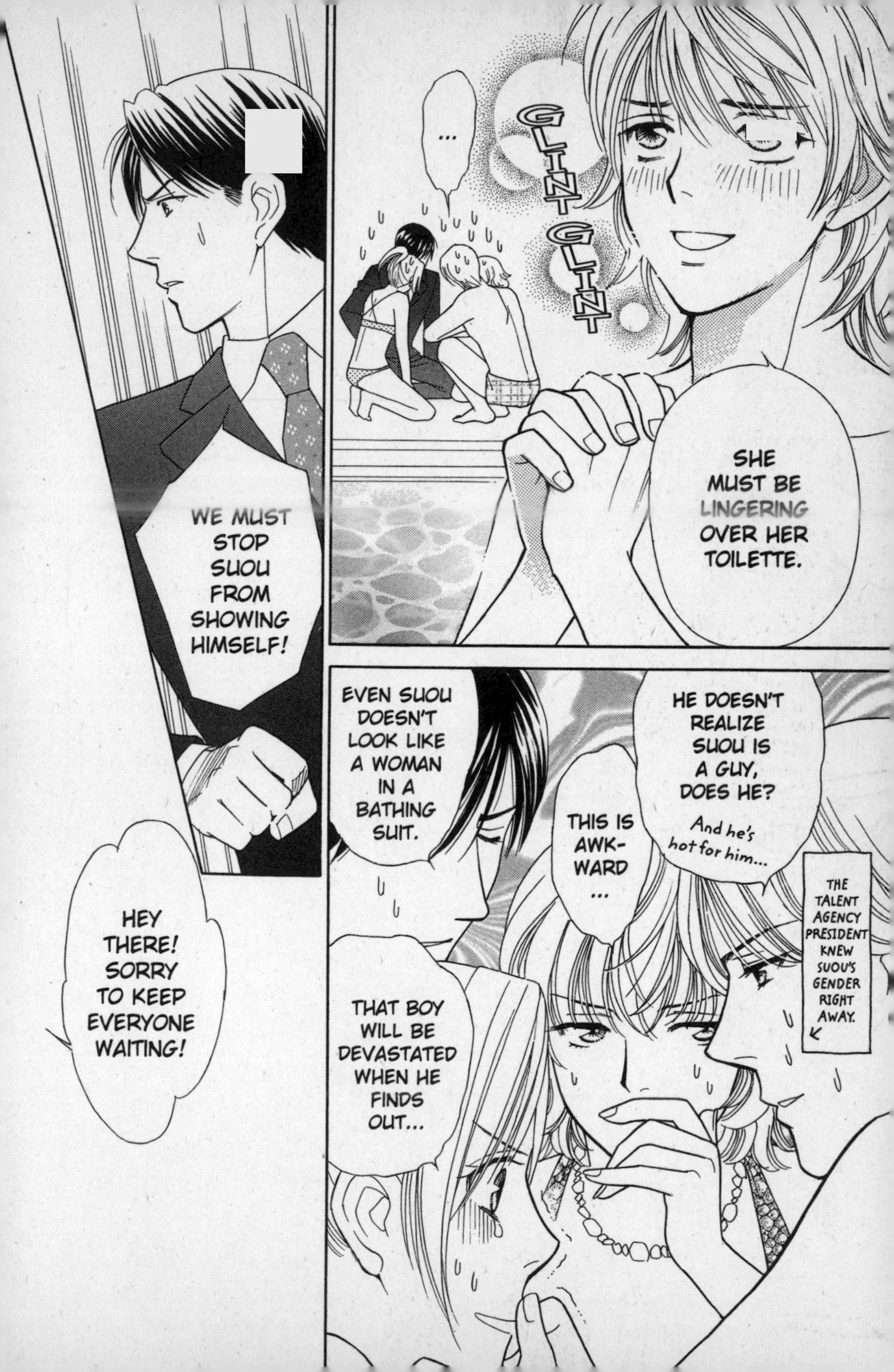
GLINT GLINT GLINT
...
SHE MUST BE LINGERING OVER HER TOILETTE.
HE DOESN'T REALIZE SUOU IS A GUY, DOES HE?
And he's hot for him...
THE TALENT AGENCY PRESIDENT KNEW SUOU'S GENDER RIGHT AWAY.
THIS IS AWK-WARD...
EVEN SUOU DOESN'T LOOK LIKE A WOMAN IN A BATHING SUIT.
THAT BOY WILL BE DEVASTATED WHEN HE FINDS OUT...
WE MUST STOP SUOU FROM SHOWING HIMSELF!
HEY THERE! SORRY TO KEEP EVERYONE WAITING!

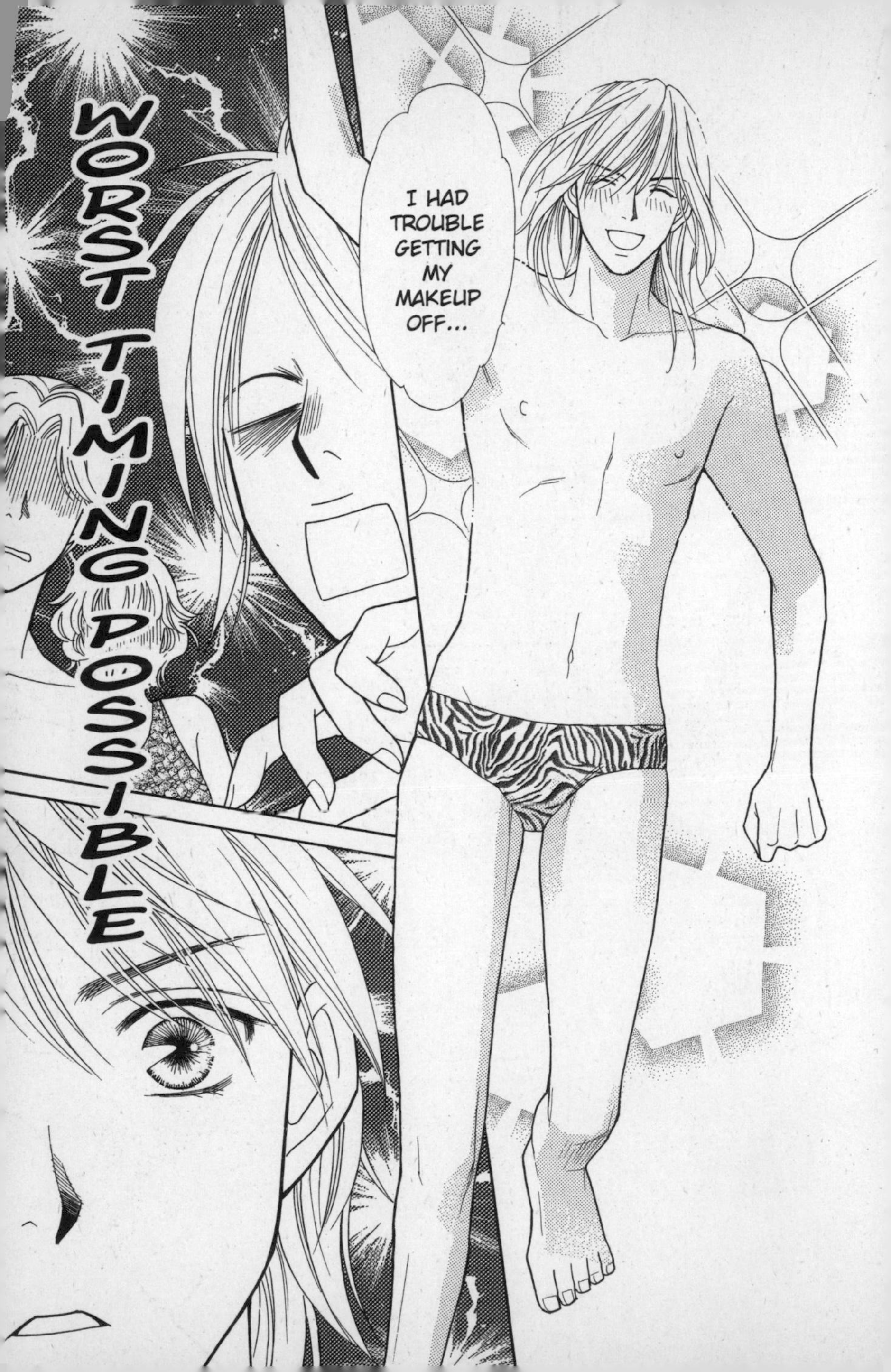
I HAD TROUBLE GETTING MY MAKEUP OFF...
WORST TIMING POSSIBLE

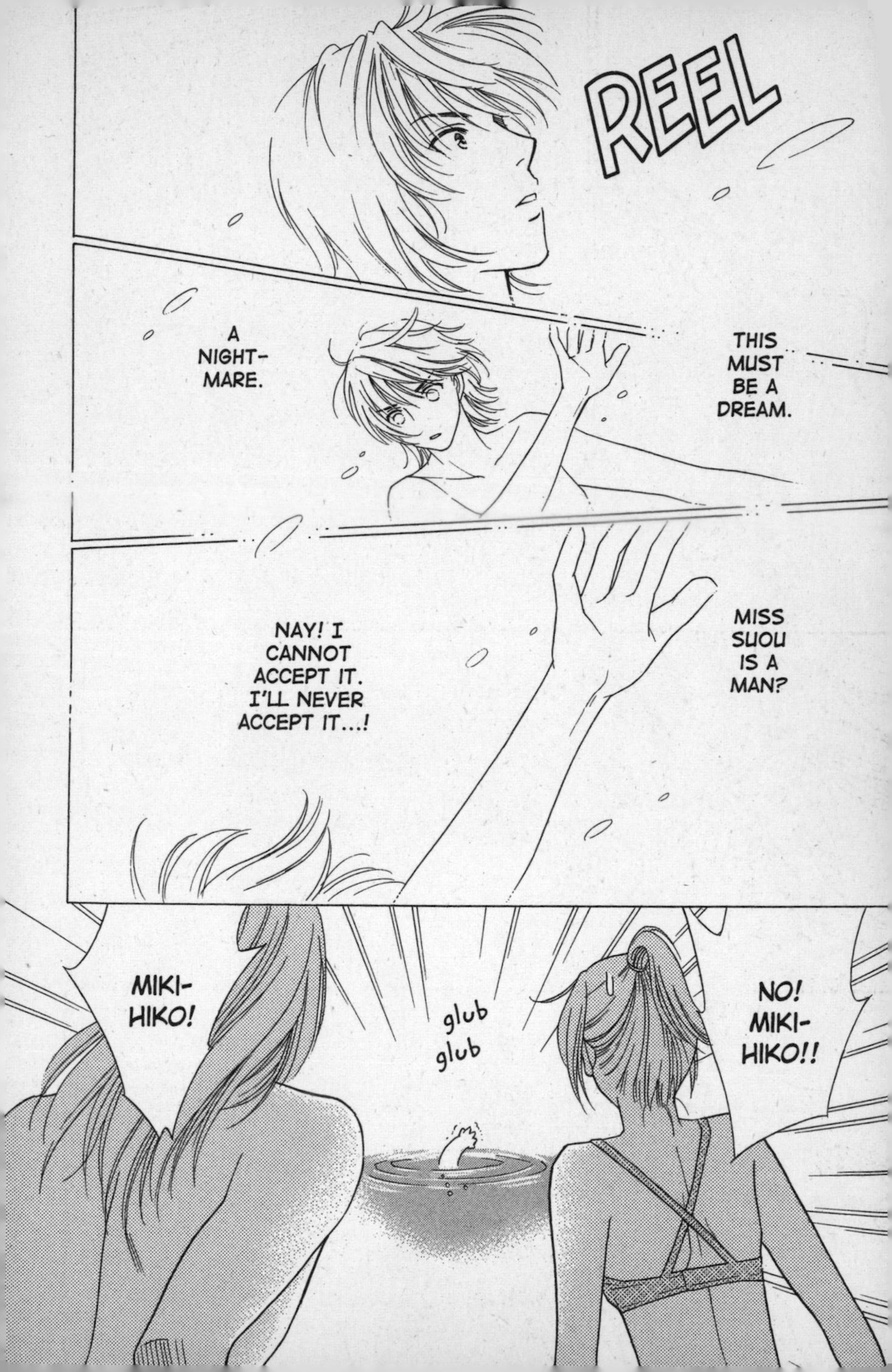
REEL
THIS MUST BE A DREAM.
A NIGHT-MARE.
MISS SUOU IS A MAN?
NAY! I CANNOT ACCEPT IT. I'LL NEVER ACCEPT IT...!
NO! MIKI-HIKO!!
glub glub
MIKI-HIKO!

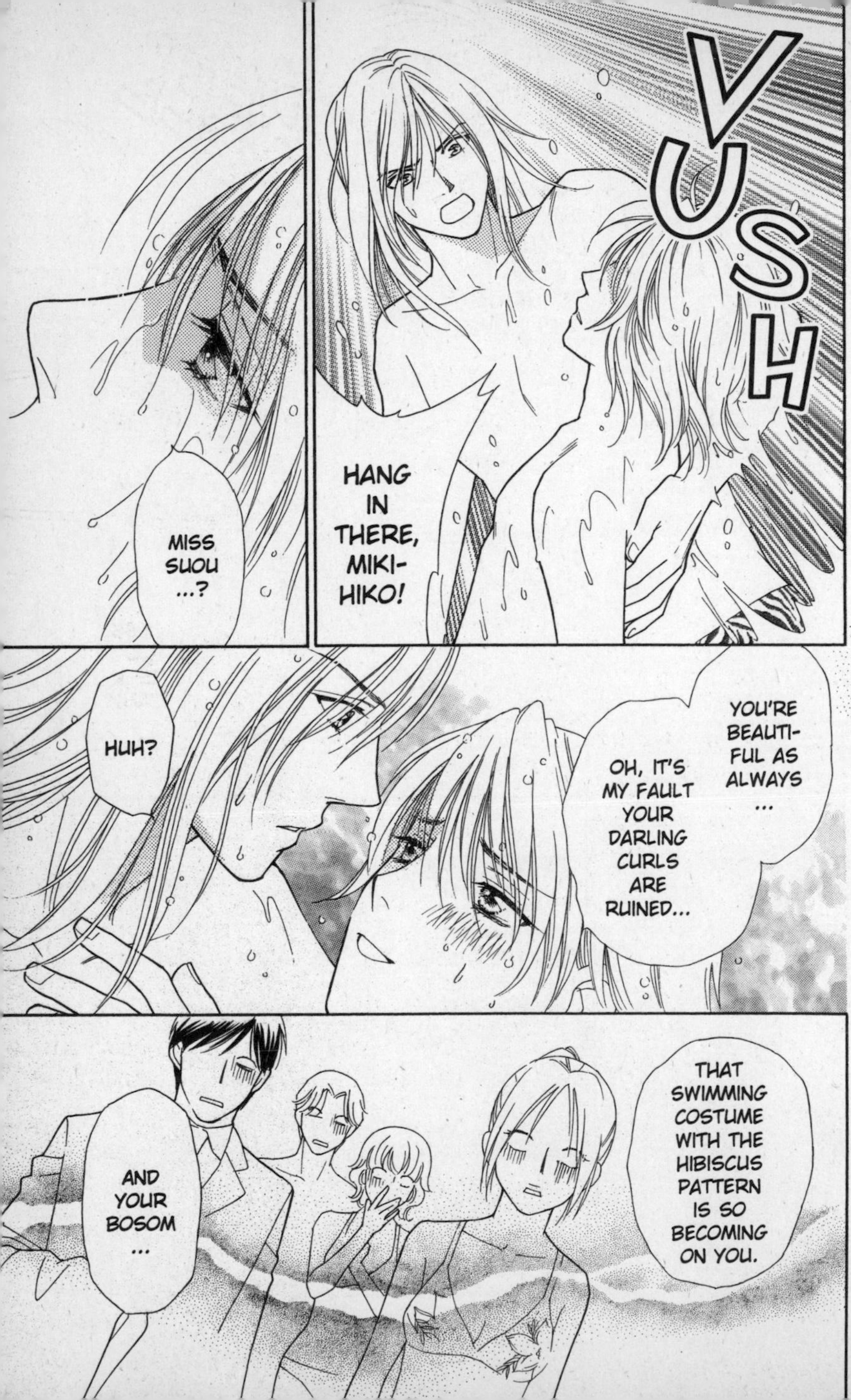
VUSH
HANG IN THERE, MIKI-HIKO!
MISS SUOU ...?
YOU'RE BEAUTI-FUL AS ALWAYS ...
OH, IT'S MY FAULT YOUR DARLING CURLS ARE RUINED...
HUH?
THAT SWIMMING COSTUME WITH THE HIBISCUS PATTERN IS SO BECOMING ON YOU.
AND YOUR BOSOM ...

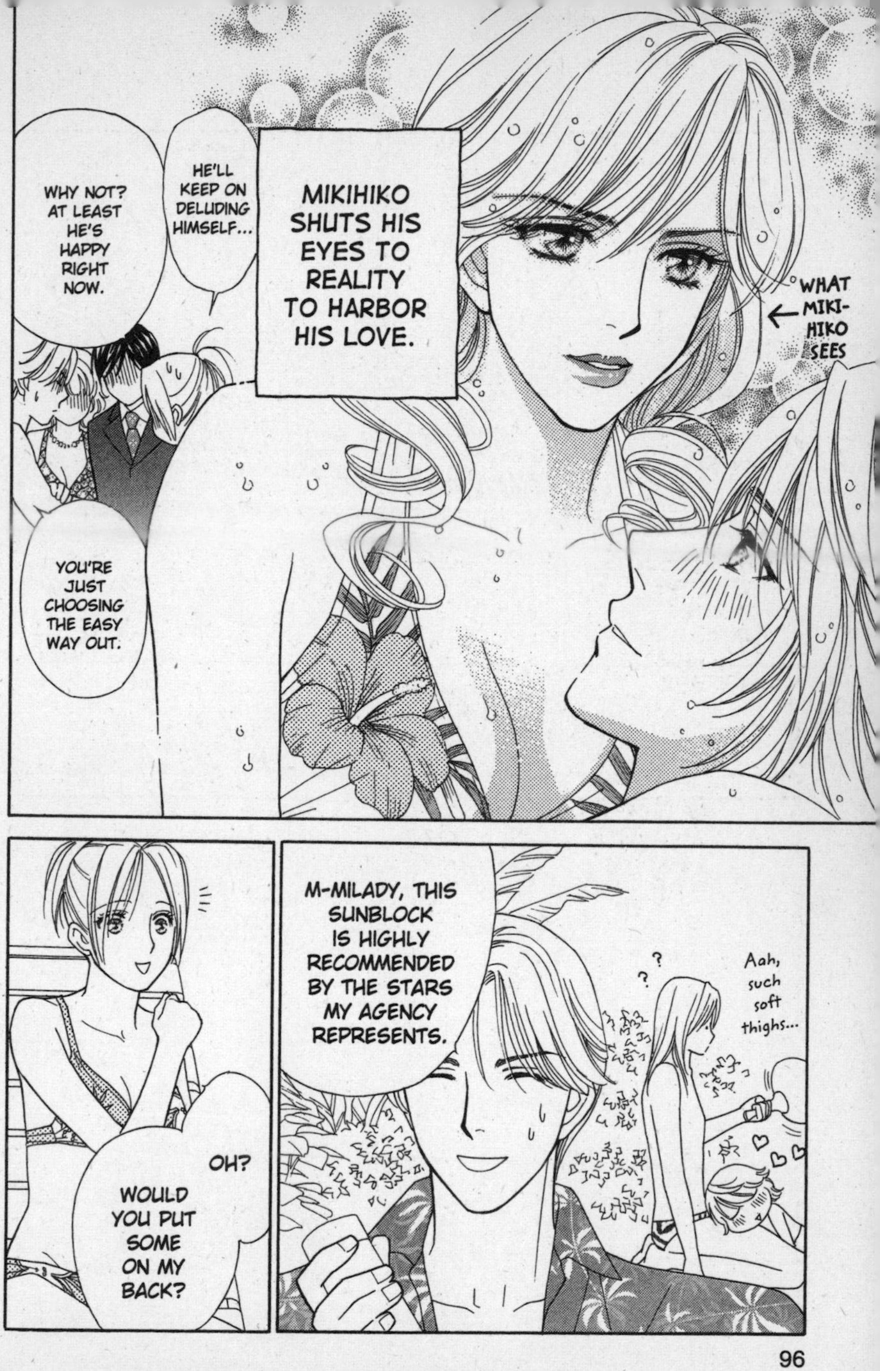
WHAT MIKI-HIKO SEES
MIKIHIKO SHUTS HIS EYES TO REALITY TO HARBOR HIS LOVE.
HE'LL KEEP ON DELUDING HIMSELF...
WHY NOT? AT LEAST HE'S HAPPY RIGHT NOW.
YOU'RE JUST CHOOSING THE EASY WAY OUT.
Aah, such soft thighs...
M-MILADY, THIS SUNBLOCK IS HIGHLY RECOMMENDED BY THE STARS MY AGENCY REPRESENTS.
OH? WOULD YOU PUT SOME ON MY BACK?

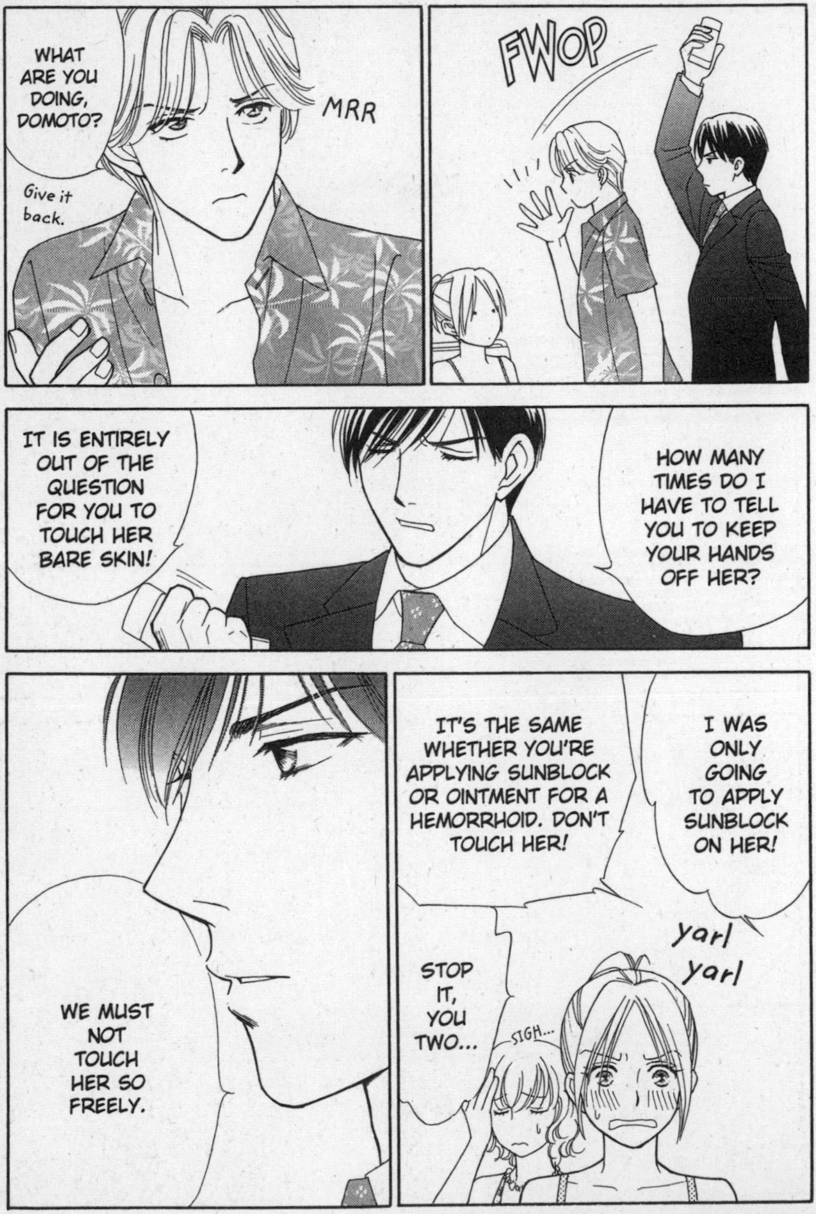
FWOP
WHAT ARE YOU DOING, DOMOTO?
MRR
Give it back.
HOW MANY TIMES DO I HAVE TO TELL YOU TO KEEP YOUR HANDS OFF HER?
IT IS ENTIRELY OUT OF THE QUESTION FOR YOU TO TOUCH HER BARE SKIN!
I WAS ONLY GOING TO APPLY SUNBLOCK ON HER!
IT'S THE SAME WHETHER YOU'RE APPLYING SUNBLOCK OR OINTMENT FOR A HEMORRHOID. DON'T TOUCH HER!
yarl yarl
STOP IT, YOU TWO...
SIGH...
WE MUST NOT TOUCH HER SO FREELY.

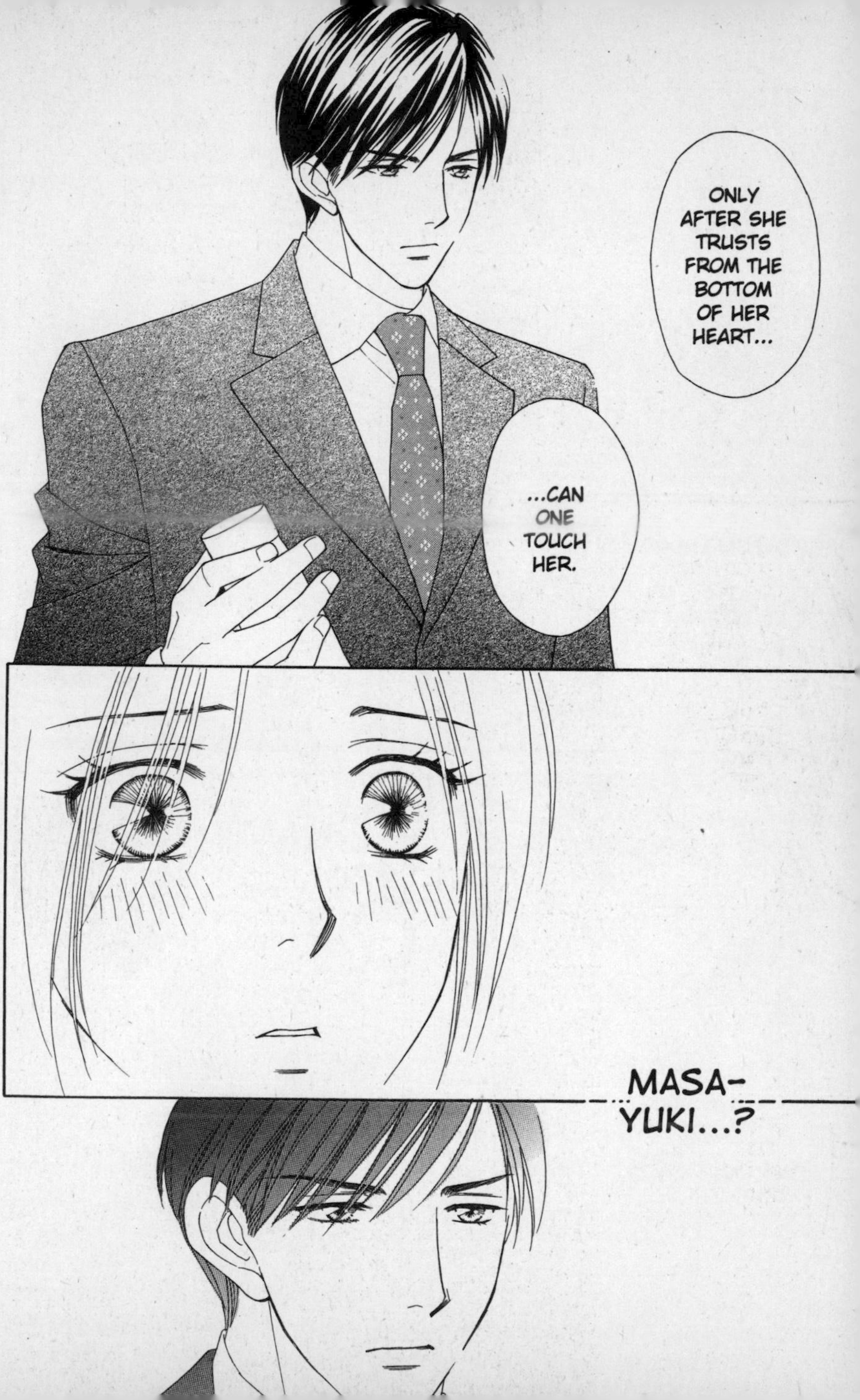
ONLY AFTER SHE TRUSTS FROM THE BOTTOM OF HER HEART...
...CAN ONE TOUCH HER.
MASA-YUKI...?

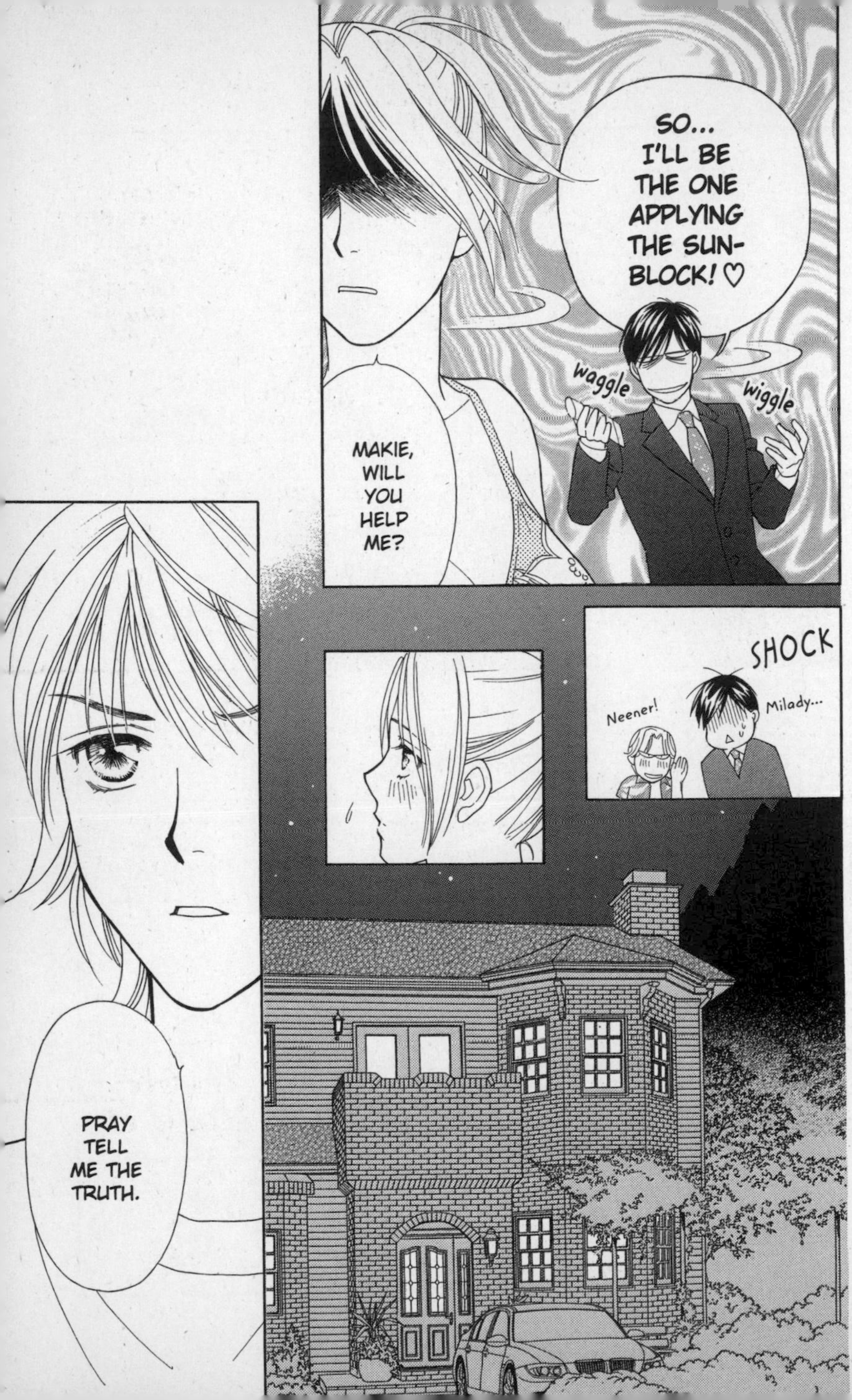
SO... I'LL BE THE ONE APPLYING THE SUN-BLOCK! ♡
wiggle
waggle
MAKIE, WILL YOU HELP ME?
SHOCK
Milady...
Neener!
PRAY TELL ME THE TRUTH.

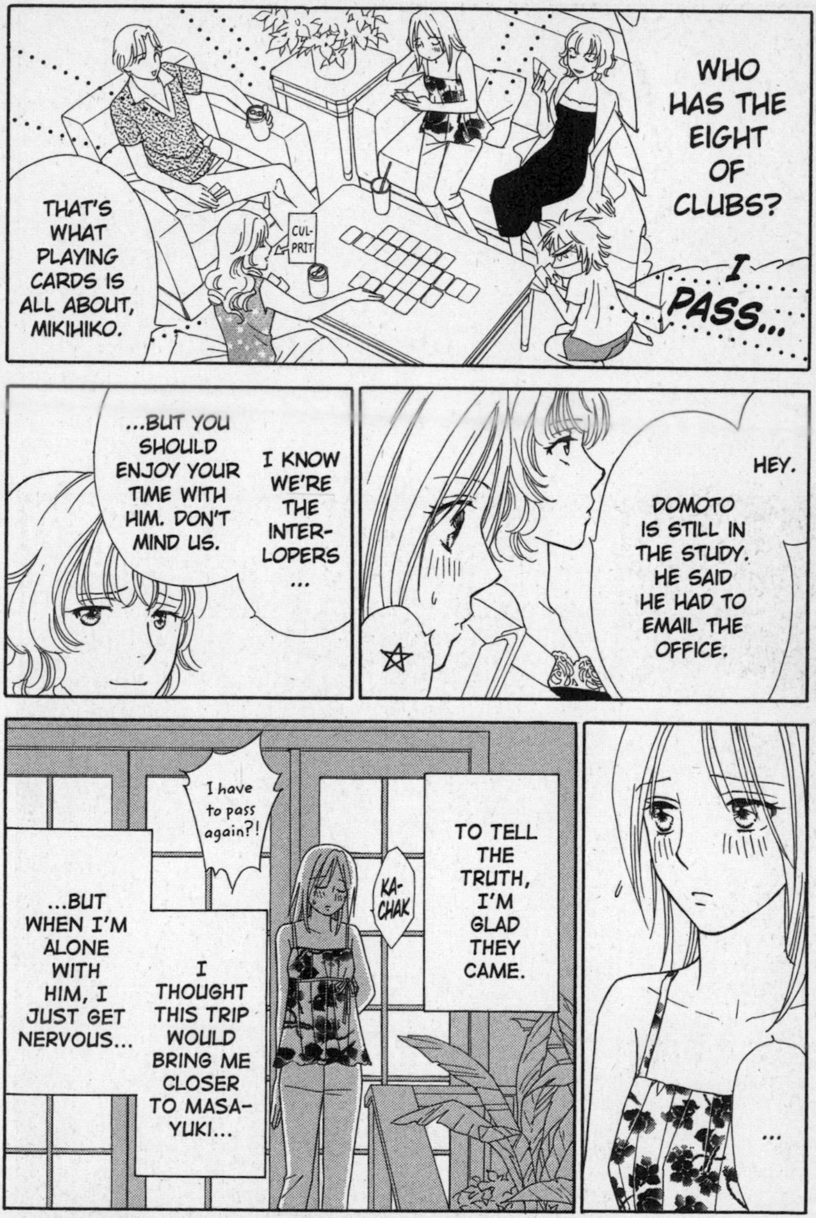
WHO HAS THE EIGHT OF CLUBS?
I PASS...
CUL-PRIT
THAT'S WHAT PLAYING CARDS IS ALL ABOUT, MIKIHIKO.
HEY.
DOMOTO IS STILL IN THE STUDY. HE SAID HE HAD TO EMAIL THE OFFICE.
I KNOW WE'RE THE INTER-LOPERS...
...BUT YOU SHOULD ENJOY YOUR TIME WITH HIM. DON'T MIND US.
...
TO TELL THE TRUTH, I'M GLAD THEY CAME.
KA-CHAK
I have to pass again?!
I THOUGHT THIS TRIP WOULD BRING ME CLOSER TO MASA-YUKI...
...BUT WHEN I'M ALONE WITH HIM, I JUST GET NERVOUS...

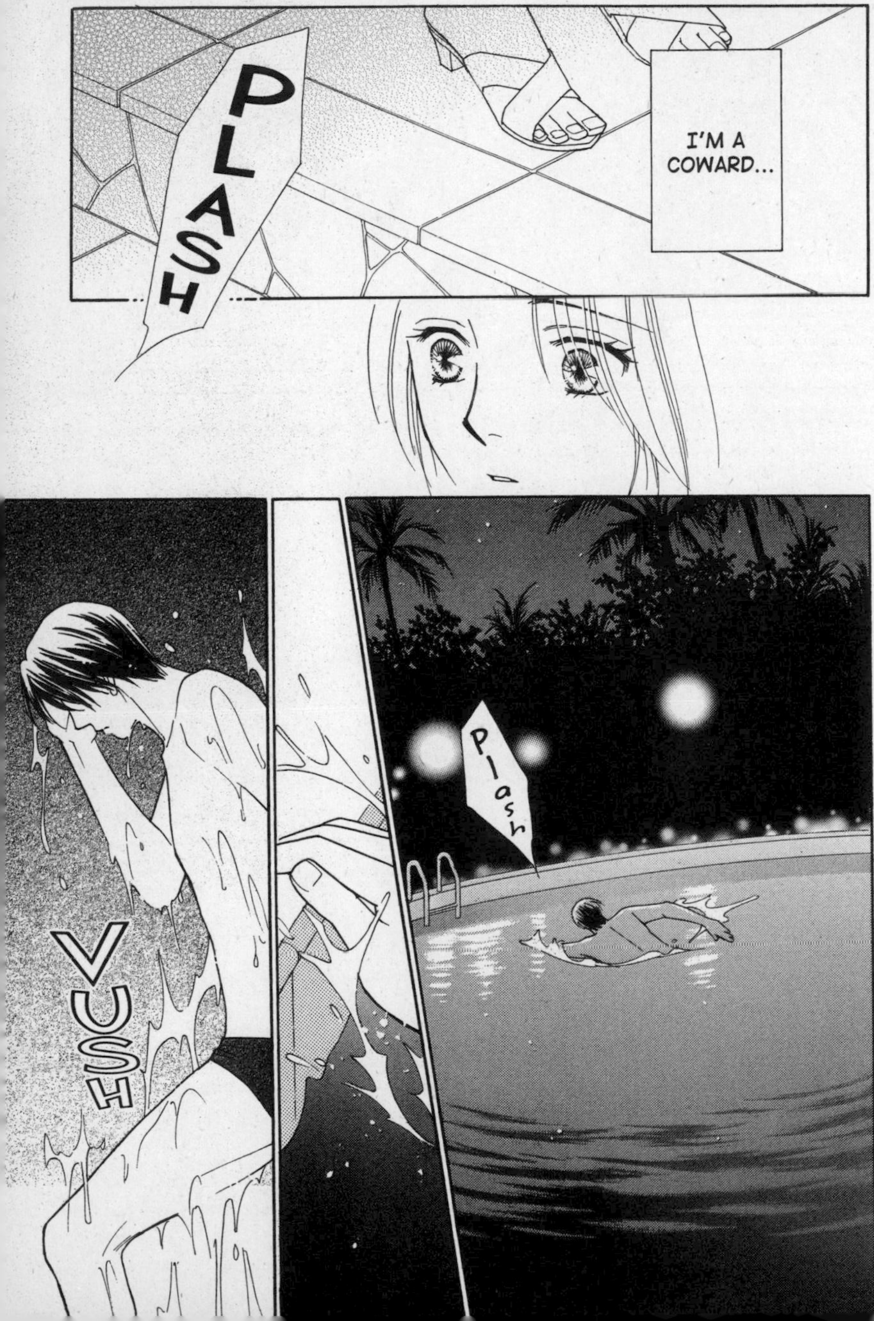
I'M A COWARD...
PLASH
Plash
VUSH

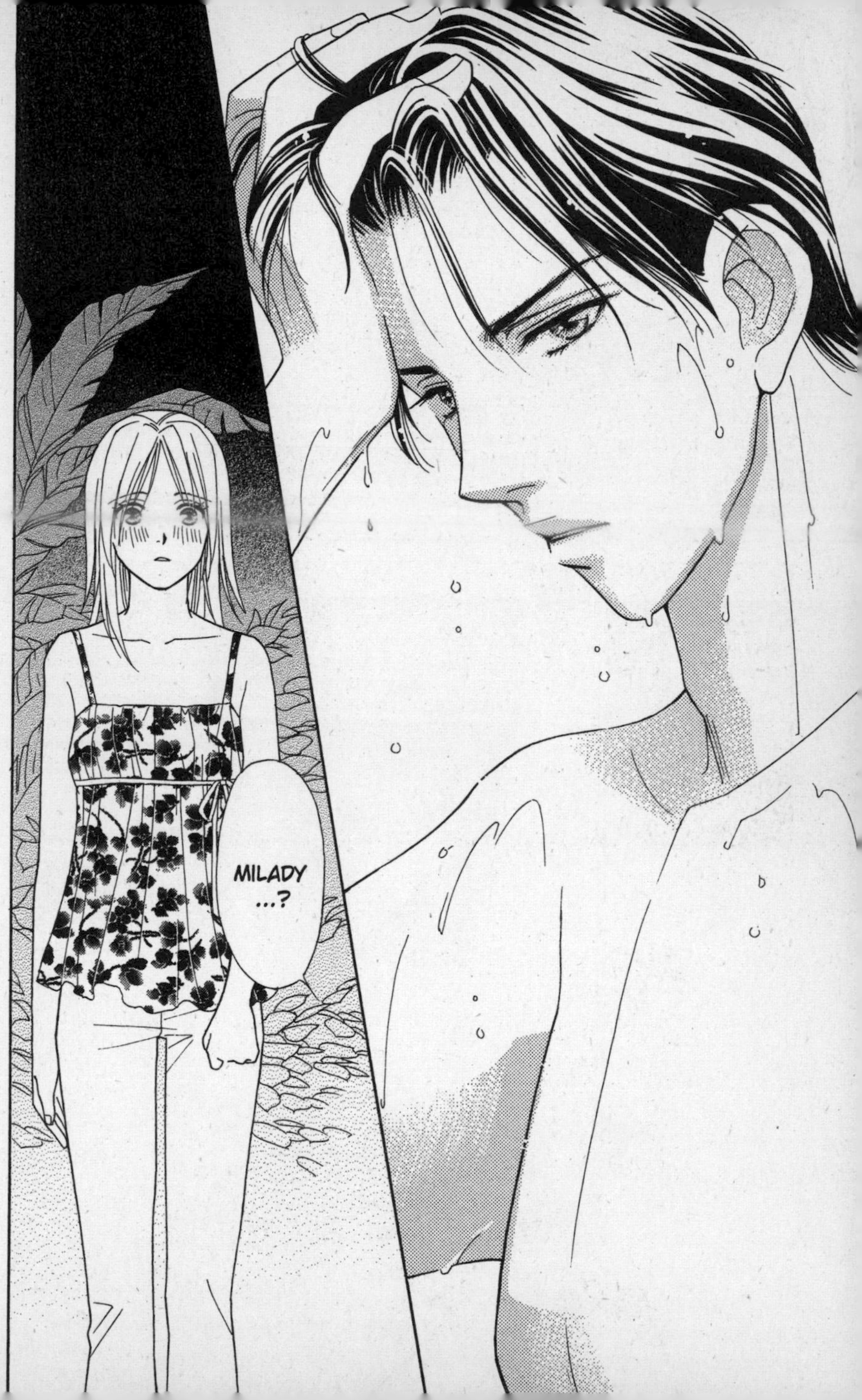
MILADY ...?

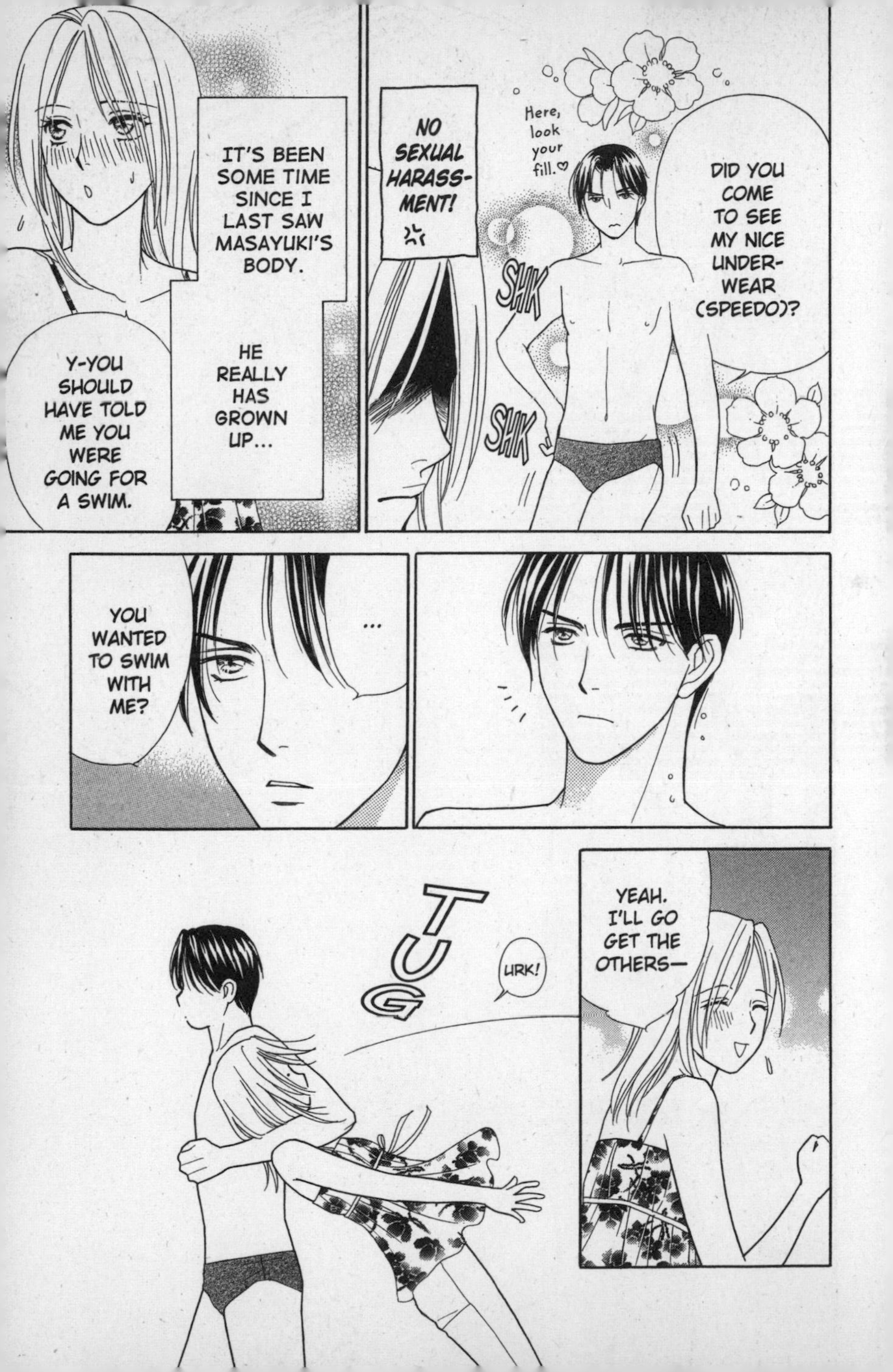
DID YOU COME TO SEE MY NICE UNDER-WEAR (SPEEDO)?
Here, look your fill.♡
SHK
SHK
NO SEXUAL HARASS-MENT!
IT'S BEEN SOME TIME SINCE I LAST SAW MASAYUKI'S BODY.
HE REALLY HAS GROWN UP...
Y-YOU SHOULD HAVE TOLD ME YOU WERE GOING FOR A SWIM.
...
YOU WANTED TO SWIM WITH ME?
YEAH. I'LL GO GET THE OTHERS—
URK!
TUG

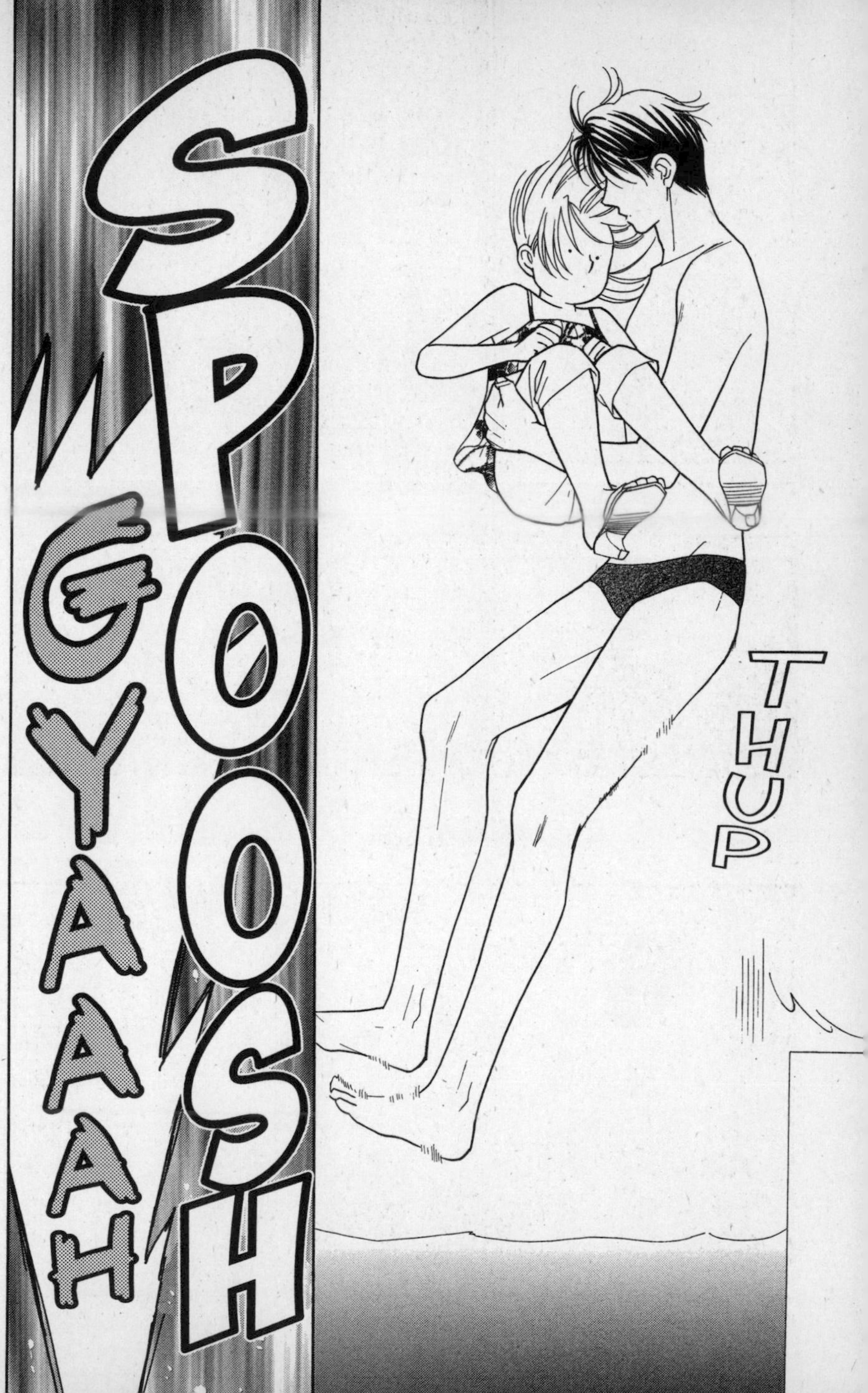
THUP
SPOOSH
GYAAAH

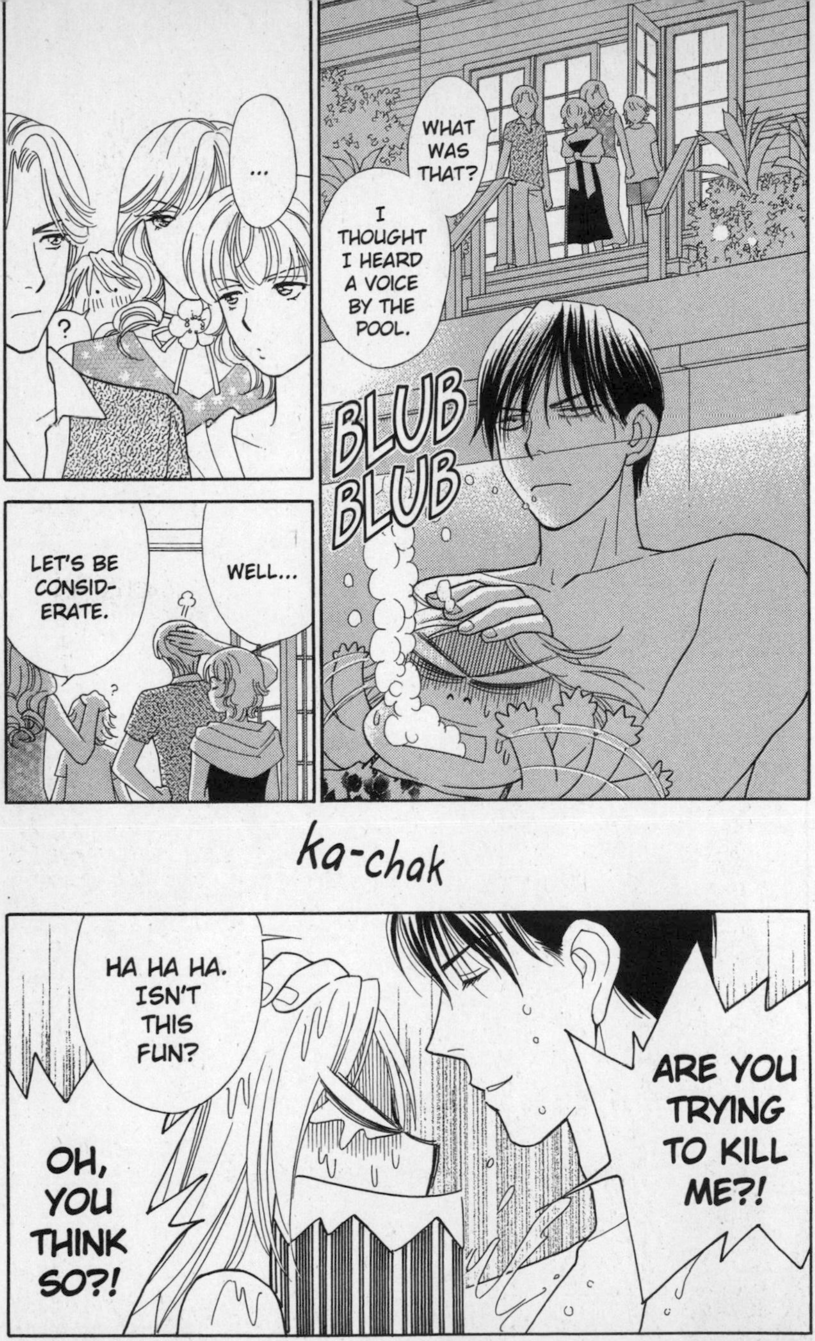

WHAT WAS THAT?
I THOUGHT I HEARD A VOICE BY THE POOL.
BLUB BLUB
...
?
WELL...
LET'S BE CONSID-ERATE.
?
ka-chak
HA HA HA. ISN'T THIS FUN?
ARE YOU TRYING TO KILL ME?!
OH, YOU THINK SO?!

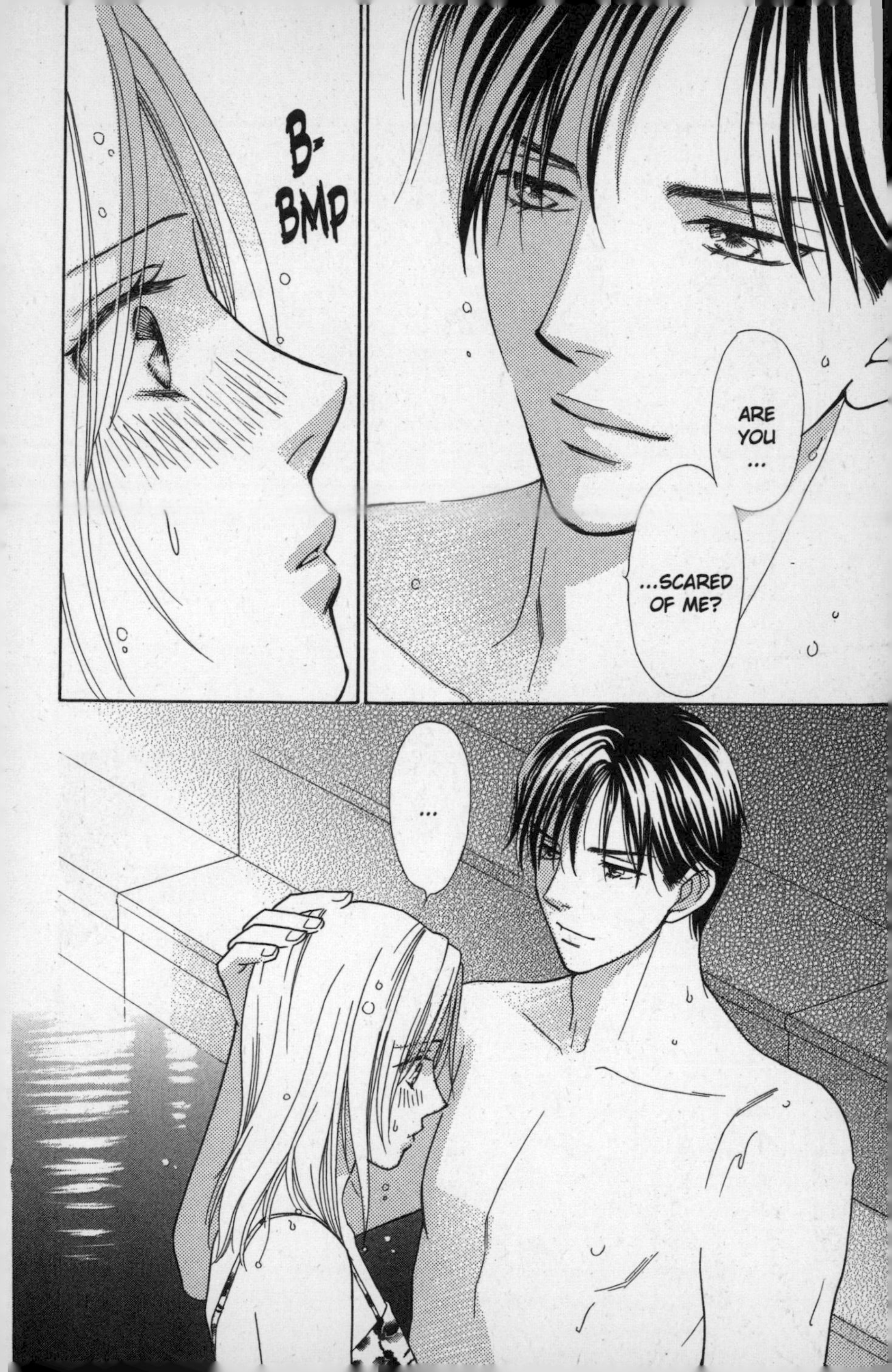
ARE YOU ...
...SCARED OF ME?
B-BMP
...

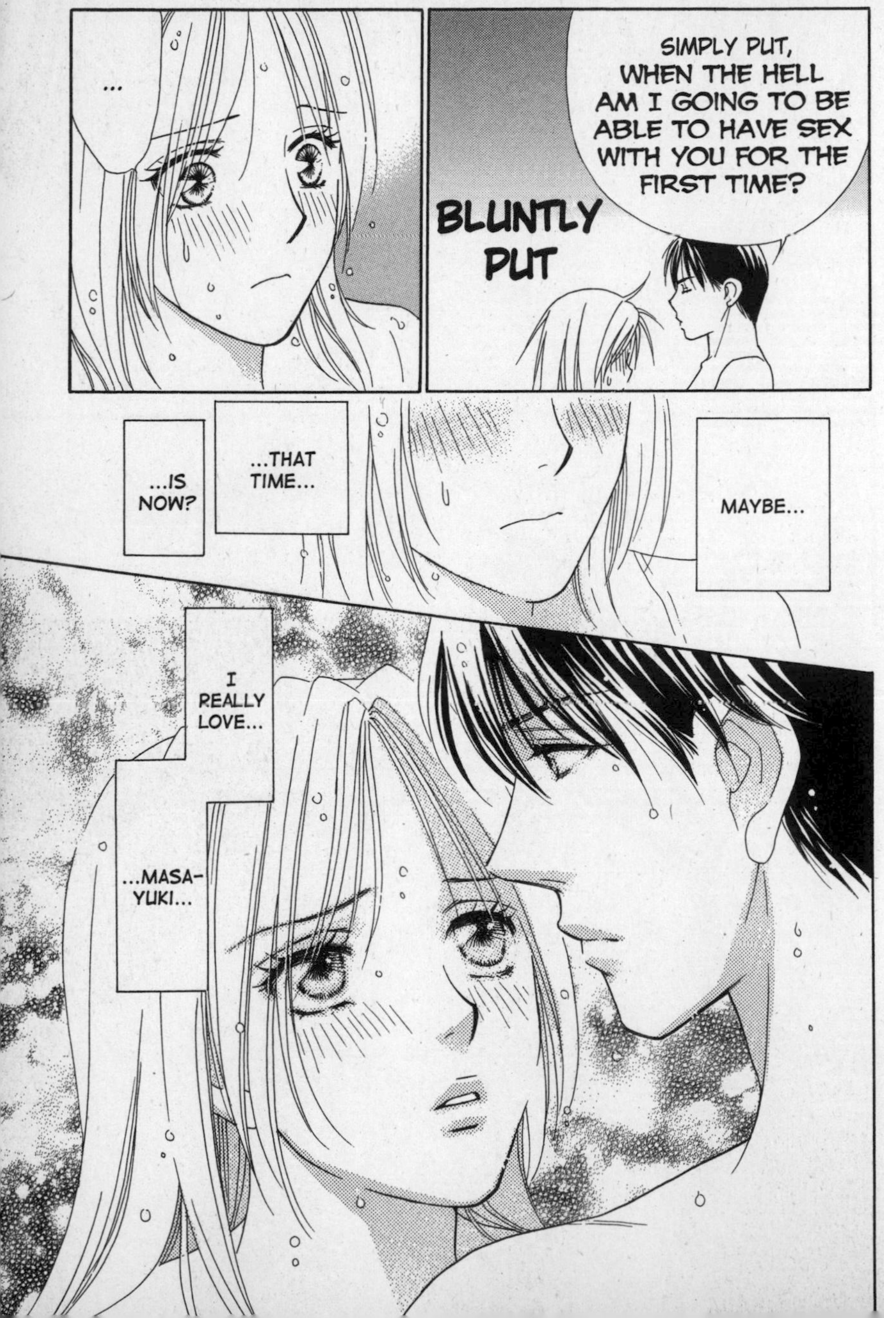
SIMPLY PUT, WHEN THE HELL AM I GOING TO BE ABLE TO HAVE SEX WITH YOU FOR THE FIRST TIME?
BLUNTLY PUT
...
MAYBE...
...THAT TIME...
...IS NOW?
I REALLY LOVE...
...MASA-YUKI...

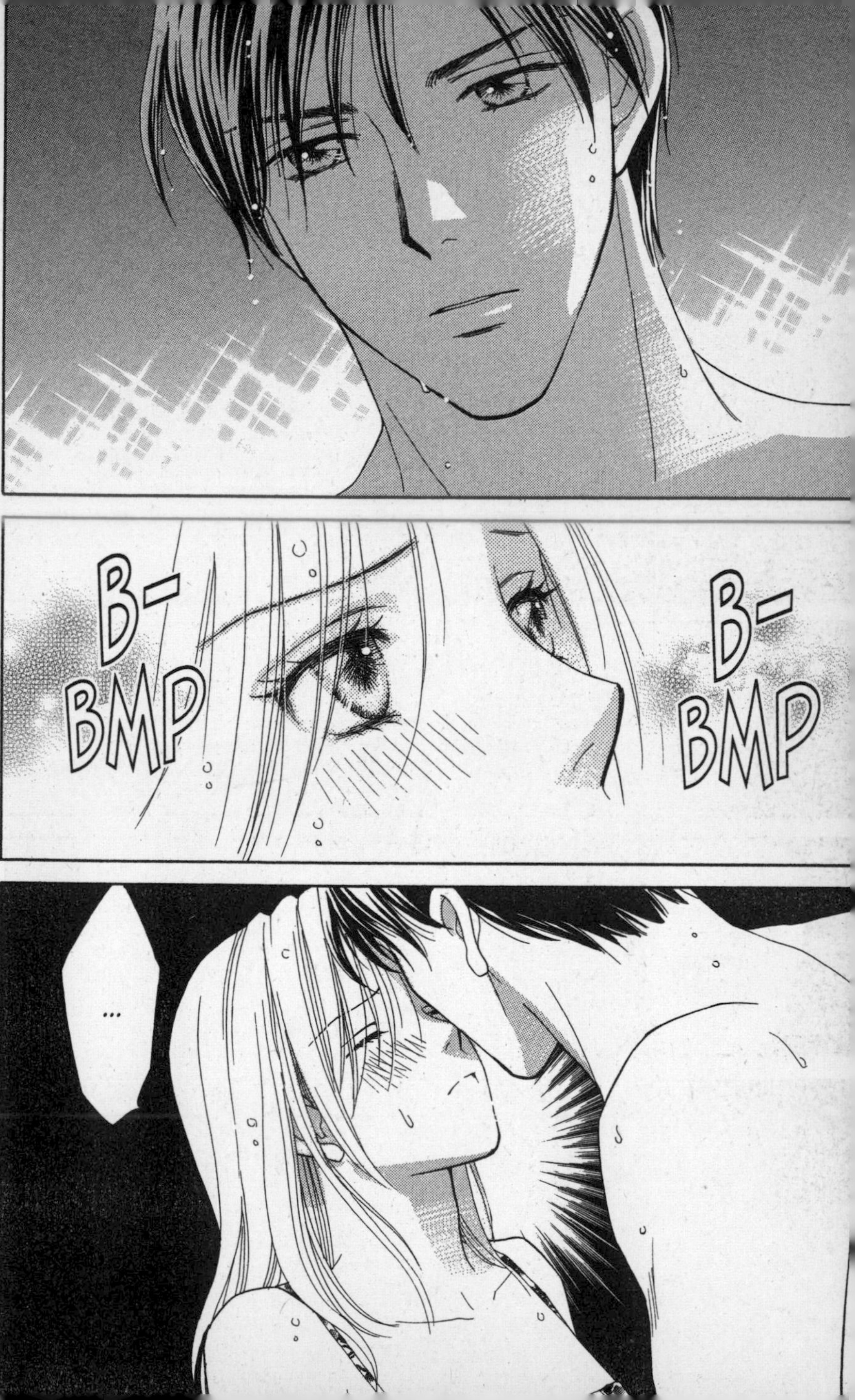
B-BMP
B-BMP
...

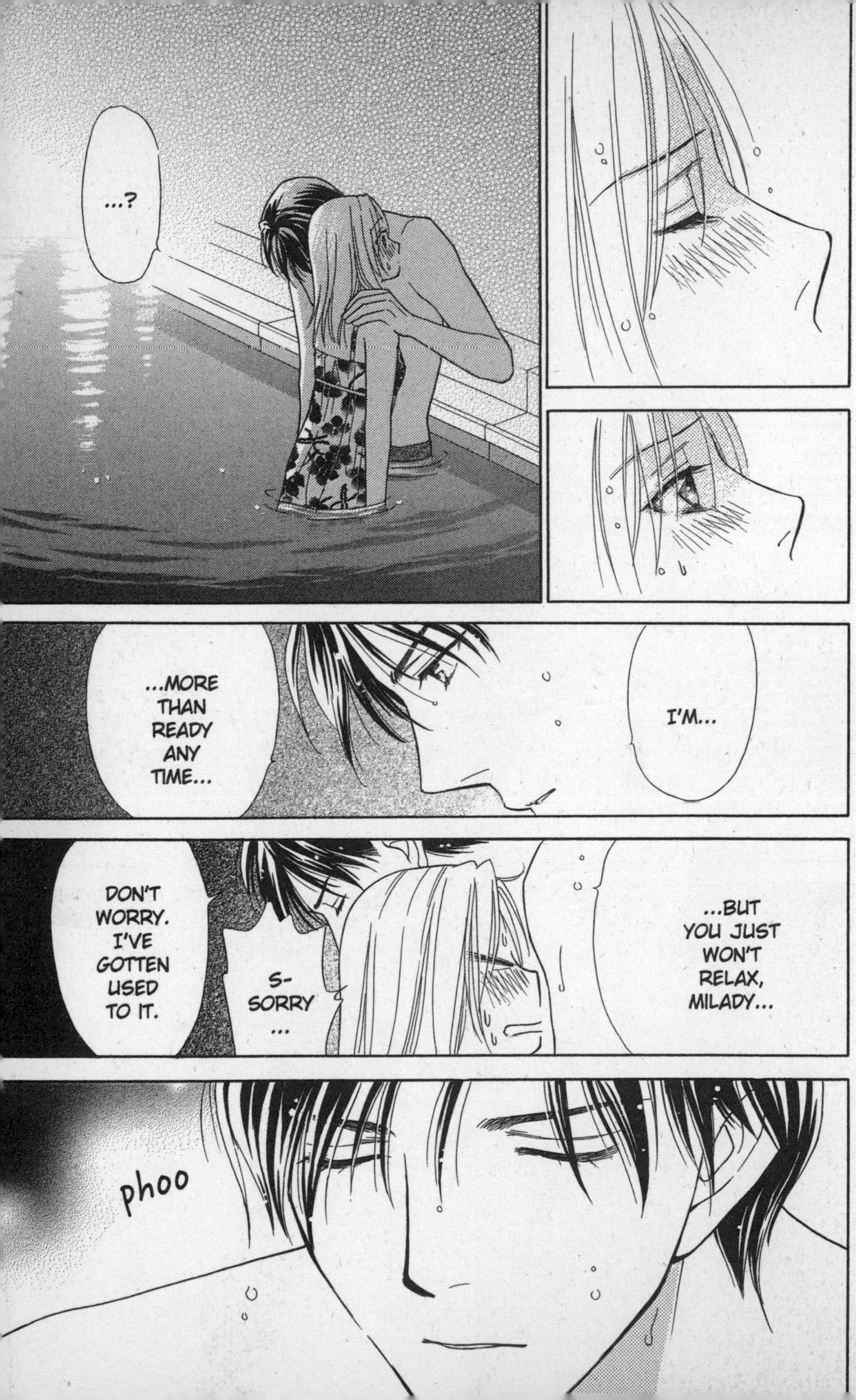
...?
I'M...
...MORE THAN READY ANY TIME...
...BUT YOU JUST WON'T RELAX, MILADY...
S-SORRY...
DON'T WORRY. I'VE GOTTEN USED TO IT.
phoo

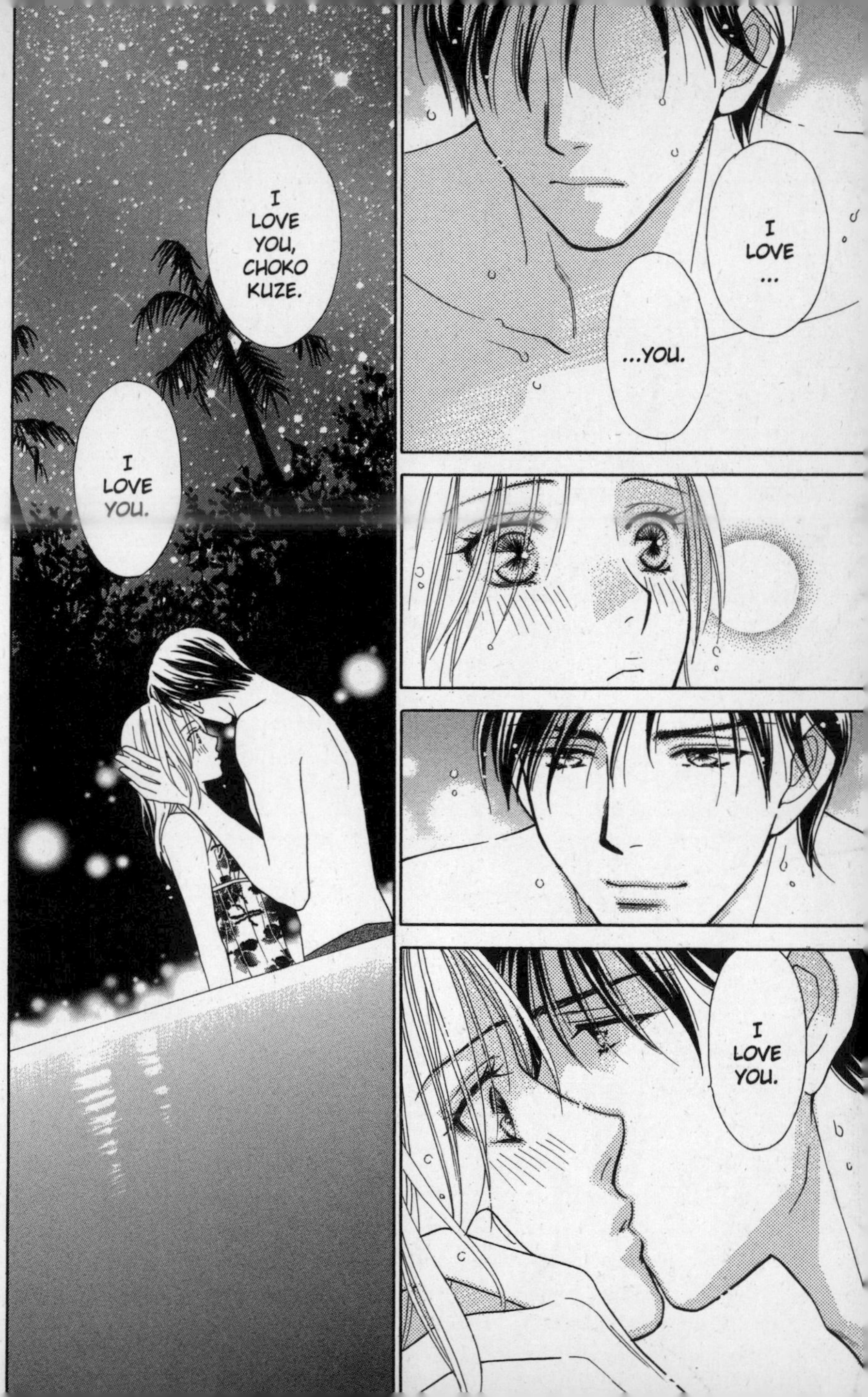
I LOVE ...
...YOU.
I LOVE YOU.
I LOVE YOU, CHOKO KUZE.
I LOVE YOU.

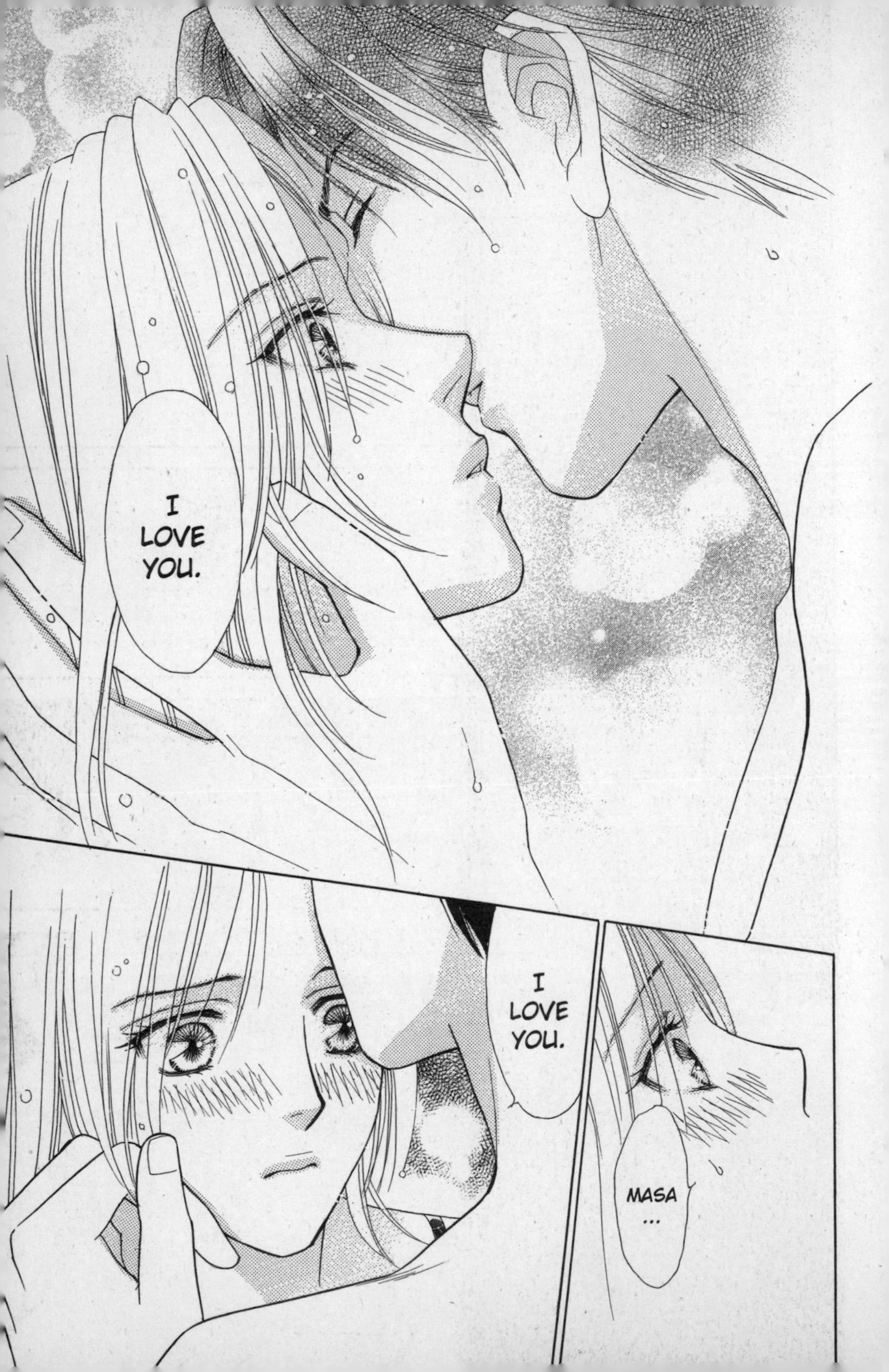
I LOVE YOU.
MASA ...
I LOVE YOU.

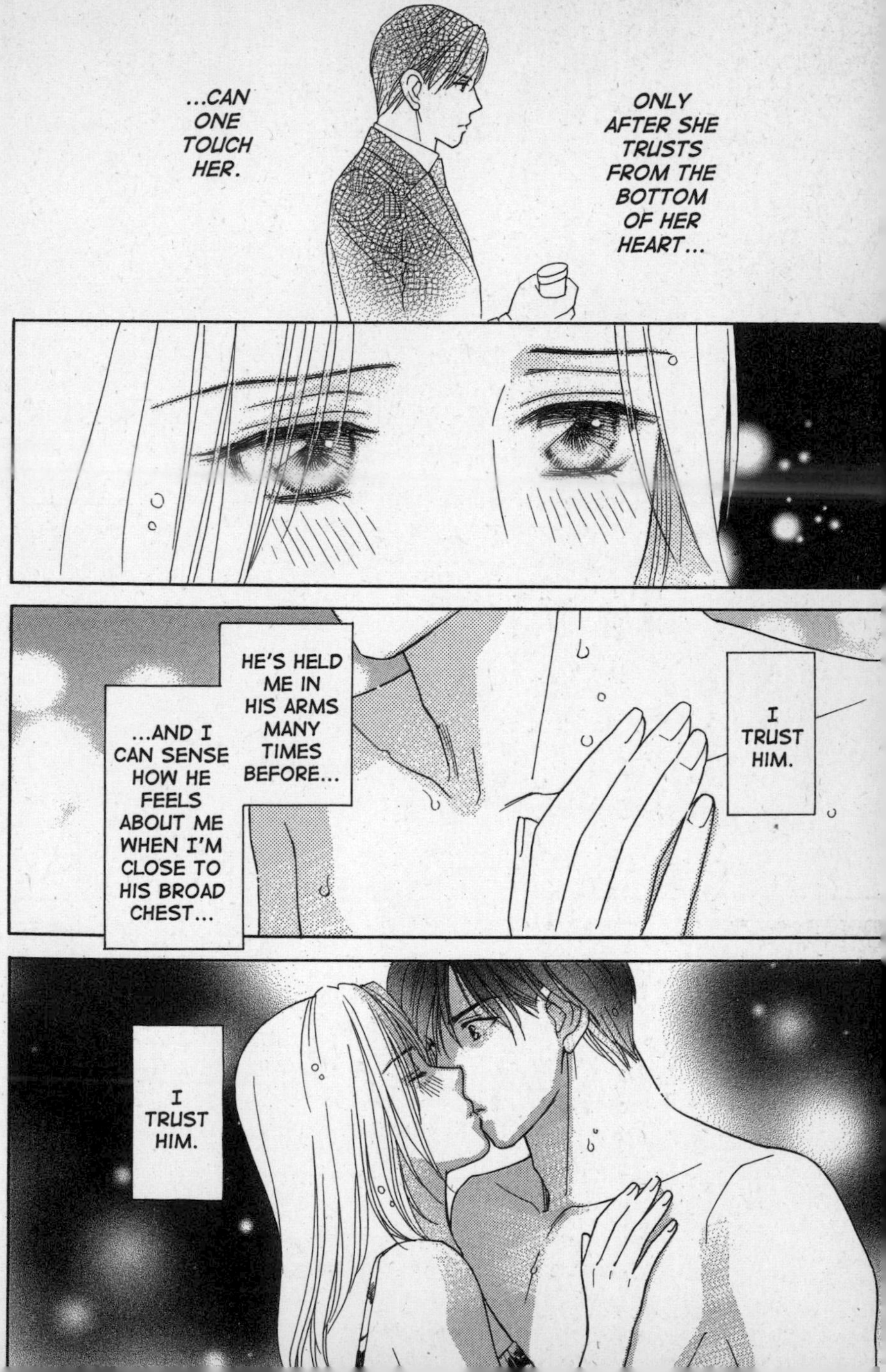
ONLY AFTER SHE TRUSTS FROM THE BOTTOM OF HER HEART...
...CAN ONE TOUCH HER.
I TRUST HIM.
HE'S HELD ME IN HIS ARMS MANY TIMES BEFORE...
...AND I CAN SENSE HOW HE FEELS ABOUT ME WHEN I'M CLOSE TO HIS BROAD CHEST...
I TRUST HIM.

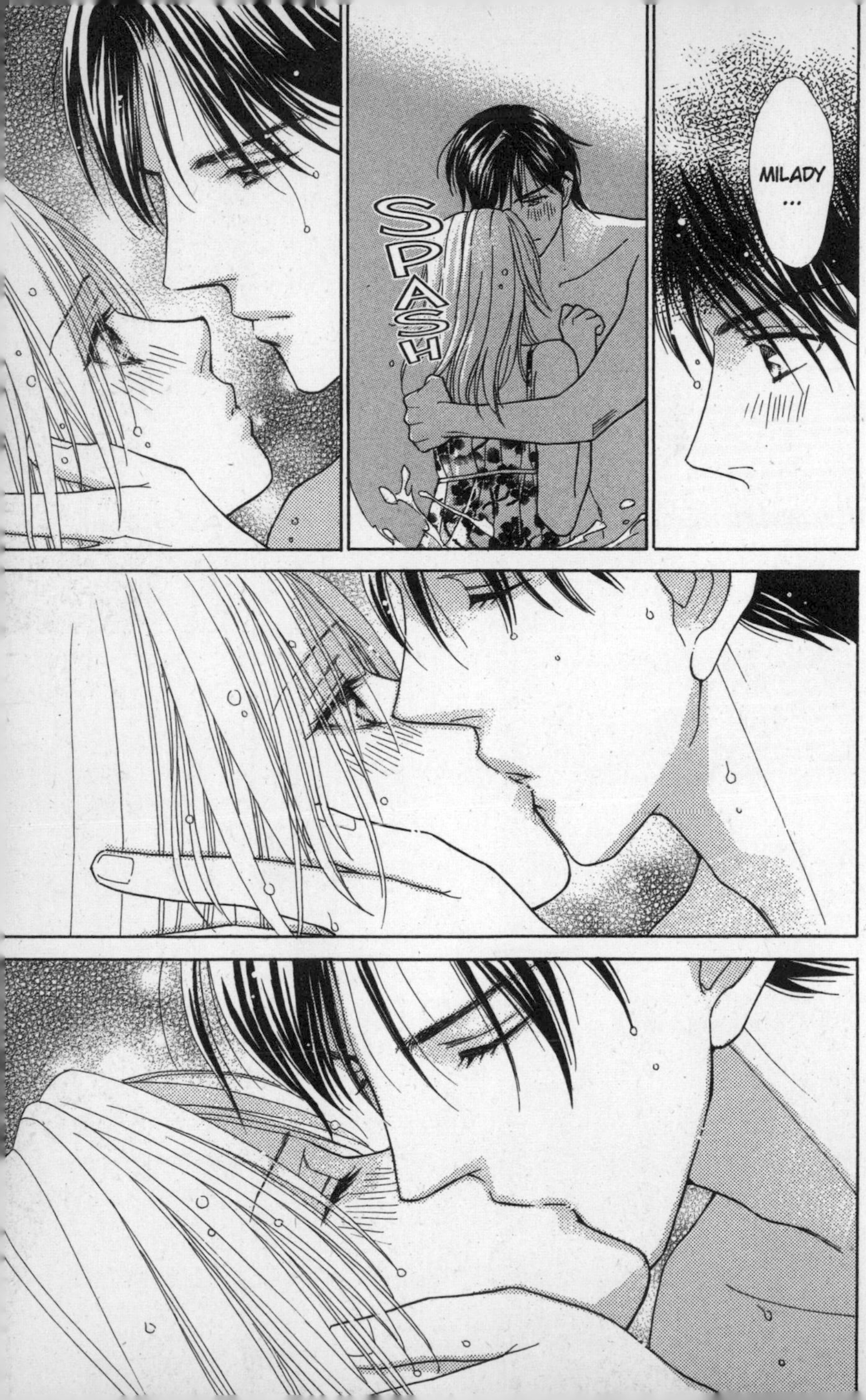
MILADY ...
SPASH

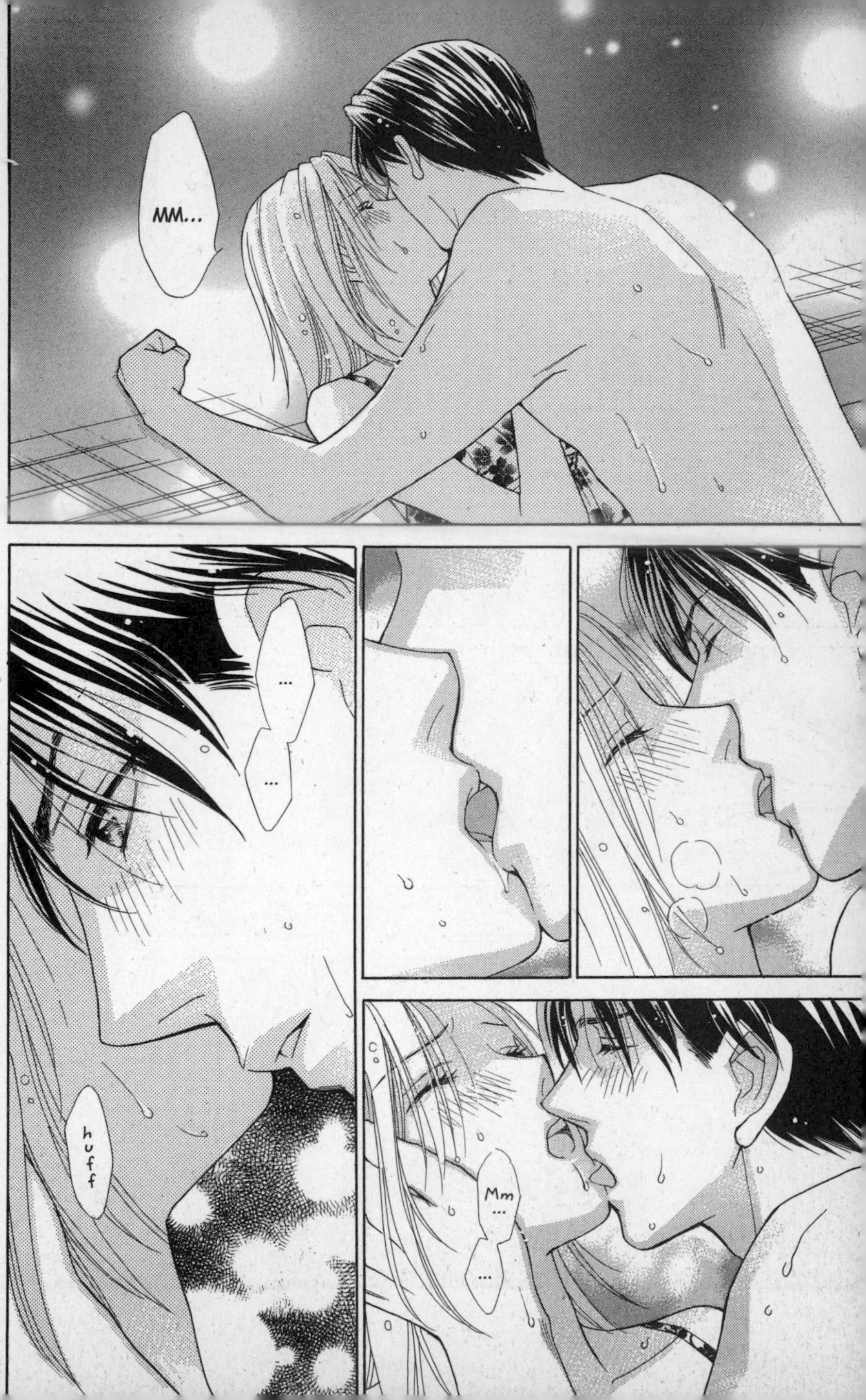
MM...
Mm
...
...
...
...
huff

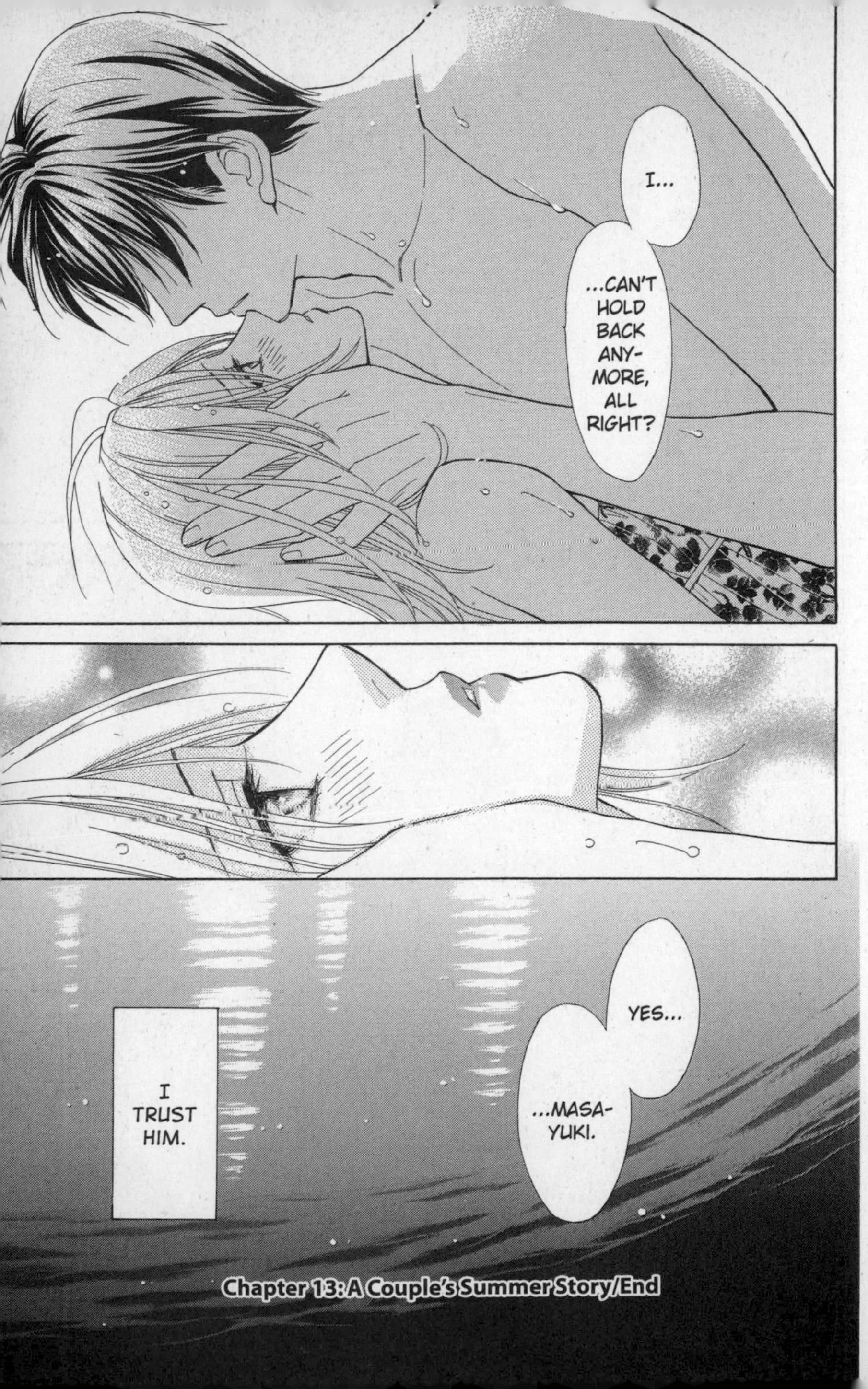
I...
...CAN'T HOLD BACK ANY-MORE, ALL RIGHT?
YES...
...MASA-YUKI.
I TRUST HIM.
Chapter 13: A Couple's Summer Story/End

SERVANT MINDSCAPE

B-BMP
B-BMP
B-BMP
B-BMP
B-BMP
B-BMP
B-BMP

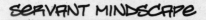

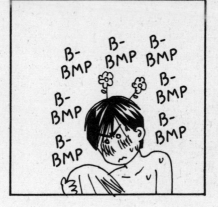

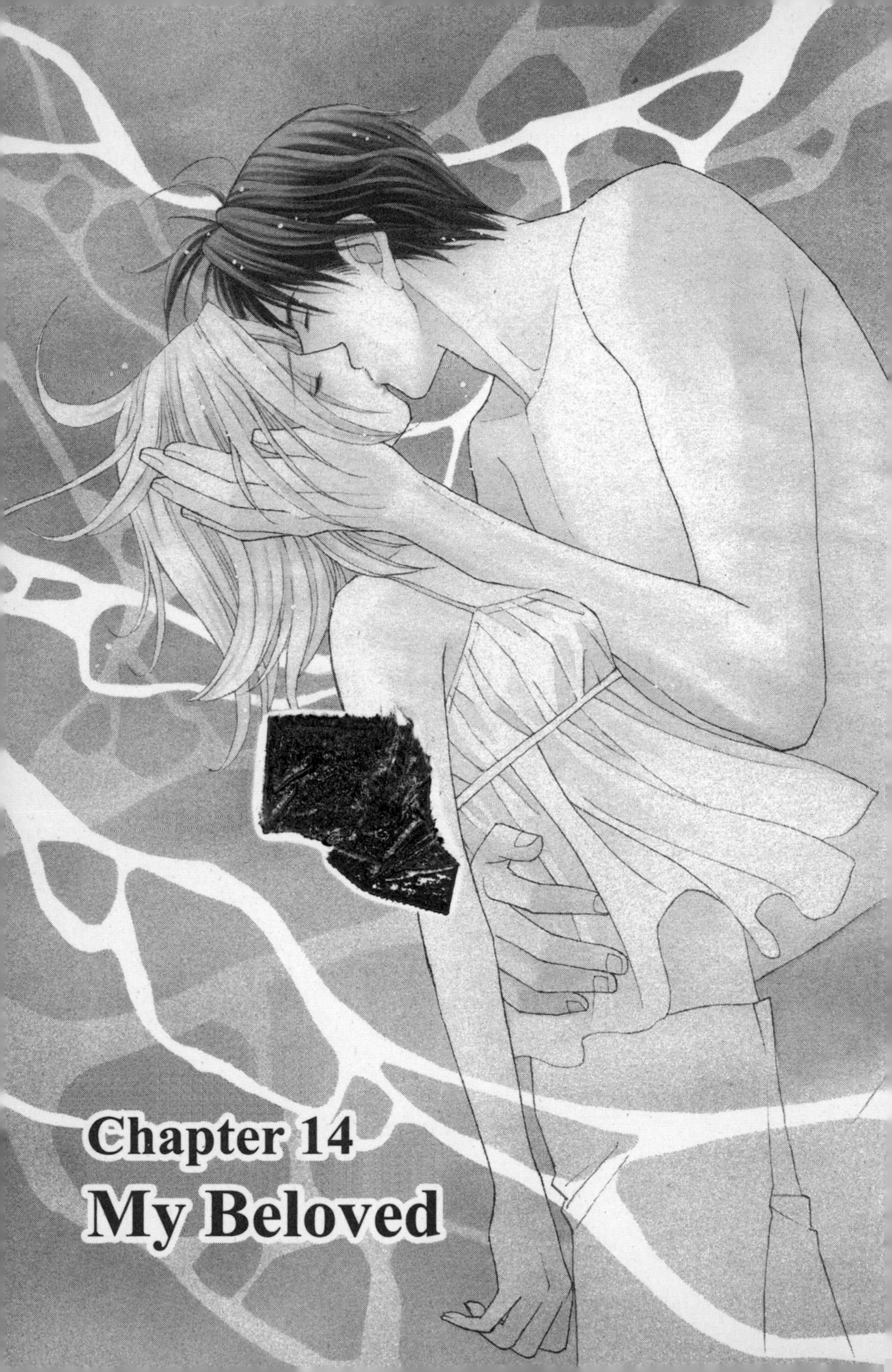

Chapter 14
My Beloved

SERVANT MINDSCAPE ②

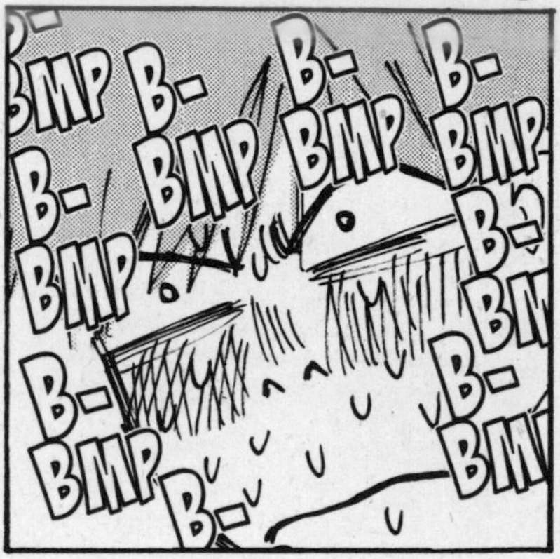
B-
BMP
B-
BMP
B-
BMP
B-
BMP
B-
BMP
B-
BMP
B-
BMP
B-

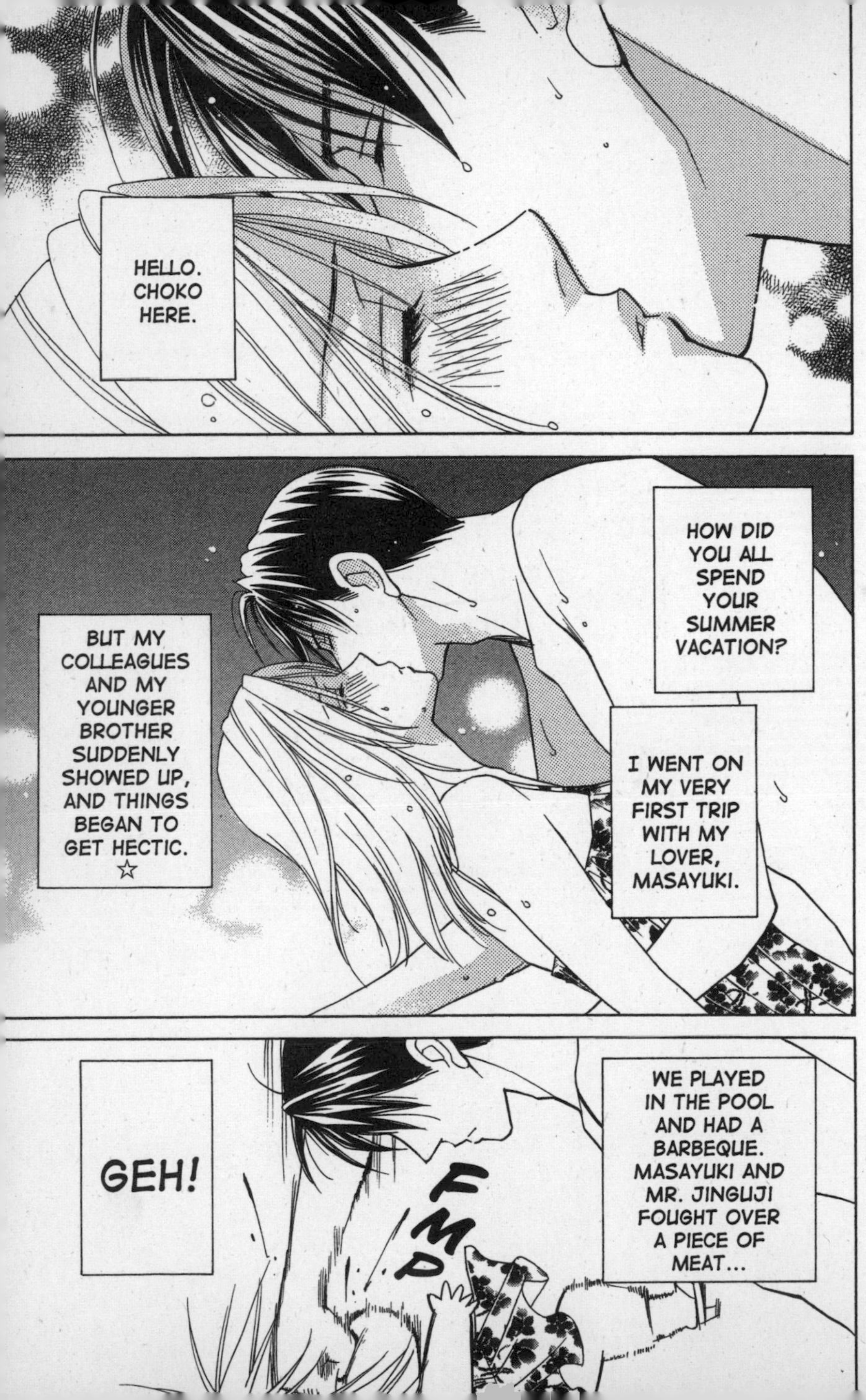
HELLO. CHOKO HERE.
HOW DID YOU ALL SPEND YOUR SUMMER VACATION?
I WENT ON MY VERY FIRST TRIP WITH MY LOVER, MASAYUKI.
BUT MY COLLEAGUES AND MY YOUNGER BROTHER SUDDENLY SHOWED UP, AND THINGS BEGAN TO GET HECTIC. ☆
WE PLAYED IN THE POOL AND HAD A BARBEQUE. MASAYUKI AND MR. JINGUJI FOUGHT OVER A PIECE OF MEAT...
FMP
GEH!

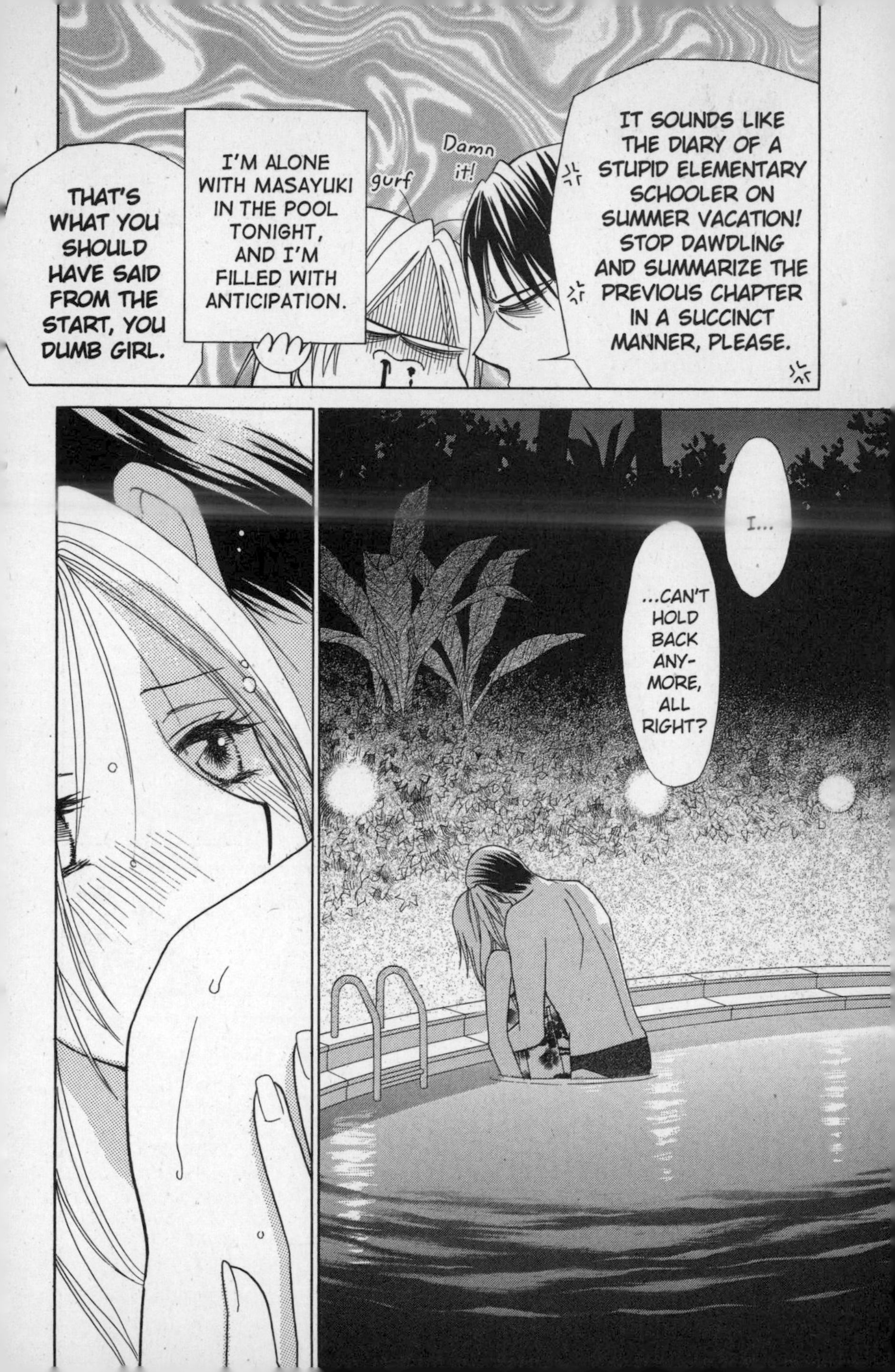
IT SOUNDS LIKE THE DIARY OF A STUPID ELEMENTARY SCHOOLER ON SUMMER VACATION! STOP DAWDLING AND SUMMARIZE THE PREVIOUS CHAPTER IN A SUCCINCT MANNER, PLEASE.
Damn it!
gurf
I'M ALONE WITH MASAYUKI IN THE POOL TONIGHT, AND I'M FILLED WITH ANTICIPATION.
THAT'S WHAT YOU SHOULD HAVE SAID FROM THE START, YOU DUMB GIRL.
I...
...CAN'T HOLD BACK ANYMORE, ALL RIGHT?

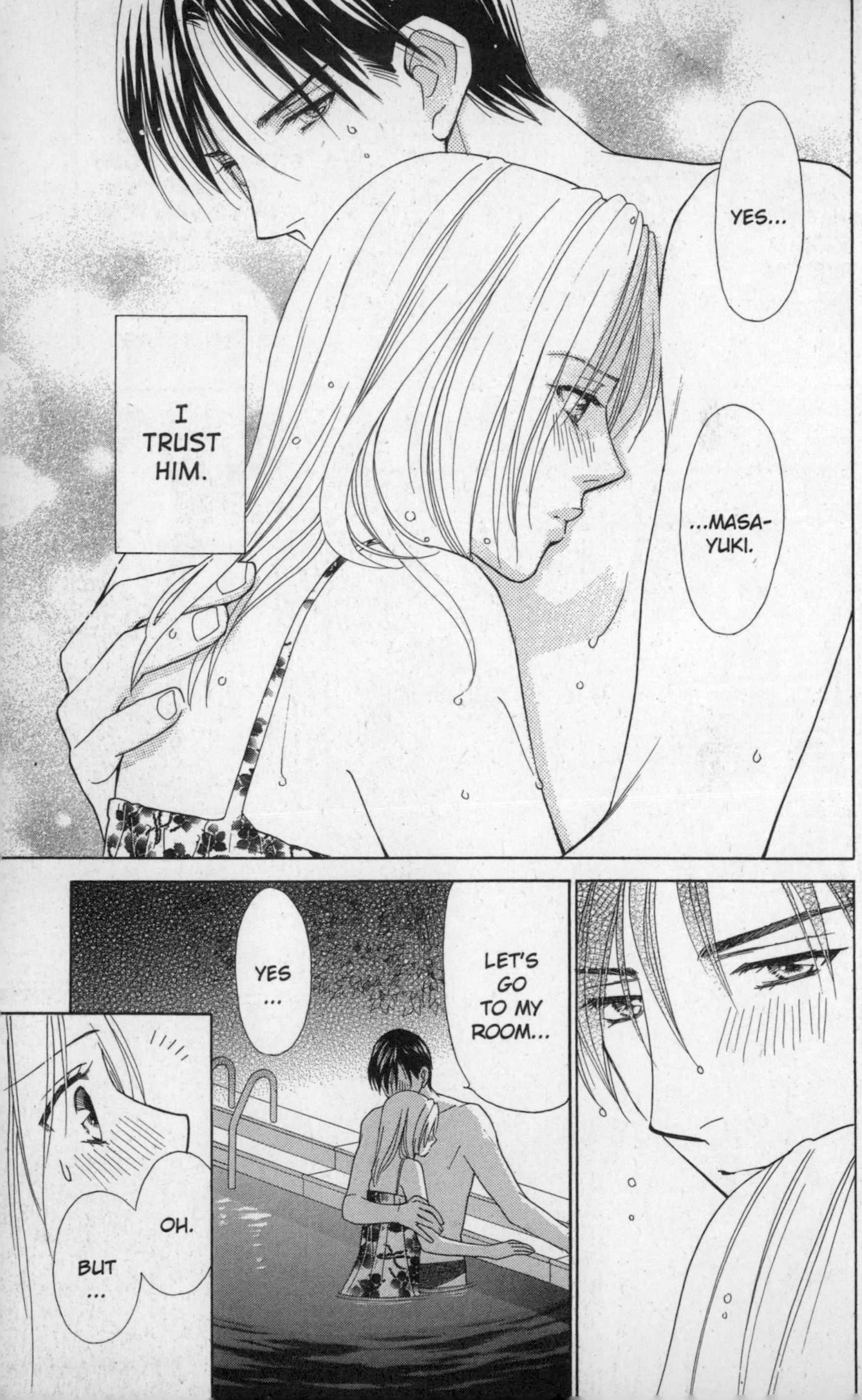
YES...
...MASA-YUKI.
I TRUST HIM.
LET'S GO TO MY ROOM...
YES ...
OH.
BUT ...

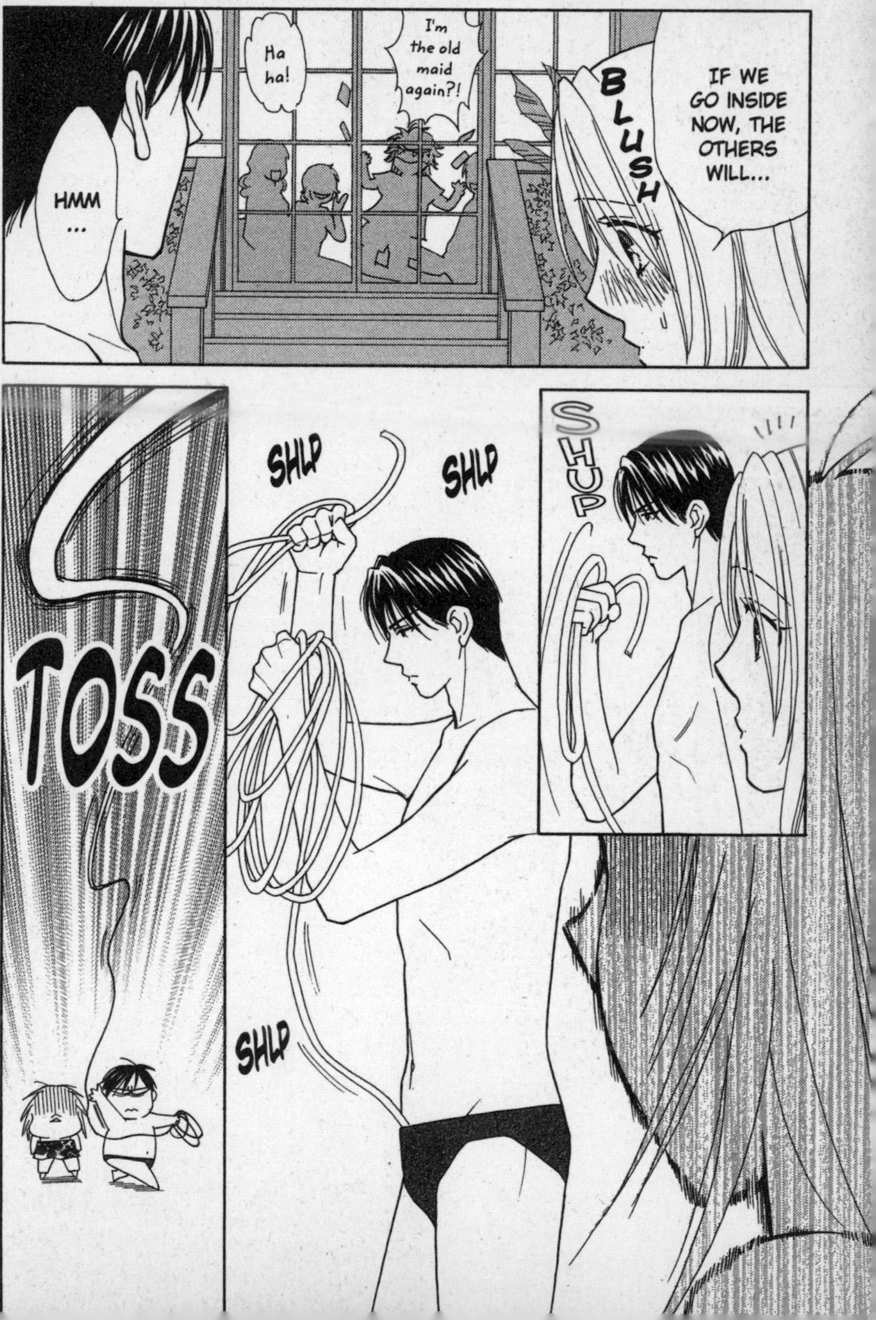
IF WE GO INSIDE NOW, THE OTHERS WILL...
BLUSH
I'm the old maid again?!
Ha ha!
HMM ...
SHUP
SHLP
SHLP
SHLP
TOSS

ILLUSTRATION BY A MANGAKA WITH 20 YEARS EXPERIENCE

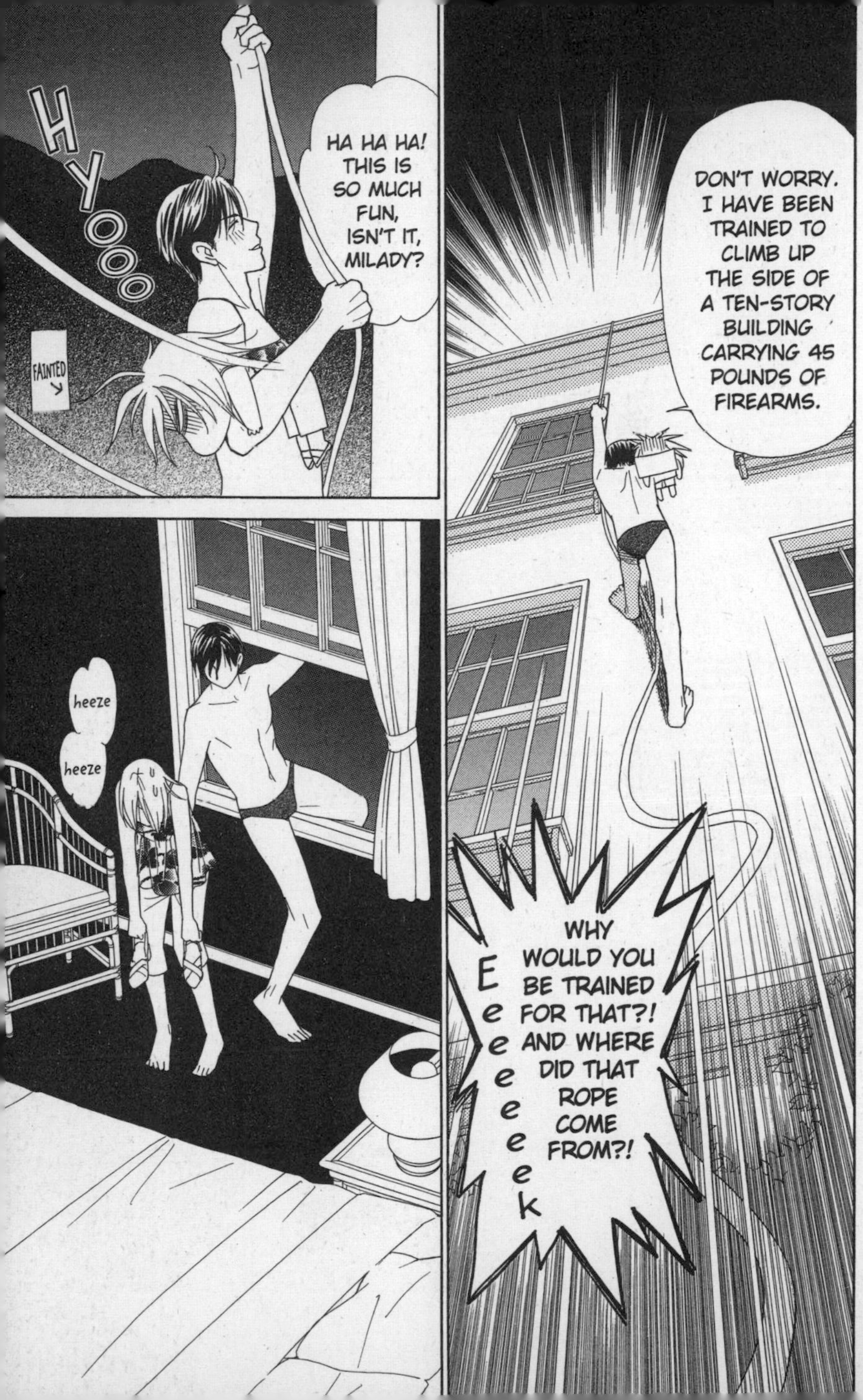

DON'T WORRY. I HAVE BEEN TRAINED TO CLIMB UP THE SIDE OF A TEN-STORY BUILDING CARRYING 45 POUNDS OF FIREARMS.
Eeeeeeeek
WHY WOULD YOU BE TRAINED FOR THAT?! AND WHERE DID THAT ROPE COME FROM?!
HYOOOO
HA HA HA! THIS IS SO MUCH FUN, ISN'T IT, MILADY?
FAINTED
heeze
heeze

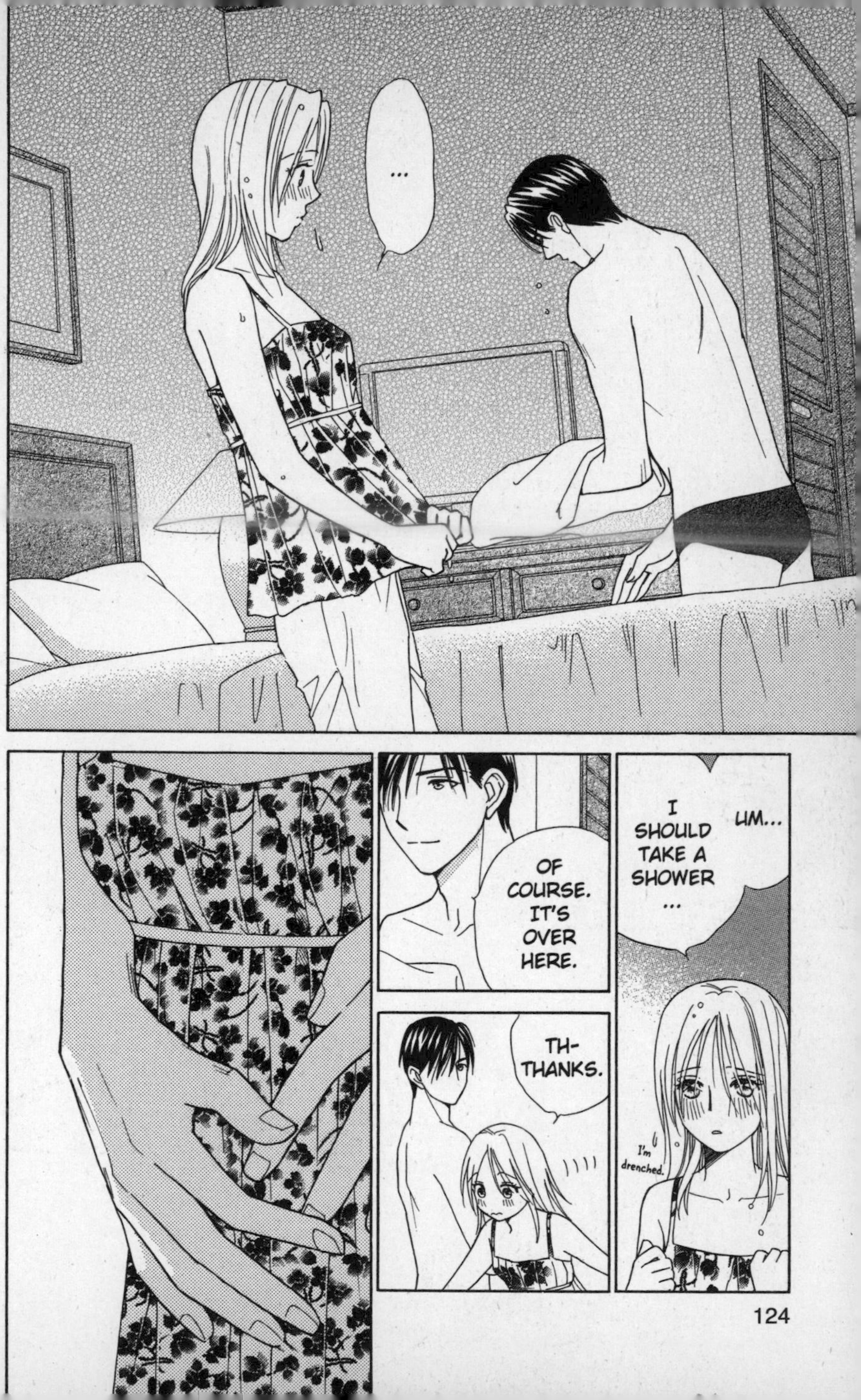
...
UM...
I SHOULD TAKE A SHOWER ...
I'm drenched.
OF COURSE. IT'S OVER HERE.
TH-THANKS.

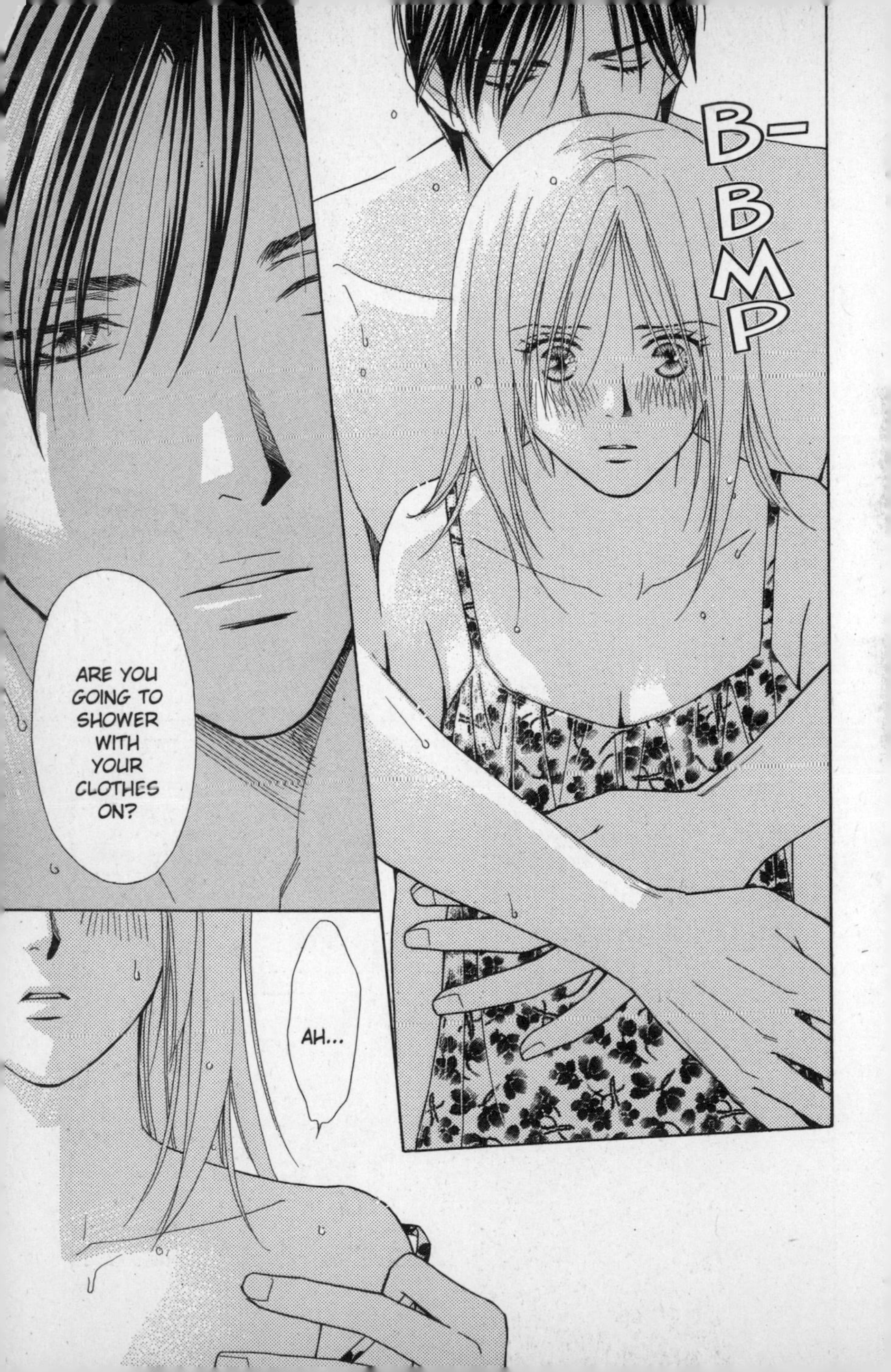
B-BMP
ARE YOU GOING TO SHOWER WITH YOUR CLOTHES ON?
AH...

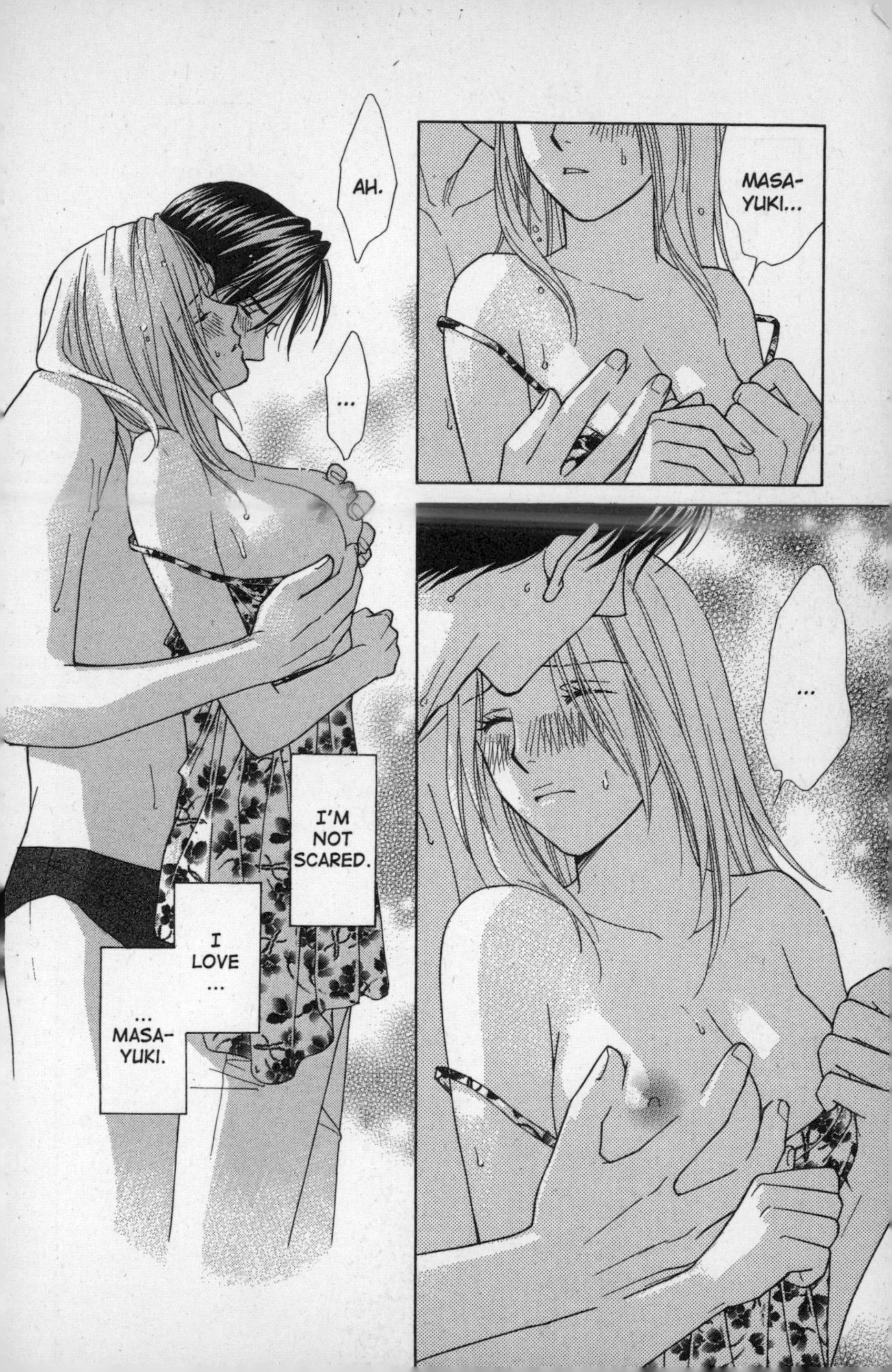
MASA-YUKI...
...
AH.
...
I'M NOT SCARED.
I LOVE ...
... MASA-YUKI.

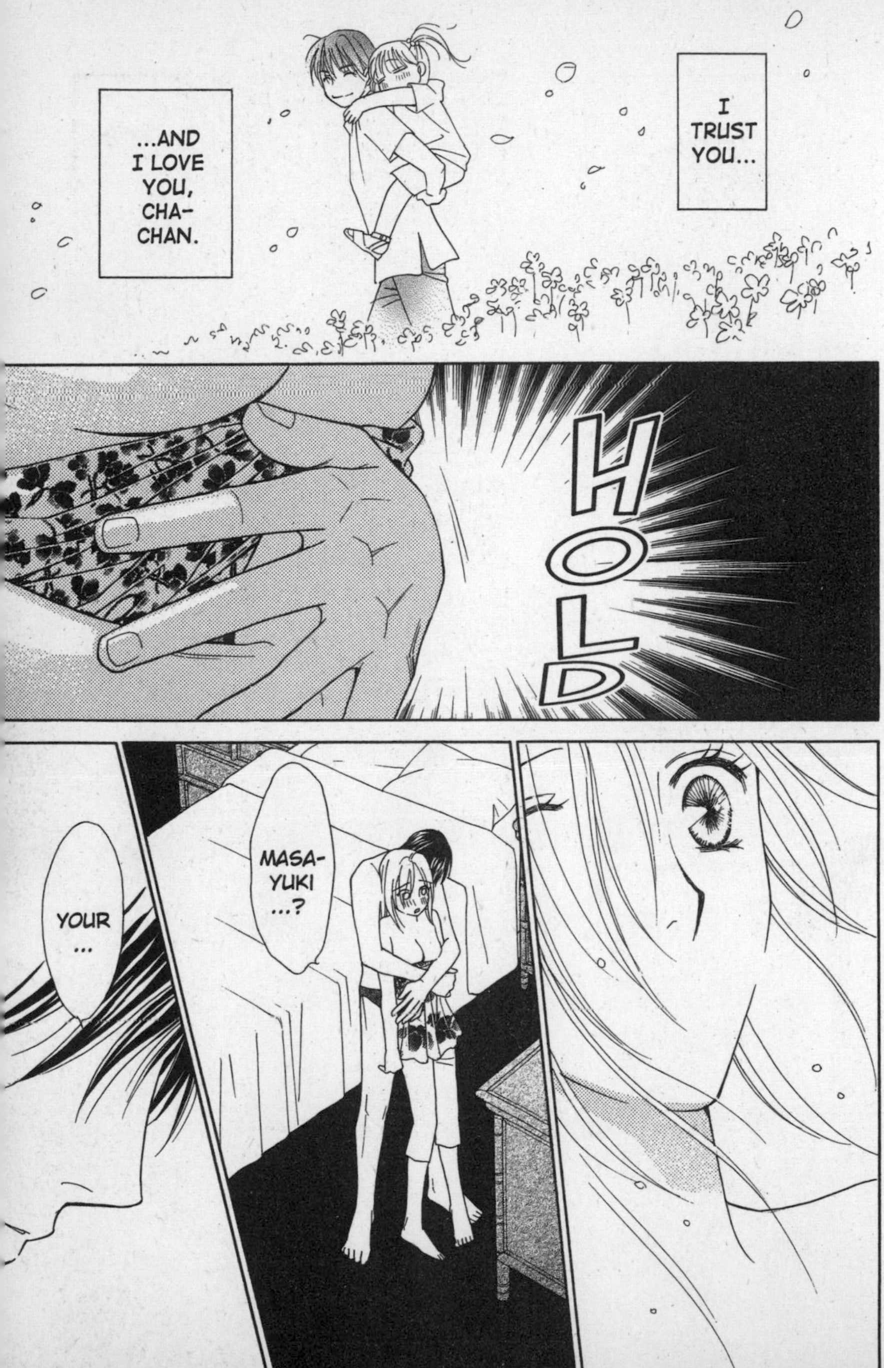
I TRUST YOU...
...AND I LOVE YOU, CHA-CHAN.
HOLD
MASA-YUKI ...?
YOUR ...

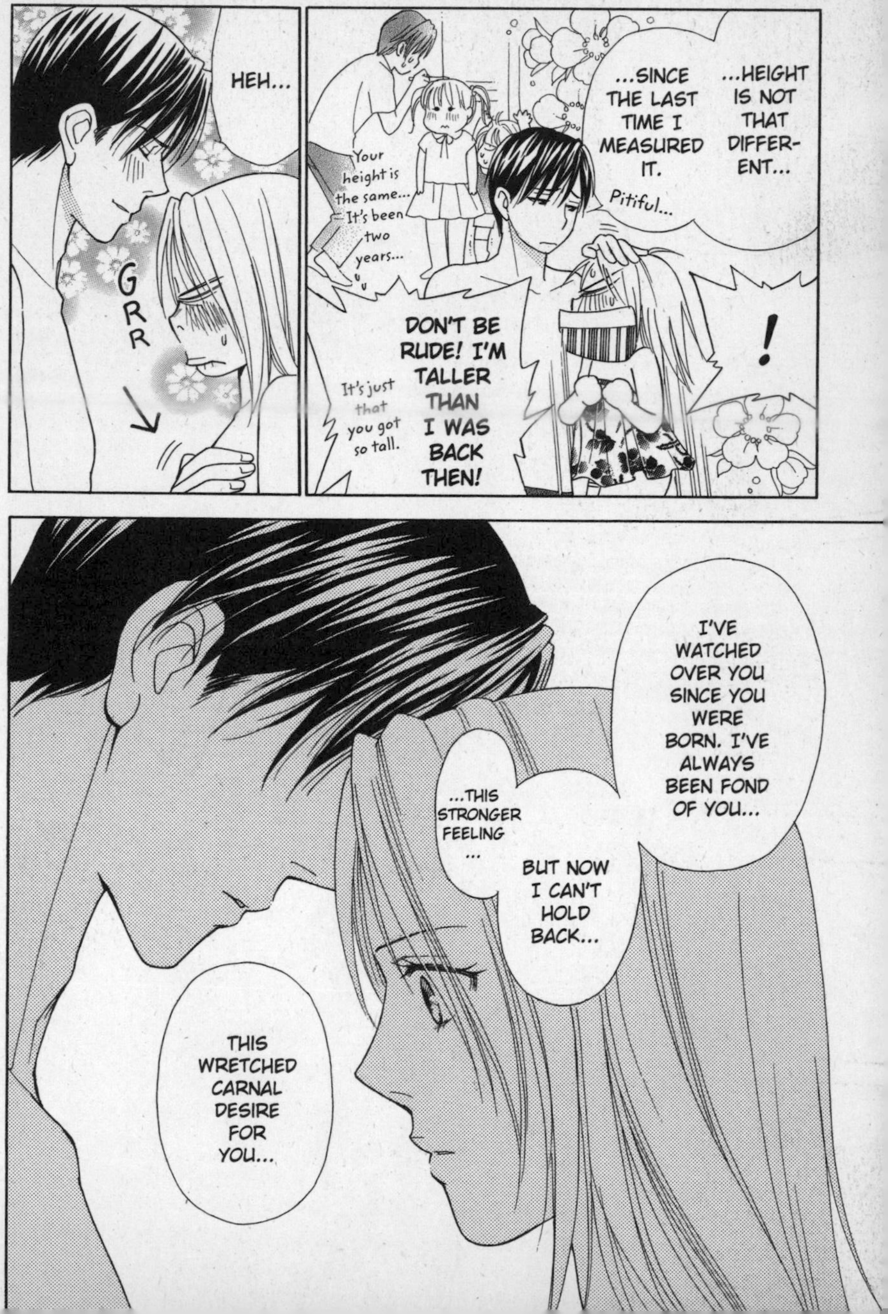
...SINCE THE LAST TIME I MEASURED IT.
...HEIGHT IS NOT THAT DIFFER-ENT...
Pitiful...
!
DON'T BE RUDE! I'M TALLER THAN I WAS BACK THEN!
It's just that you got so tall.
Your height is the same... It's been two years...
HEH...
GRR
I'VE WATCHED OVER YOU SINCE YOU WERE BORN. I'VE ALWAYS BEEN FOND OF YOU...
...THIS STRONGER FEELING ...
BUT NOW I CAN'T HOLD BACK...
THIS WRETCHED CARNAL DESIRE FOR YOU...

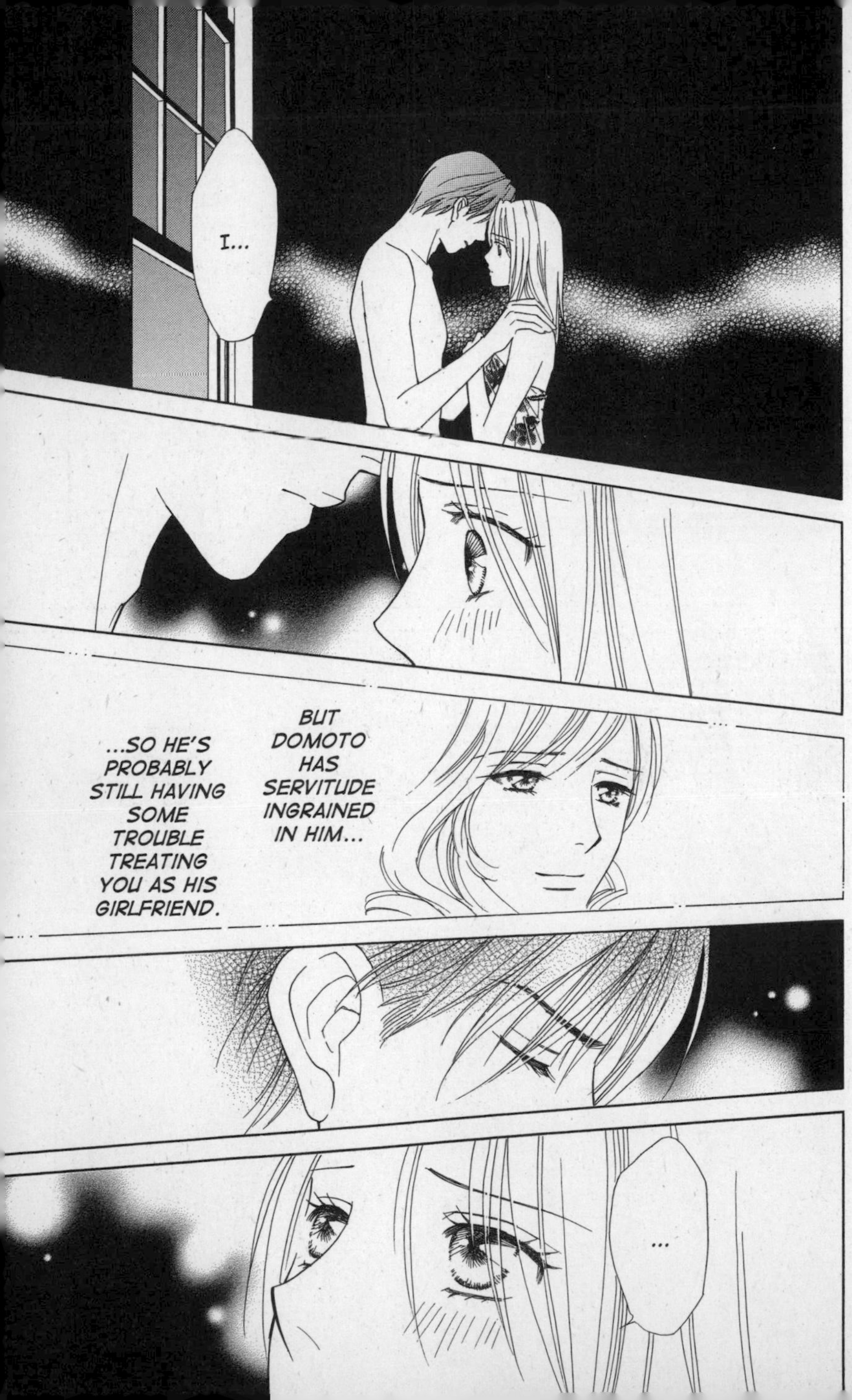
I...
BUT DOMOTO HAS SERVITUDE INGRAINED IN HIM...
...SO HE'S PROBABLY STILL HAVING SOME TROUBLE TREATING YOU AS HIS GIRLFRIEND.
...

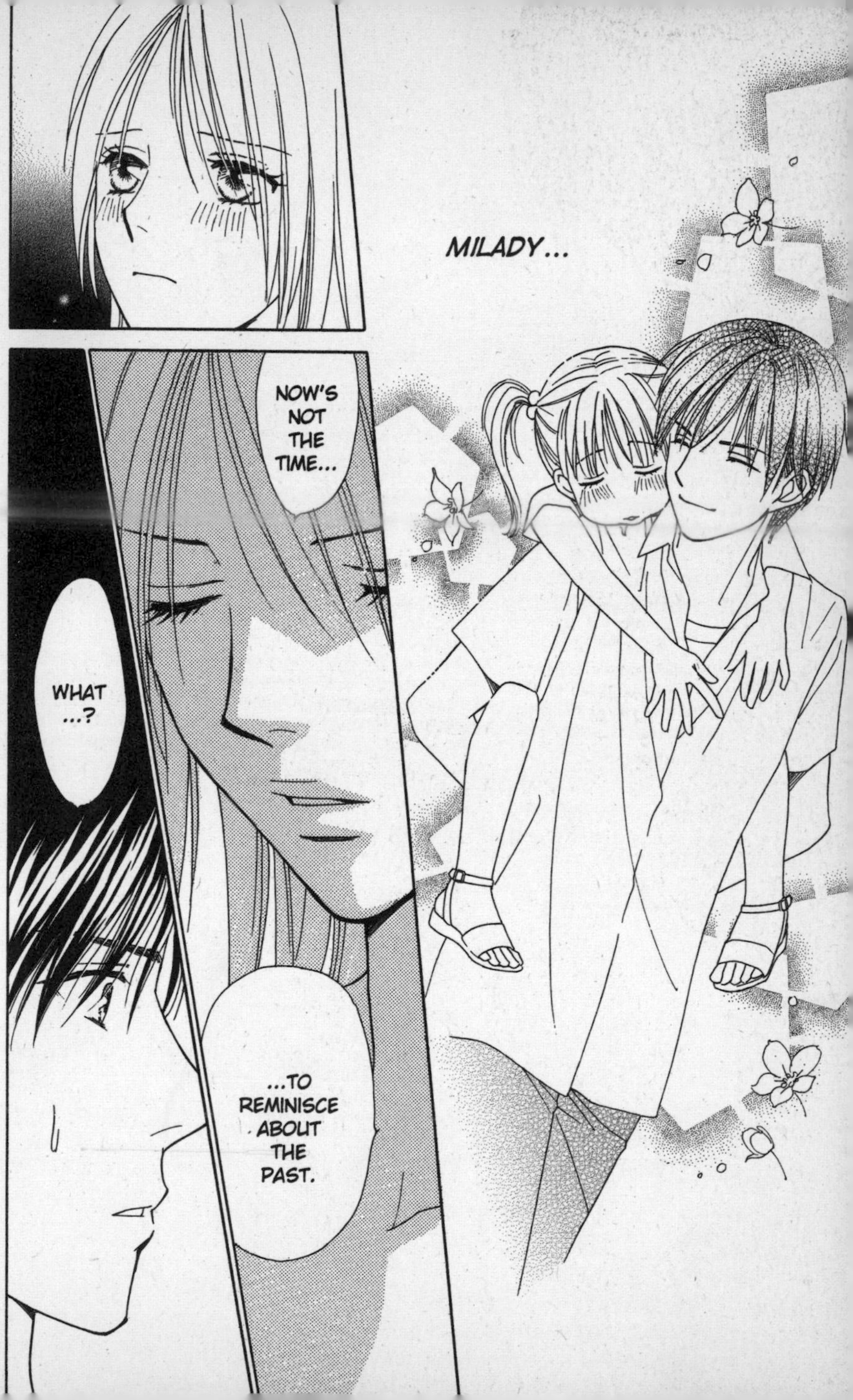
MILADY...
NOW'S NOT THE TIME...
WHAT ...?
...TO REMINISCE ABOUT THE PAST.

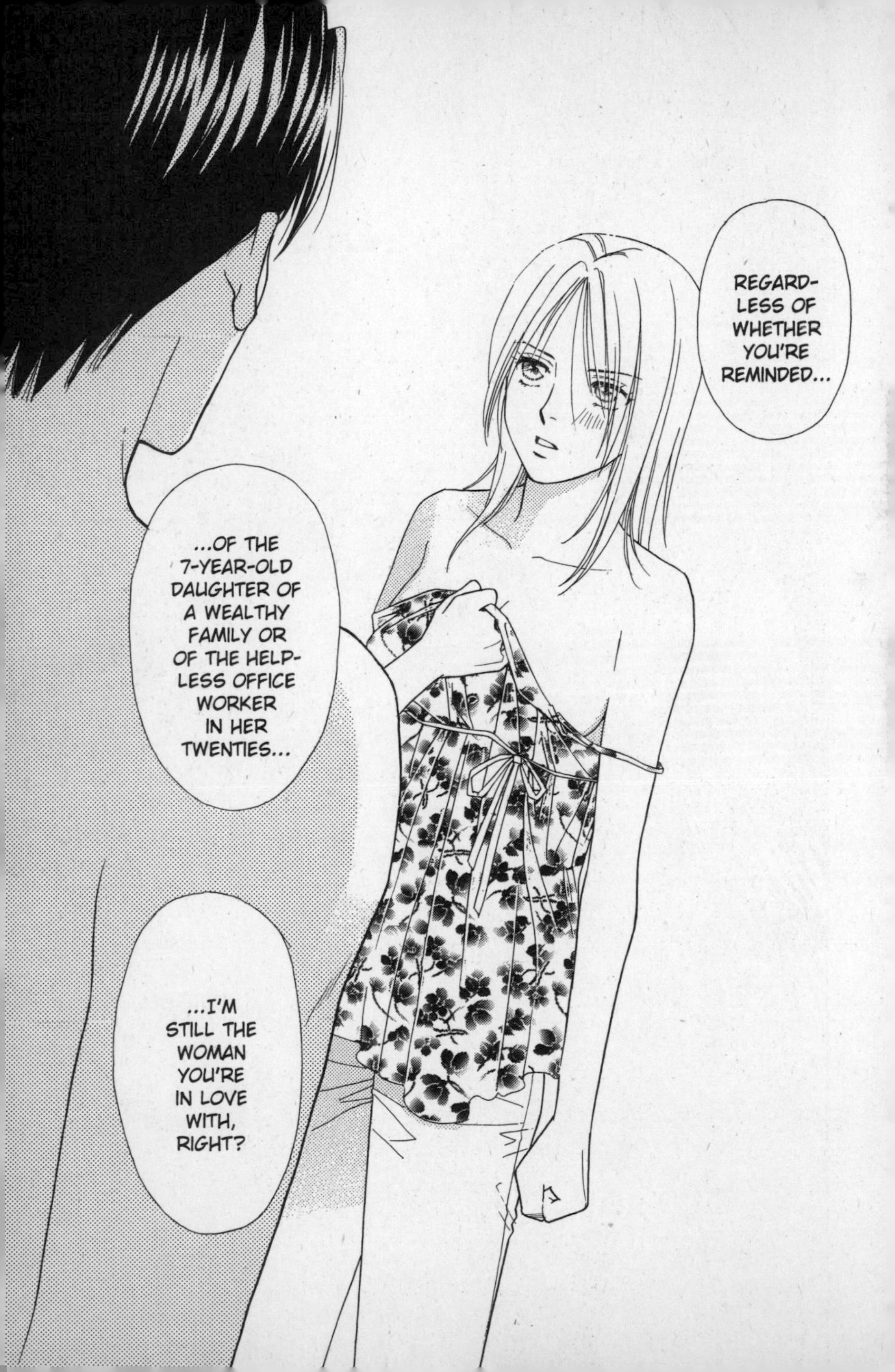
REGARD-LESS OF WHETHER YOU'RE REMINDED...
...OF THE 7-YEAR-OLD DAUGHTER OF A WEALTHY FAMILY OR OF THE HELP-LESS OFFICE WORKER IN HER TWENTIES...
...I'M STILL THE WOMAN YOU'RE IN LOVE WITH, RIGHT?

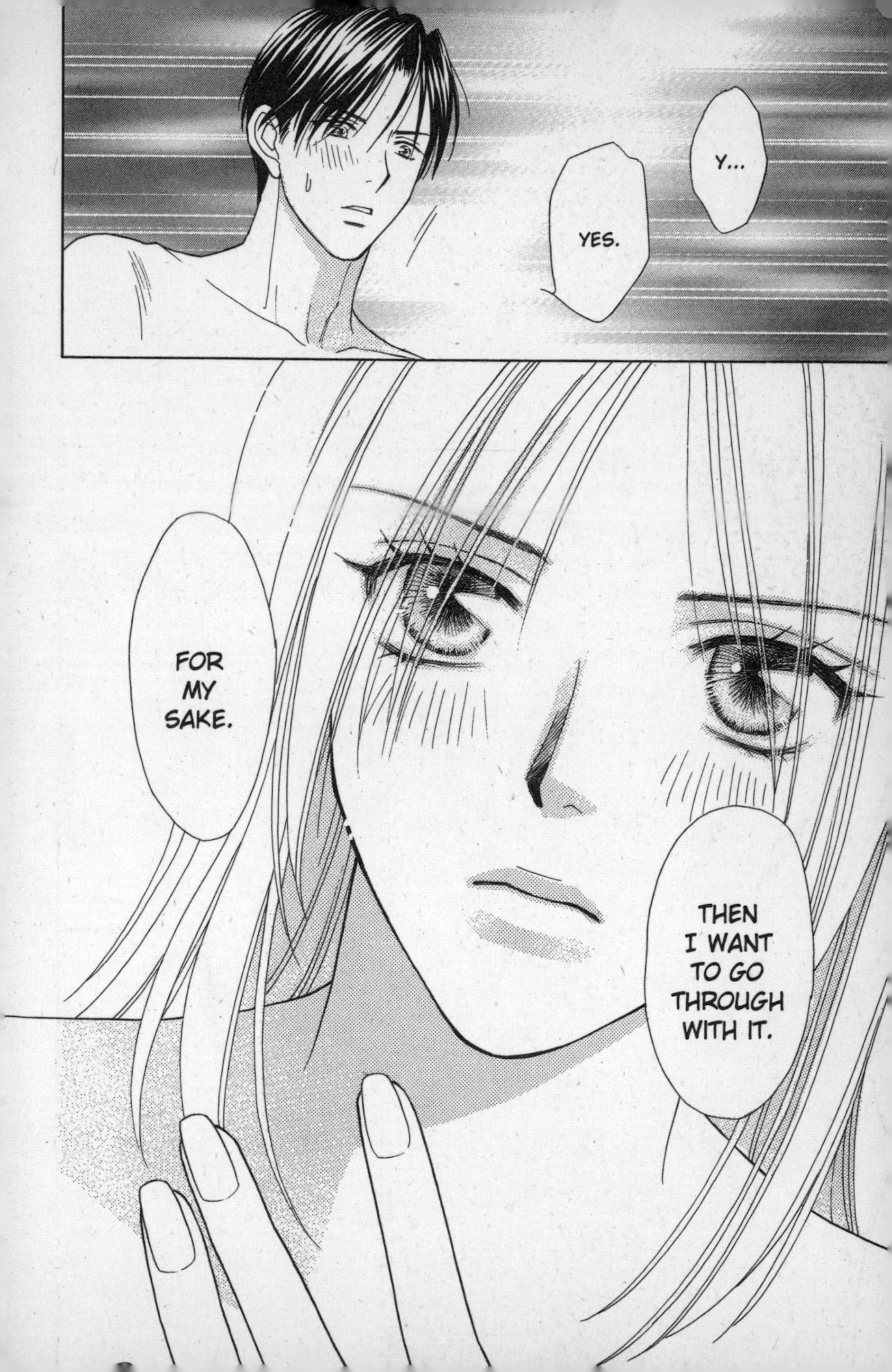
Y...
YES.
THEN I WANT TO GO THROUGH WITH IT.
FOR MY SAKE.

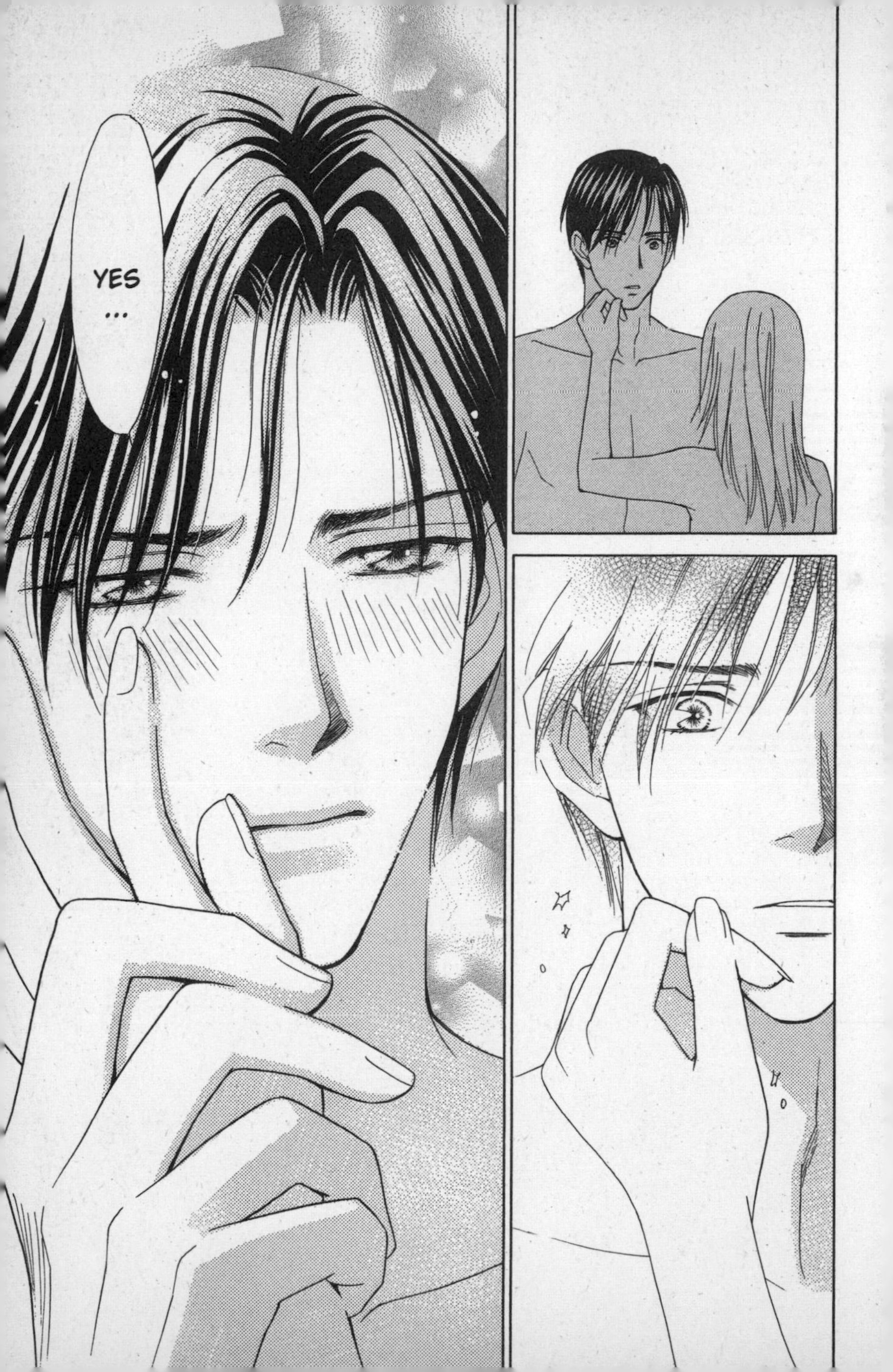
YES
...

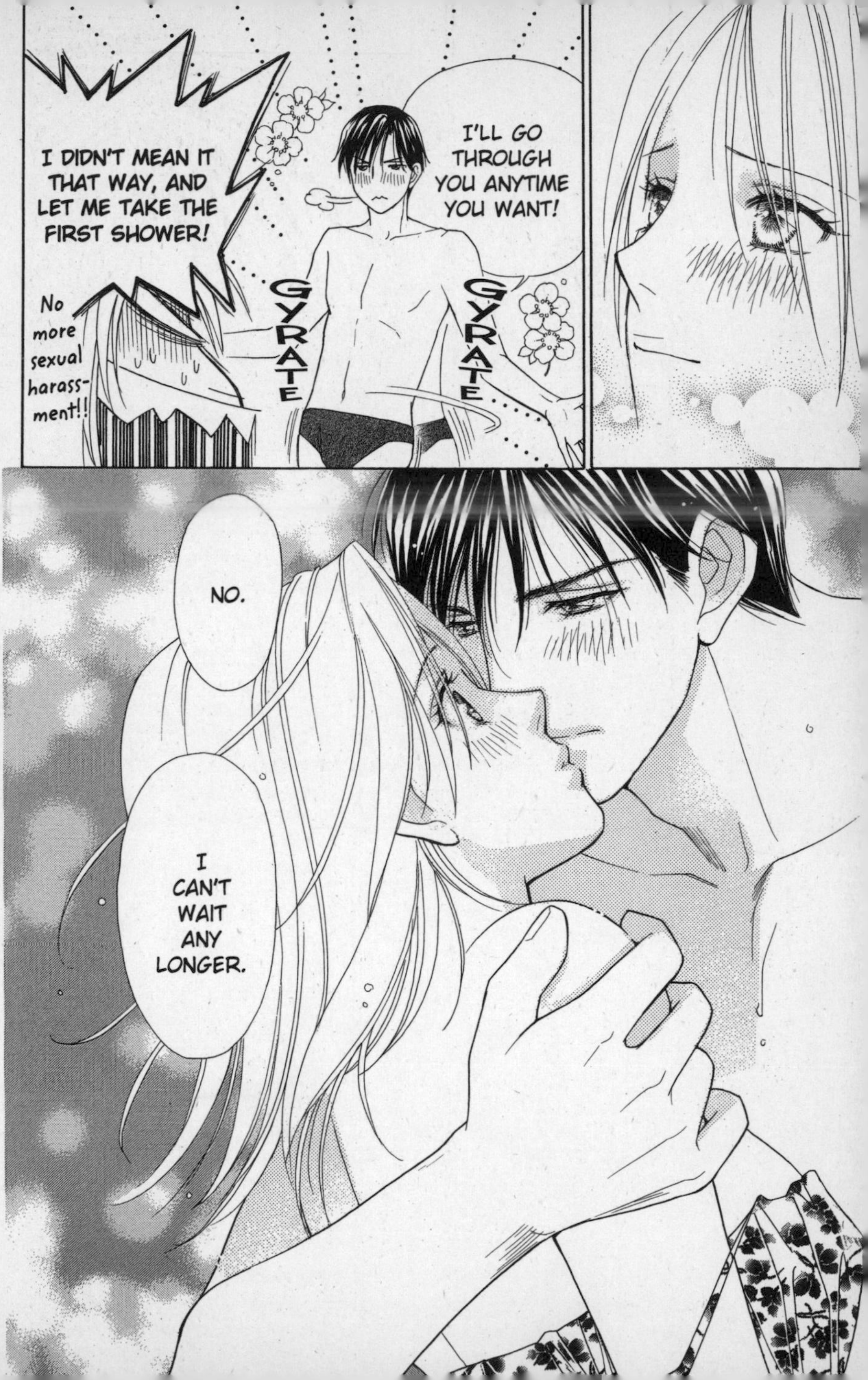

I'LL GO THROUGH YOU ANYTIME YOU WANT!
I DIDN'T MEAN IT THAT WAY, AND LET ME TAKE THE FIRST SHOWER!
GYRATE
GYRATE
No more sexual harassment!!
NO.
I CAN'T WAIT ANY LONGER.

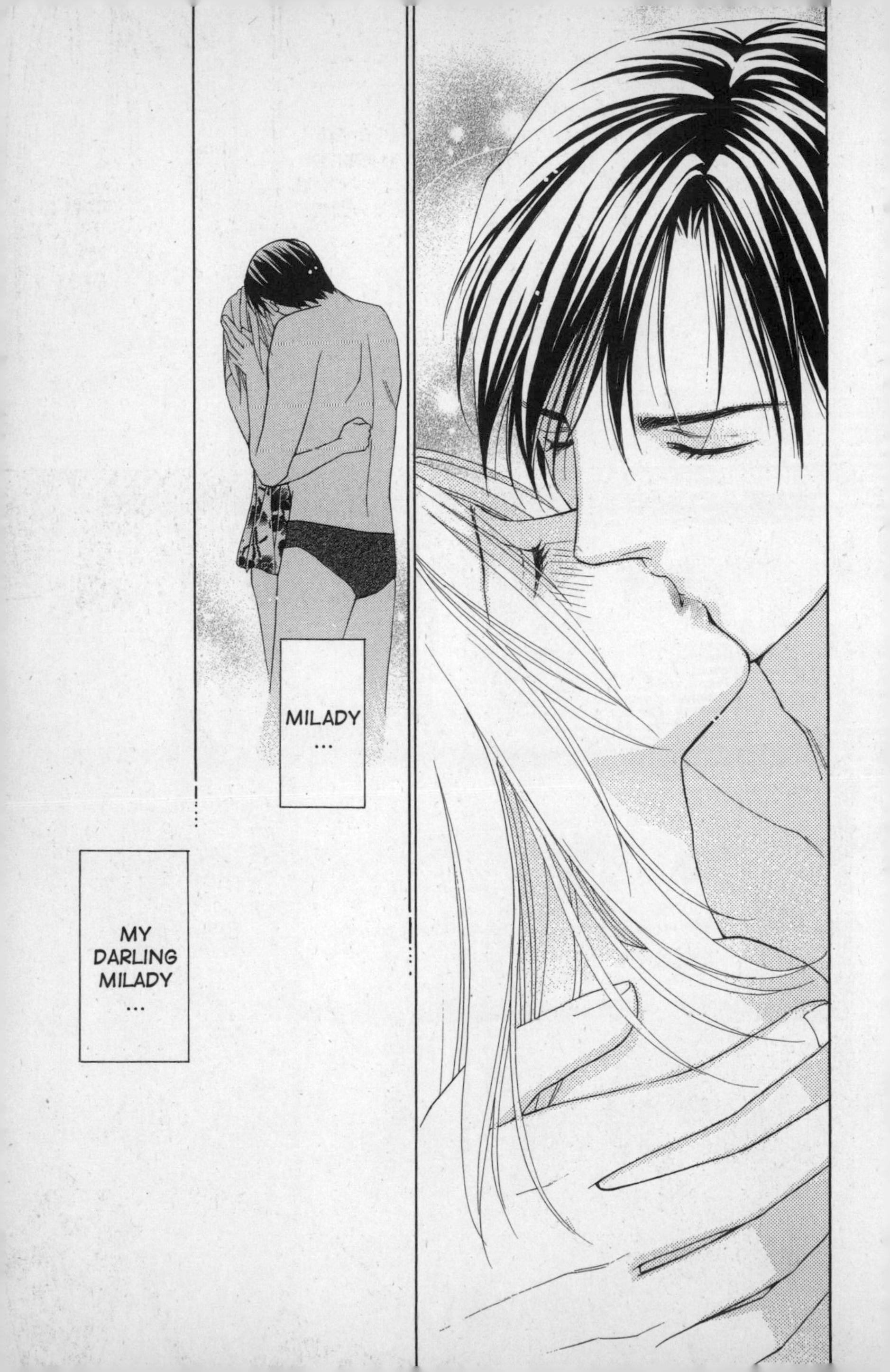
MILADY ...
MY DARLING MILADY ...

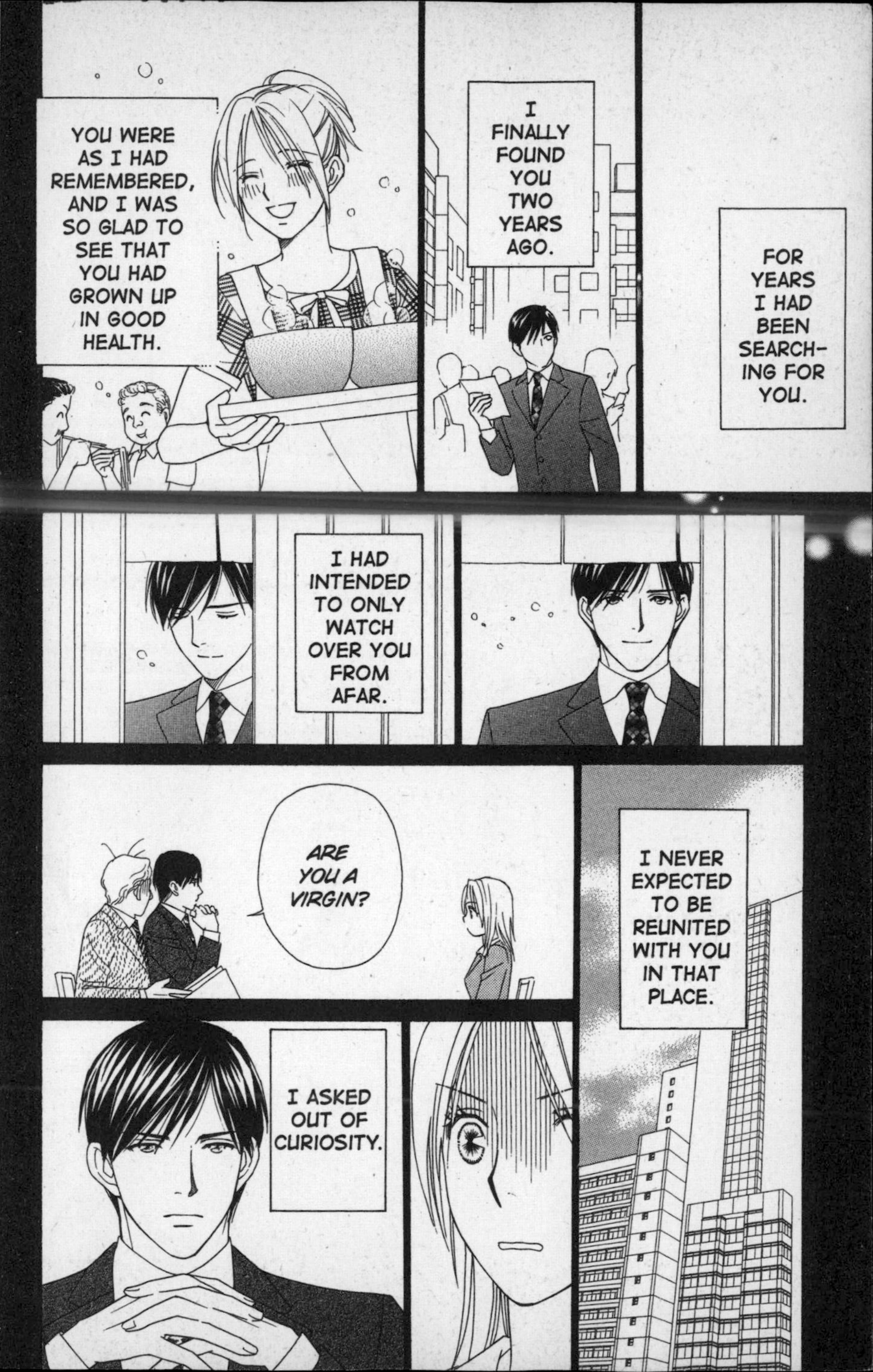
FOR YEARS I HAD BEEN SEARCHING FOR YOU.
I FINALLY FOUND YOU TWO YEARS AGO.
YOU WERE AS I HAD REMEMBERED, AND I WAS SO GLAD TO SEE THAT YOU HAD GROWN UP IN GOOD HEALTH.
I HAD INTENDED TO ONLY WATCH OVER YOU FROM AFAR.
I NEVER EXPECTED TO BE REUNITED WITH YOU IN THAT PLACE.
ARE YOU A VIRGIN?
I ASKED OUT OF CURIOSITY.

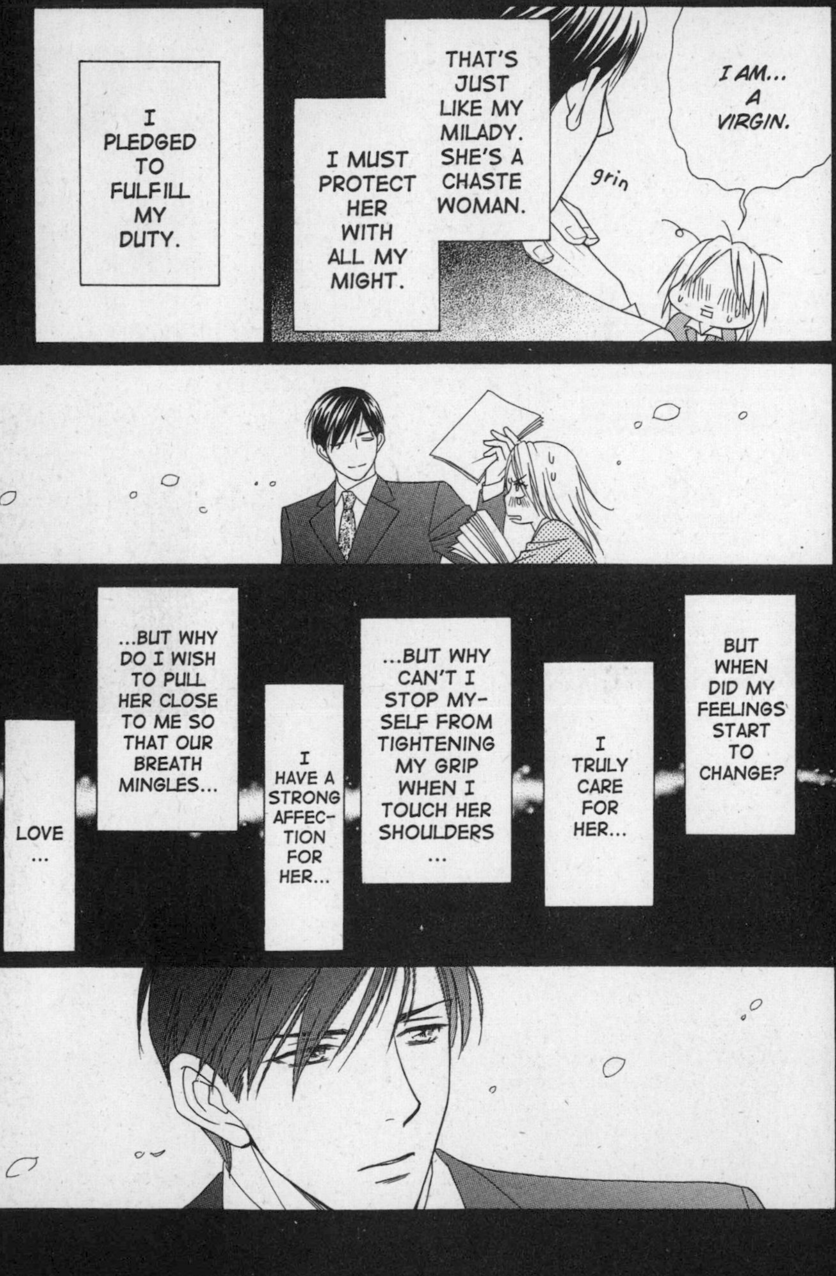
I AM... A VIRGIN.
grin
THAT'S JUST LIKE MY MILADY. SHE'S A CHASTE WOMAN.
I MUST PROTECT HER WITH ALL MY MIGHT.
I PLEDGED TO FULFILL MY DUTY.
BUT WHEN DID MY FEELINGS START TO CHANGE?
I TRULY CARE FOR HER...
...BUT WHY CAN'T I STOP MY-SELF FROM TIGHTENING MY GRIP WHEN I TOUCH HER SHOULDERS...
I HAVE A STRONG AFFEC-TION FOR HER...
...BUT WHY DO I WISH TO PULL HER CLOSE TO ME SO THAT OUR BREATH MINGLES...
LOVE...

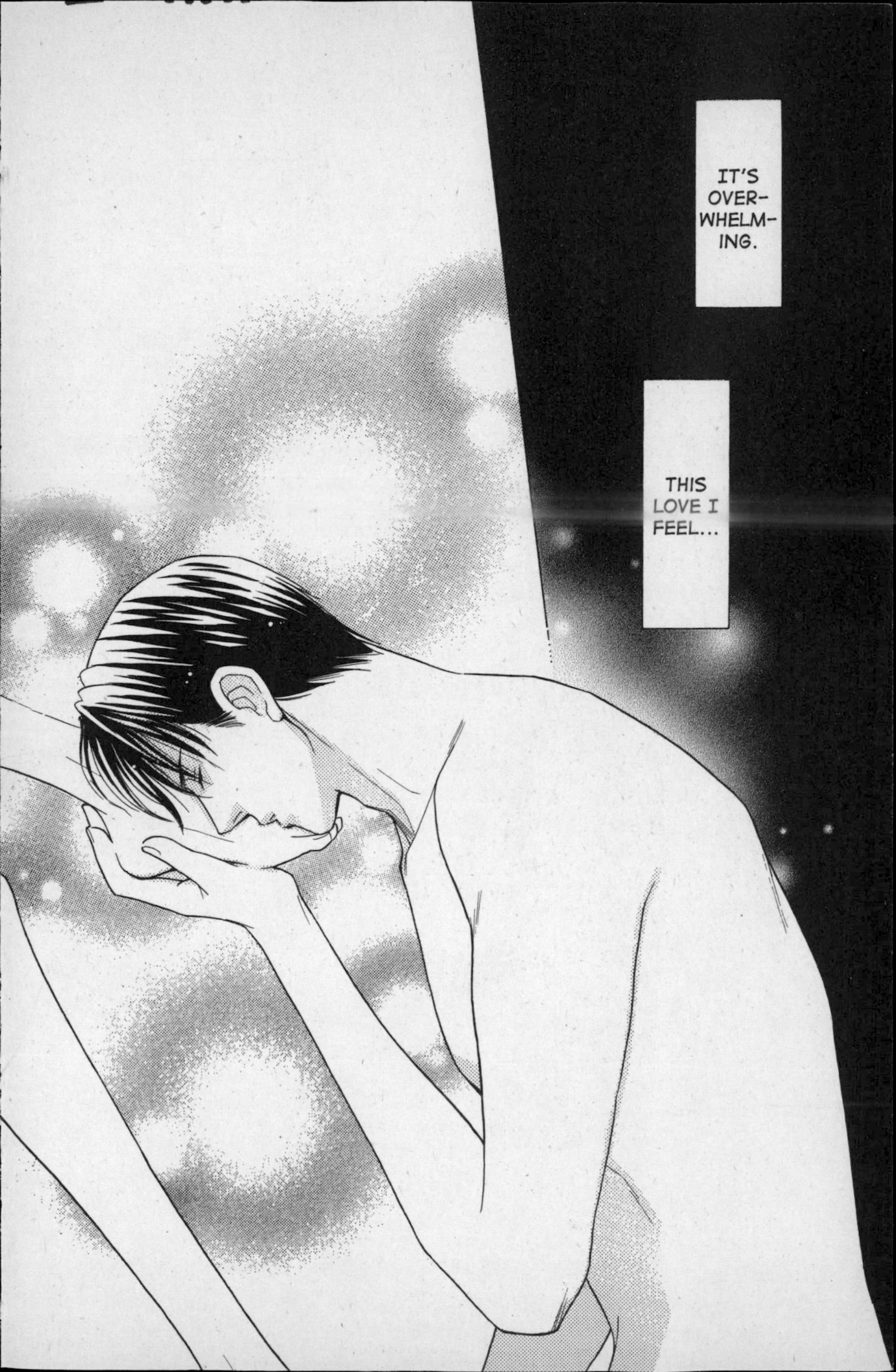
IT'S OVER-WHELMING.
THIS LOVE I FEEL...

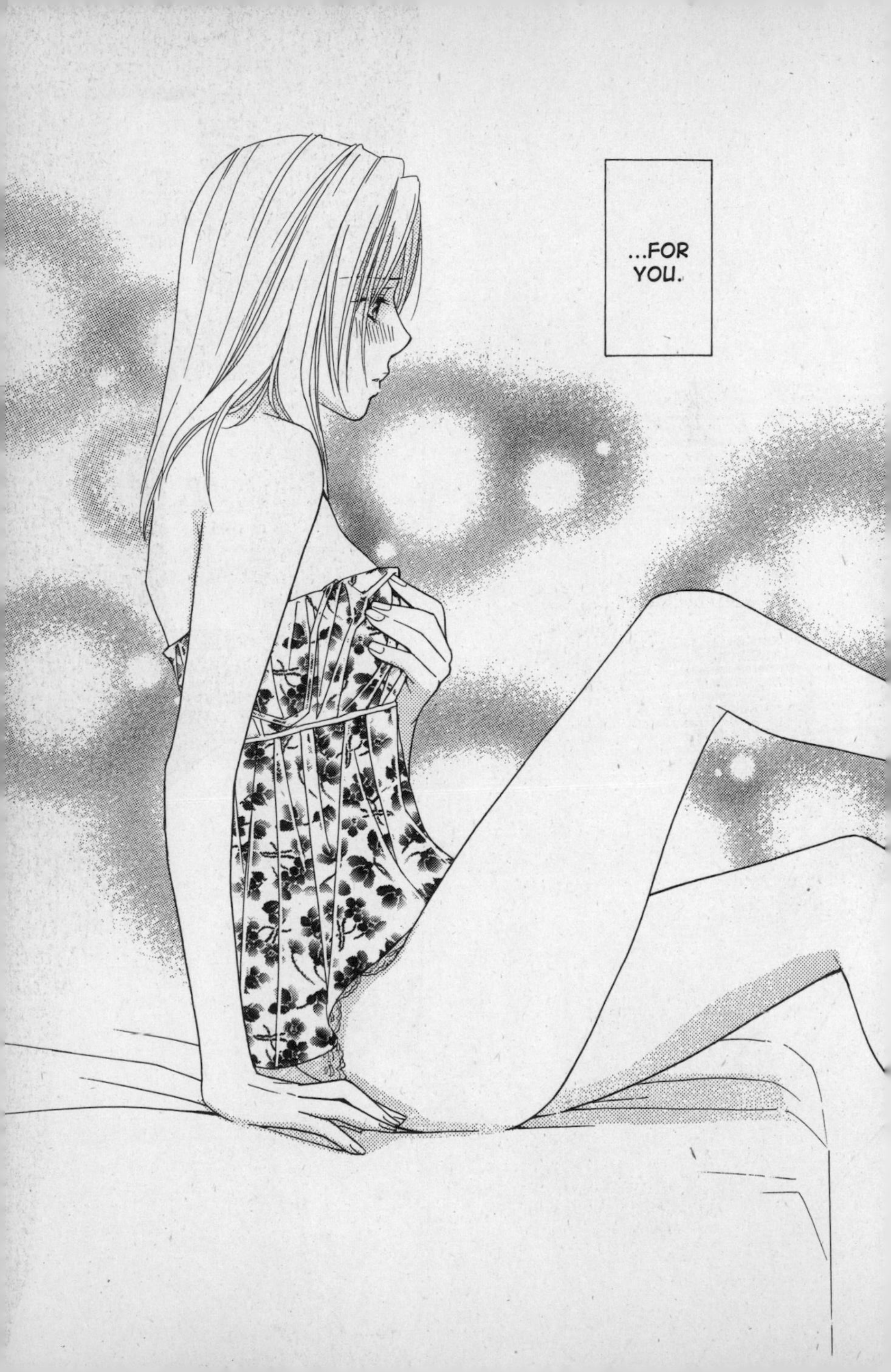
...FOR YOU.

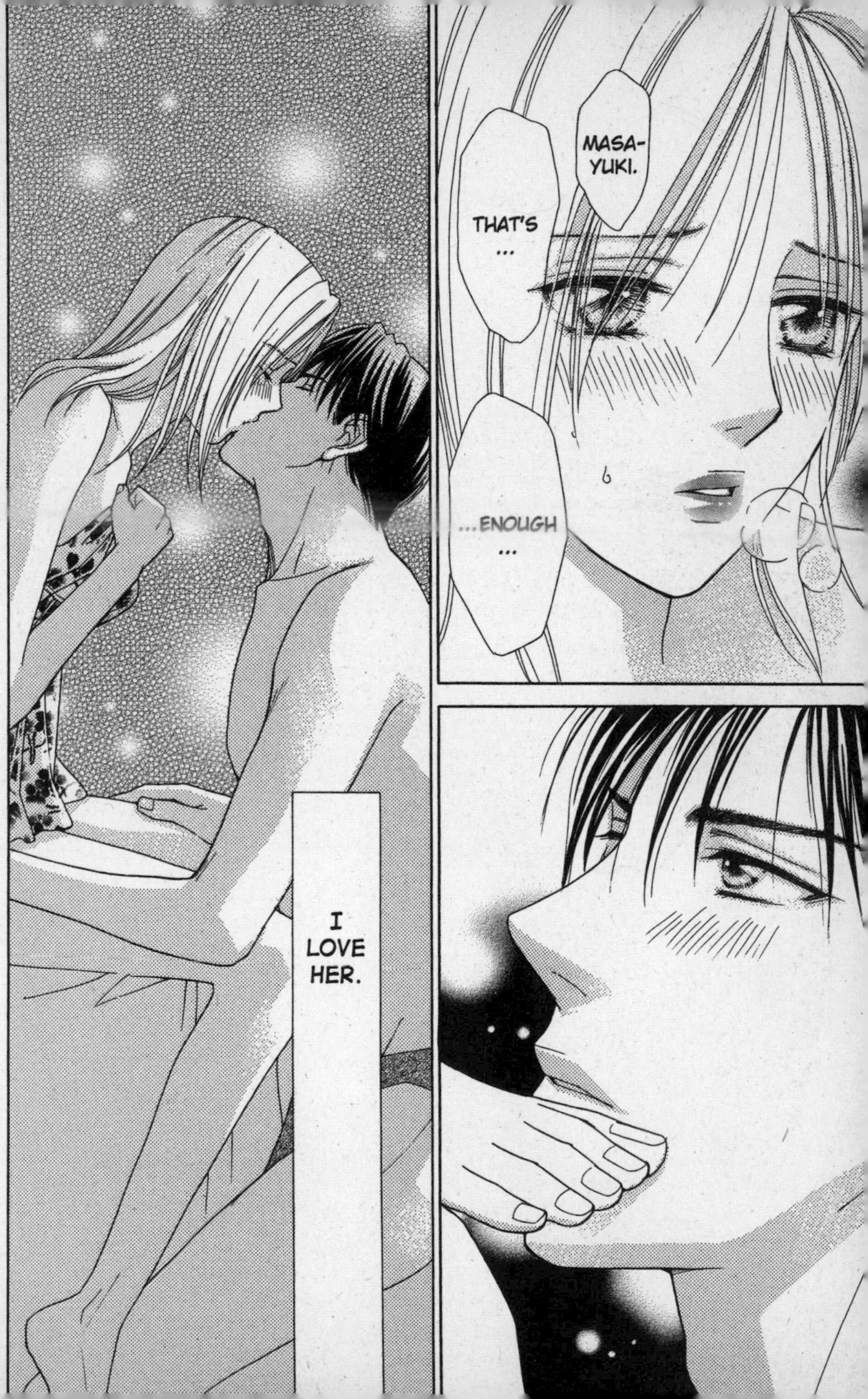
MASA-YUKI.
THAT'S ...
...ENOUGH ...
I LOVE HER.

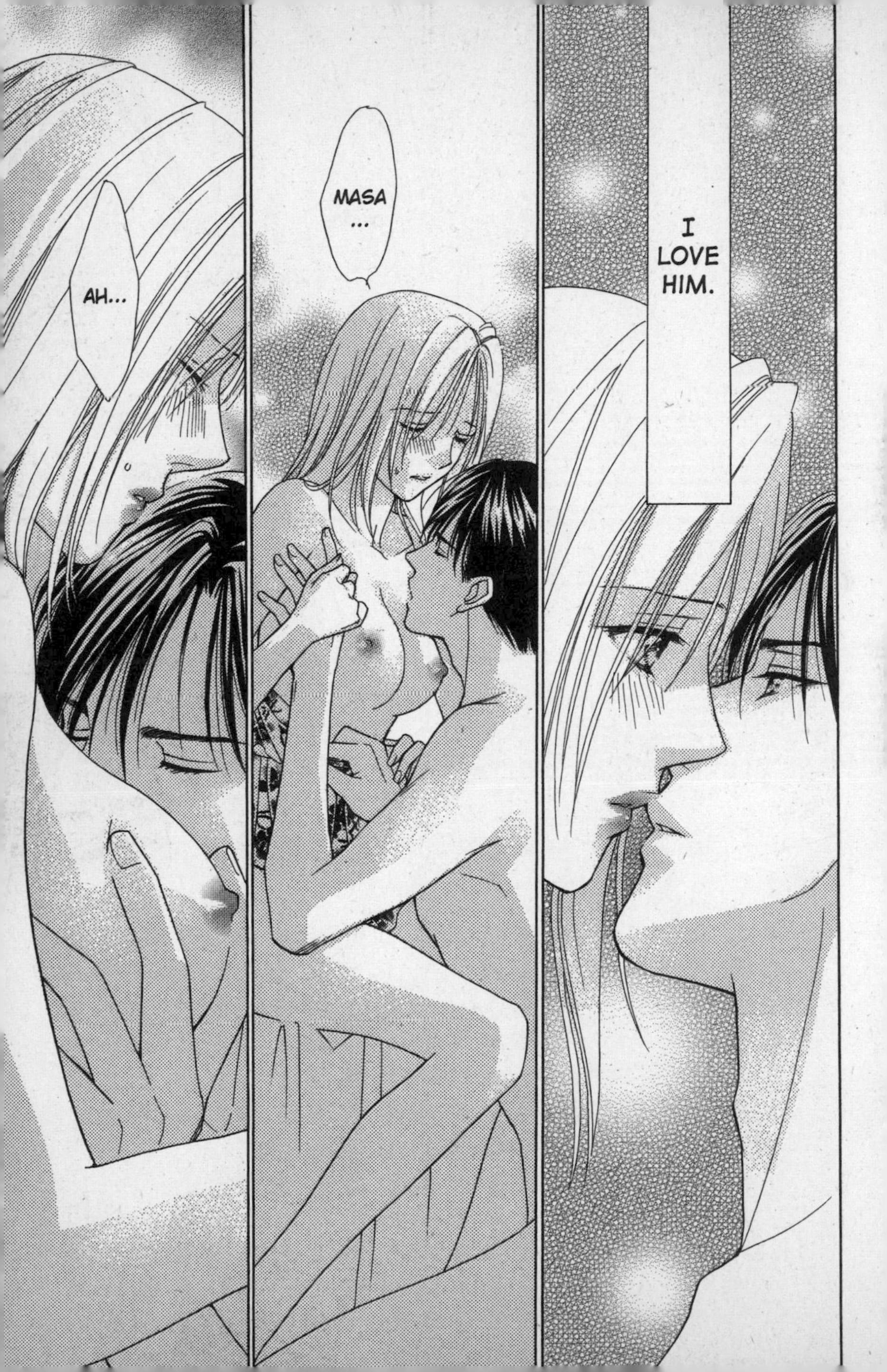
I LOVE HIM.
MASA ...
AH...

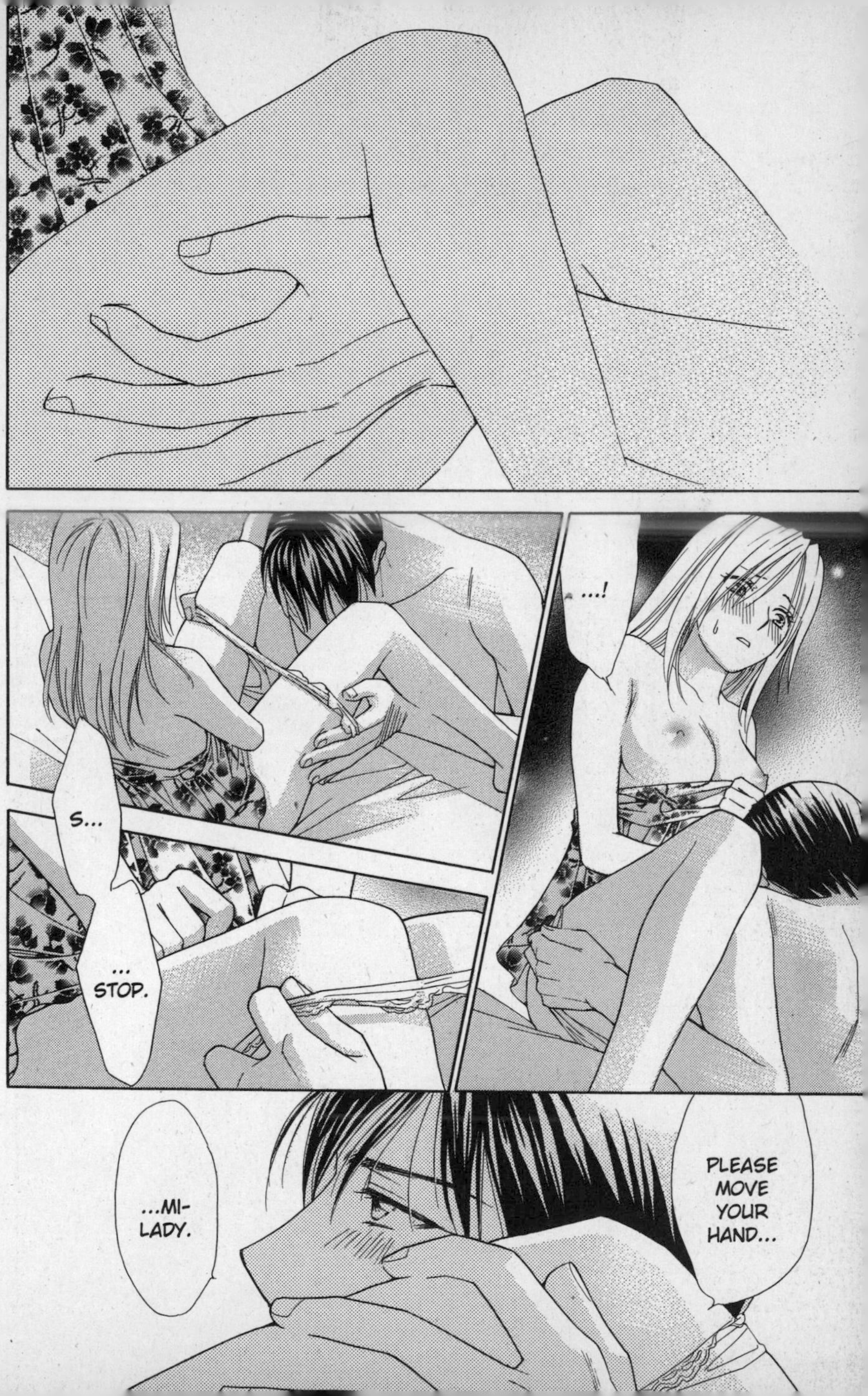
...!
S...
...STOP.
PLEASE MOVE YOUR HAND...
...MI-LADY.

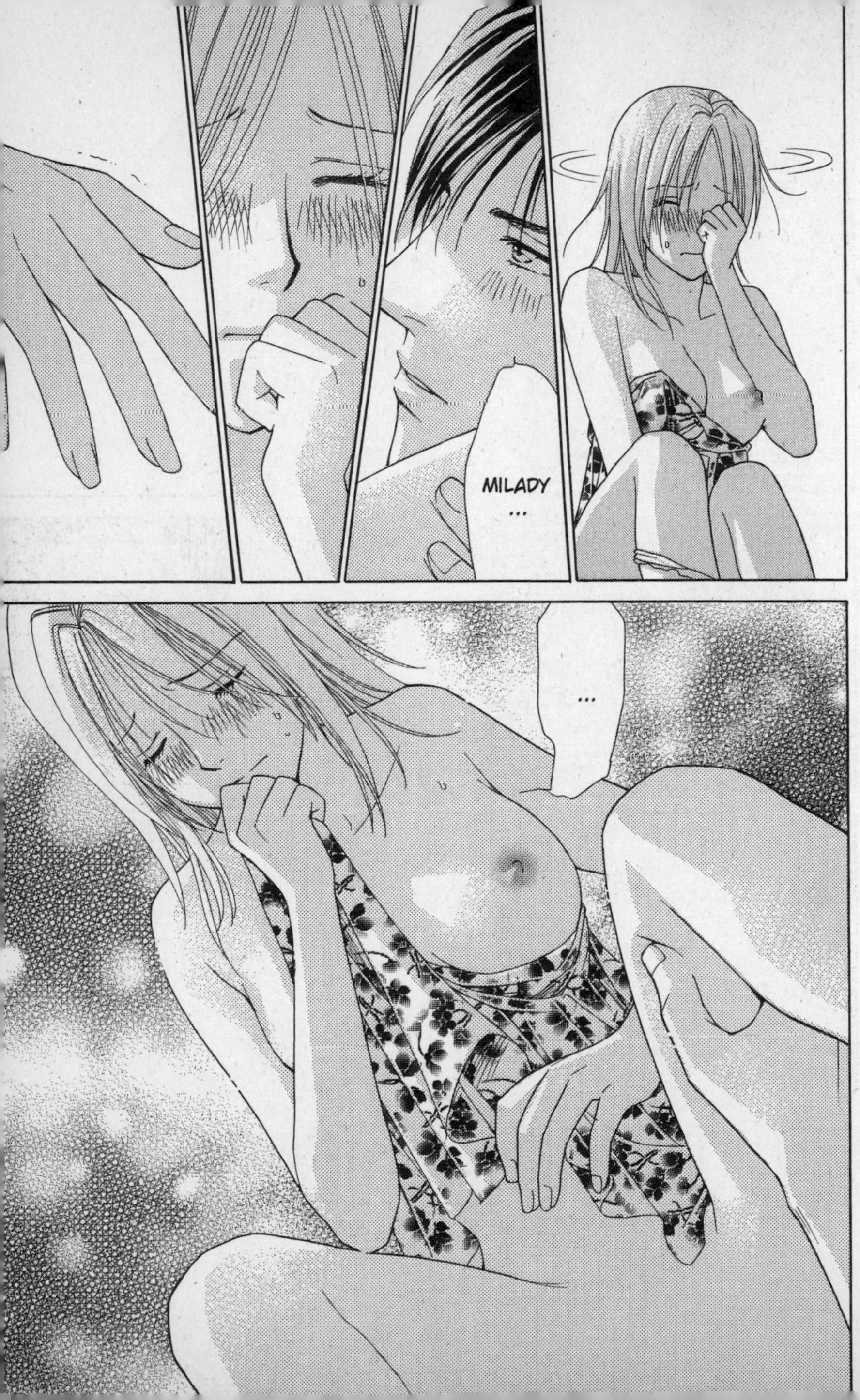
MILADY
...
...

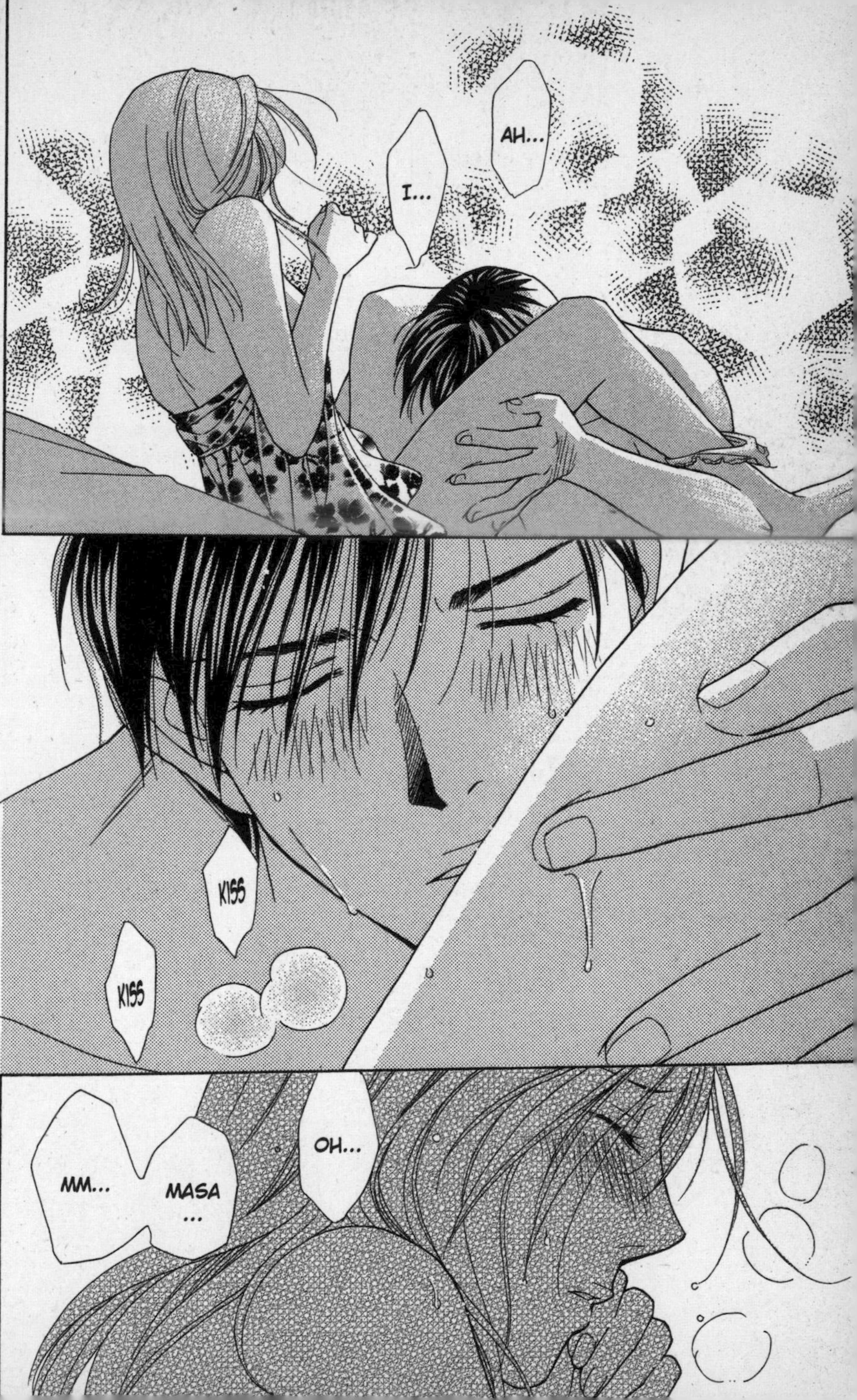
AH...
I...
KISS
KISS
OH...
MASA ...
MM...

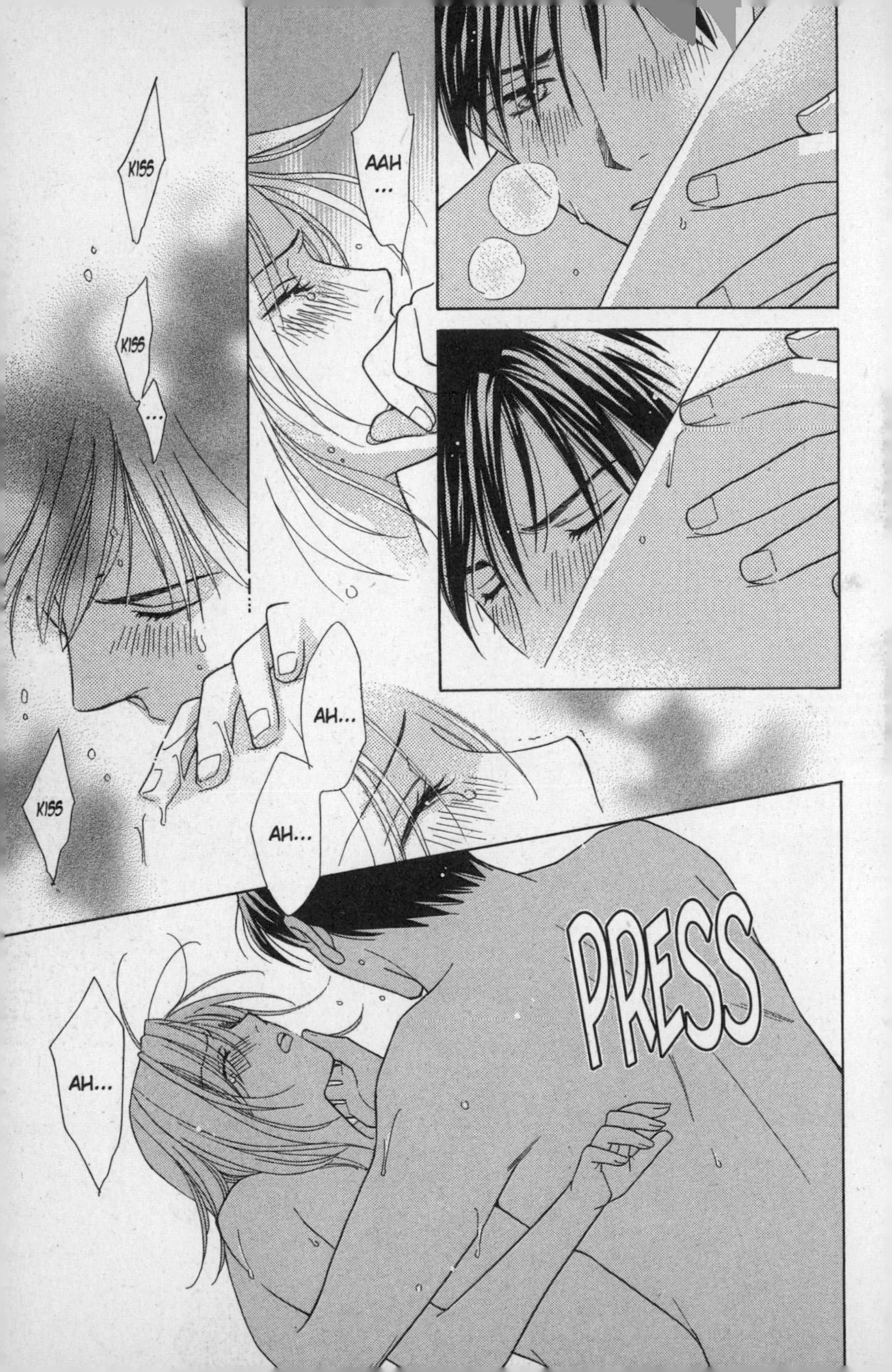
AAH
...
KISS
KISS
...
AH...
AH...
KISS
PRESS
AH...

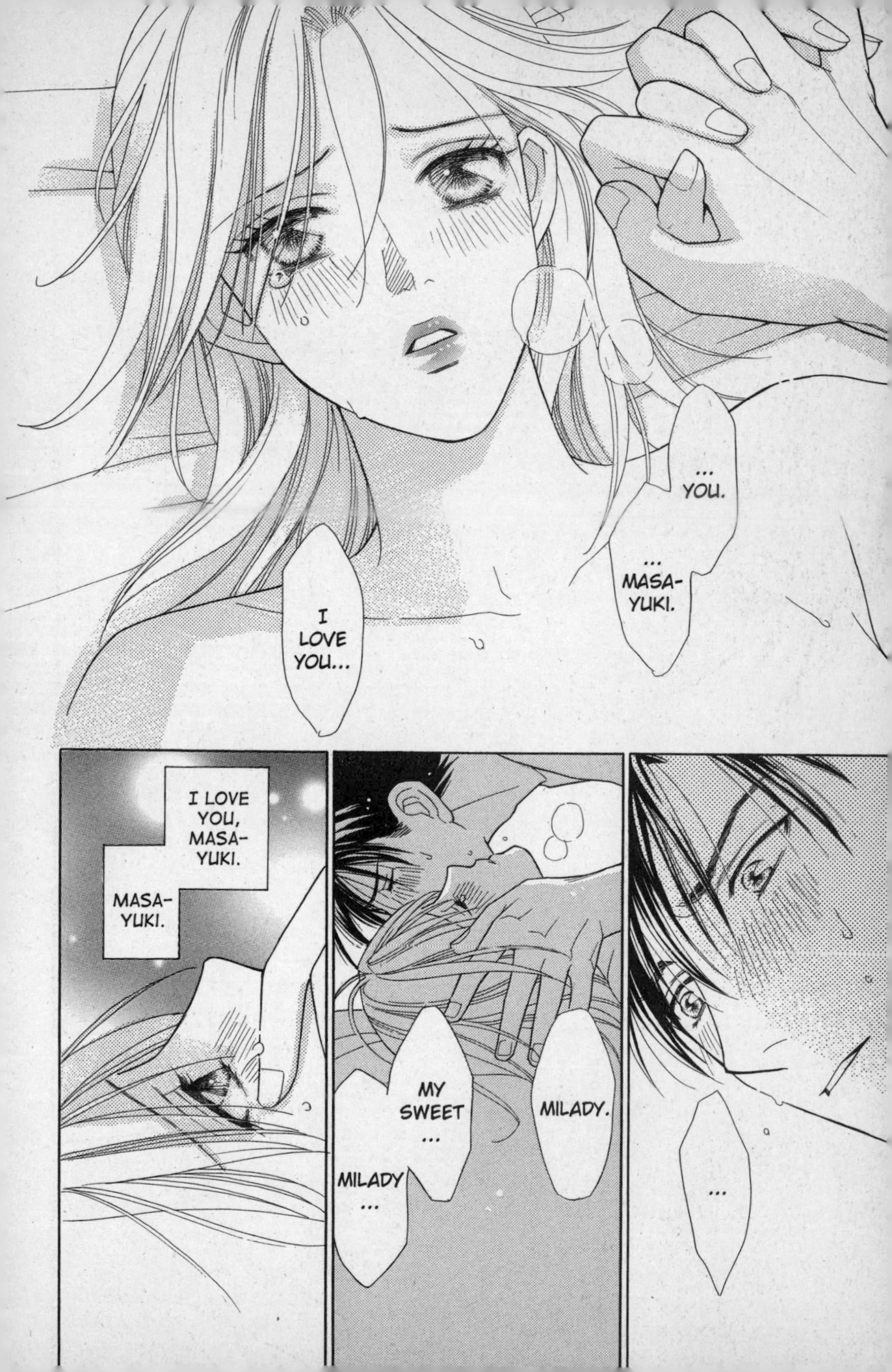
... YOU.
... MASA-YUKI.
I LOVE YOU...
...
MILADY.
MY SWEET ...
MILADY ...
I LOVE YOU, MASA-YUKI.
MASA-YUKI.

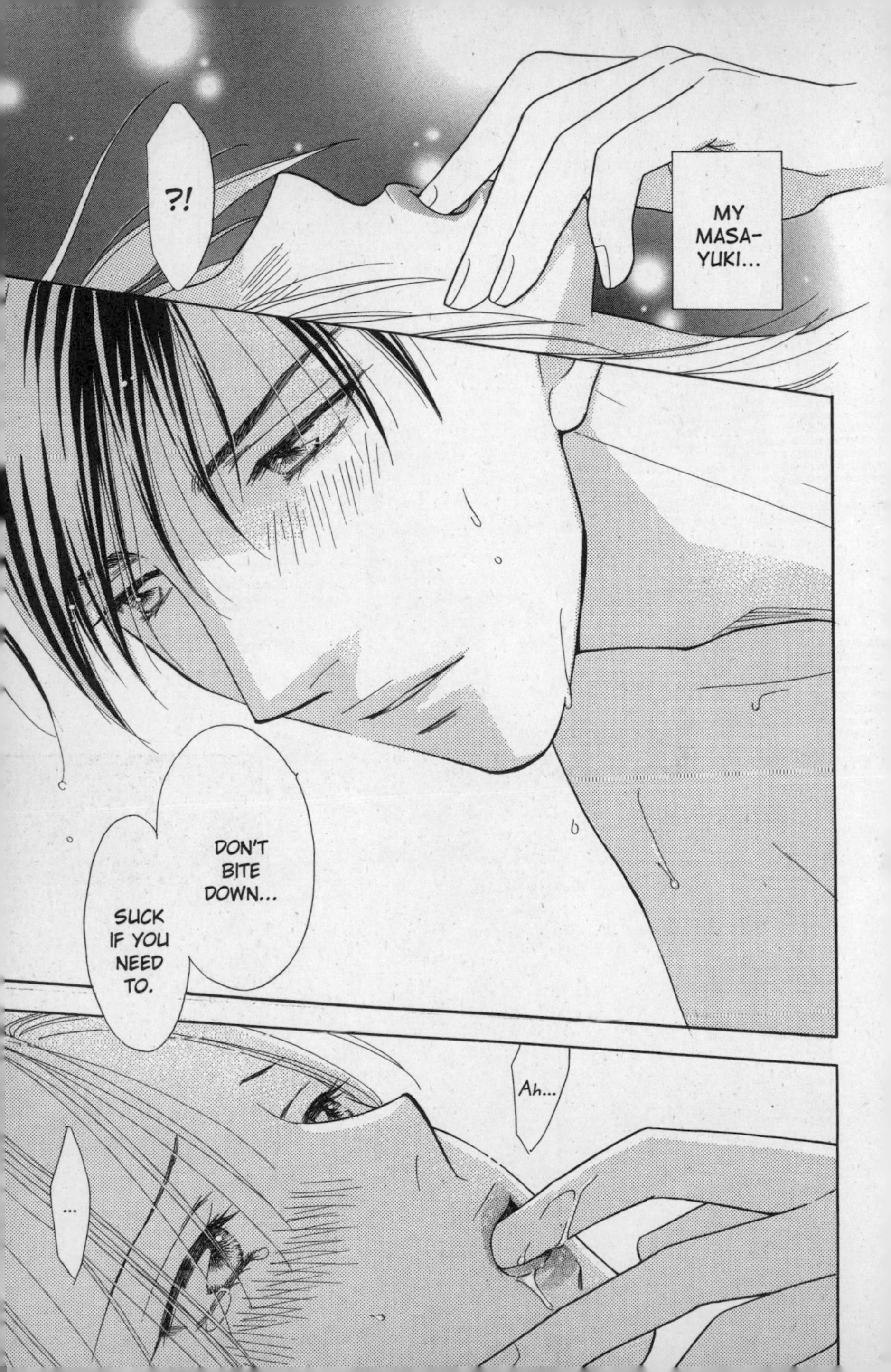
MY MASA-YUKI...
?!
DON'T BITE DOWN...
SUCK IF YOU NEED TO.
Ah...
...

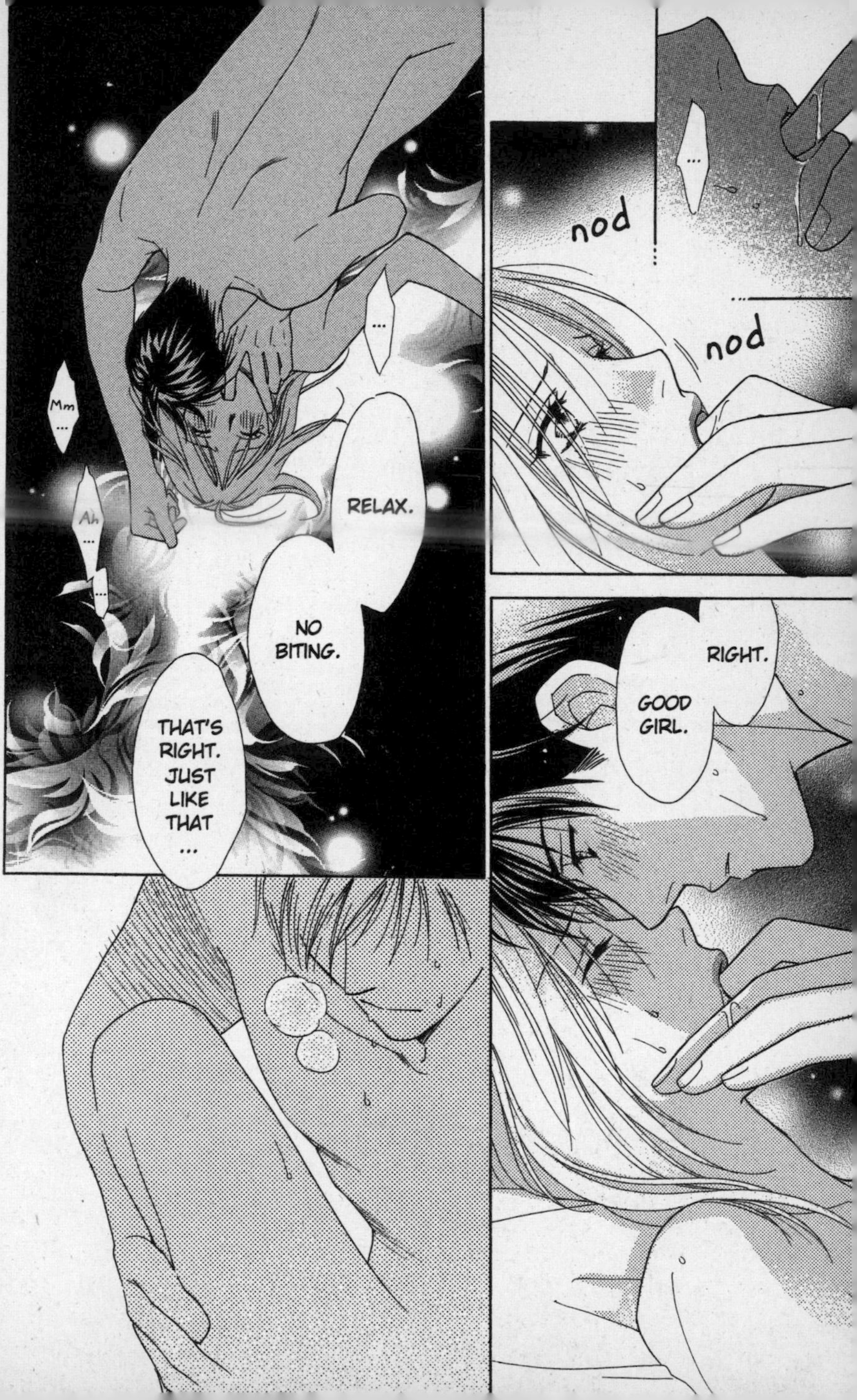
...
nod
...
nod
RIGHT.
GOOD GIRL.
...
Mm ...
Ah ...
...
RELAX.
NO BITING.
THAT'S RIGHT. JUST LIKE THAT ...

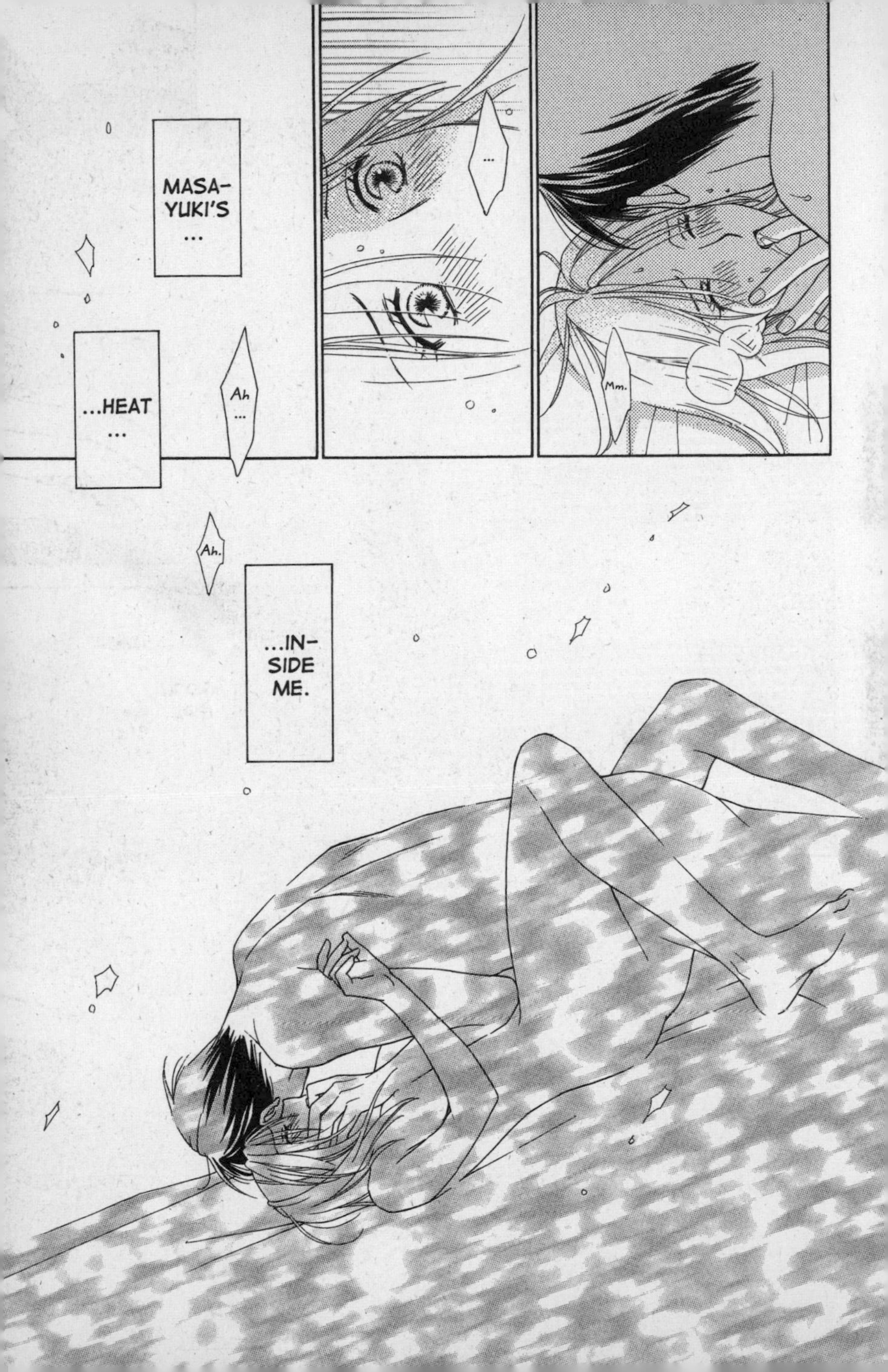
Mm.
...
MASA-YUKI'S ...
Ah ...
...HEAT ...
Ah.
...IN-SIDE ME.

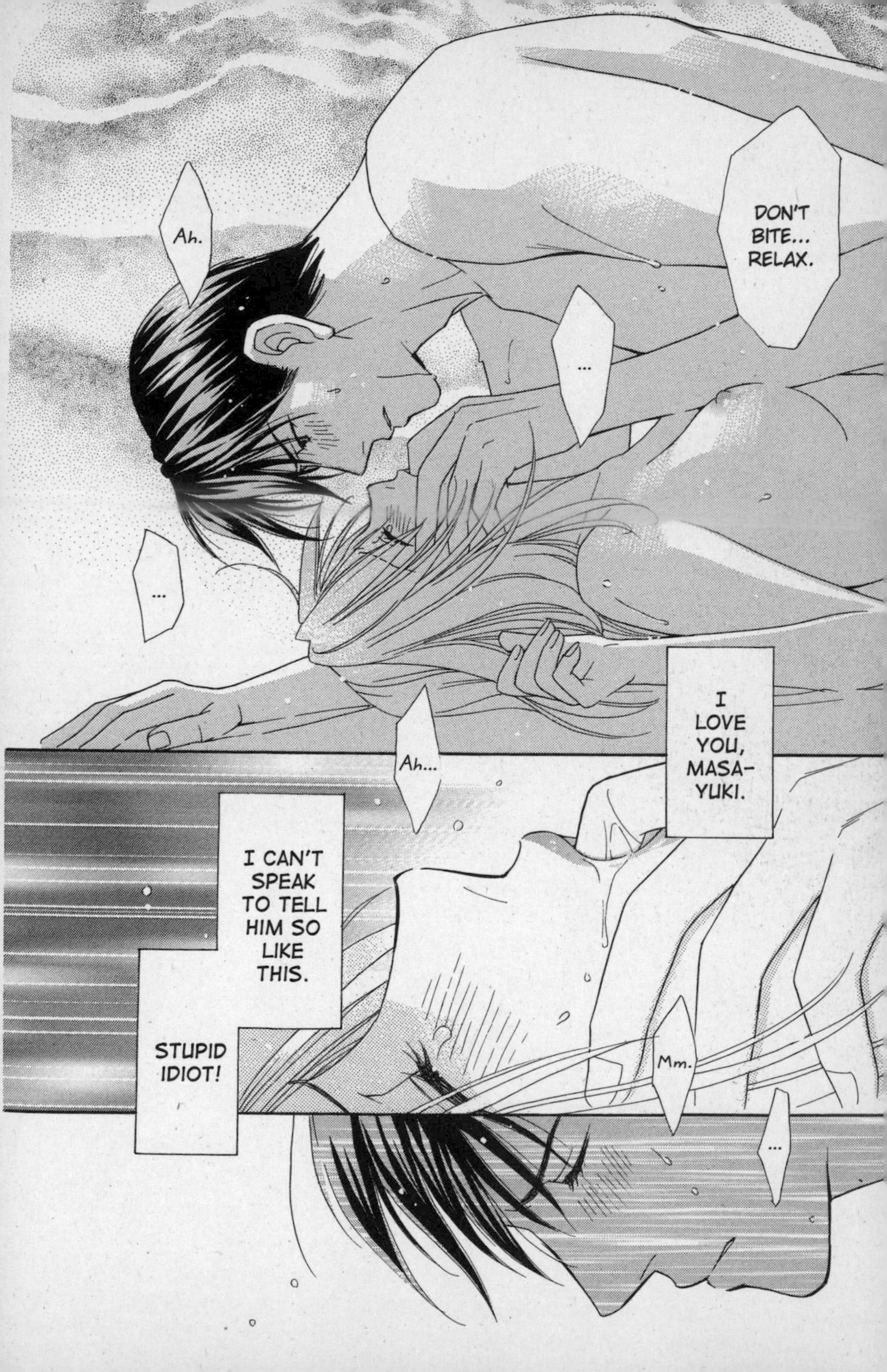
DON'T BITE... RELAX.
...
Ah.
...
I LOVE YOU, MASA-YUKI.
Ah...
Mm.
...
I CAN'T SPEAK TO TELL HIM SO LIKE THIS.
STUPID IDIOT!

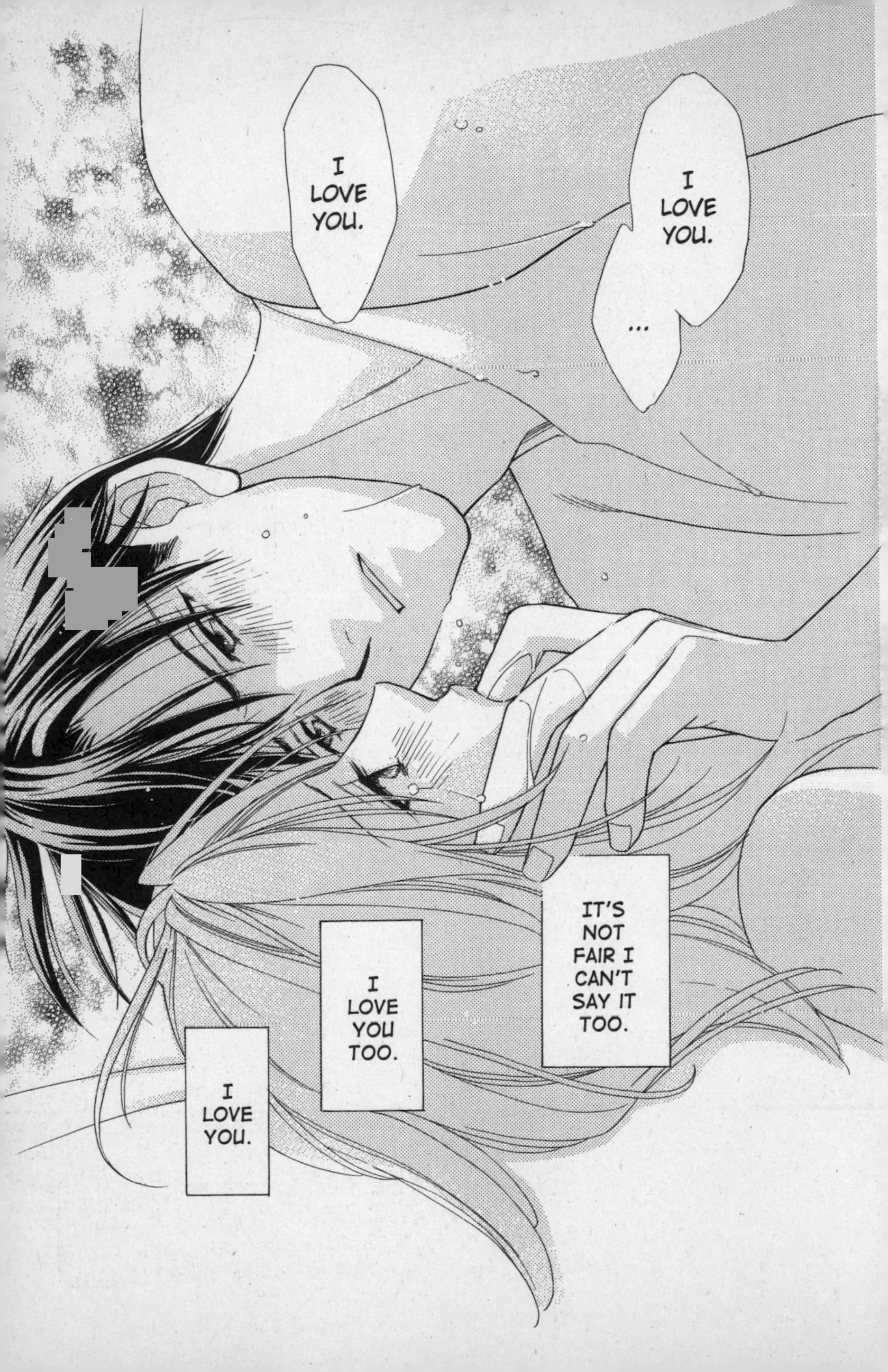
I LOVE YOU. ...
I LOVE YOU.
IT'S NOT FAIR I CAN'T SAY IT TOO.
I LOVE YOU TOO.
I LOVE YOU.

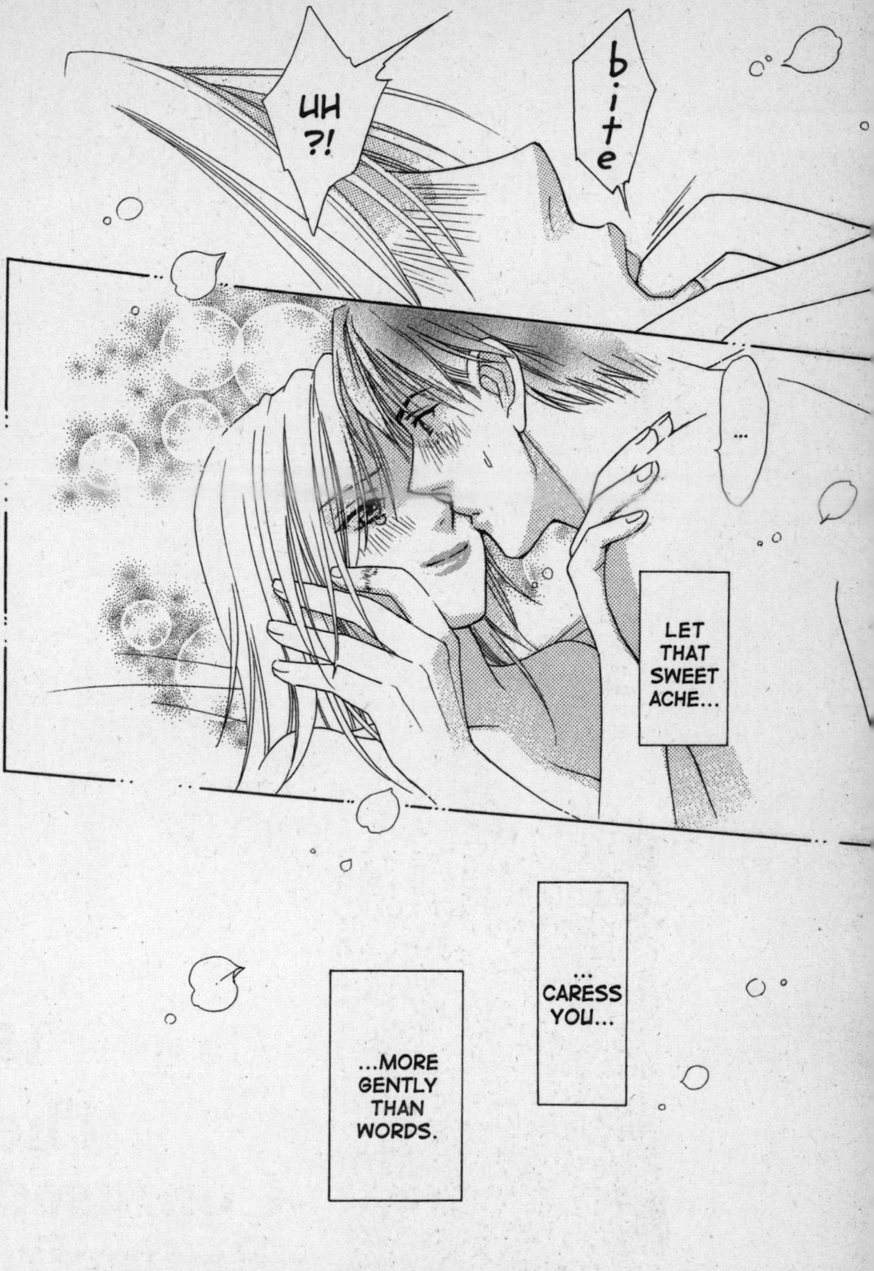
bite
UH ?!
...
LET THAT SWEET ACHE...
... CARESS YOU...
...MORE GENTLY THAN WORDS.

Chapter 14: My Beloved/End

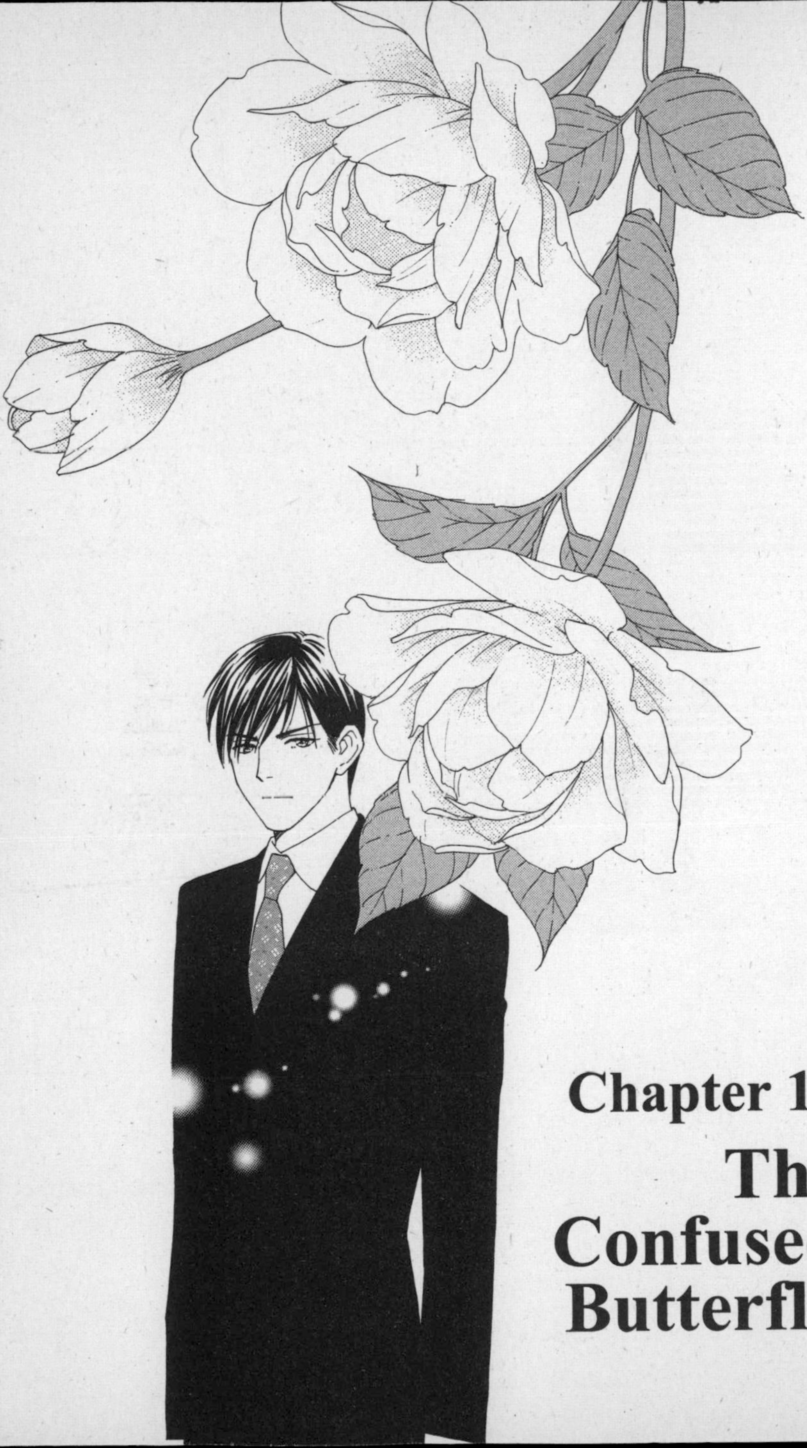

Chapter 15
The Confused Butterfly

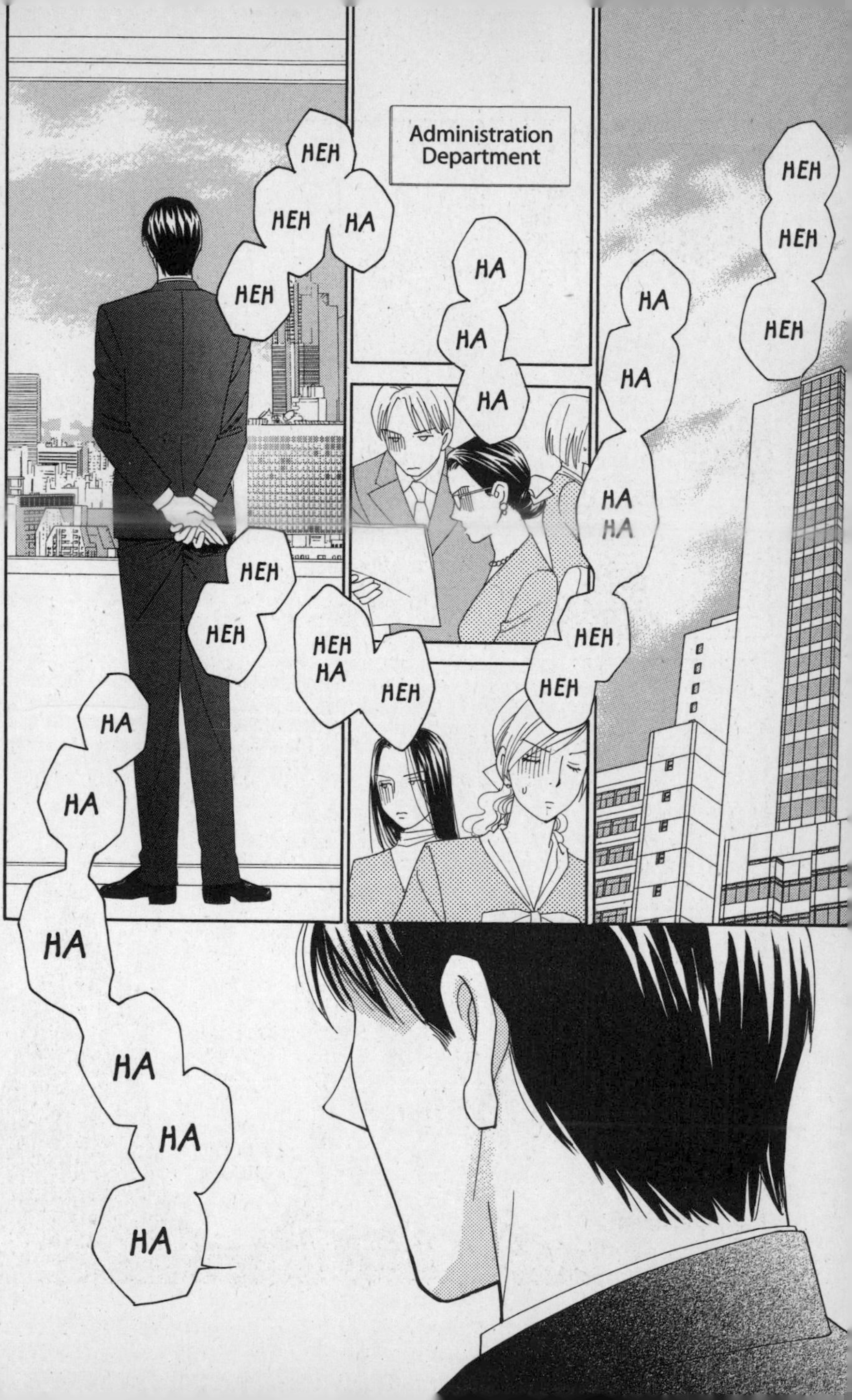
HEH HEH HEH
HA HA HA HA HA HEH HEH
Administration Department
HA HA HA
HEH HEH HA HEH
HEH HEH
HEH HA HEH
HA HA HA HA HA HA

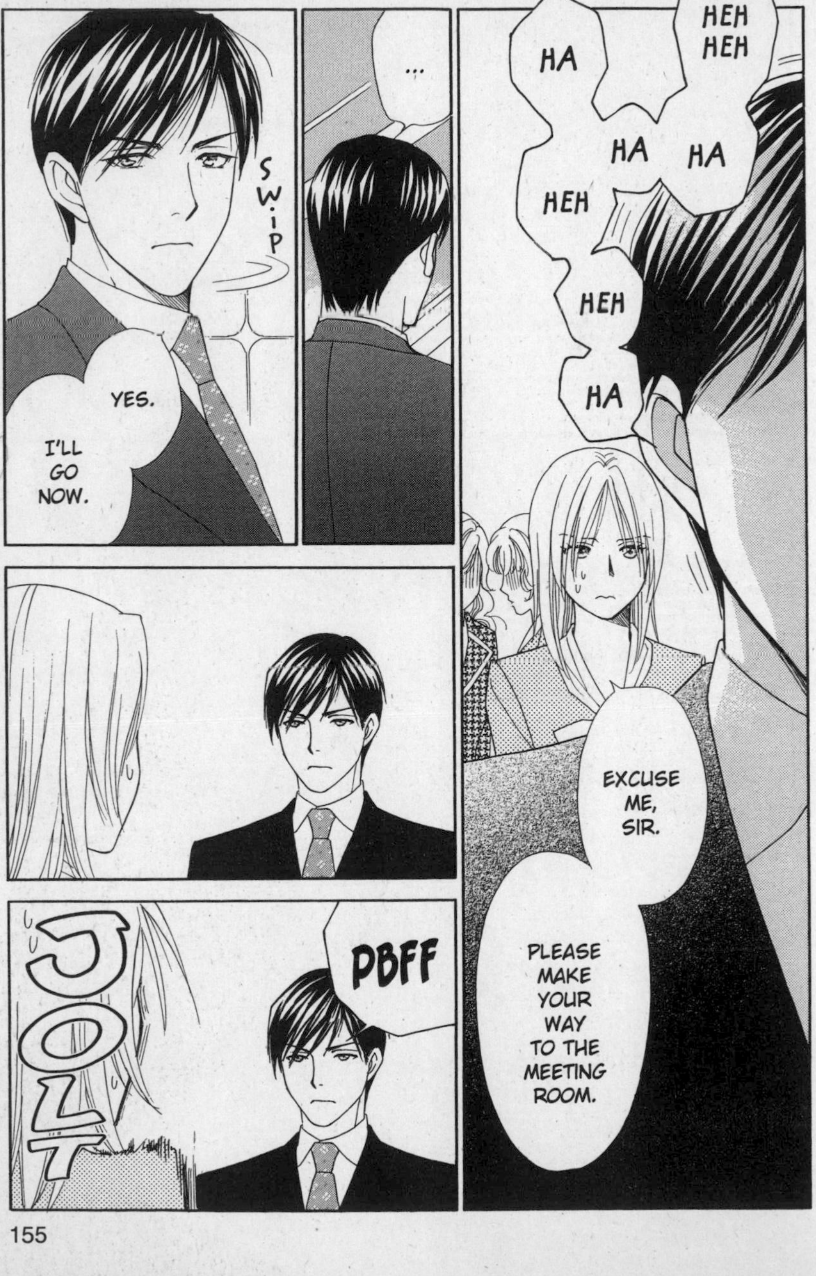
HEH HEH
HA
HA
HA
HEH
HEH
HA
EXCUSE ME, SIR.
PLEASE MAKE YOUR WAY TO THE MEETING ROOM.
...
SWIP
YES.
I'LL GO NOW.
PBFF
JOLT

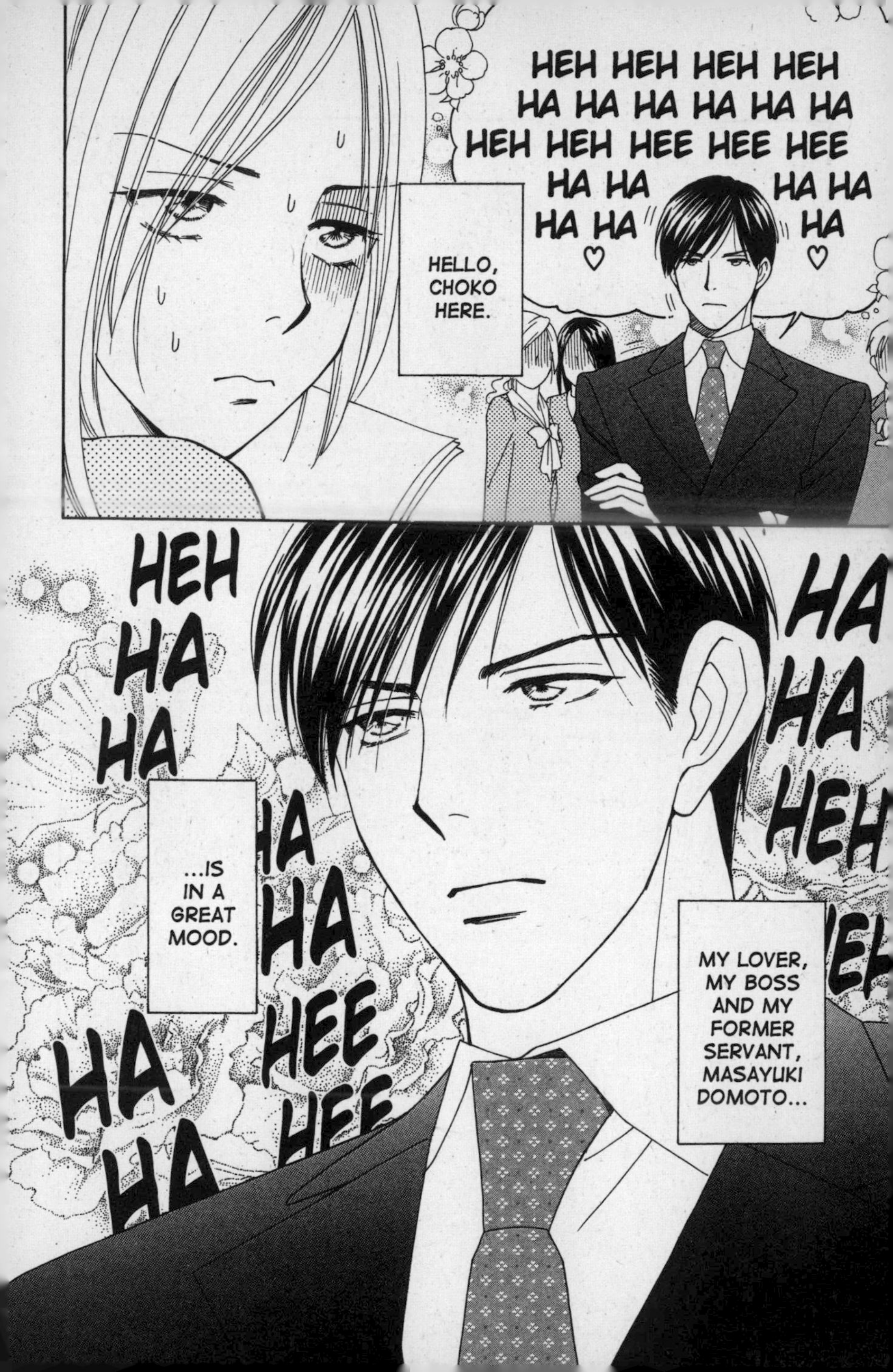
HEH HEH HEH HEH
HA HA HA HA HA HA
HEH HEH HEE HEE HEE
HA HA HA HA
HA HA HA
HELLO, CHOKO HERE.
HA HA HEH
MY LOVER, MY BOSS AND MY FORMER SERVANT, MASAYUKI DOMOTO...
...IS IN A GREAT MOOD.
HA HA HEE
HEH HA HA
HA HA

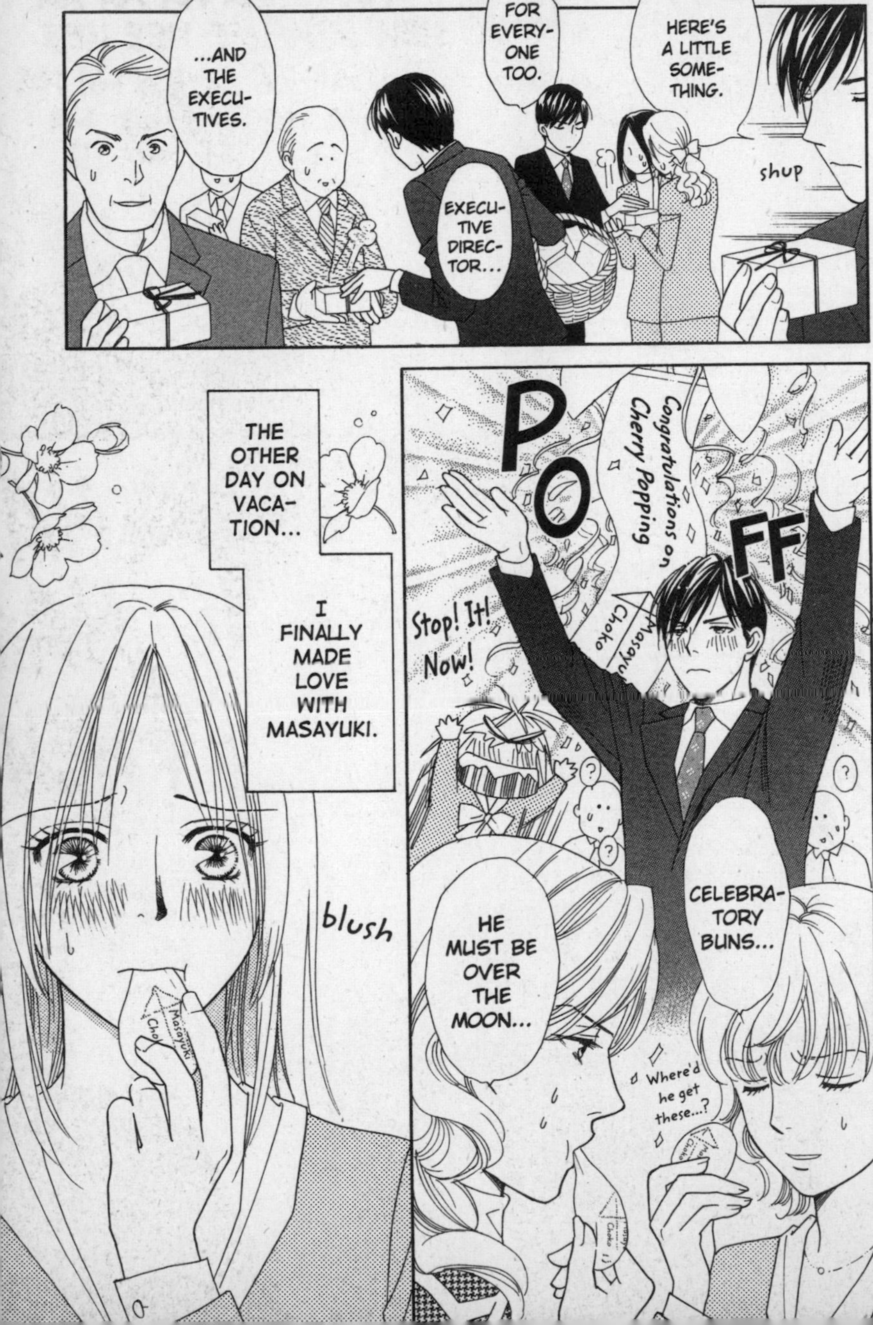
HERE'S A LITTLE SOME-THING.
shup
FOR EVERY-ONE TOO.
EXECU-TIVE DIREC-TOR...
...AND THE EXECU-TIVES.
POFF
Congratulations on Cherry Popping
Stop! It! Now!
CELEBRA-TORY BUNS...
HE MUST BE OVER THE MOON...
Where'd he get these...?
THE OTHER DAY ON VACA-TION...
I FINALLY MADE LOVE WITH MASAYUKI.
blush

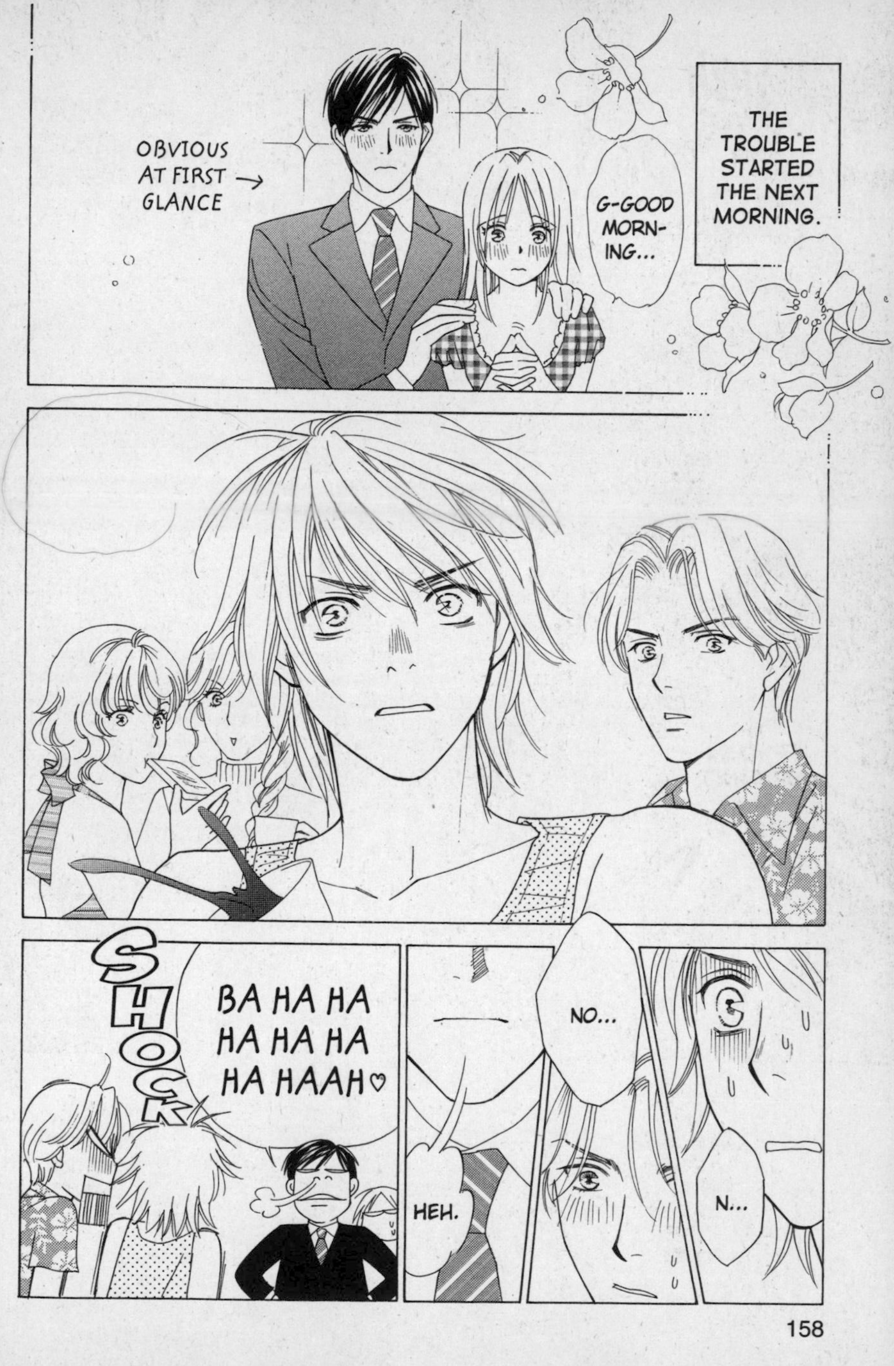
THE TROUBLE STARTED THE NEXT MORNING.
G-GOOD MORNING-ING...
OBVIOUS AT FIRST GLANCE
N...
NO...
HEH.
SHOCK
BA HA HA HA HA HA HA HAAH♡

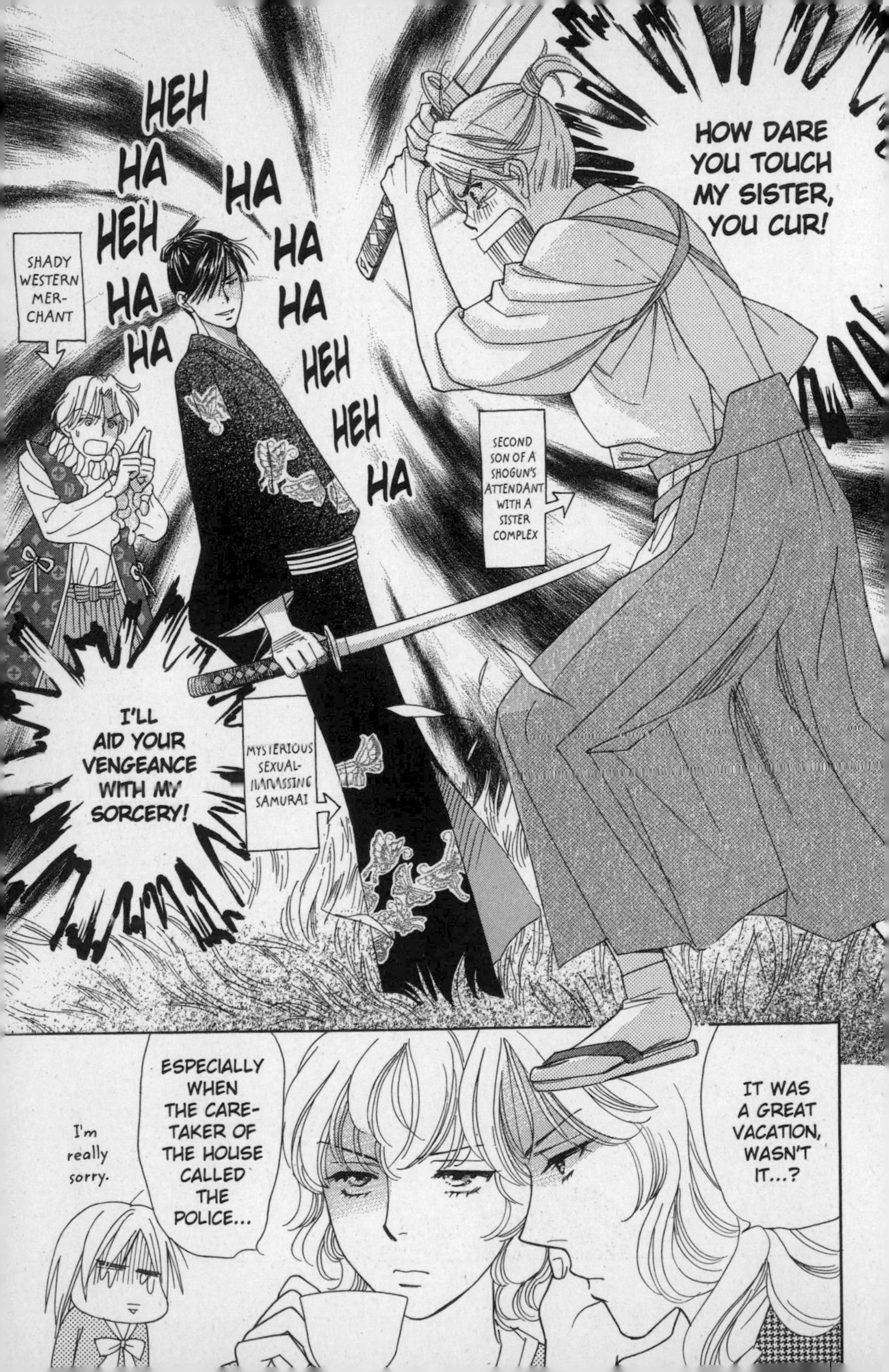
HOW DARE YOU TOUCH MY SISTER, YOU CUR!
SECOND SON OF A SHOGUN'S ATTENDANT WITH A SISTER COMPLEX
HEH HA HEH HA HA HA
HA HA HA HEH HEH HA
SHADY WESTERN MER-CHANT
MYSTERIOUS SEXUAL-HARASSING SAMURAI
I'LL AID YOUR VENGEANCE WITH MY SORCERY!
IT WAS A GREAT VACATION, WASN'T IT...?
ESPECIALLY WHEN THE CARE-TAKER OF THE HOUSE CALLED THE POLICE...
I'm really sorry.

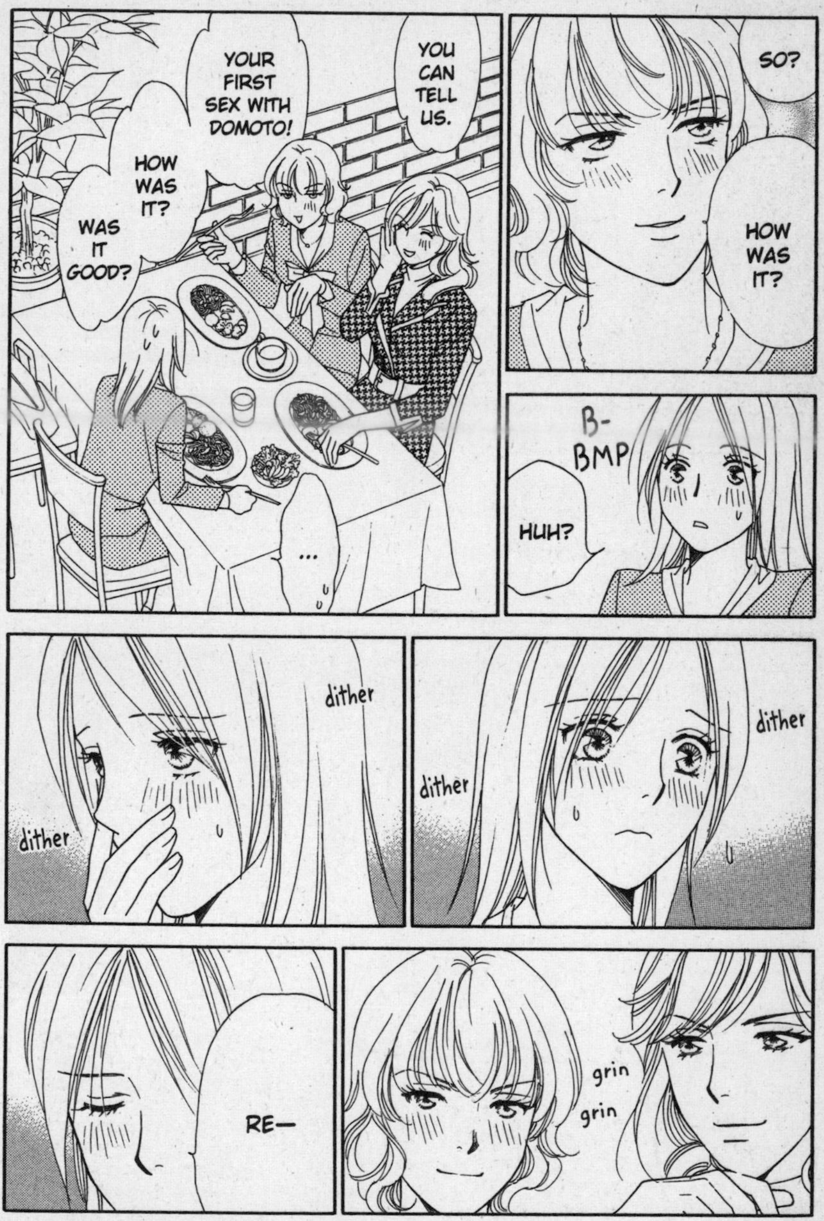
SO?
HOW WAS IT?
B-BMP
HUH?
YOU CAN TELL US.
YOUR FIRST SEX WITH DOMOTO!
HOW WAS IT?
WAS IT GOOD?
...
dither
dither
dither
dither
grin
grin
RE—

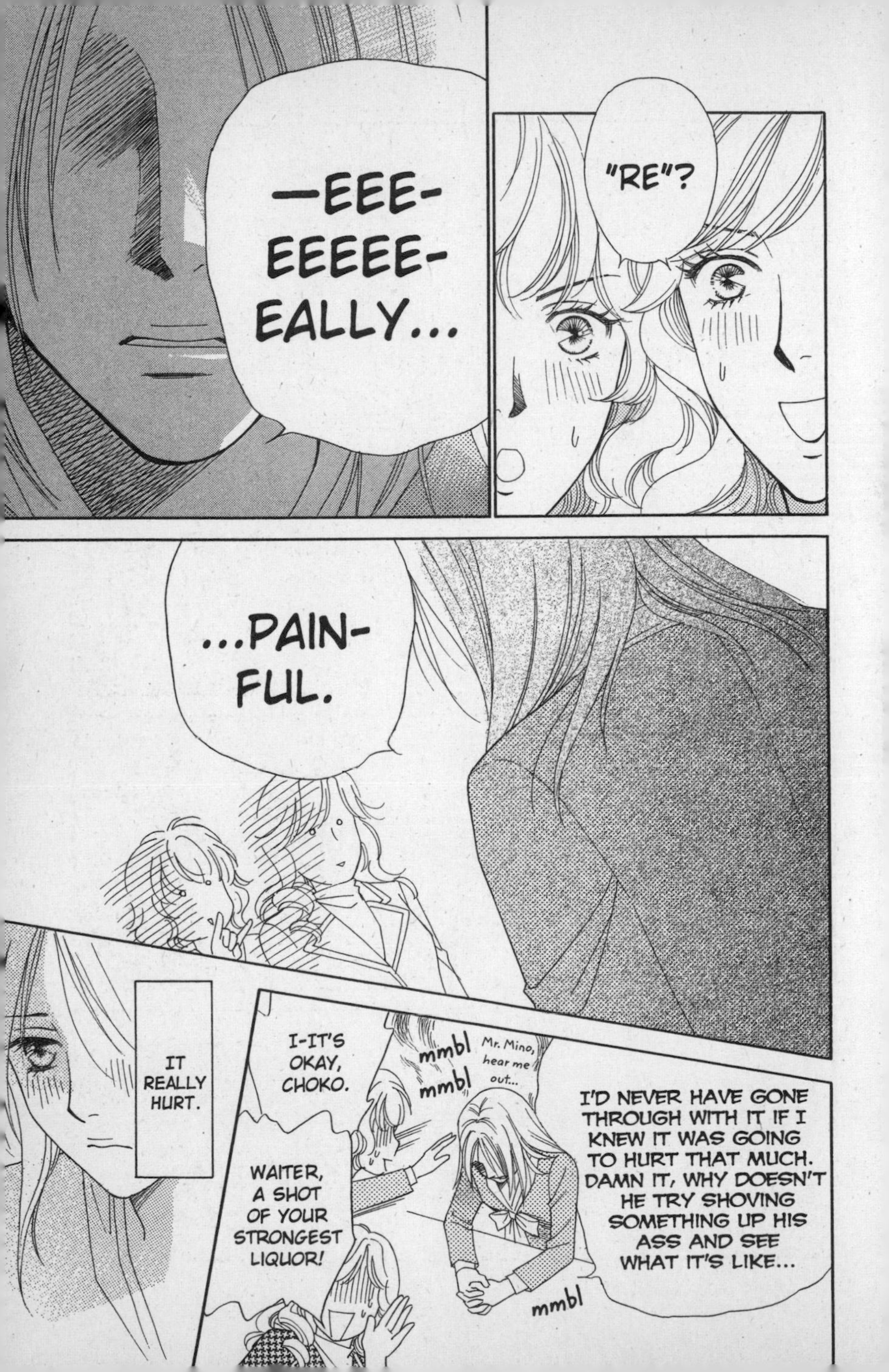
"RE"?
—EEE-EEEEE-EALLY...
...PAIN-FUL.
Mr. Mino, hear me out...
mmbl
mmbl
I'D NEVER HAVE GONE THROUGH WITH IT IF I KNEW IT WAS GOING TO HURT THAT MUCH. DAMN IT, WHY DOESN'T HE TRY SHOVING SOMETHING UP HIS ASS AND SEE WHAT IT'S LIKE...
I-IT'S OKAY, CHOKO.
WAITER, A SHOT OF YOUR STRONGEST LIQUOR!
mmbl
IT REALLY HURT.

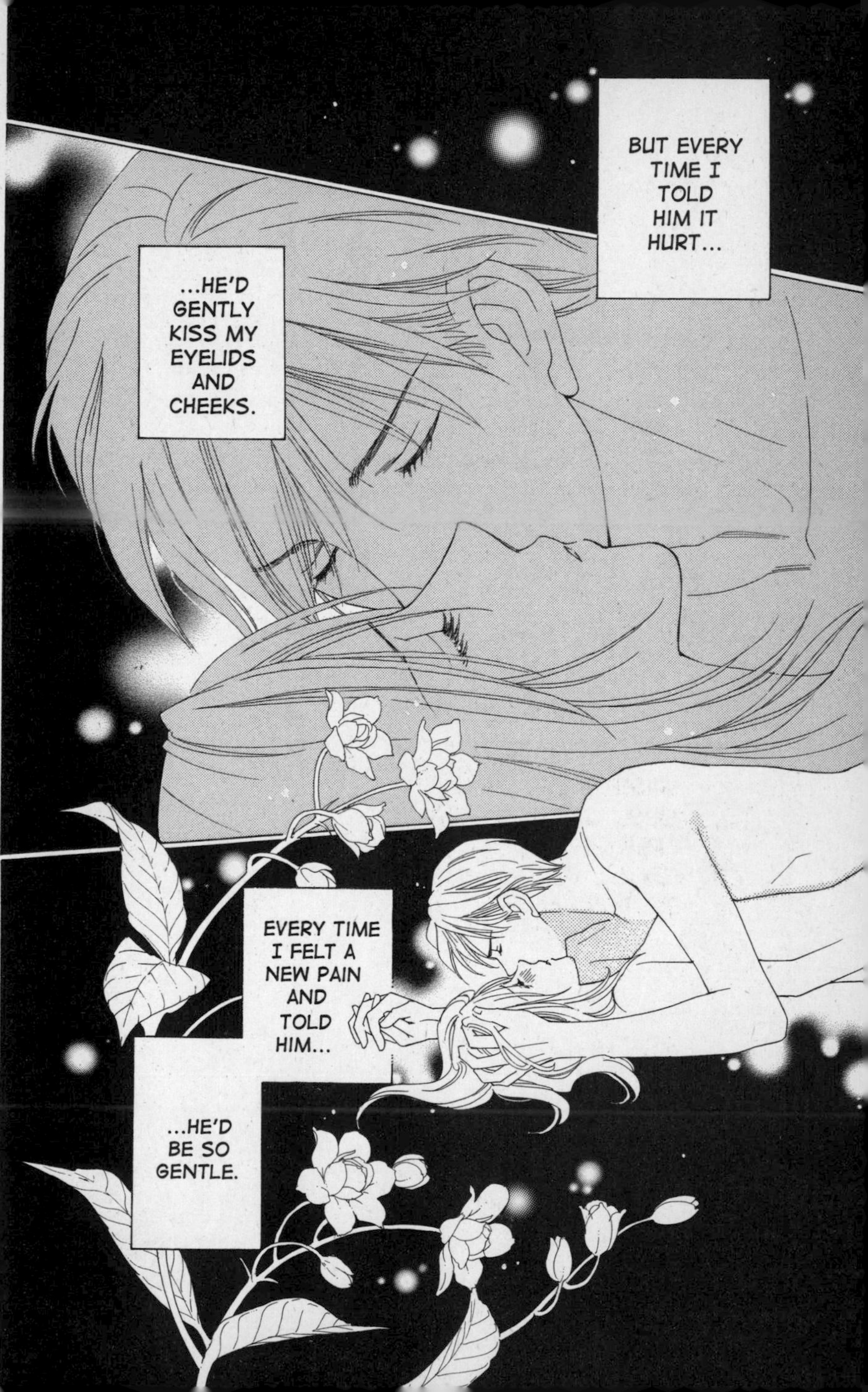
BUT EVERY TIME I TOLD HIM IT HURT...
...HE'D GENTLY KISS MY EYELIDS AND CHEEKS.
EVERY TIME I FELT A NEW PAIN AND TOLD HIM...
...HE'D BE SO GENTLE.

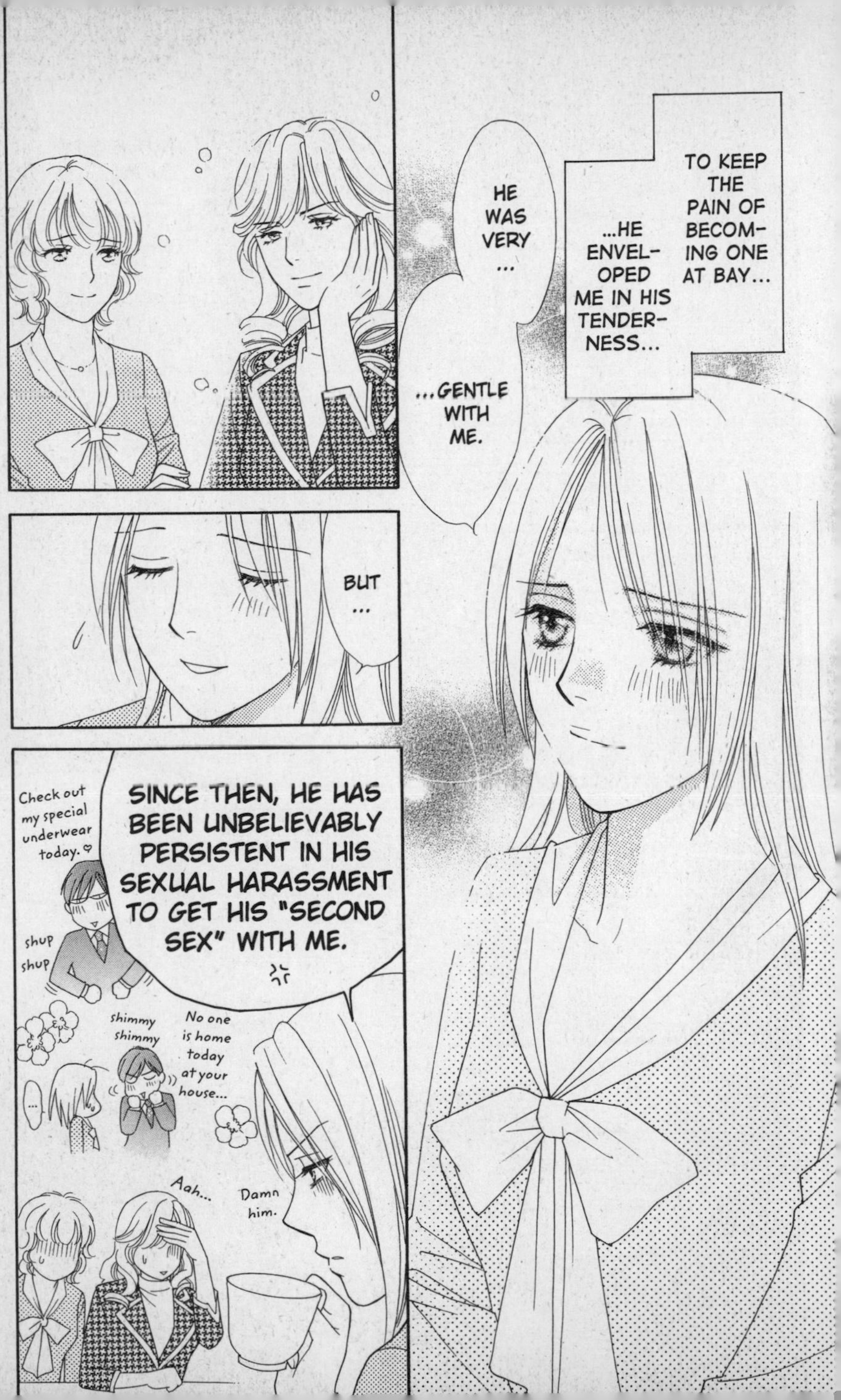
TO KEEP THE PAIN OF BECOMING ONE AT BAY...
...HE ENVELOPED ME IN HIS TENDERNESS...
HE WAS VERY ...
...GENTLE WITH ME.
BUT ...
SINCE THEN, HE HAS BEEN UNBELIEVABLY PERSISTENT IN HIS SEXUAL HARASSMENT TO GET HIS "SECOND SEX" WITH ME.
Check out my special underwear today. ♡
shup shup
No one is home today at your house...
shimmy shimmy
...
Damn him.
Aah...

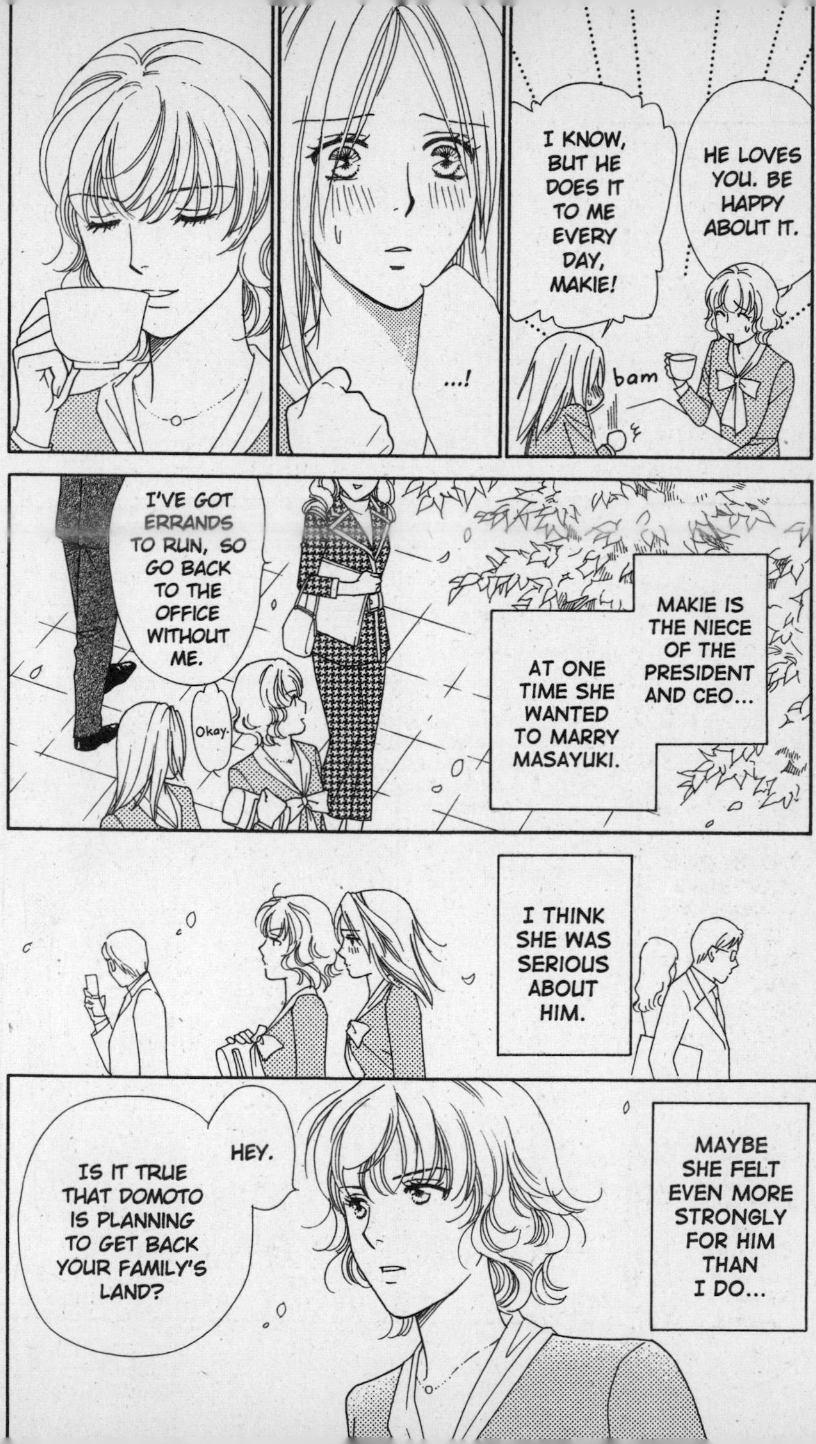
HE LOVES YOU. BE HAPPY ABOUT IT.
I KNOW, BUT HE DOES IT TO ME EVERY DAY, MAKIE!
bam
...!
MAKIE IS THE NIECE OF THE PRESIDENT AND CEO...
AT ONE TIME SHE WANTED TO MARRY MASAYUKI.
I'VE GOT ERRANDS TO RUN, SO GO BACK TO THE OFFICE WITHOUT ME.
Okay.
I THINK SHE WAS SERIOUS ABOUT HIM.
MAYBE SHE FELT EVEN MORE STRONGLY FOR HIM THAN I DO...
HEY.
IS IT TRUE THAT DOMOTO IS PLANNING TO GET BACK YOUR FAMILY'S LAND?

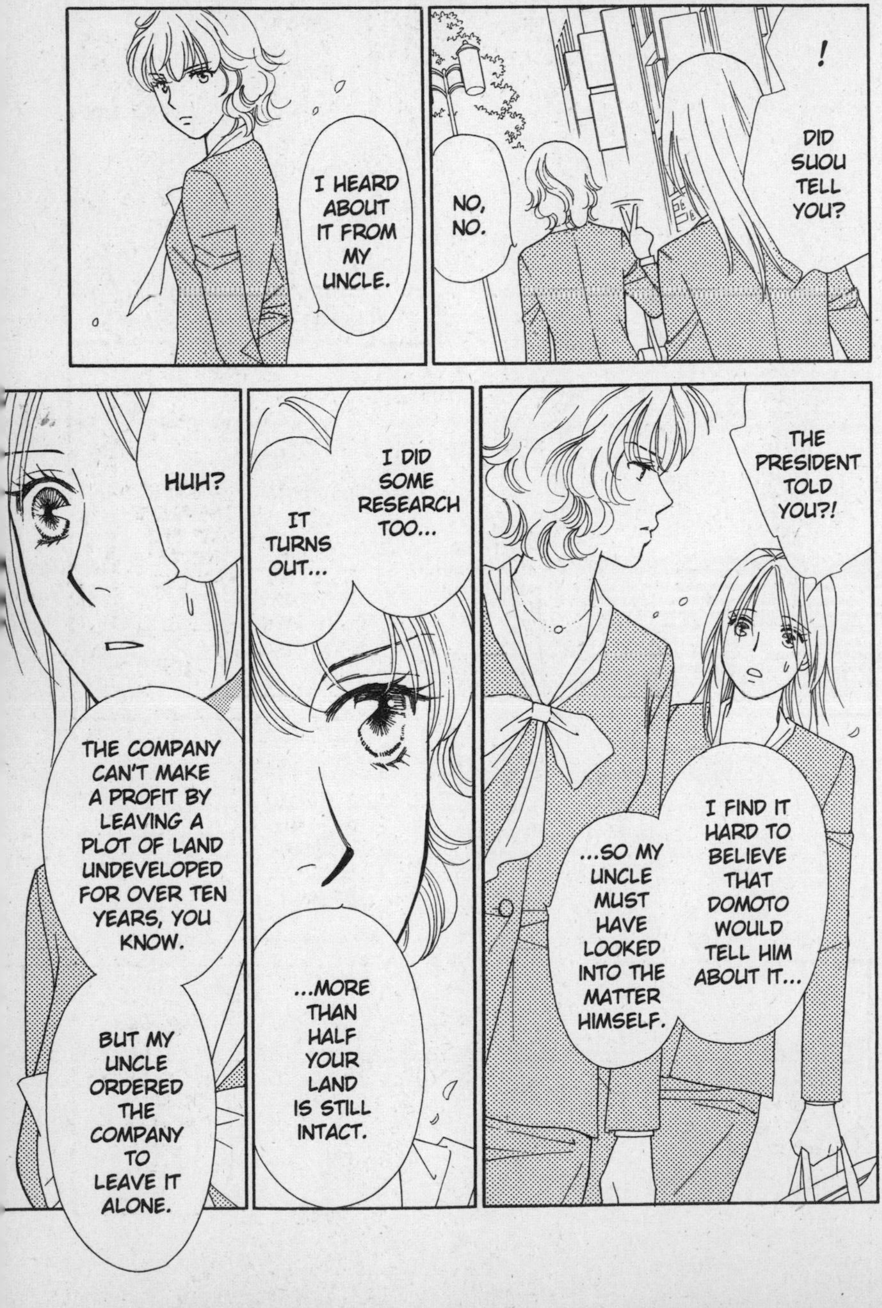
!
DID SUOU TELL YOU?
NO, NO.
I HEARD ABOUT IT FROM MY UNCLE.
THE PRESIDENT TOLD YOU?!
I FIND IT HARD TO BELIEVE THAT DOMOTO WOULD TELL HIM ABOUT IT...
...SO MY UNCLE MUST HAVE LOOKED INTO THE MATTER HIMSELF.
I DID SOME RESEARCH TOO...
IT TURNS OUT...
...MORE THAN HALF YOUR LAND IS STILL INTACT.
HUH?
THE COMPANY CAN'T MAKE A PROFIT BY LEAVING A PLOT OF LAND UNDEVELOPED FOR OVER TEN YEARS, YOU KNOW.
BUT MY UNCLE ORDERED THE COMPANY TO LEAVE IT ALONE.

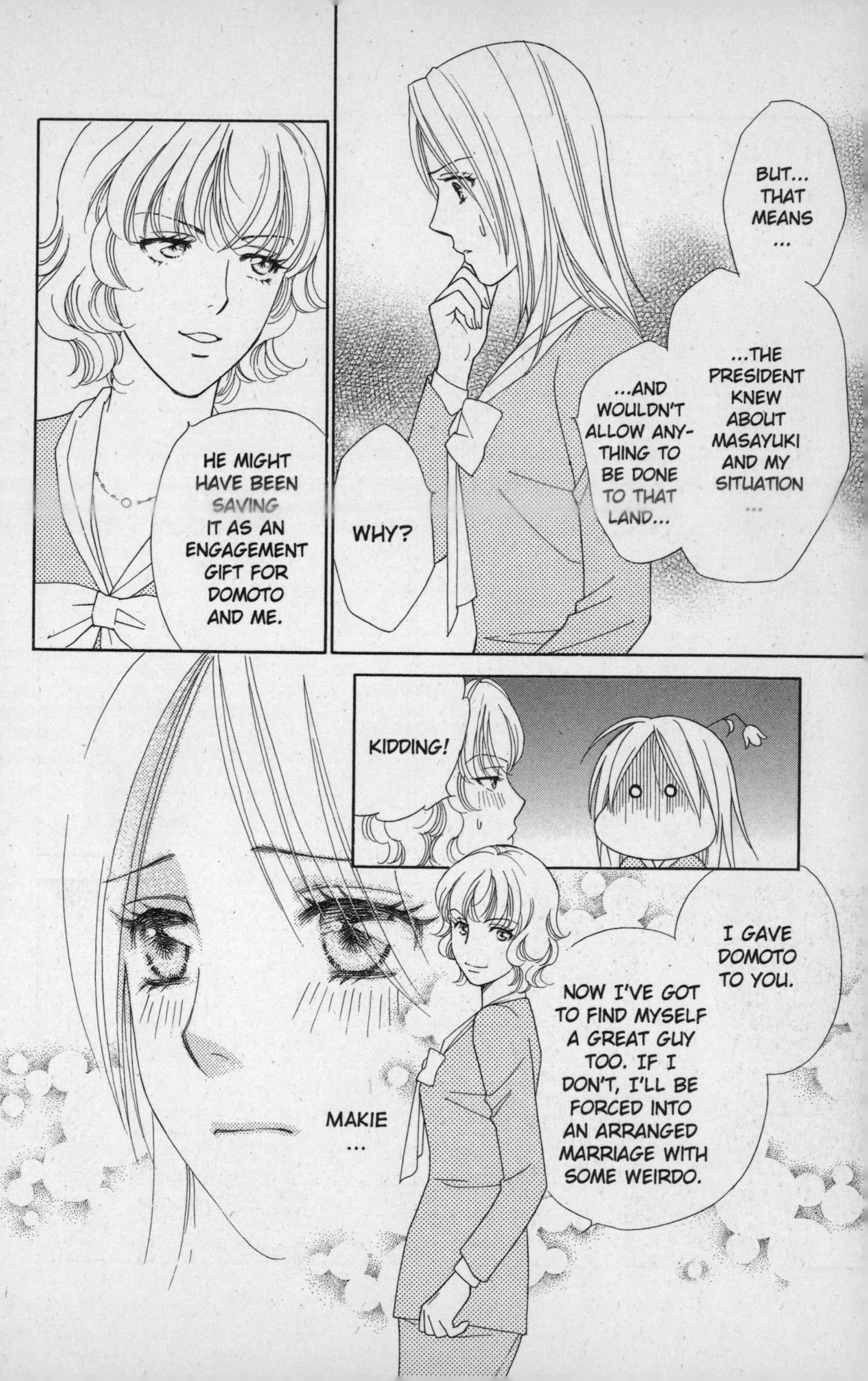
BUT... THAT MEANS ...
...THE PRESIDENT KNEW ABOUT MASAYUKI AND MY SITUATION ...
...AND WOULDN'T ALLOW ANY-THING TO BE DONE TO THAT LAND...
WHY?
HE MIGHT HAVE BEEN SAVING IT AS AN ENGAGEMENT GIFT FOR DOMOTO AND ME.
KIDDING!
I GAVE DOMOTO TO YOU.
NOW I'VE GOT TO FIND MYSELF A GREAT GUY TOO. IF I DON'T, I'LL BE FORCED INTO AN ARRANGED MARRIAGE WITH SOME WEIRDO.
MAKIE ...

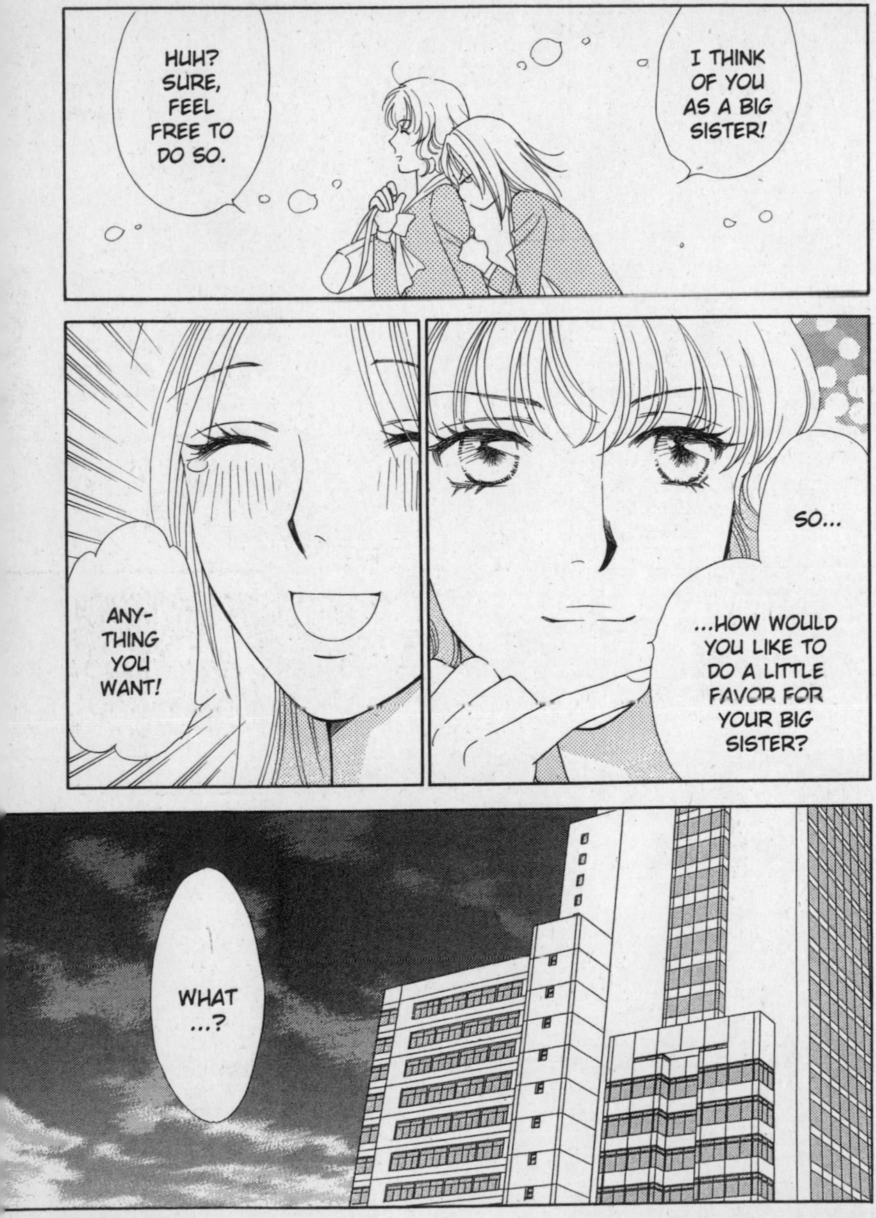
I THINK OF YOU AS A BIG SISTER!
HUH? SURE, FEEL FREE TO DO SO.
SO...
...HOW WOULD YOU LIKE TO DO A LITTLE FAVOR FOR YOUR BIG SISTER?
ANY-THING YOU WANT!
WHAT ...?

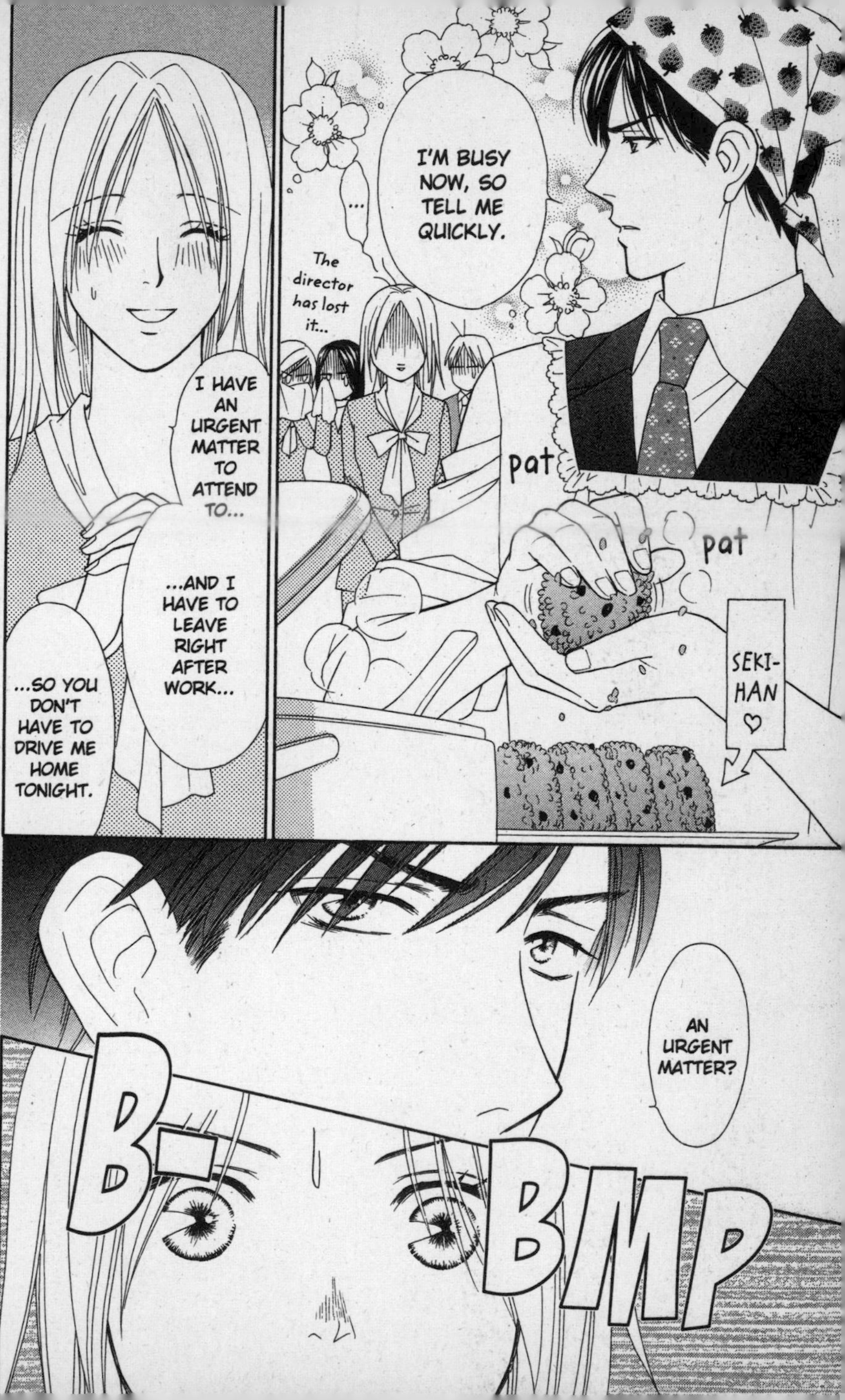
I'M BUSY NOW, SO TELL ME QUICKLY.
...
The director has lost it...
pat
pat
SEKI-HAN ♡
I HAVE AN URGENT MATTER TO ATTEND TO...
...AND I HAVE TO LEAVE RIGHT AFTER WORK...
...SO YOU DON'T HAVE TO DRIVE ME HOME TONIGHT.
AN URGENT MATTER?
B-BMP

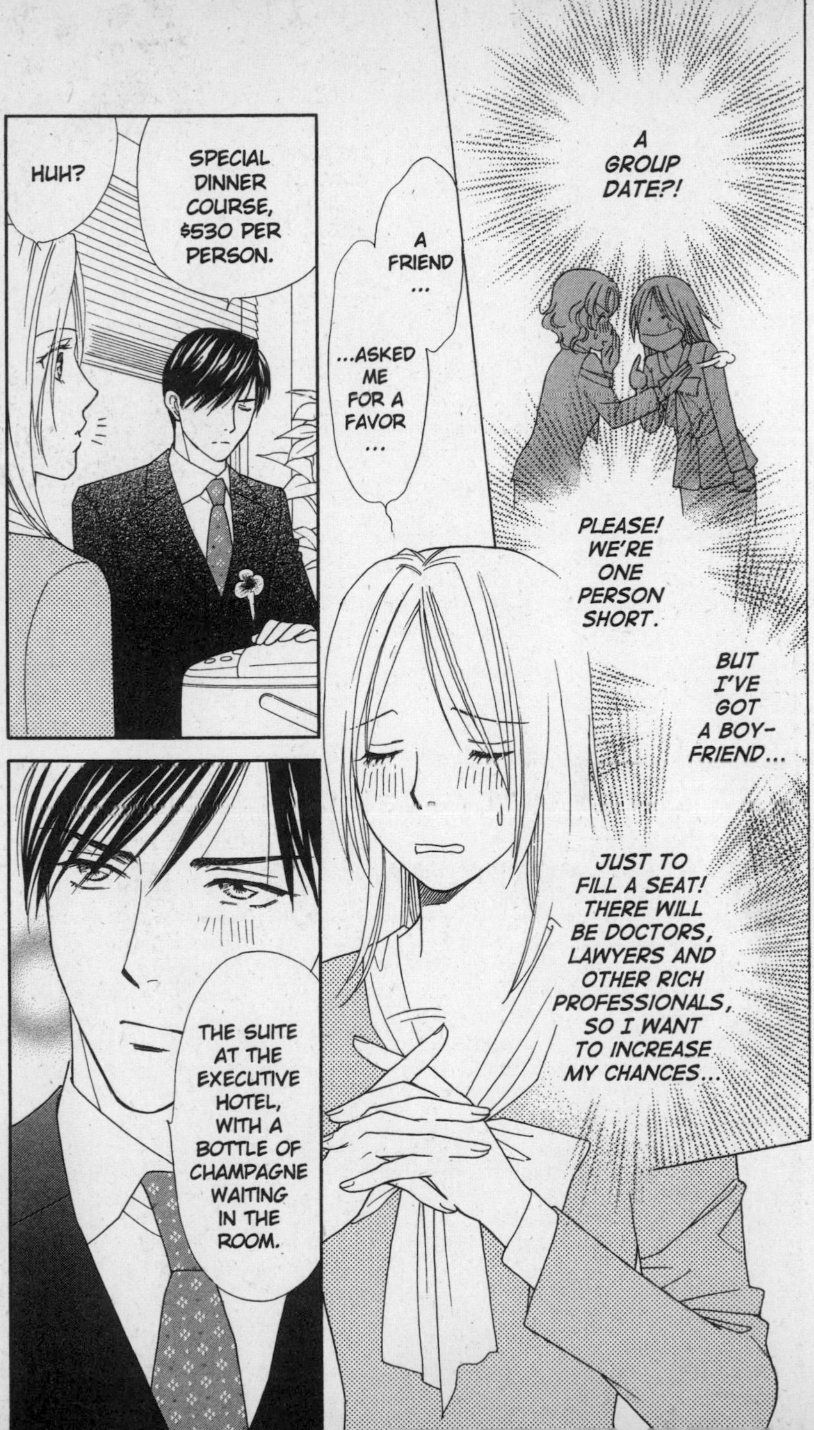
A FRIEND ...
...ASKED ME FOR A FAVOR ...
A GROUP DATE?!
PLEASE! WE'RE ONE PERSON SHORT.
BUT I'VE GOT A BOY-FRIEND...
JUST TO FILL A SEAT! THERE WILL BE DOCTORS, LAWYERS AND OTHER RICH PROFESSIONALS, SO I WANT TO INCREASE MY CHANCES...
SPECIAL DINNER COURSE, $530 PER PERSON.
HUH?
THE SUITE AT THE EXECUTIVE HOTEL, WITH A BOTTLE OF CHAMPAGNE WAITING IN THE ROOM.

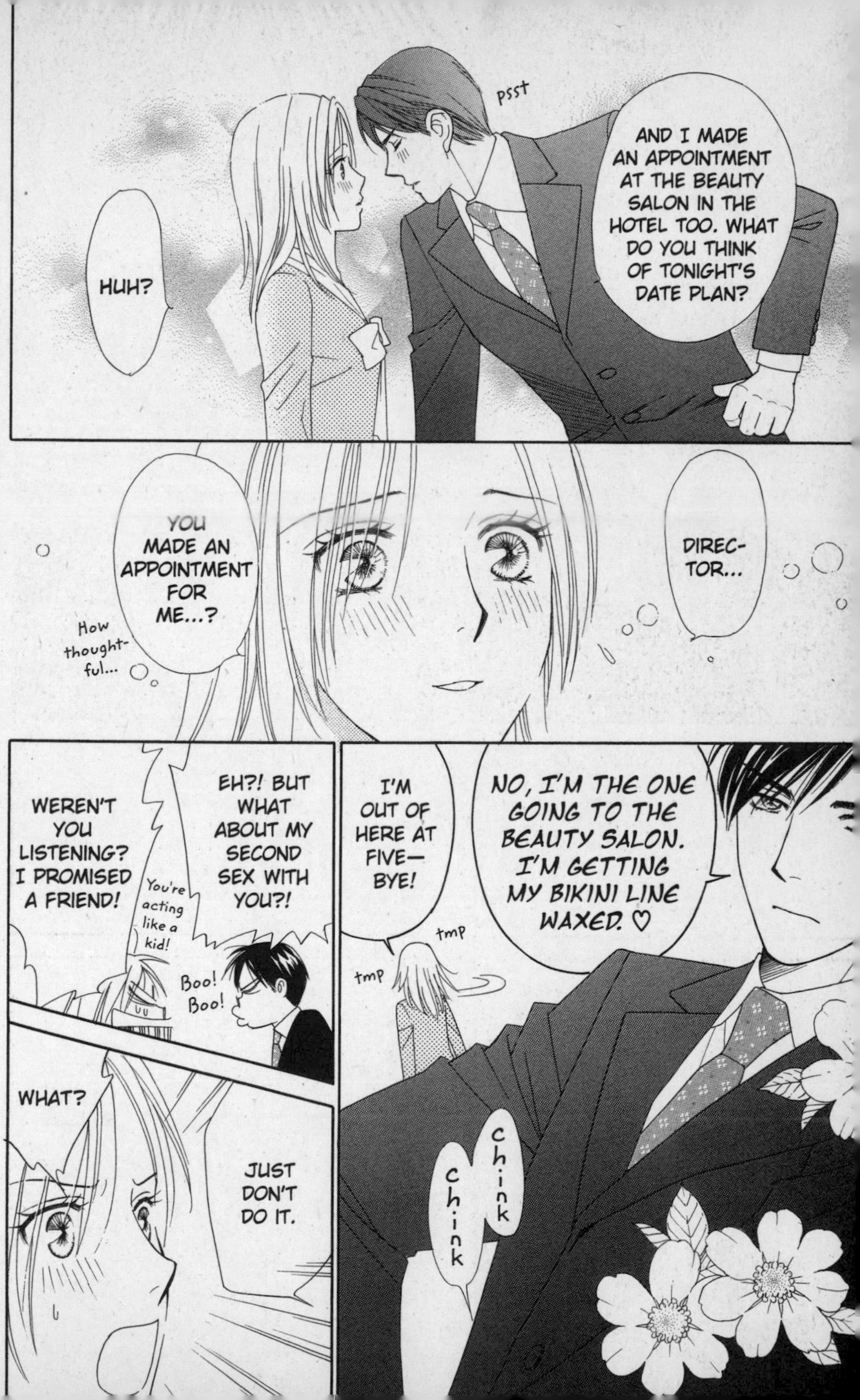
psst
AND I MADE AN APPOINTMENT AT THE BEAUTY SALON IN THE HOTEL TOO. WHAT DO YOU THINK OF TONIGHT'S DATE PLAN?
HUH?
DIREC-TOR...
YOU MADE AN APPOINTMENT FOR ME...?
How thought-ful...
NO, I'M THE ONE GOING TO THE BEAUTY SALON. I'M GETTING MY BIKINI LINE WAXED. ♡
I'M OUT OF HERE AT FIVE—BYE!
tmp
tmp
chink
chink
EH?! BUT WHAT ABOUT MY SECOND SEX WITH YOU?!
WEREN'T YOU LISTENING? I PROMISED A FRIEND!
You're acting like a kid!
Boo! Boo!
JUST DON'T DO IT.
WHAT?

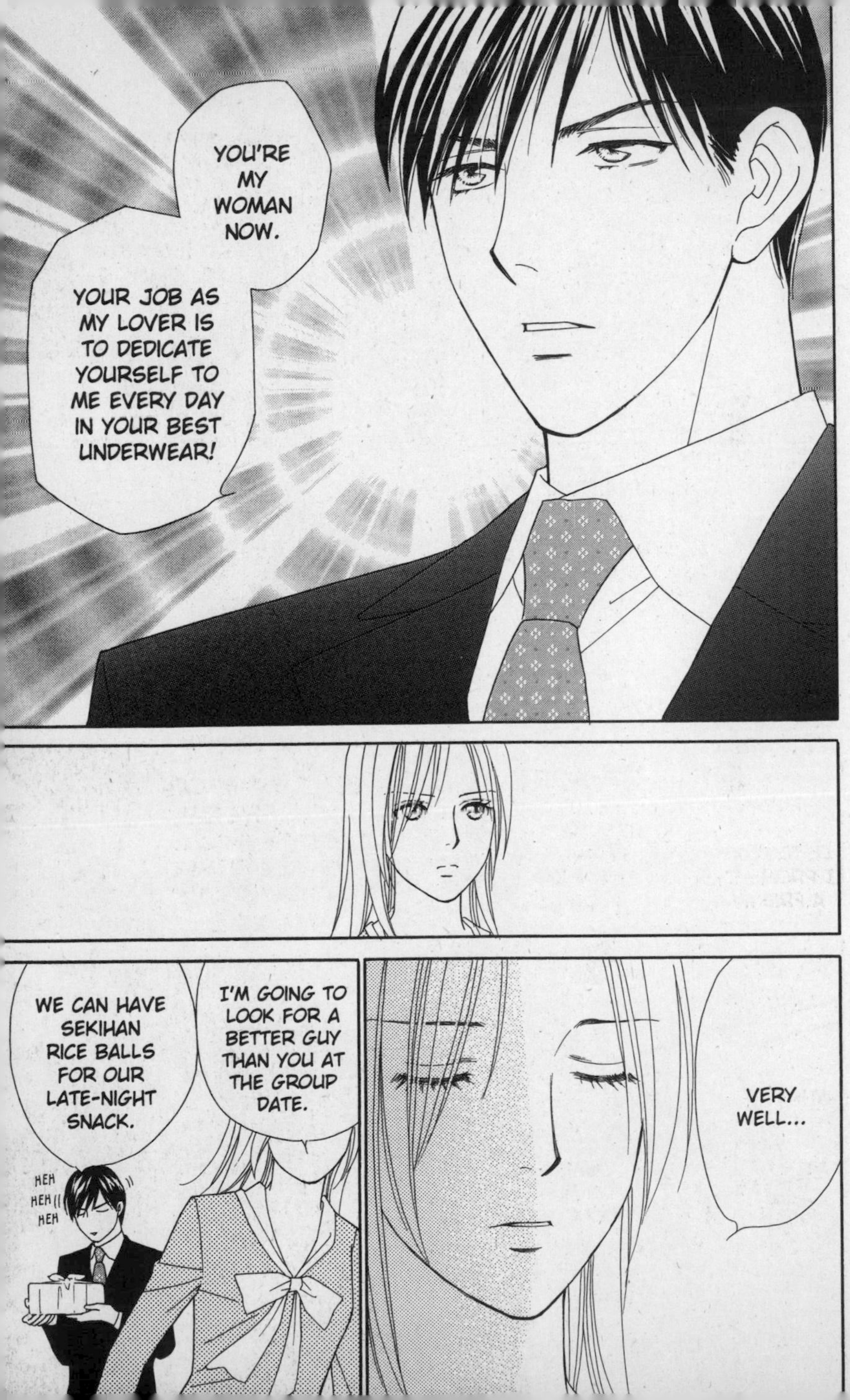
YOU'RE MY WOMAN NOW.
YOUR JOB AS MY LOVER IS TO DEDICATE YOURSELF TO ME EVERY DAY IN YOUR BEST UNDERWEAR!
VERY WELL...
I'M GOING TO LOOK FOR A BETTER GUY THAN YOU AT THE GROUP DATE.
WE CAN HAVE SEKIHAN RICE BALLS FOR OUR LATE-NIGHT SNACK.
HEH HEH HEH

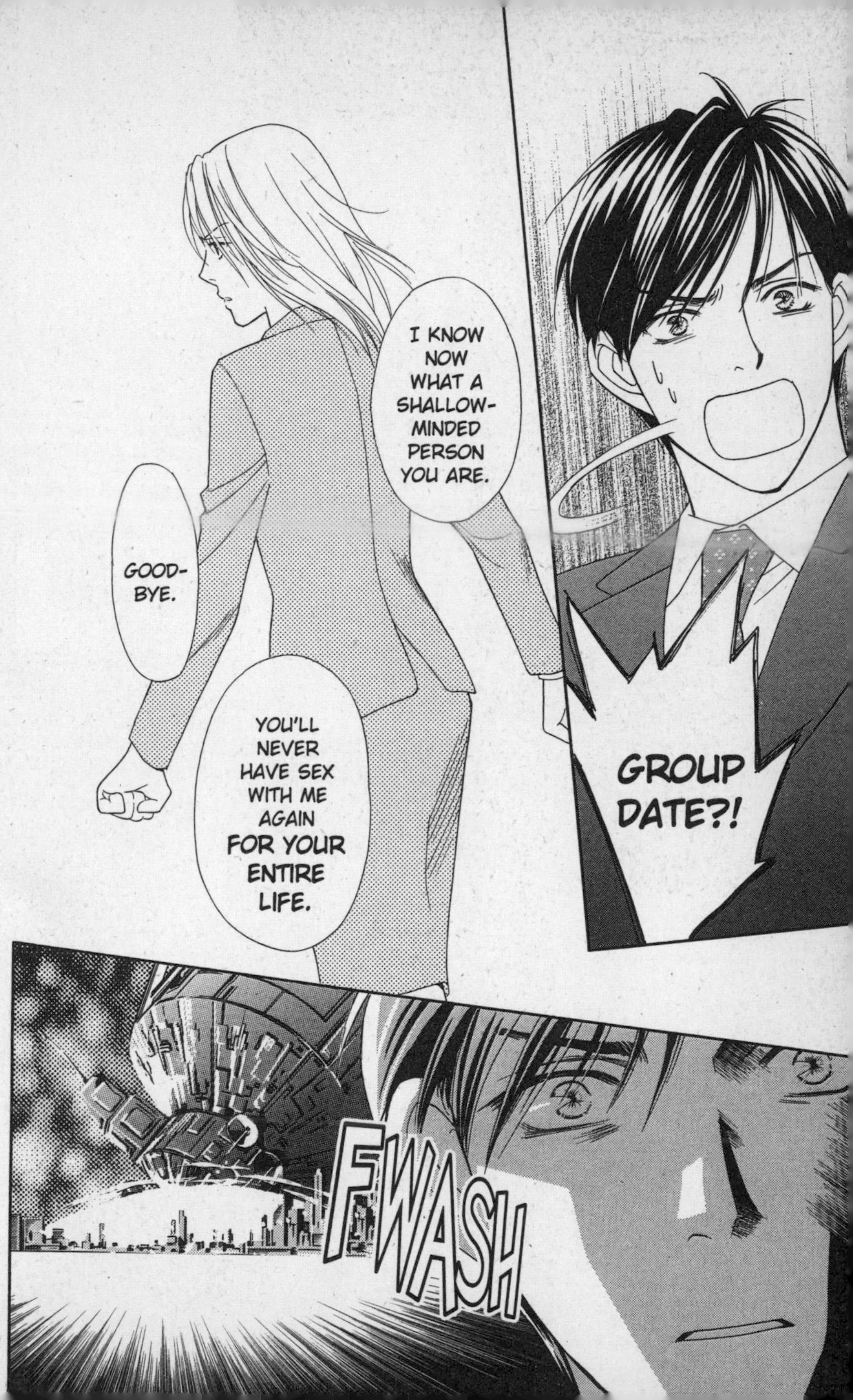
GROUP DATE?!
I KNOW NOW WHAT A SHALLOW-MINDED PERSON YOU ARE.
GOOD-BYE.
YOU'LL NEVER HAVE SEX WITH ME AGAIN FOR YOUR ENTIRE LIFE.
FWASH

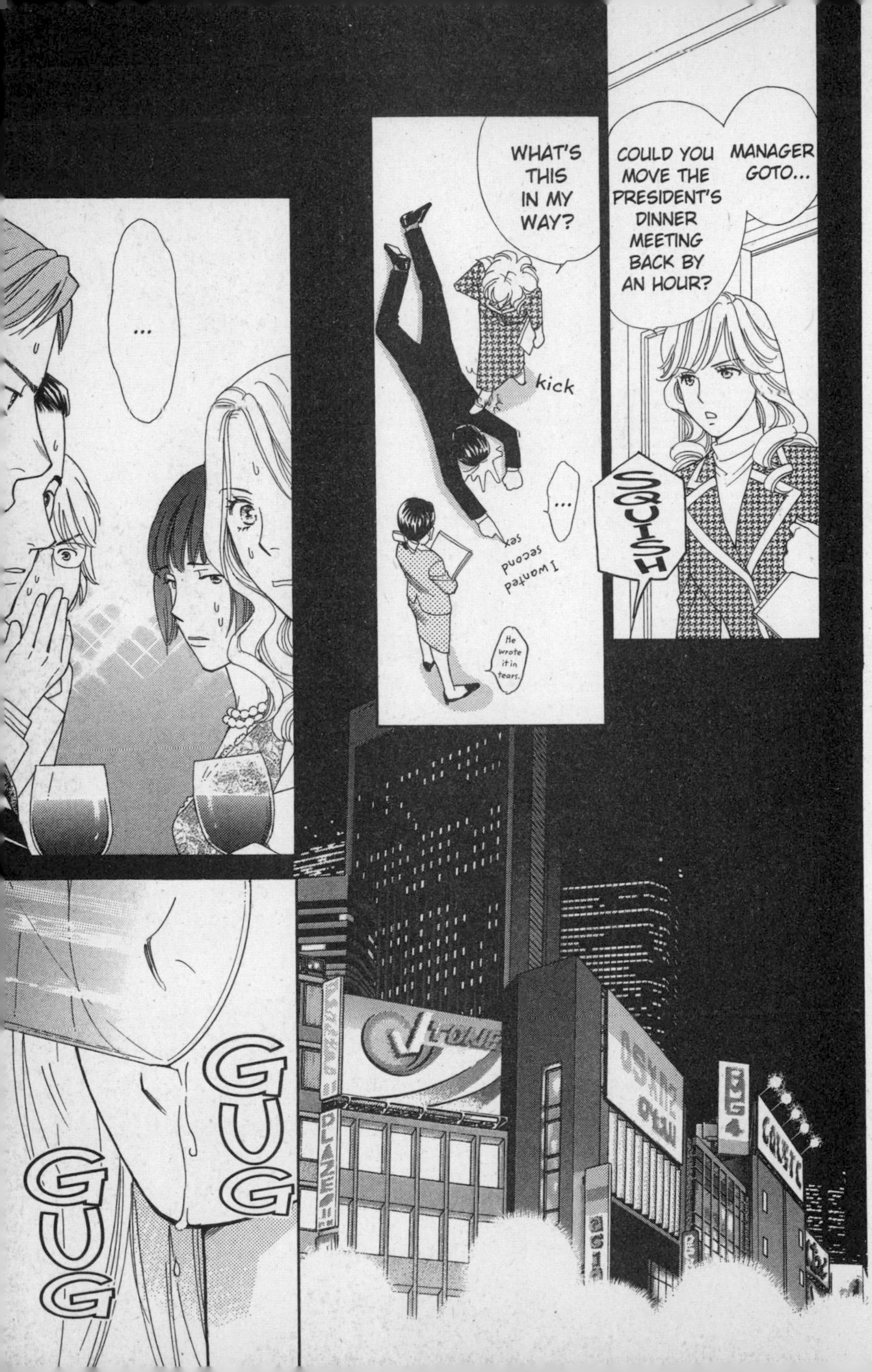
MANAGER GOTO...
COULD YOU MOVE THE PRESIDENT'S DINNER MEETING BACK BY AN HOUR?
SQUISH
WHAT'S THIS IN MY WAY?
kick
...
I wanted second sex
He wrote it in tears.
...
GUG
GUG

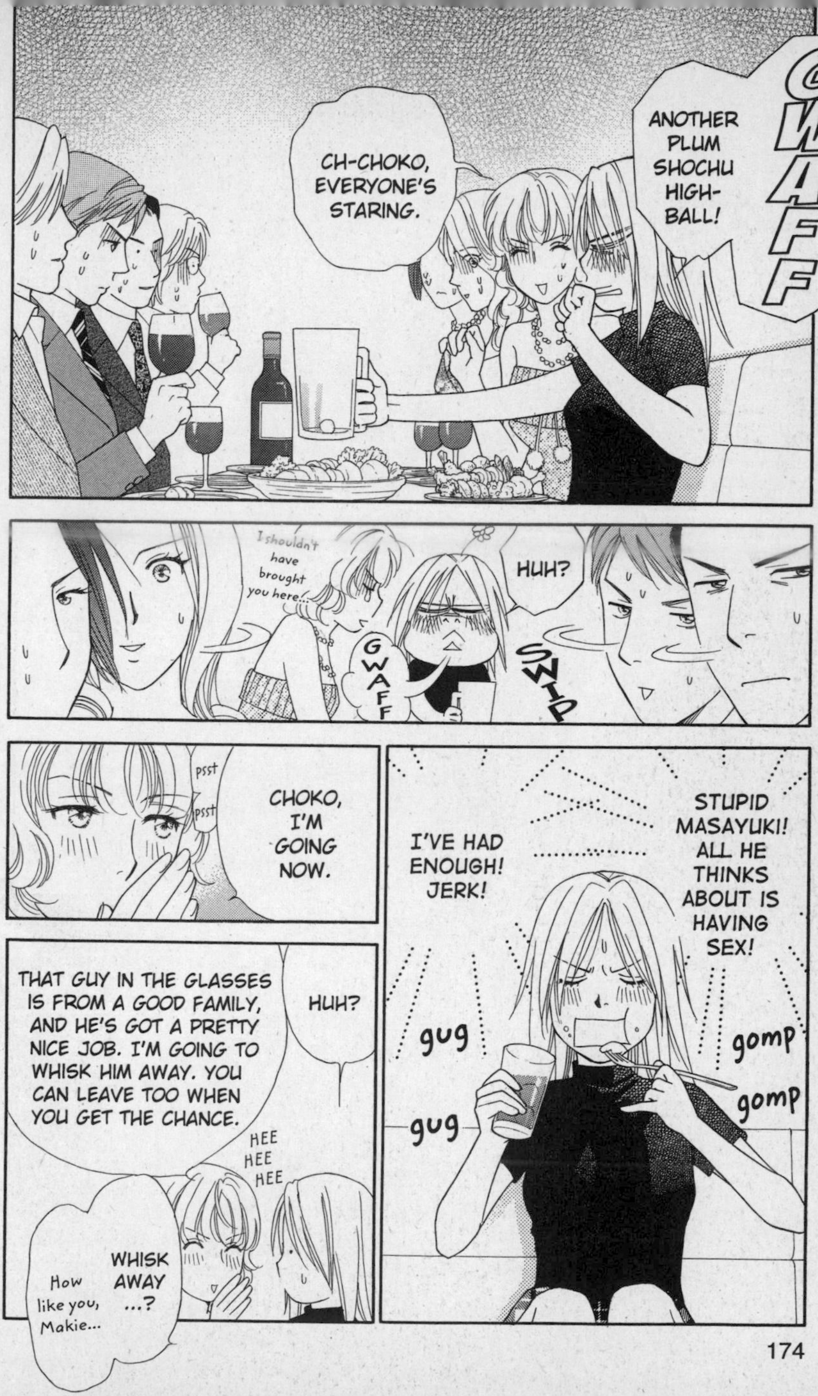
GWAFF
ANOTHER PLUM SHOCHU HIGH-BALL!
CH-CHOKO, EVERYONE'S STARING.
HUH?
SWIP
GWAFF
I shouldn't have brought you here...
STUPID MASAYUKI! ALL HE THINKS ABOUT IS HAVING SEX!
I'VE HAD ENOUGH! JERK!
gomp
gomp
gug
gug
psst
psst
CHOKO, I'M GOING NOW.
THAT GUY IN THE GLASSES IS FROM A GOOD FAMILY, AND HE'S GOT A PRETTY NICE JOB. I'M GOING TO WHISK HIM AWAY. YOU CAN LEAVE TOO WHEN YOU GET THE CHANCE.
HUH?
HEE HEE HEE
WHISK AWAY ...?
How like you, Makie...

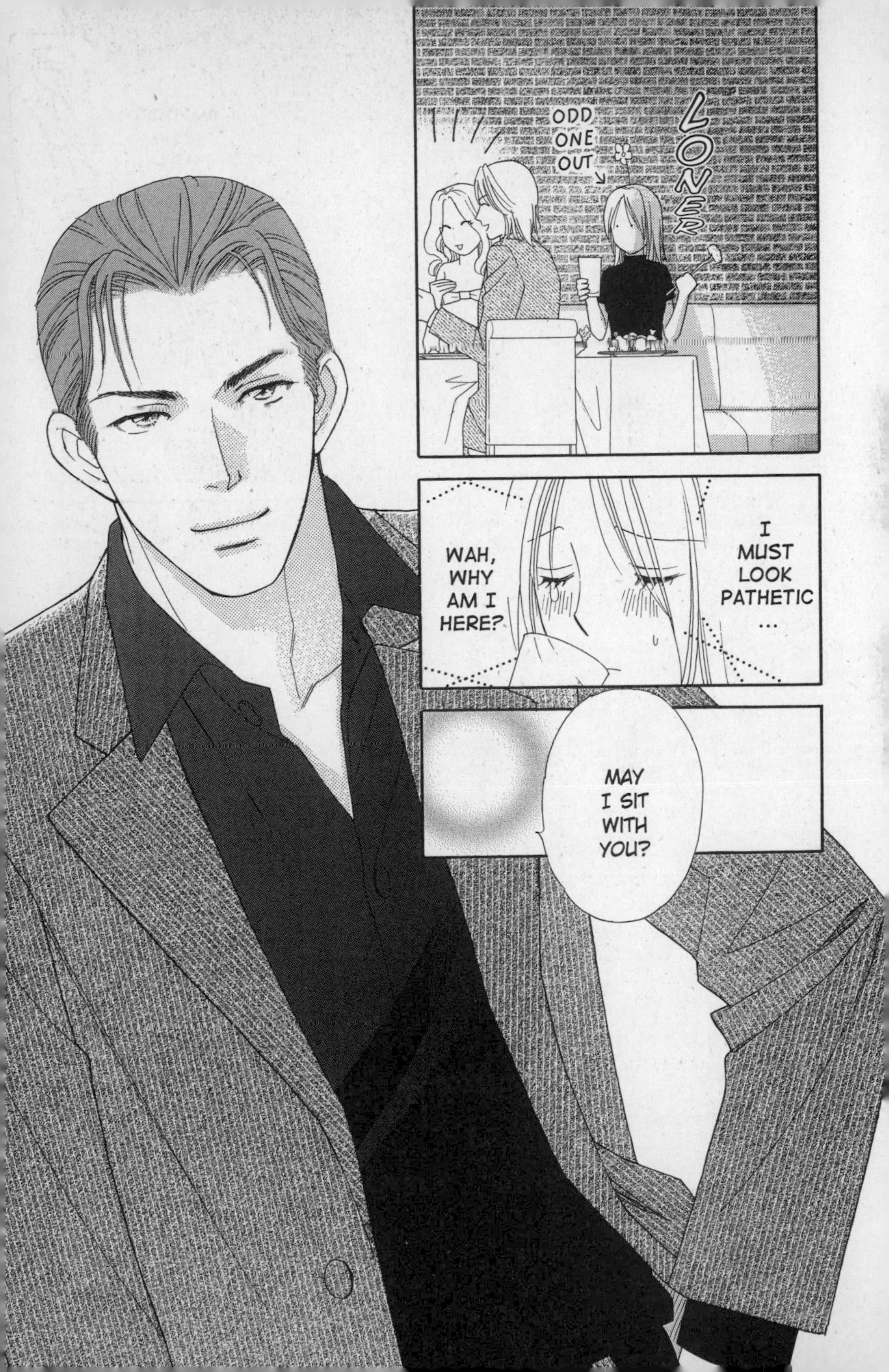
LONER
ODD ONE OUT
I MUST LOOK PATHETIC ...
WAH, WHY AM I HERE?
MAY I SIT WITH YOU?

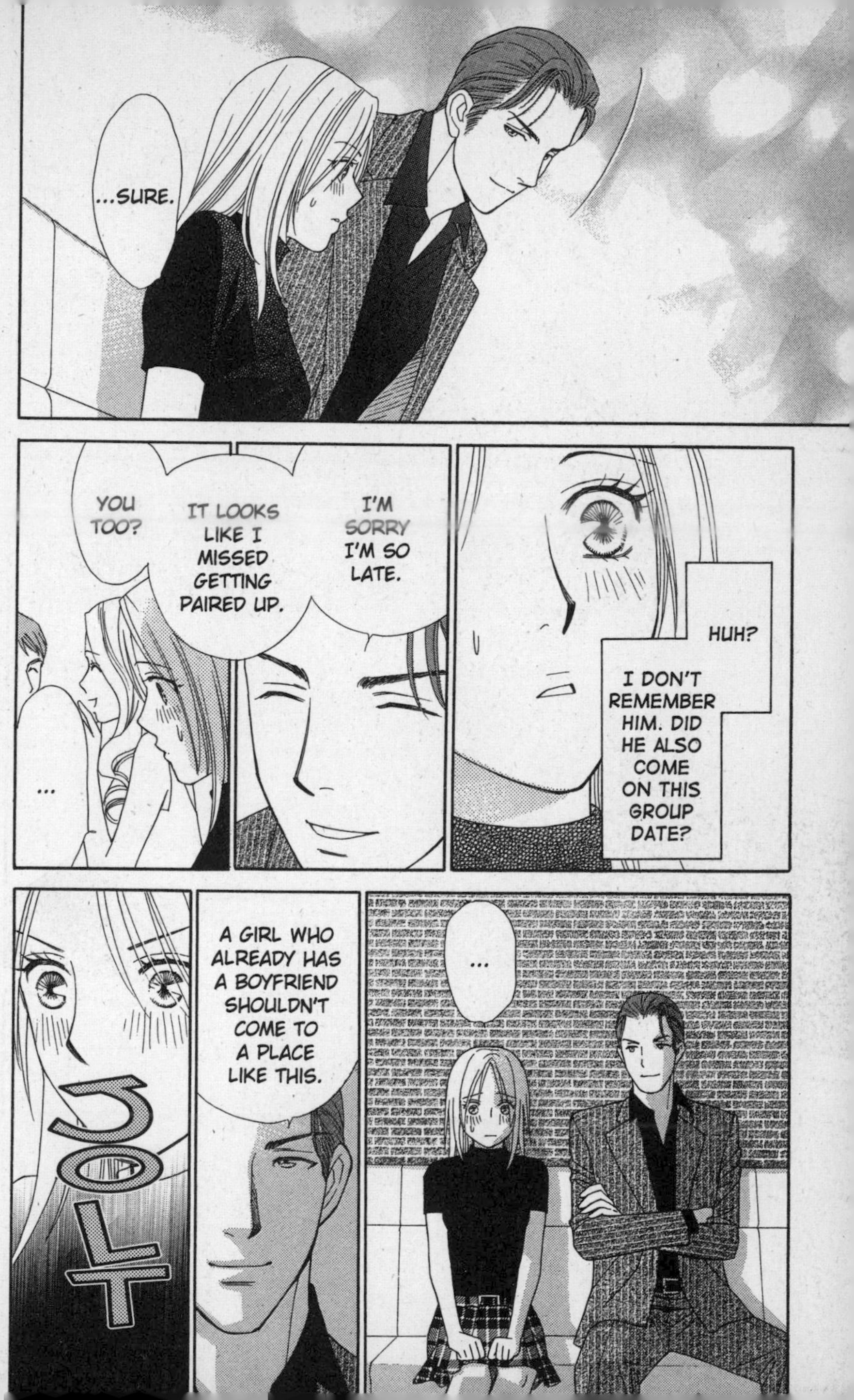
...SURE.
HUH?
I DON'T REMEMBER HIM. DID HE ALSO COME ON THIS GROUP DATE?
I'M SORRY I'M SO LATE.
IT LOOKS LIKE I MISSED GETTING PAIRED UP.
YOU TOO?
...
...
A GIRL WHO ALREADY HAS A BOYFRIEND SHOULDN'T COME TO A PLACE LIKE THIS.
JOLT

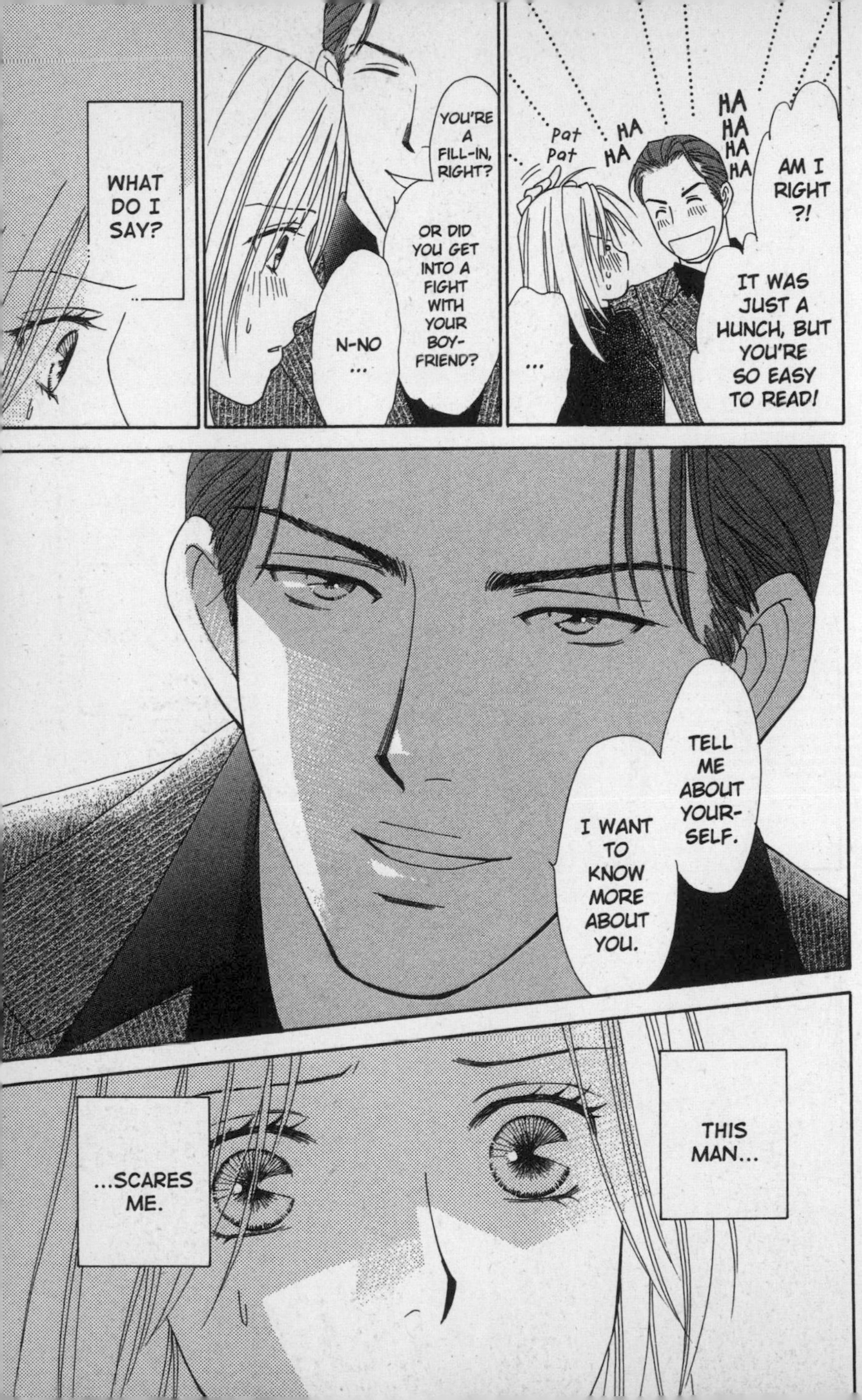
AM I RIGHT ?!
HA HA HA HA
HA HA
Pat Pat
IT WAS JUST A HUNCH, BUT YOU'RE SO EASY TO READ!
...
YOU'RE A FILL-IN, RIGHT?
OR DID YOU GET INTO A FIGHT WITH YOUR BOY-FRIEND?
N-NO ...
WHAT DO I SAY?
TELL ME ABOUT YOUR-SELF.
I WANT TO KNOW MORE ABOUT YOU.
THIS MAN...
...SCARES ME.

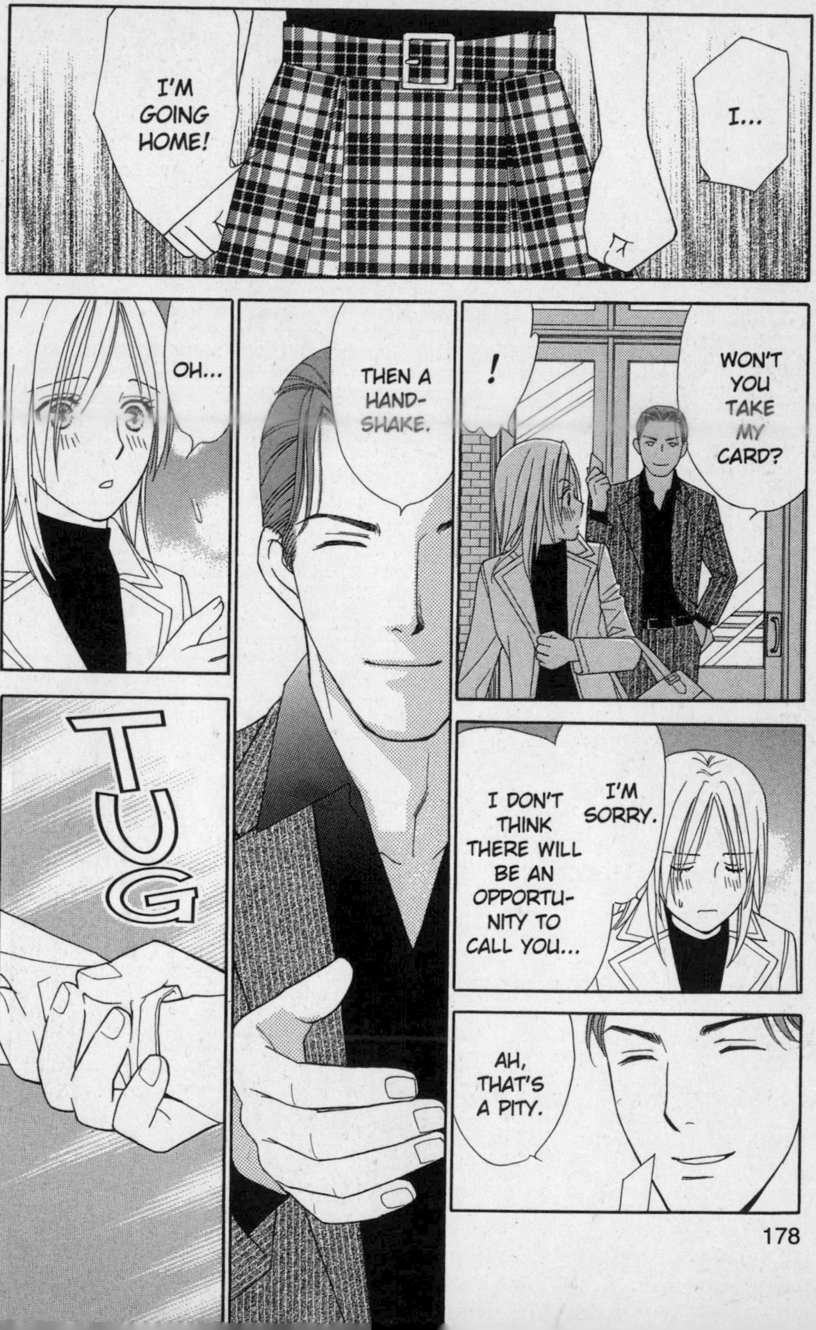
I...
I'M GOING HOME!
WON'T YOU TAKE MY CARD?
!
I'M SORRY.
I DON'T THINK THERE WILL BE AN OPPORTUNITY TO CALL YOU...
AH, THAT'S A PITY.
THEN A HAND-SHAKE.
OH...
TUG

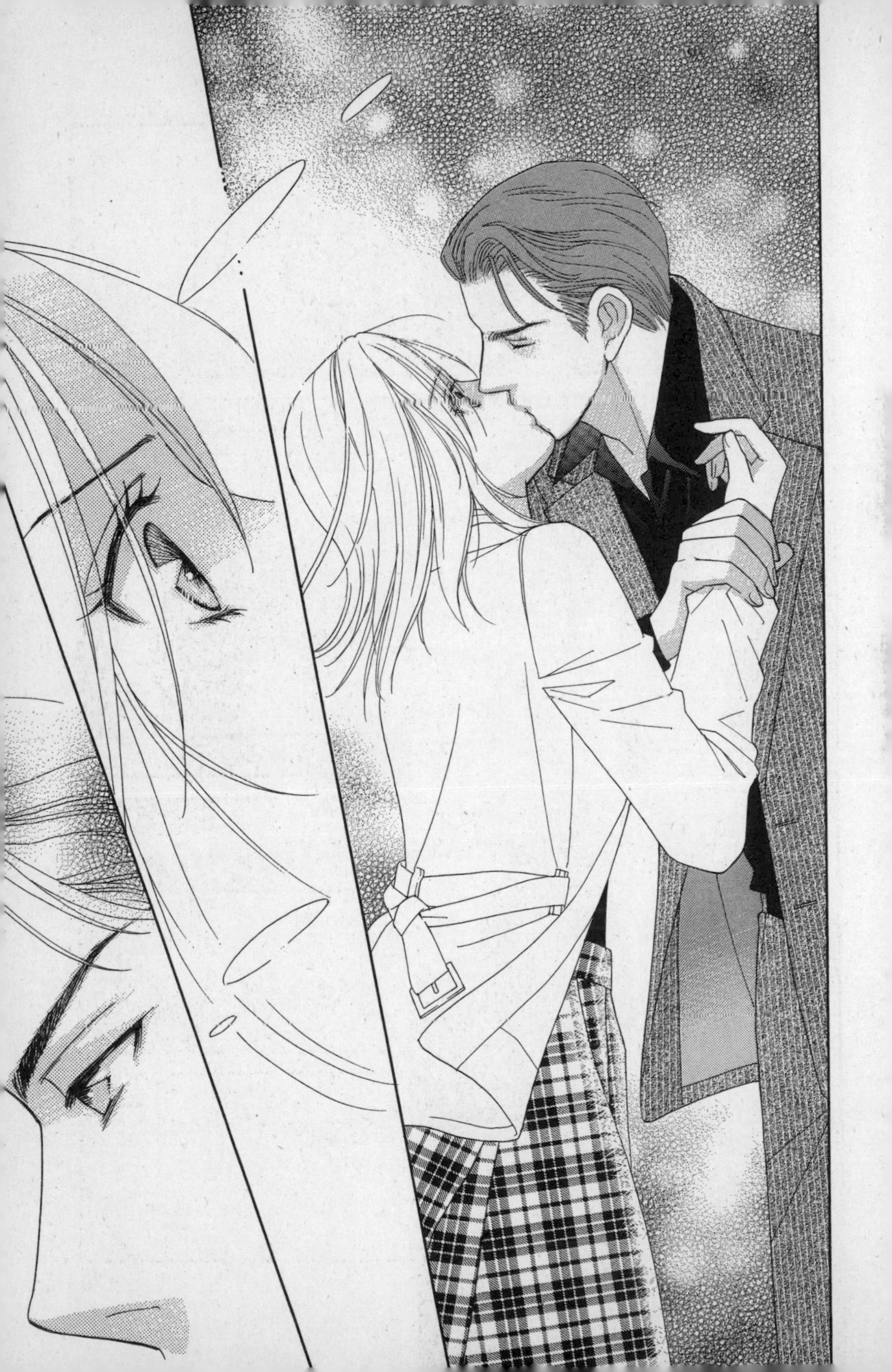

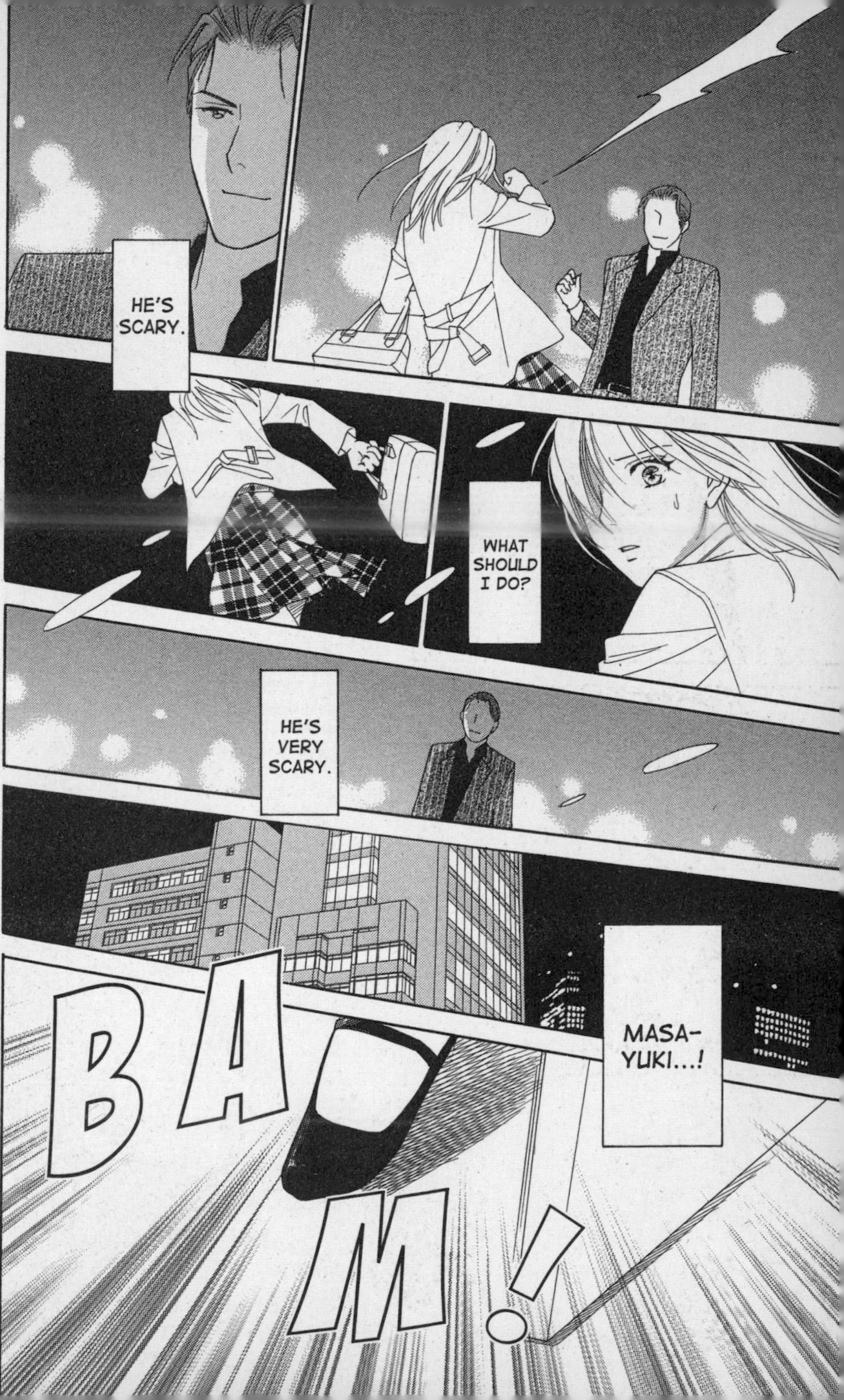
HE'S SCARY.
WHAT SHOULD I DO?
HE'S VERY SCARY.
MASA-YUKI...!
BAM!

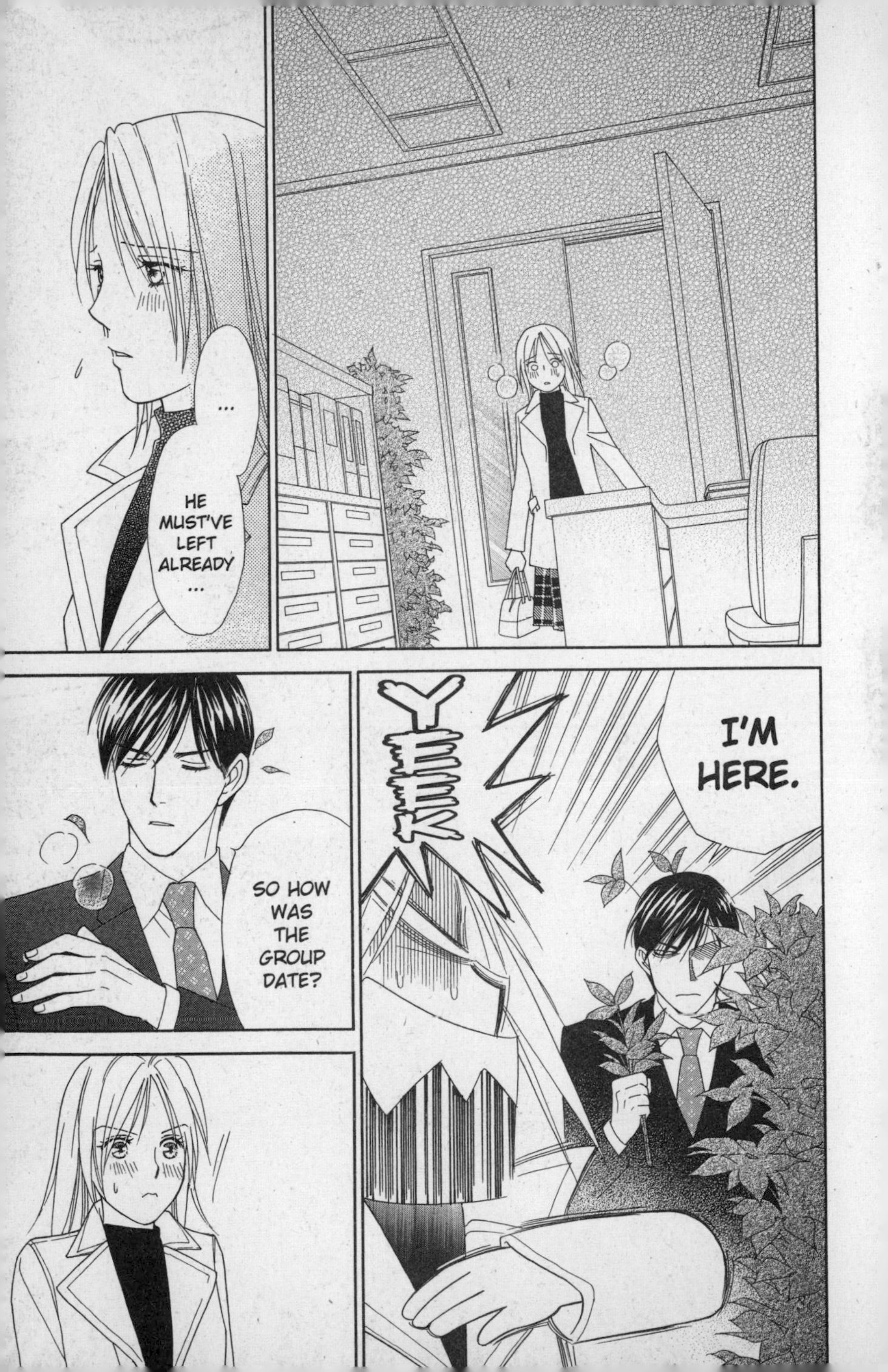
...
HE MUST'VE LEFT ALREADY ...
I'M HERE.
YEEK
SO HOW WAS THE GROUP DATE?

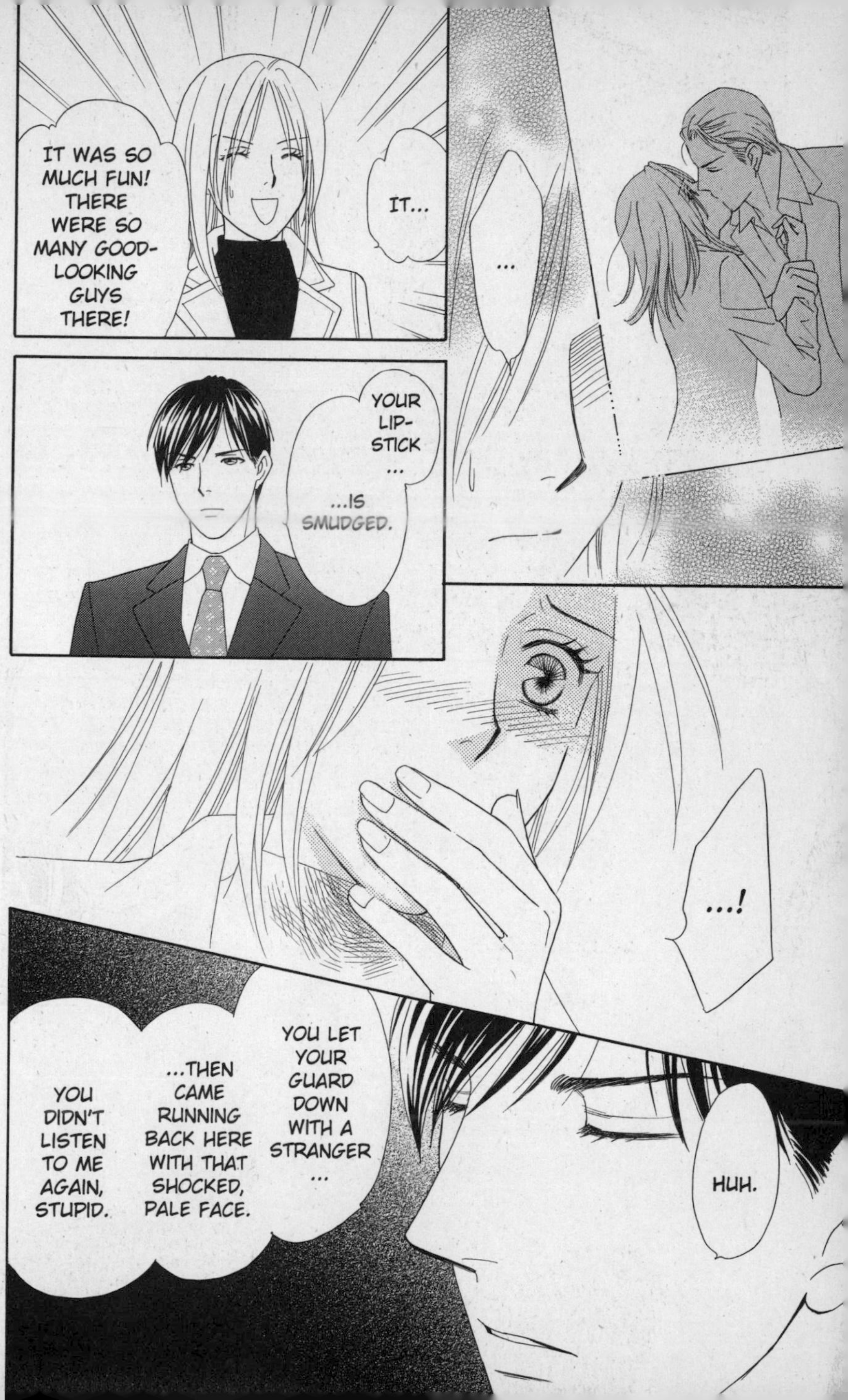
...
IT...
IT WAS SO MUCH FUN! THERE WERE SO MANY GOOD-LOOKING GUYS THERE!
YOUR LIP-STICK ...
...IS SMUDGED.
...!
HUH.
YOU LET YOUR GUARD DOWN WITH A STRANGER ...
...THEN CAME RUNNING BACK HERE WITH THAT SHOCKED, PALE FACE.
YOU DIDN'T LISTEN TO ME AGAIN, STUPID.

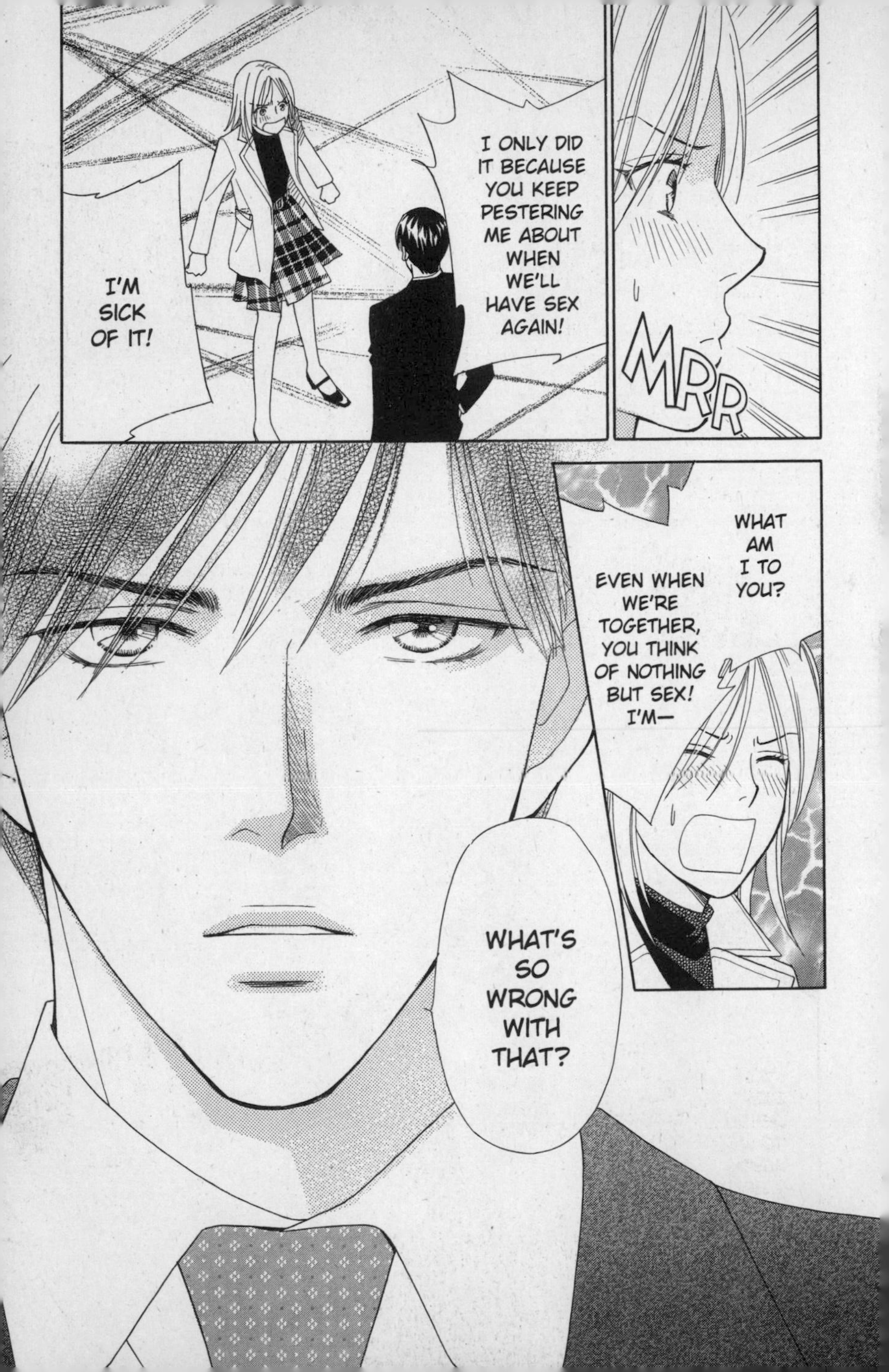
MRR
I ONLY DID IT BECAUSE YOU KEEP PESTERING ME ABOUT WHEN WE'LL HAVE SEX AGAIN!
I'M SICK OF IT!
WHAT AM I TO YOU?
EVEN WHEN WE'RE TOGETHER, YOU THINK OF NOTHING BUT SEX! I'M—
WHAT'S SO WRONG WITH THAT?

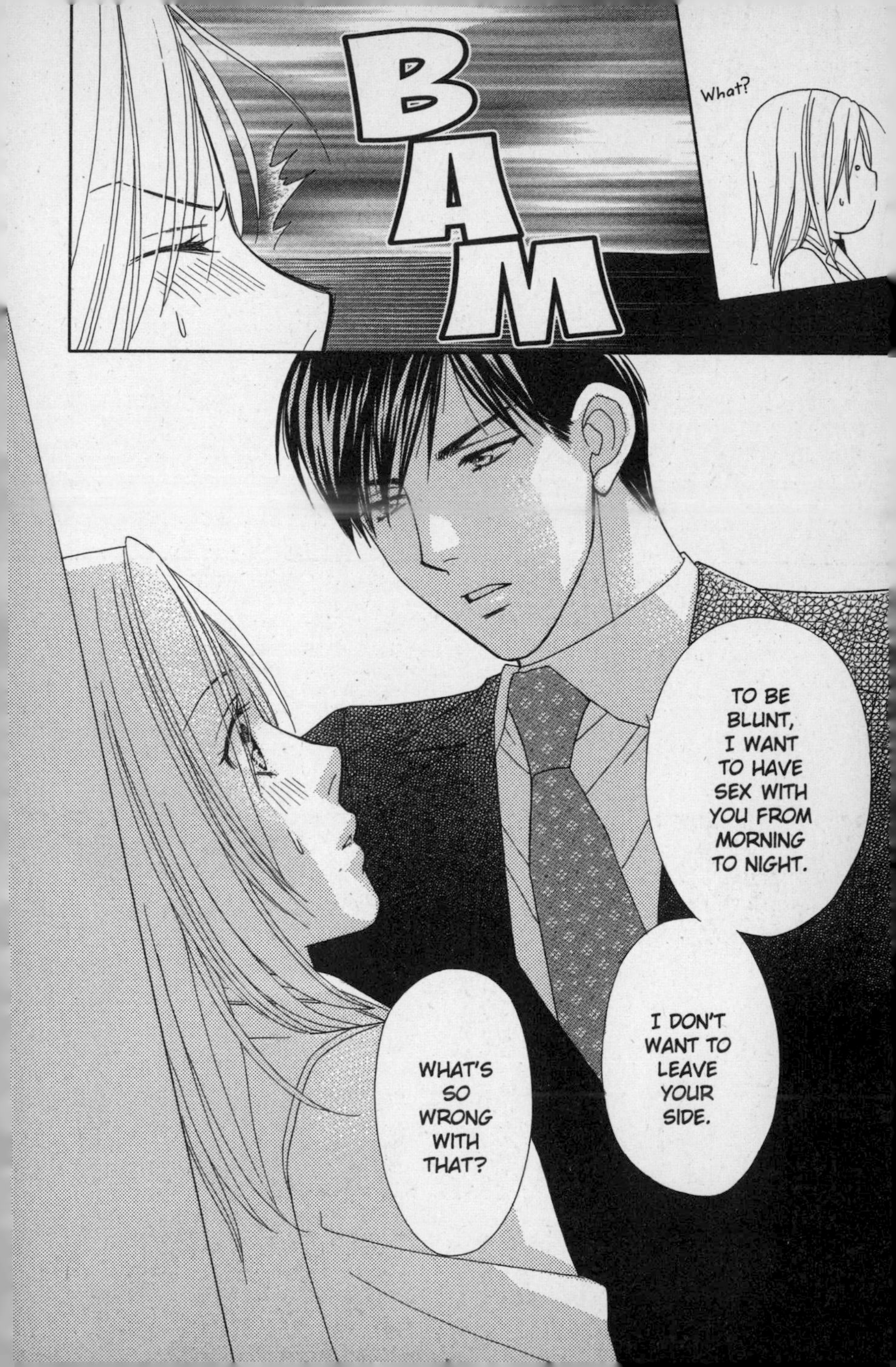
What?
BAM
TO BE BLUNT, I WANT TO HAVE SEX WITH YOU FROM MORNING TO NIGHT.
I DON'T WANT TO LEAVE YOUR SIDE.
WHAT'S SO WRONG WITH THAT?

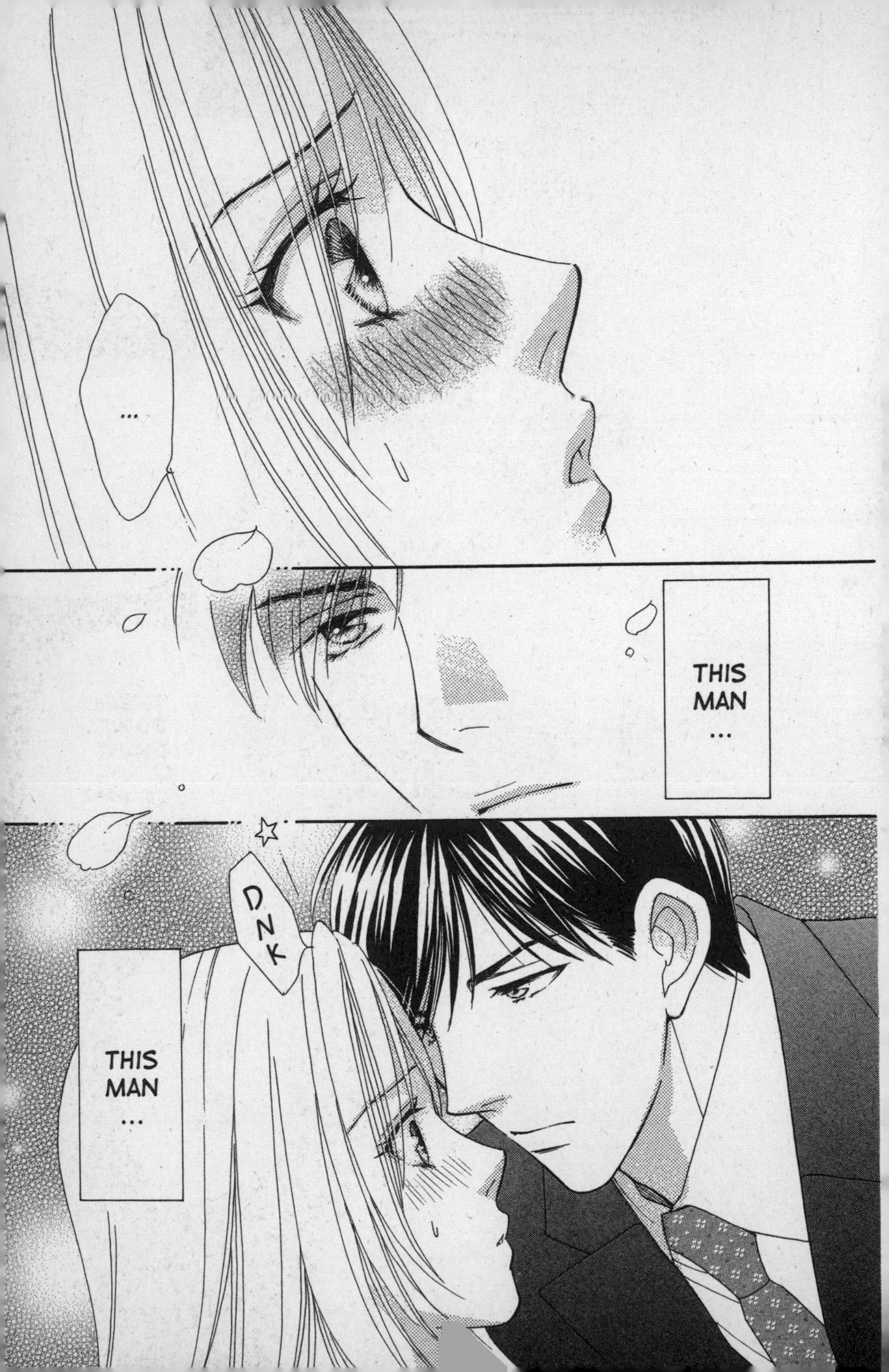
...
THIS MAN ...
DNK
THIS MAN ...

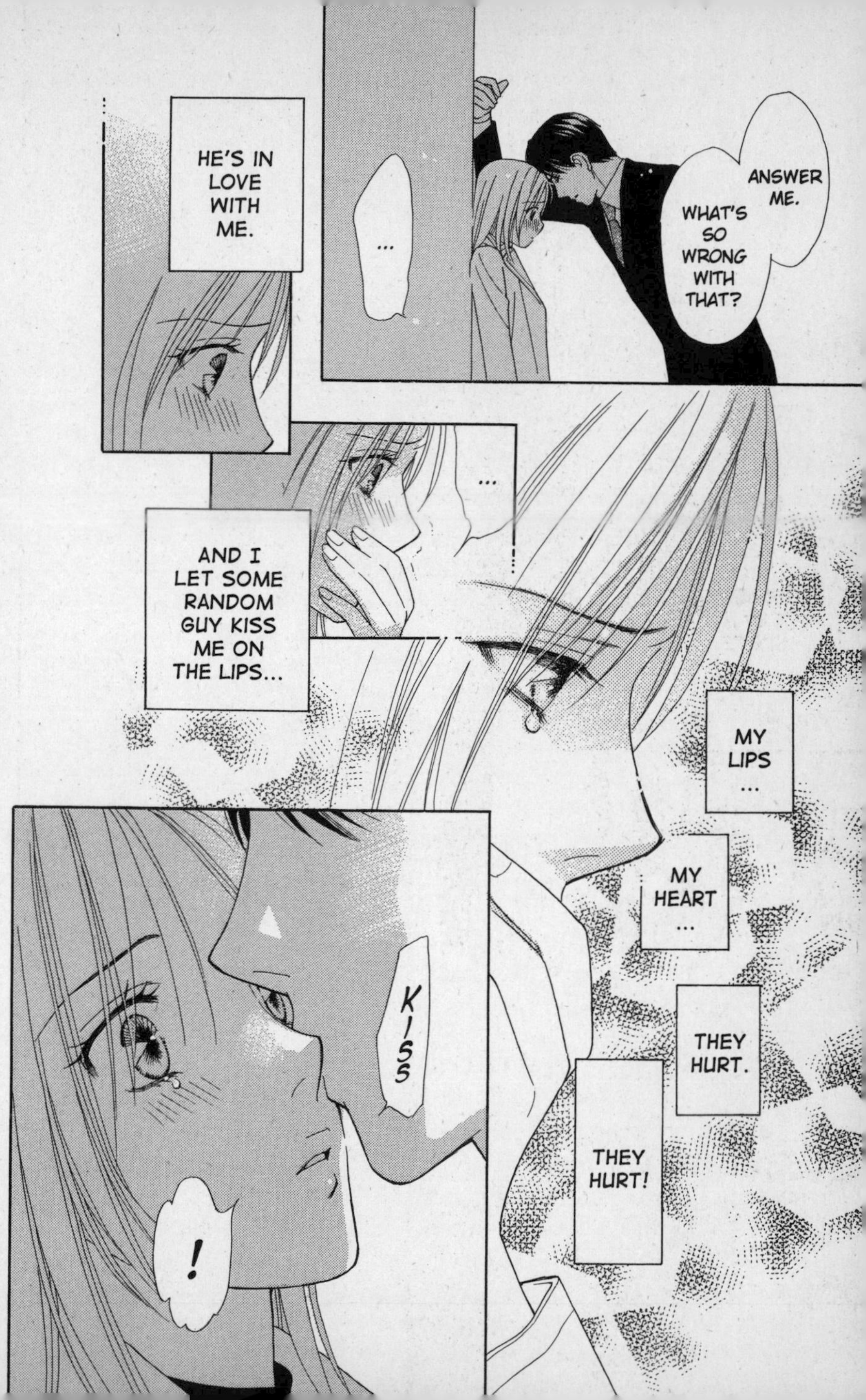
ANSWER ME.
WHAT'S SO WRONG WITH THAT?
...
HE'S IN LOVE WITH ME.
...
AND I LET SOME RANDOM GUY KISS ME ON THE LIPS...
MY LIPS...
MY HEART...
THEY HURT.
THEY HURT!
KISS
!

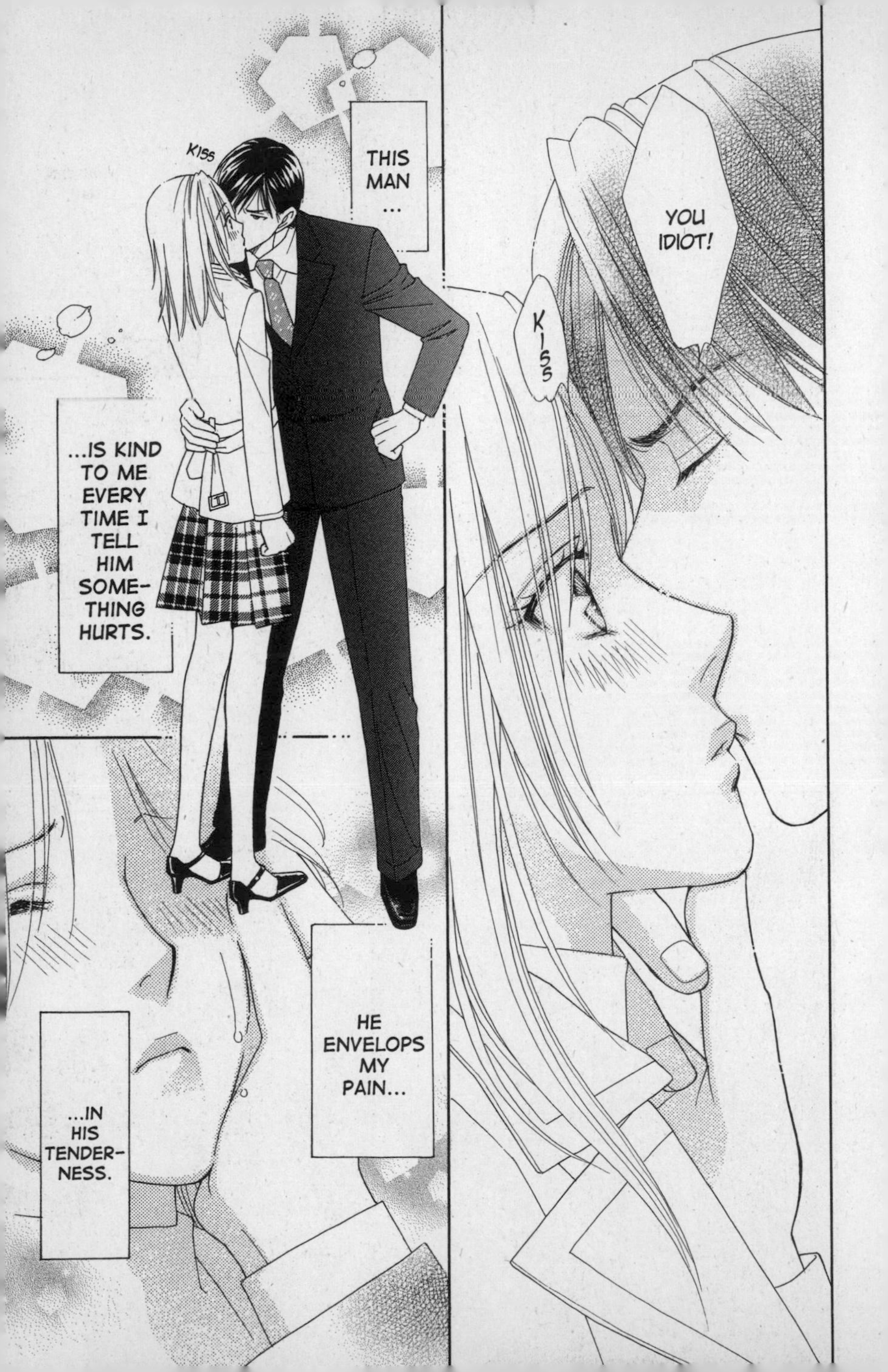
YOU IDIOT!
KISS
THIS MAN...
KISS
...IS KIND TO ME EVERY TIME I TELL HIM SOME-THING HURTS.
HE ENVELOPS MY PAIN...
...IN HIS TENDER-NESS.

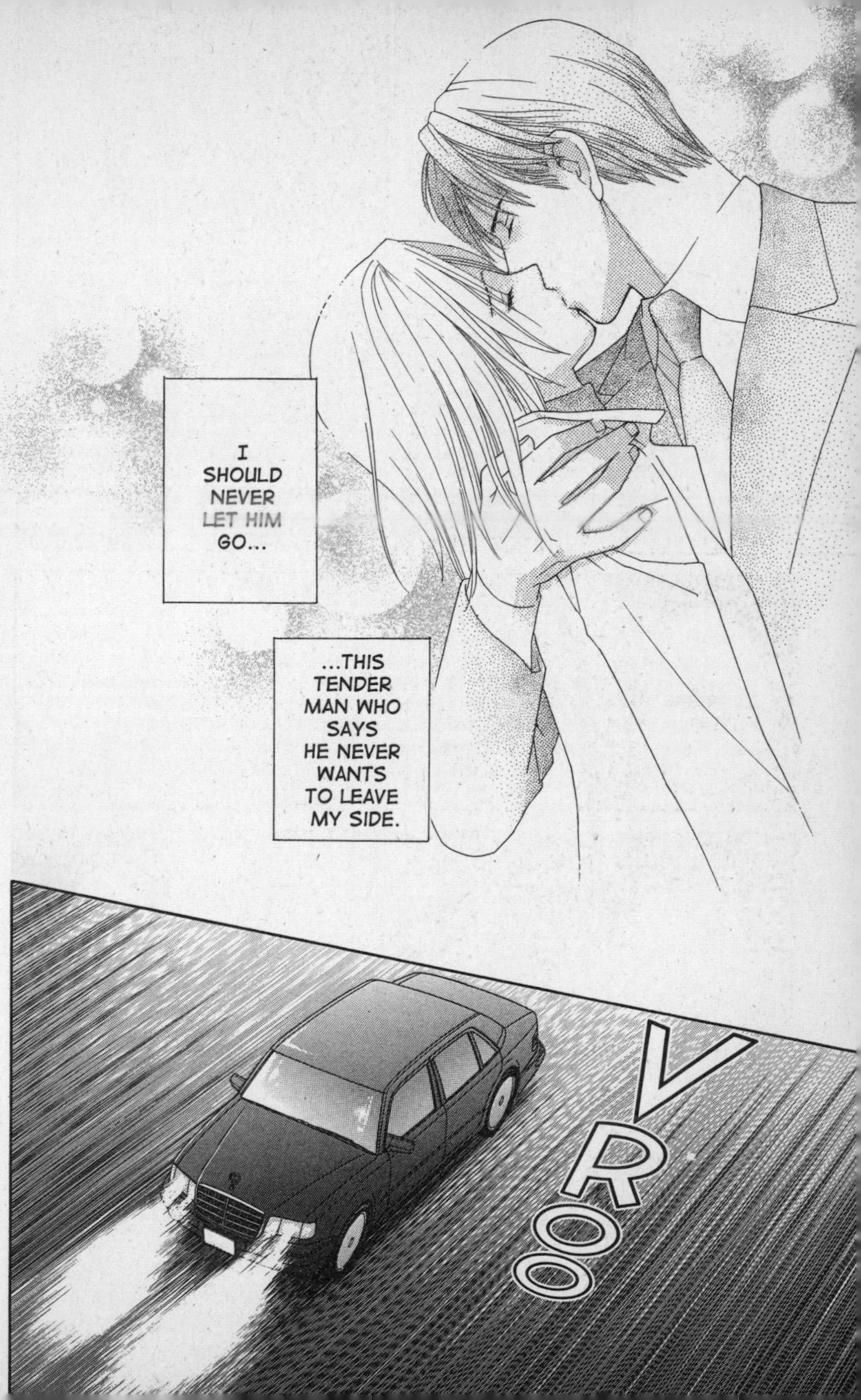
I SHOULD NEVER LET HIM GO...
...THIS TENDER MAN WHO SAYS HE NEVER WANTS TO LEAVE MY SIDE.
VROOO

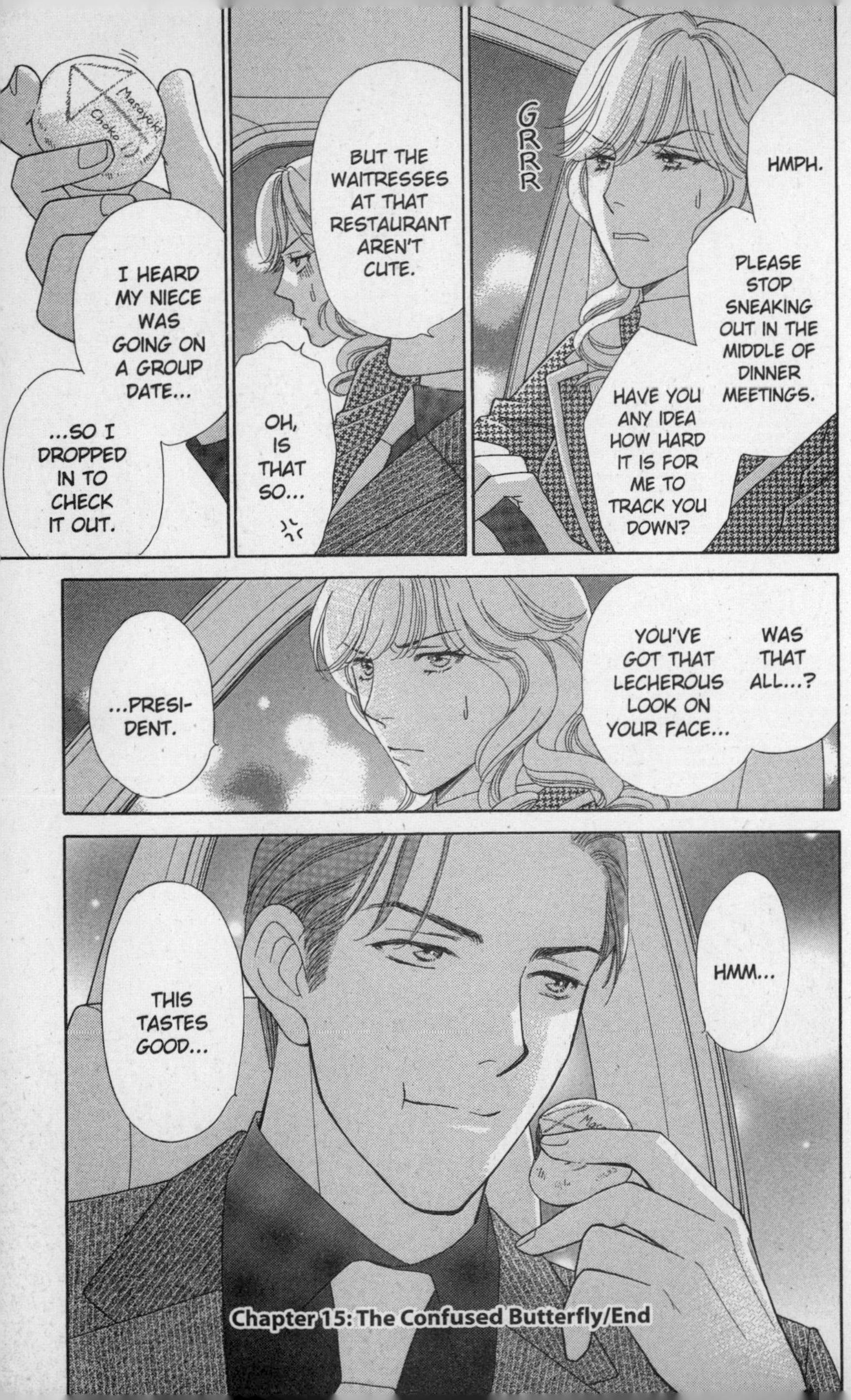
GRRR
HMPH.
PLEASE STOP SNEAKING OUT IN THE MIDDLE OF DINNER MEETINGS.
HAVE YOU ANY IDEA HOW HARD IT IS FOR ME TO TRACK YOU DOWN?
BUT THE WAITRESSES AT THAT RESTAURANT AREN'T CUTE.
OH, IS THAT SO...
Masayuki
Choko
I HEARD MY NIECE WAS GOING ON A GROUP DATE...
...SO I DROPPED IN TO CHECK IT OUT.
WAS THAT ALL...?
YOU'VE GOT THAT LECHEROUS LOOK ON YOUR FACE...
...PRESIDENT.
HMM...
THIS TASTES GOOD...
Chapter 15: The Confused Butterfly/End

FROM THE AUTHOR

Thank you for reading volume 3 of *Butterflies, Flowers*...♡
Well... At last. Finally... Ha ha ha...
I'm more than aware that the characters I draw are not normal, but I never thought Masayuki would turn out to be such a weirdo. Eeek.

This is the story of Masayuki, who has served his lady since childhood and has grown up to become a fine sexual-harassing servant. Please look forward to the next chapter of the somewhat half-baked drama series for morning TV: *Cha-chan*.♡

Okay, my head is somewhat half-baked too... Please tell us what you think about this series.♡

Nancy Thistlethwaite, Editor
VIZ Media, LLC
295 Bay Street
San Francisco, CA 94133

吉原由起
Yuki Yoshihara
12/2006

You know, there's a café now that calls customers "Milady"...
But I'd rather be called "Your Majesty" than "Milady"... by people like Fersen and Oscar.
Oh really.

Butterflies, Flowers

Notes

Page 1:   Shichi-Go-San is a rite of passage in celebration of girls who are 3 and 7 years old, and boys who are 3 and 5 years old. Children of these ages and their families visit Shinto shrines on November 15 to pray for their future and well being.

Page 22:   Tackey & Tsubasa is a J-pop duo.

Page 37:   "Zeon" is a reference to *Mobile Suit Gundam*. In the series, the Principality of Zeon starts a war of independence with Earth.

Page 50:   "Welcome home, Master" is what the waitstaff at butler cafés would say to greet their customers.

Page 51:   Hikaru G*nji was a popular male J-pop group that often performed on roller skates. "Paradise Galaxy" (*Paradise Ginga*) is a song of theirs.

Page 90:   Ayaya is the nickname for Aya Matsuura. She was in a commercial for Yofuku no Aoyama, a men's apparel store. Shuzo Matsuoka is a former professional tennis player who was in a commercial for a different men's apparel store, Shinshifuku no Konaka.

Page 157: Domoto is giving out *kohaku manju*, a steamed bun that is often served at celebratory occasions.

Page 190: Fersen and Oscar are characters from *The Rose of Versailles*.

About the Author

Yuki Yoshihara was born in Tokyo on February 11. She wanted to become a mangaka since elementary school and debuted in 1988 with *Chanel no Sasayaki*. She is the author of numerous series including *Darling wa Namamono ni Tsuki* and *Itadakimasu*. Yoshihara's favorite band is the Pet Shop Boys, and she keeps her TV tuned to the Mystery Channel.

BUTTERFLIES, FLOWERS

Vol. 3

Shojo Beat Edition

STORY AND ART BY

YUKI YOSHIHARA

Original Japanese edition "CHOU YO HANA YO"
published by SHOGAKUKAN Inc.

Adaptation/Nancy Thistlethwaite
Translation/Tetsuichiro Miyaki
Touch-up Art & Lettering/Freeman Wong
Design/Hidemi Sahara
Editor/Nancy Thistlethwaite

VP, Production/Alvin Lu
VP, Sales & Product Marketing/Gonzalo Ferreyra
VP, Creative/Linda Espinosa
Publisher/Hyoe Narita

Printed in the U.S.A.

Published by VIZ Media, LLC
P.O. Box 77010
San Francisco, CA 94107

10 9 8 7 6 5 4 3 2 1
First printing, June 2010

viz media
www.viz.com

RATED M FOR MATURE

PARENTAL ADVISORY
BUTTERFLIES, FLOWERS is rated M for MATURE and is recommended for ages 18 and up.
ratings.viz.com

Shojo Beat
www.shojobeat.com

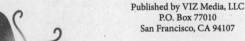

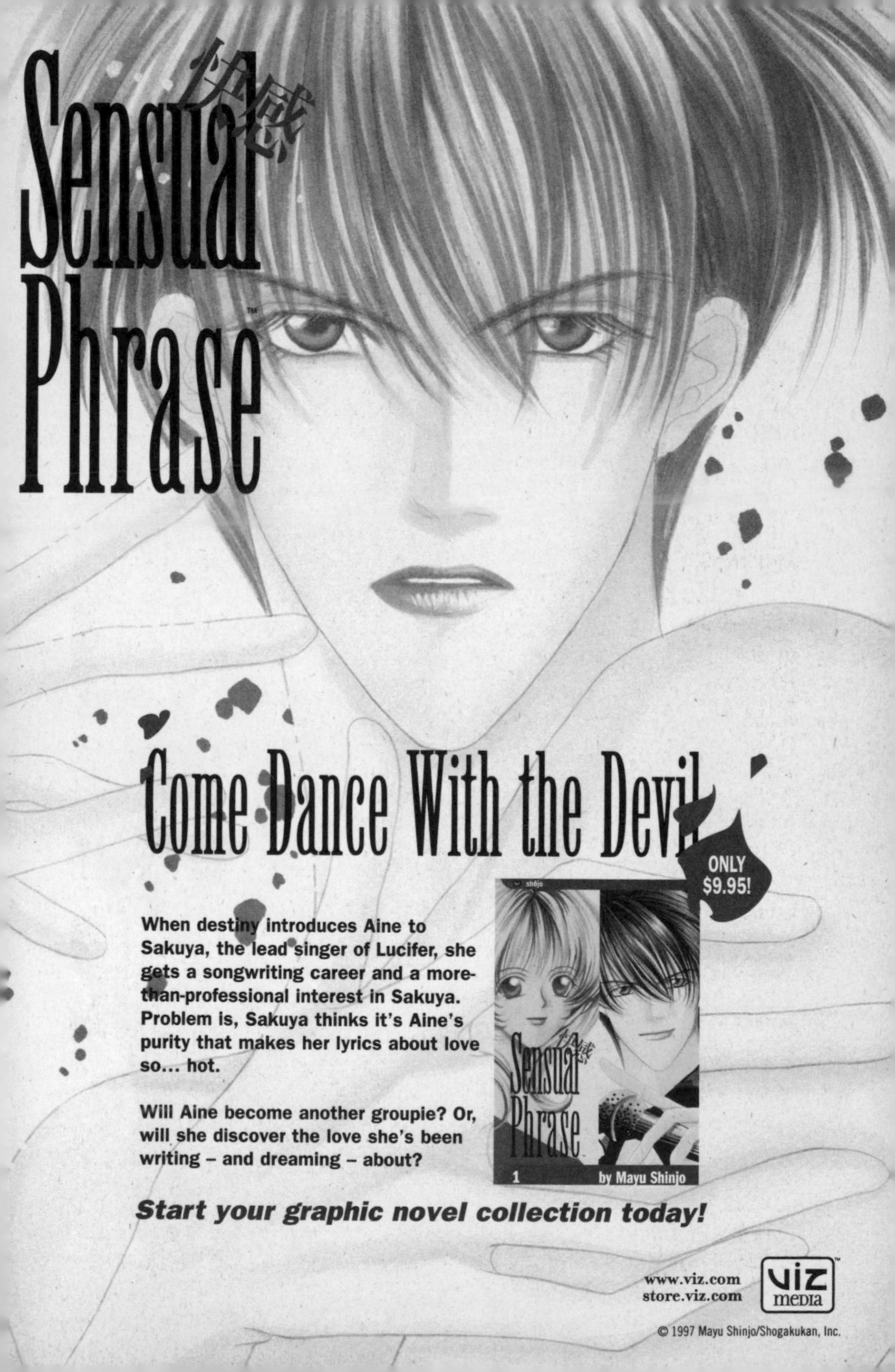
Sensual Phrase™
快感
Come Dance With the Devil
ONLY $9.95!
When destiny introduces Aine to Sakuya, the lead singer of Lucifer, she gets a songwriting career and a more-than-professional interest in Sakuya. Problem is, Sakuya thinks it's Aine's purity that makes her lyrics about love so... hot.
Will Aine become another groupie? Or, will she discover the love she's been writing – and dreaming – about?
shōjo
Sensual Phrase
1
by Mayu Shinjo
Start your graphic novel collection today!
www.viz.com
store.viz.com
VIZ media
© 1997 Mayu Shinjo/Shogakukan, Inc.

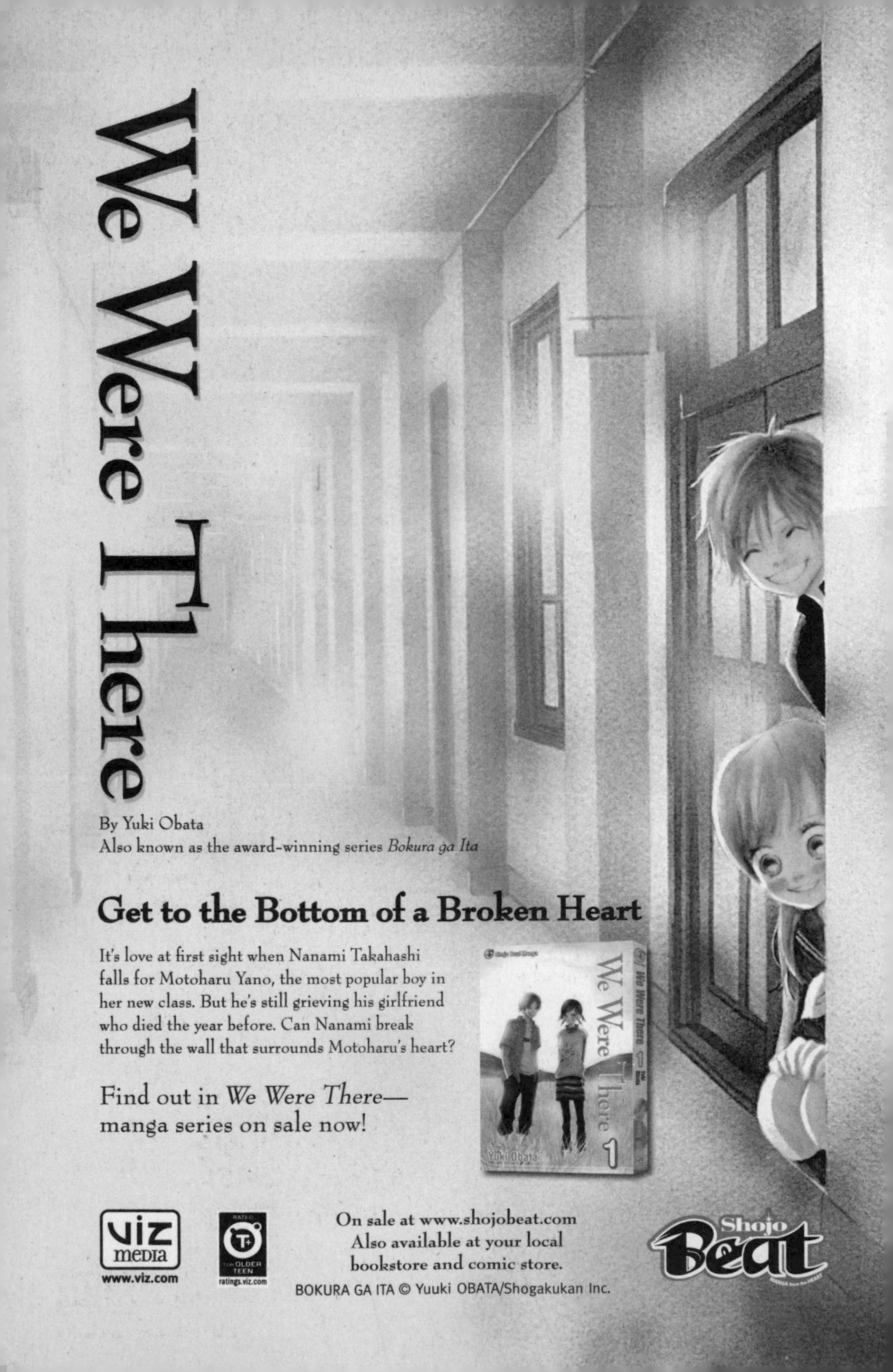
We Were There
By Yuki Obata
Also known as the award-winning series *Bokura ga Ita*
Get to the Bottom of a Broken Heart
It's love at first sight when Nanami Takahashi falls for Motoharu Yano, the most popular boy in her new class. But he's still grieving his girlfriend who died the year before. Can Nanami break through the wall that surrounds Motoharu's heart?
Find out in *We Were There*—manga series on sale now!
We Were There
Yuki Obata
1
VIZ media
www.viz.com
RATED T+ FOR OLDER TEEN
ratings.viz.com
On sale at www.shojobeat.com
Also available at your local bookstore and comic store.
BOKURA GA ITA © Yuuki OBATA/Shogakukan Inc.
Shojo Beat
MANGA from the HEART

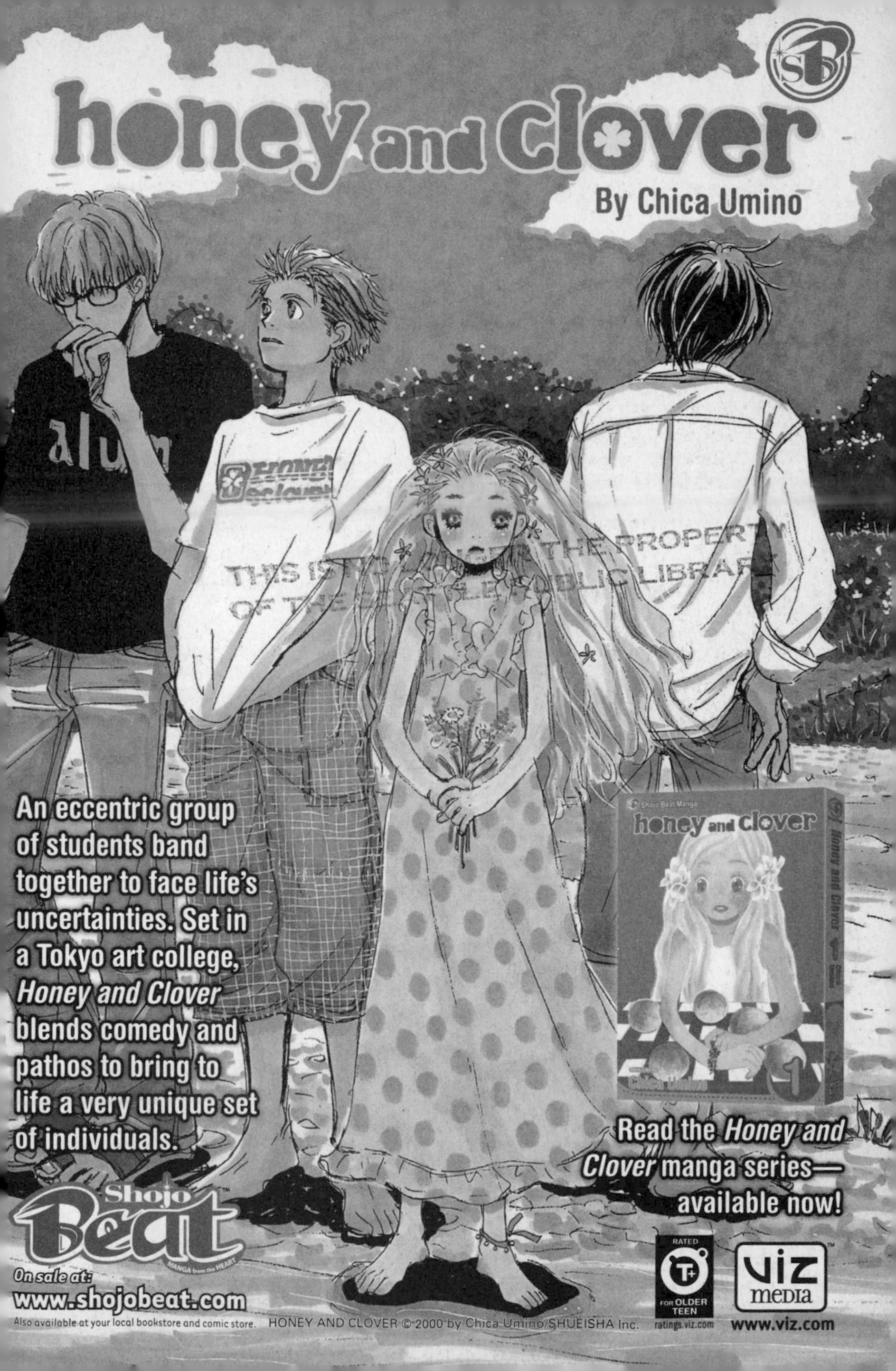
honey and clover
By Chica Umino
An eccentric group of students band together to face life's uncertainties. Set in a Tokyo art college, *Honey and Clover* blends comedy and pathos to bring to life a very unique set of individuals.
Shojo Beat Manga
honey and clover
Chica Umino
1
Read the *Honey and Clover* manga series—available now!
Shojo Beat
MANGA from the HEART
On sale at:
www.shojobeat.com
Also available at your local bookstore and comic store.
HONEY AND CLOVER © 2000 by Chica Umino/SHUEISHA Inc.
RATED T+ FOR OLDER TEEN
ratings.viz.com
VIZ media
www.viz.com

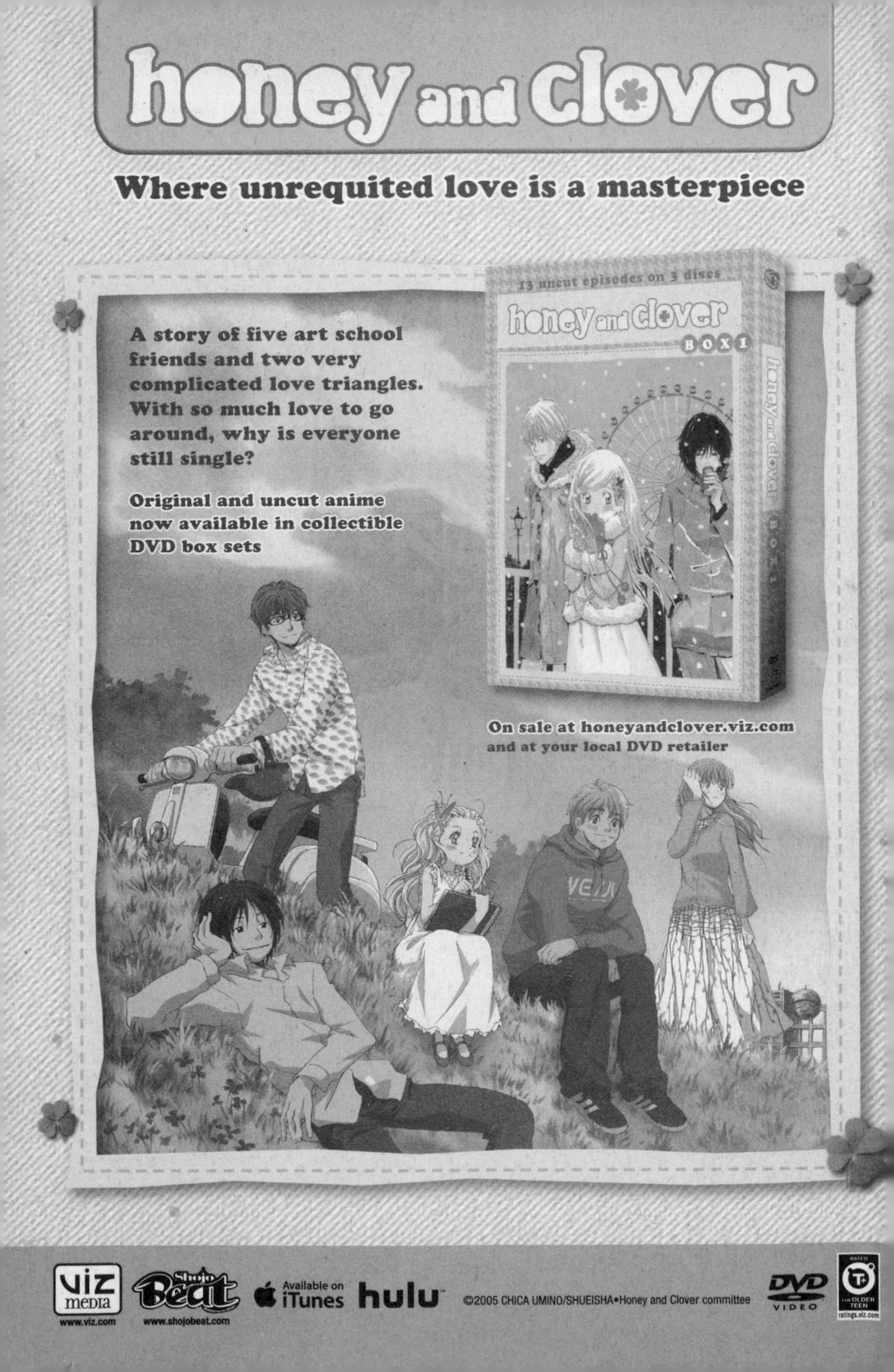
honey and clover
Where unrequited love is a masterpiece
13 uncut episodes on 3 discs
honey and clover
BOX 1
A story of five art school friends and two very complicated love triangles. With so much love to go around, why is everyone still single?
Original and uncut anime now available in collectible DVD box sets
On sale at honeyandclover.viz.com and at your local DVD retailer
viz media
www.viz.com
Shojo Beat
www.shojobeat.com
Available on iTunes
hulu
©2005 CHICA UMINO/SHUEISHA•Honey and Clover committee
DVD VIDEO
RATED T+ FOR OLDER TEEN
ratings.viz.com